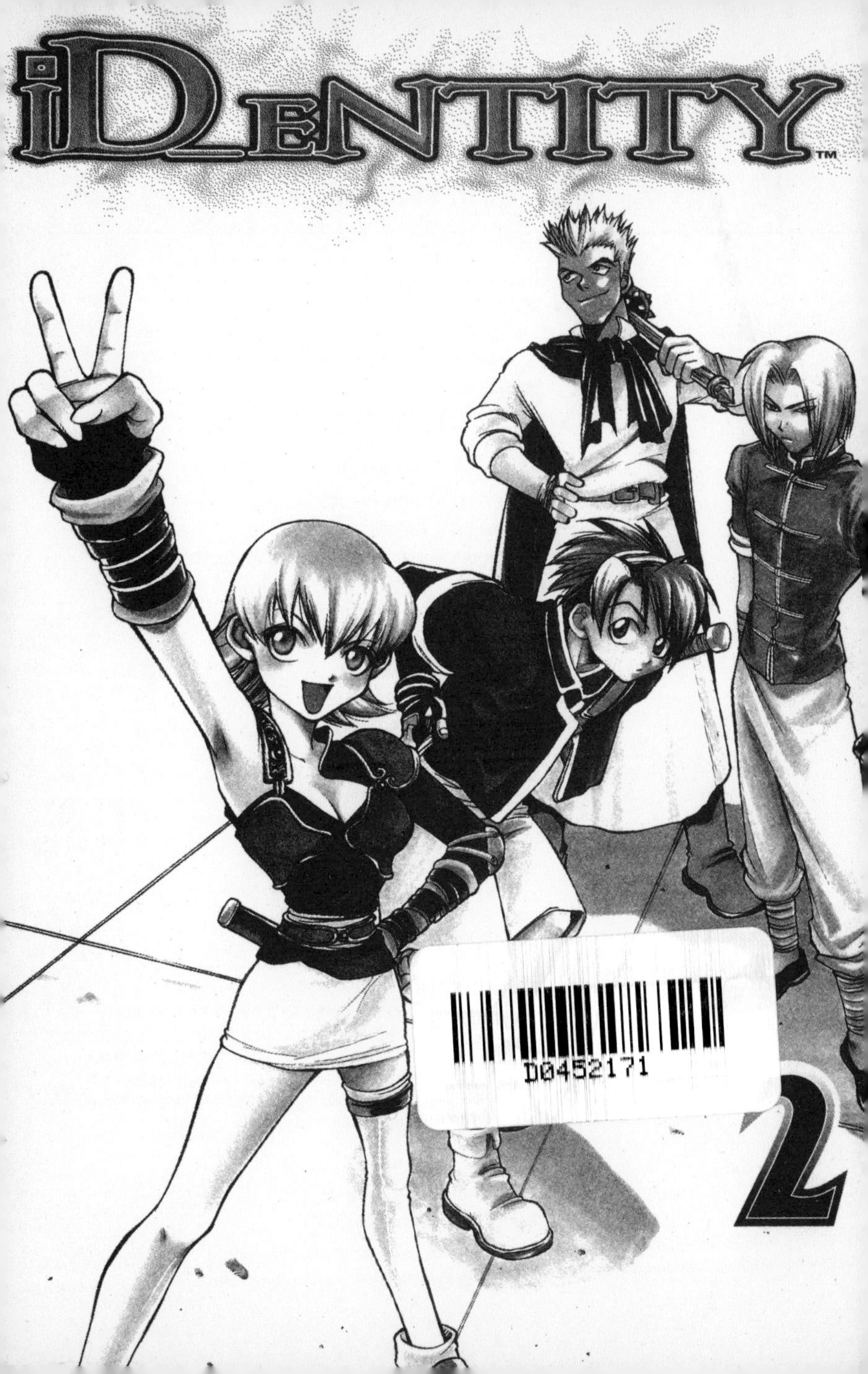
iDENTITY™
2

iD_eNTITY Vol. 2
Written by Hee-Joon Son
Illustrated by Youn-Kyung Kim

Translation - Sarah Kim
English Adaptation - Jason Dietrich
Copy Editor - Suzanne Waldman
Retouch and Lettering - Jeanine Han
Production Artist - Lucas Rivera
Cover Design - Jorge Negrete

Editor - Tim Beedle
Digital Imaging Manager - Chris Buford
Pre-Press Manager - Antonio DePietro
Production Managers - Jennifer Miller and Mutsumi Miyazaki
Art Director - Matt Alford
Managing Editor - Jill Freshney
VP of Production - Ron Klamert
Editor-in-Chief - Mike Kiley
President and C.O.O. - John Parker
Publisher and C.E.O. - Stuart Levy

A  TOKYOPOP® Manga

TOKYOPOP Inc.
5900 Wilshire Blvd. Suite 2000
Los Angeles, CA 90036

E-mail: info@TOKYOPOP.com
Come visit us online at www.TOKYOPOP.com

ISBN: 1-59532-346-5
First TOKYOPOP printing: July 2005
10 9 8 7 6 5 4 3 2 1
Printed in Canada

iDeNTITY™

vOL. 2

wRITTEN bY hEE-jOON sON
iLLUSTRATED bY yOUN-kYUNG kIM

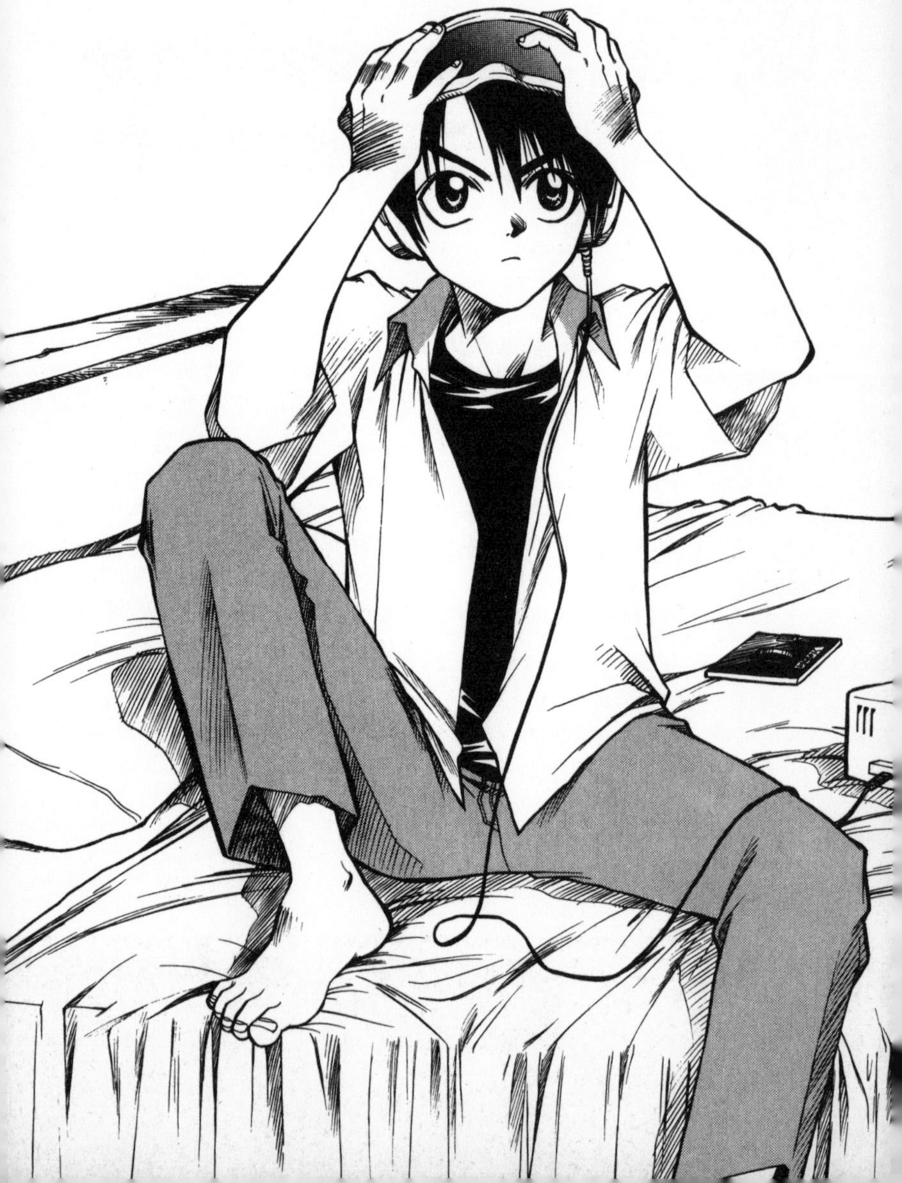

PASSWORD RECOGNIZED…

IDENTITY CONFIRMED…

ACCESSING PAST VOLUME FILE…

In real life, Jang-Gun, Kwan-Su and Woon-Suk are average kids
with average problems, but in the virtual world of Lost Saga, they're
Team Triple Threat. Using the screen names Roto, Boromid and Ah-
Dol, they've become heroes to countless NPCs and legends among
gamers everywhere. But you don't become a hero without making a
few enemies along the way. Whether it's the sorcerer-turned-bounty
hunter Aradon the Black, the troublesome team of thieves known
as The Fallen Angels or the bratty little debugger Myriah, Team
Triple Threat had better watch their back and be ready for anything,
because in Lost Saga nothing is what it seems and murder can happen with a click of a mouse.

TRANSMISSION COMPLETE…

LOGGING OFF…

iD_eNTITY rOGUE'S gALLERY_

tHE cITIZENS oF lOST sAGA_

TEAM TRIPLE THREAT

Roto = Jang-Gun

SORCERER

When Jang-Gun isn't cracking the books, he's cracking monster skulls as Roto, a sword-swinging sorcerer in his favorite online role-playing game, Lost Saga. Even though he's possibly the world's biggest game-geek and usually looks like he just rolled out of bed, the ladies inexplicably find him attractive. Maybe he made a good saving throw…

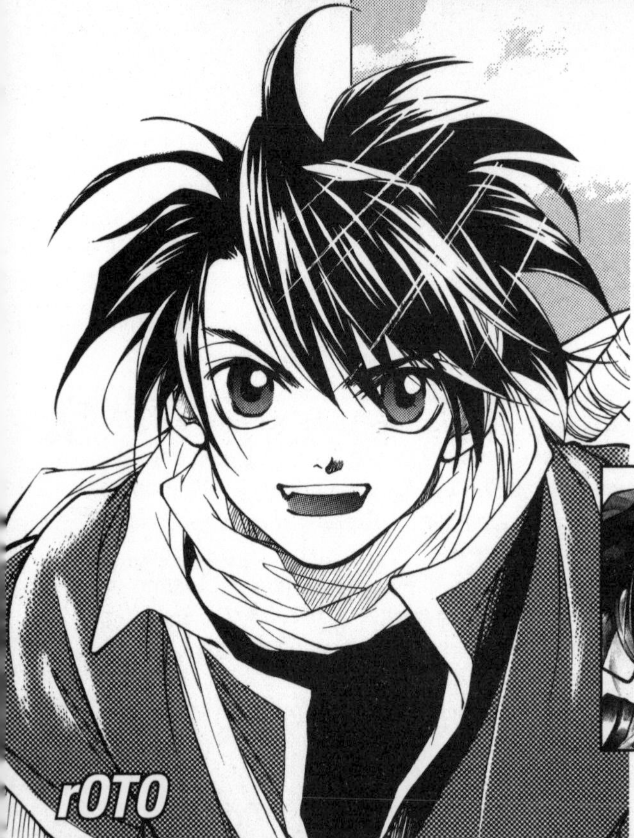
rOTO

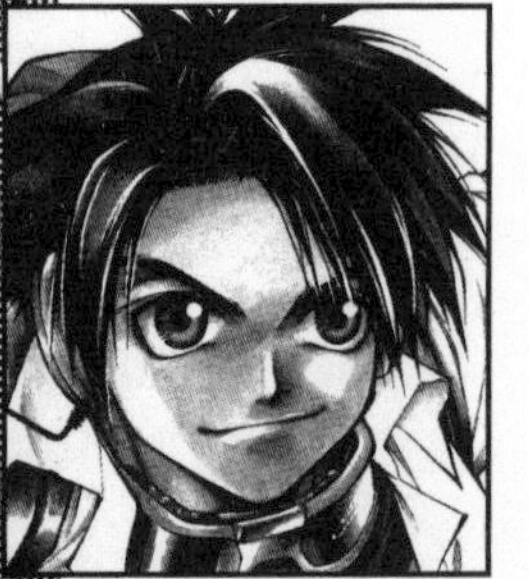

jANG-gUN

Team Triple Threat (cont'd)

Boromid = Kwan-Su

PRIEST

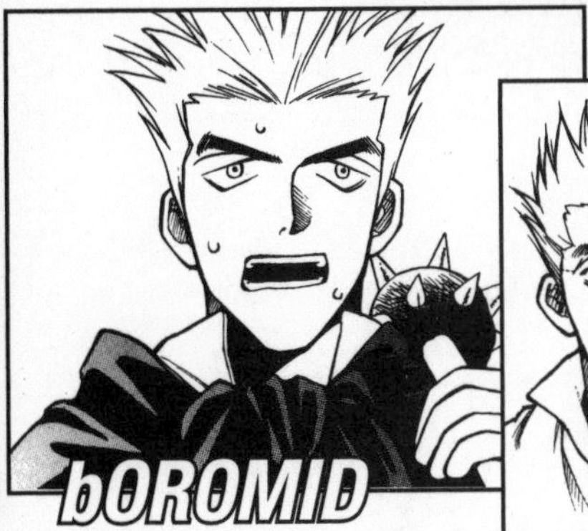
bOROMID

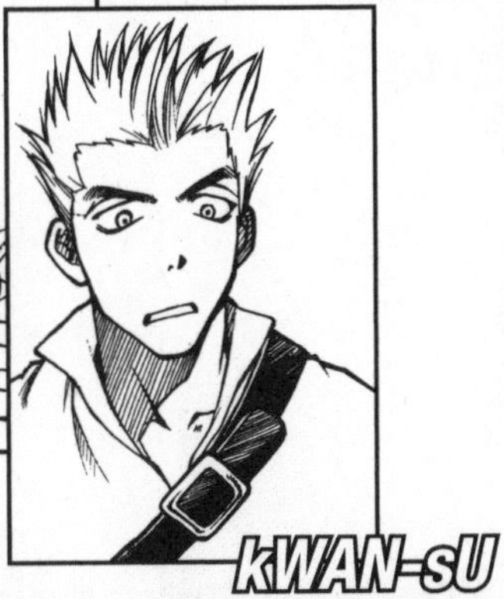
kWAN-sU

An indifferent student at best, Kwan-Su spends his nights as Boromid, a wild-card of a priest. Boromid's as likely to get his friends in over their heads as he is to keep them in the Game with his healing prayers. Now if he could only get the ladies to see his sensitive side…

Ah-Dol = Woon-Suk

WARRIOR

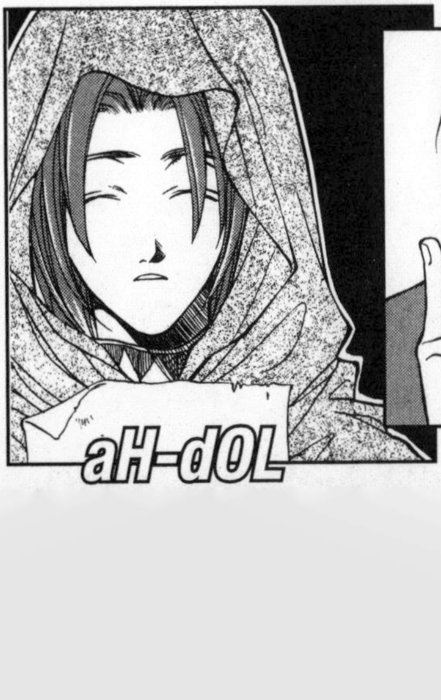
aH-dOL

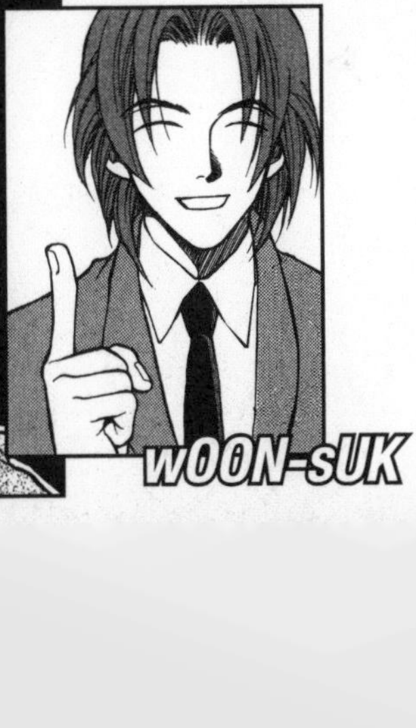
wOON-sUK

As Ah-Dol, the warrior, Woon-Suk is the glue that keeps Team Triple Threat together. The strong and silent type, he'd rather let his knuckle-dusters do the talking.

iD_eNTITY rOGUE'S gALLERY_

tHE cITIZENS oF lOST sAGA_(cont'd)

THE FALLEN ANGELS = THE LOVELY ANGELS

THIEVES

tHE fALLEN aNGELS

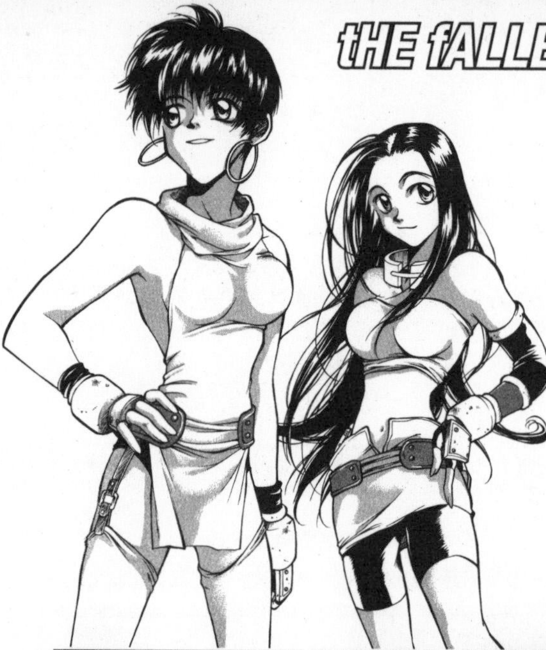

These two hot sisters are master-level thieves called ***"The Fallen Angels"*** in the world of the Game. In the real world, they're the pop singing sensation ***"The Lovely Angels."***

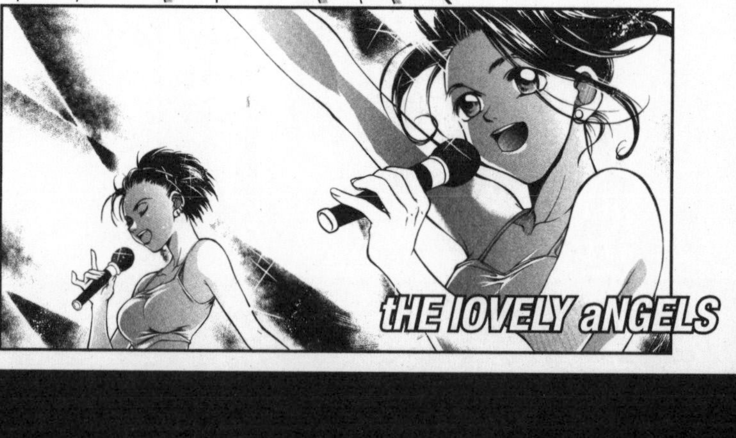
tHE lOVELY aNGELS

K.C. = Jin-Mee

THIEF

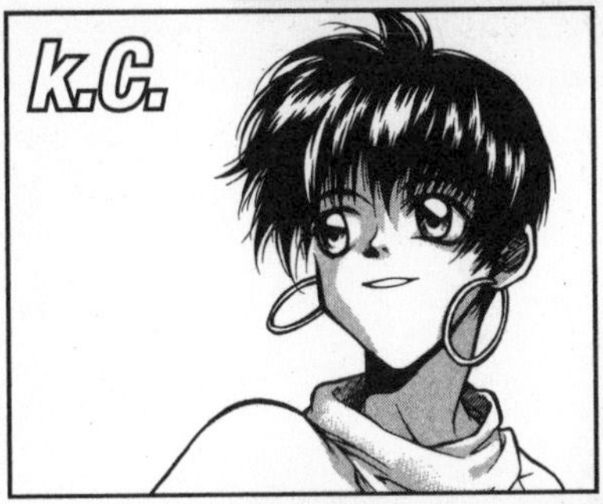
k.C.

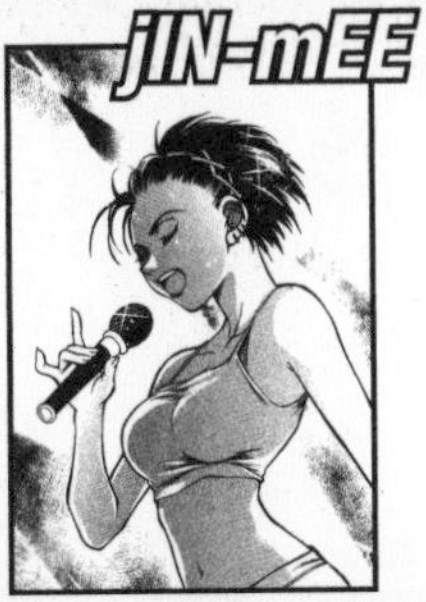
jIN-mEE

Offline, Jin-Mee is one half of the famous pop idol group ***"The Lovely Angels."*** Online, she lets her hair down as part of the master-level thief duo, ***"The Fallen Angels."***

Julie = Gina

THIEF

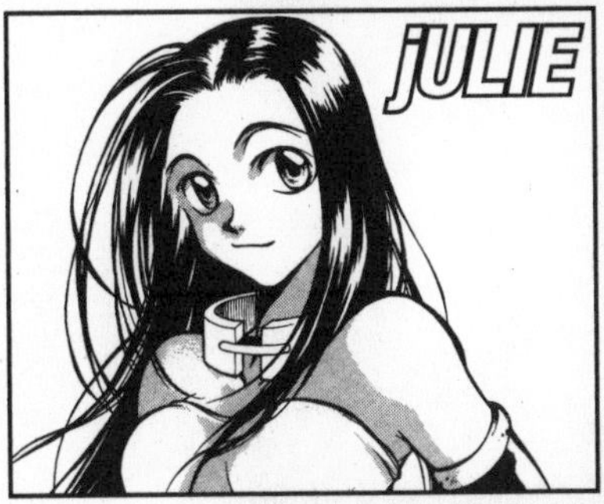
jULIE

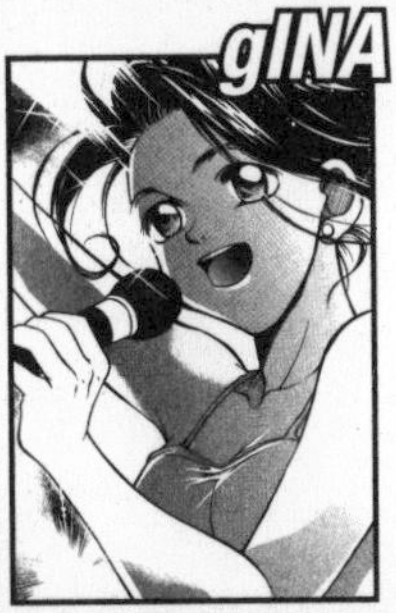
gINA

Julie may call herself a treasure hunter, but she's a cat burglar at heart. In the Game's world, Julie and her sister have a score to settle with ***Team Triple Threat.*** In the real world, Gina is a pop singer who is frustrated with the obligations of her demanding lifestyle.

Yoon-Ji

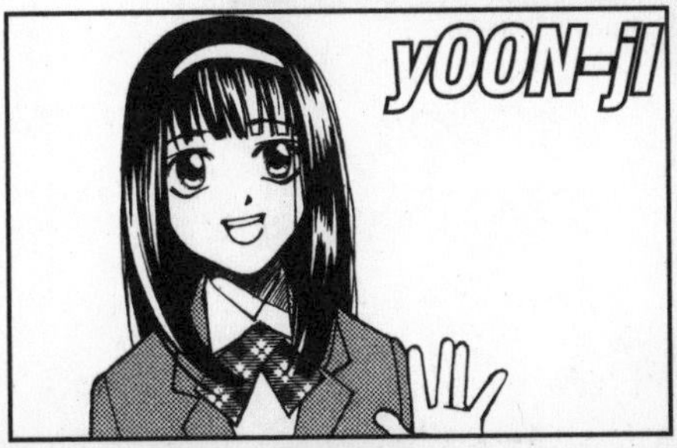
yOON-ji

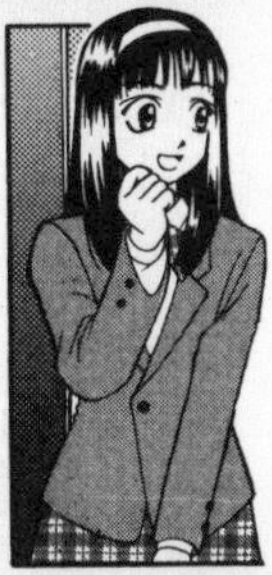

Classroom cutie with a crush on Jang-Gun.

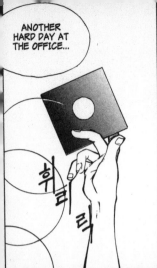

ANOTHER HARD DAY AT THE OFFICE...

HONEY, I'M HOME! DID YOU MISS ME?

BEEP!

PLEASE UPDATE YOUR USER ID CARD...

WHAT? IT'S BEEN A YEAR ALREADY?

IF I HAVE TO GET AN UPDATE...

...THAT MEANS TODAY IS MY BIRTHDAY!

HOW COULD I FORGET THAT? I'M SUCH A SPACE CADET!

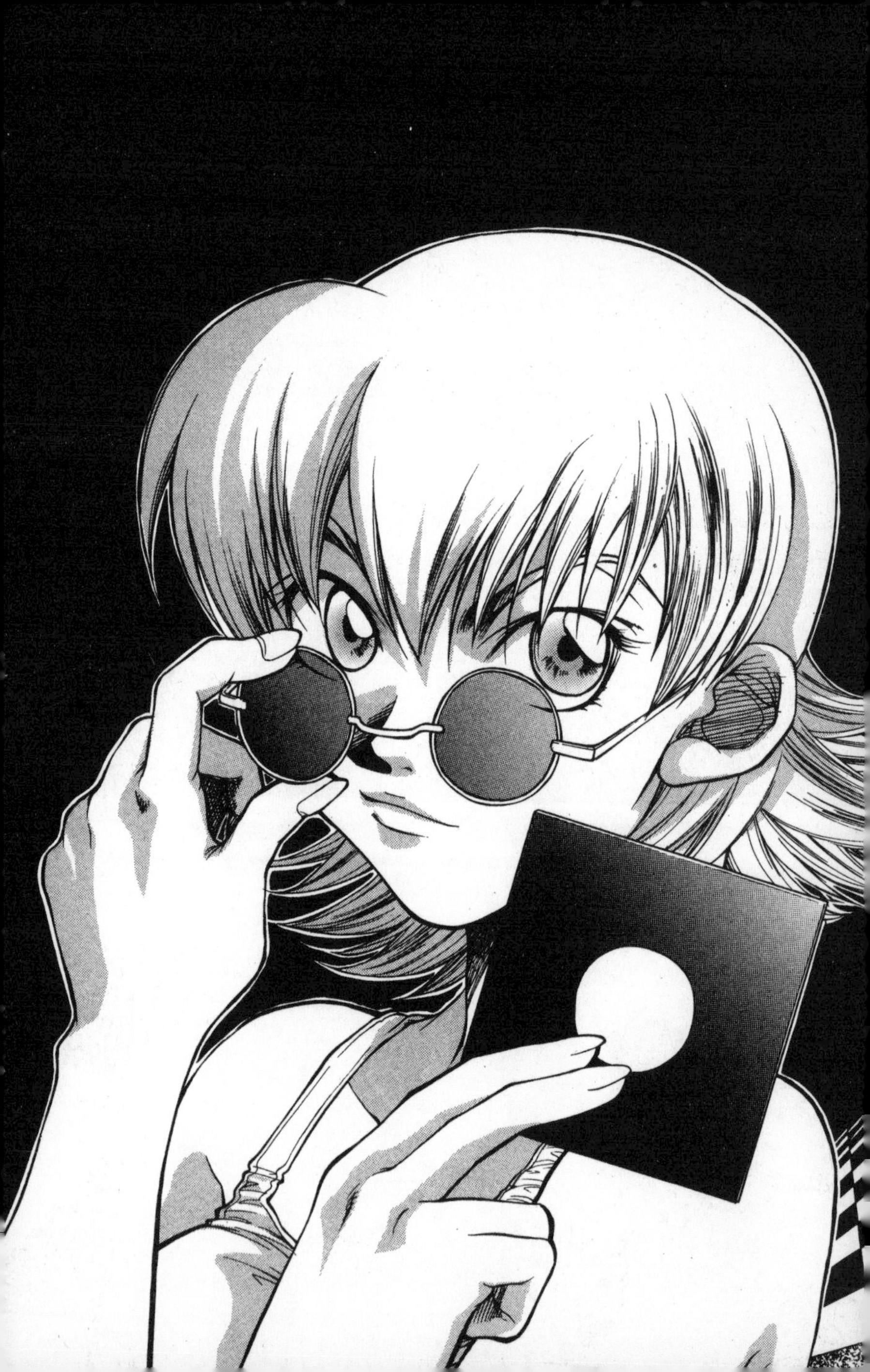

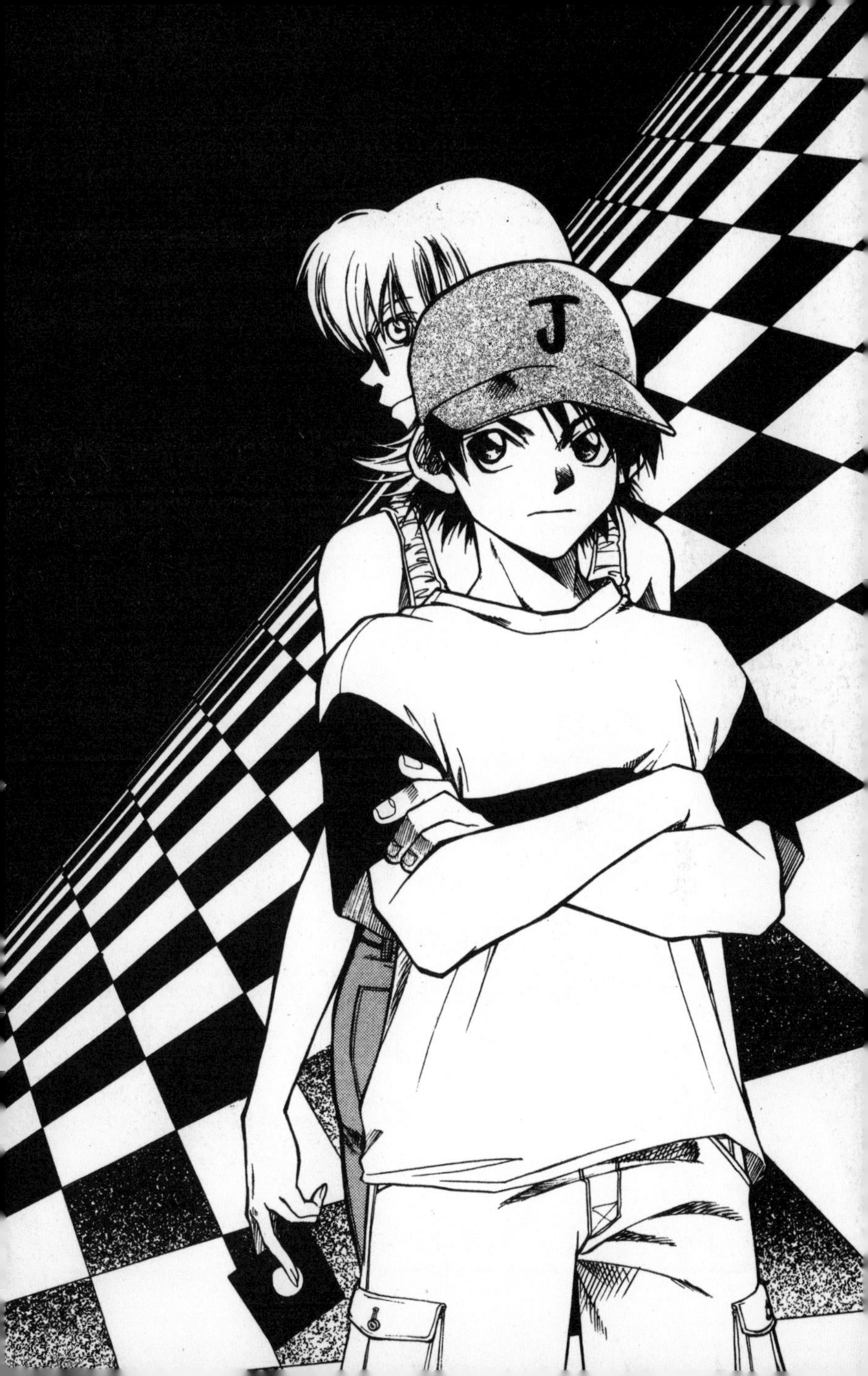
J

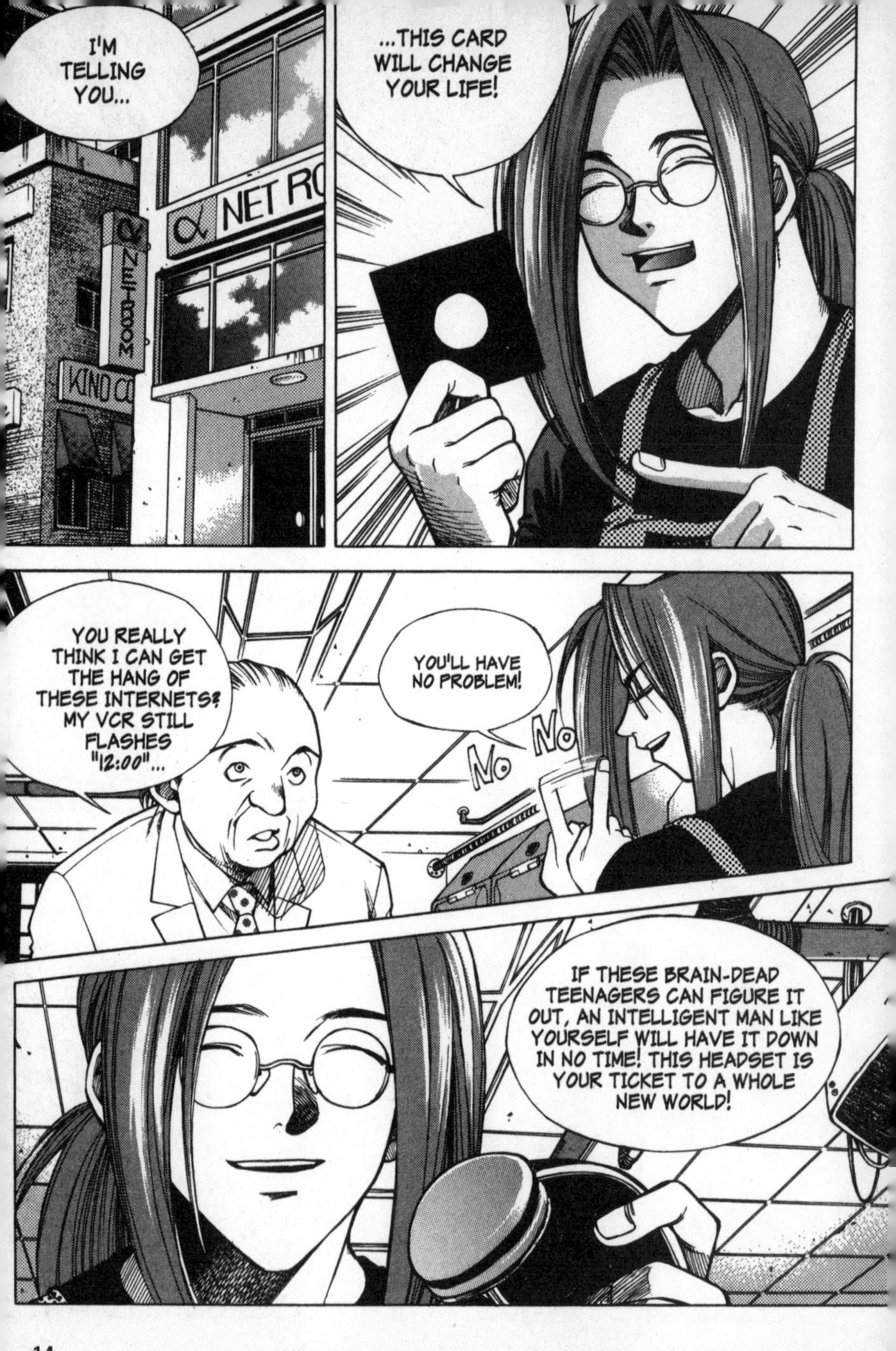
I'M TELLING YOU...
NET RO
NETROOM
KIND CO
...THIS CARD WILL CHANGE YOUR LIFE!
YOU REALLY THINK I CAN GET THE HANG OF THESE INTERNETS? MY VCR STILL FLASHES "12:00"...
YOU'LL HAVE NO PROBLEM!
No No
IF THESE BRAIN-DEAD TEENAGERS CAN FIGURE IT OUT, AN INTELLIGENT MAN LIKE YOURSELF WILL HAVE IT DOWN IN NO TIME! THIS HEADSET IS YOUR TICKET TO A WHOLE NEW WORLD!

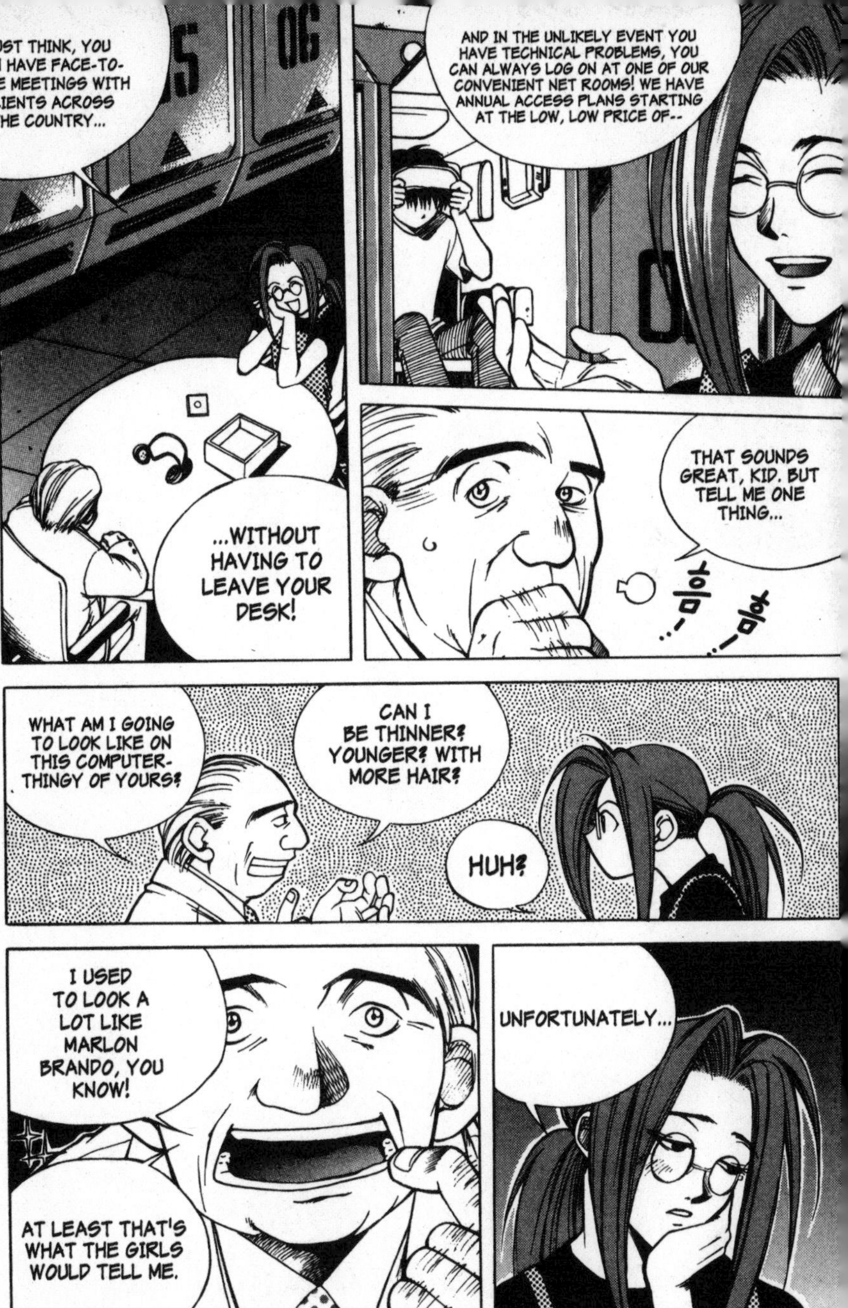

JUST THINK, YOU CAN HAVE FACE-TO-FACE MEETINGS WITH CLIENTS ACROSS THE COUNTRY...
...WITHOUT HAVING TO LEAVE YOUR DESK!
AND IN THE UNLIKELY EVENT YOU HAVE TECHNICAL PROBLEMS, YOU CAN ALWAYS LOG ON AT ONE OF OUR CONVENIENT NET ROOMS! WE HAVE ANNUAL ACCESS PLANS STARTING AT THE LOW, LOW PRICE OF--
THAT SOUNDS GREAT, KID. BUT TELL ME ONE THING...
흠...
흠...
WHAT AM I GOING TO LOOK LIKE ON THIS COMPUTER-THINGY OF YOURS?
CAN I BE THINNER? YOUNGER? WITH MORE HAIR?
HUH?
I USED TO LOOK A LOT LIKE MARLON BRANDO, YOU KNOW!
AT LEAST THAT'S WHAT THE GIRLS WOULD TELL ME.
UNFORTUNATELY...

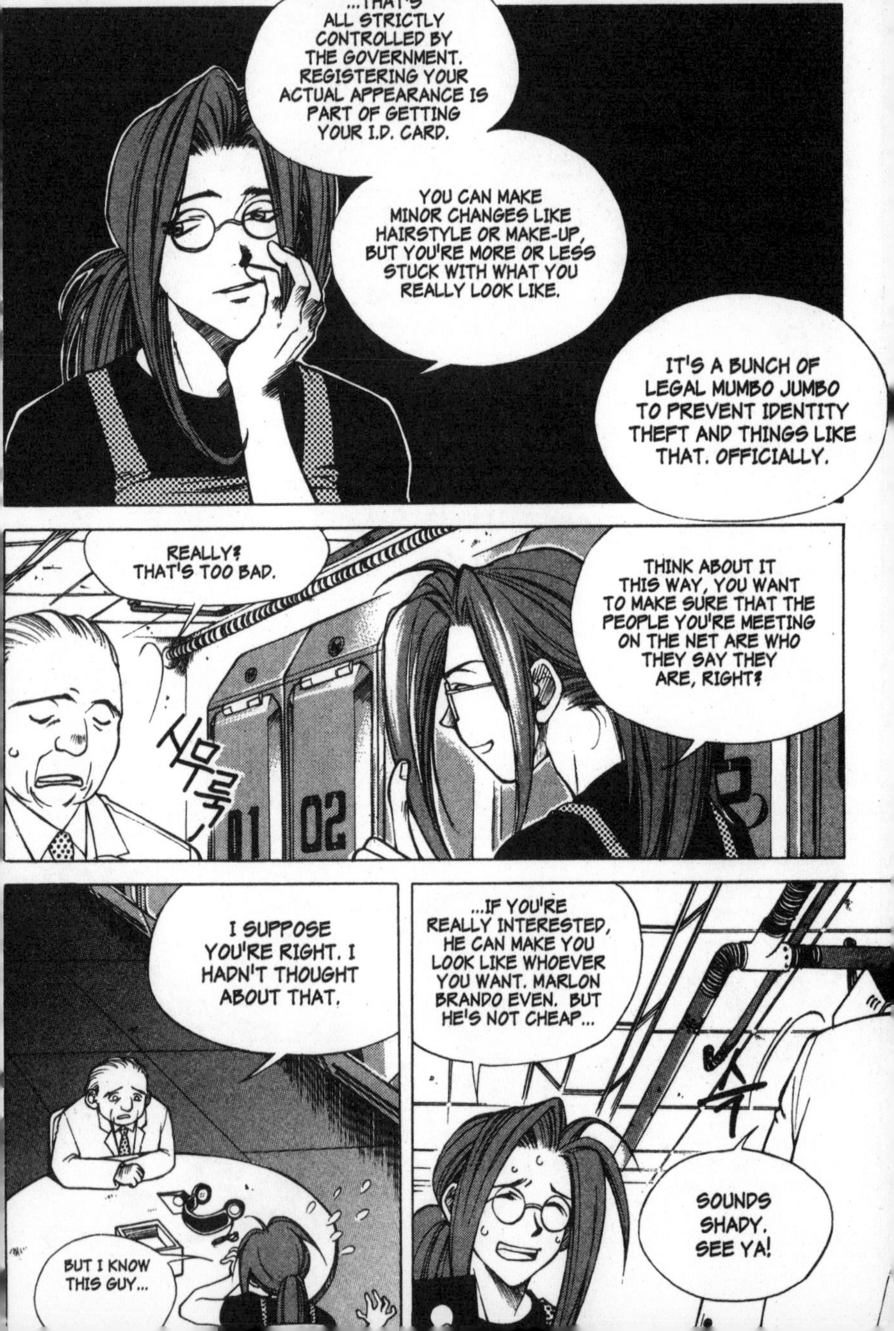
...THAT'S ALL STRICTLY CONTROLLED BY THE GOVERNMENT. REGISTERING YOUR ACTUAL APPEARANCE IS PART OF GETTING YOUR I.D. CARD.
YOU CAN MAKE MINOR CHANGES LIKE HAIRSTYLE OR MAKE-UP, BUT YOU'RE MORE OR LESS STUCK WITH WHAT YOU REALLY LOOK LIKE.
IT'S A BUNCH OF LEGAL MUMBO JUMBO TO PREVENT IDENTITY THEFT AND THINGS LIKE THAT. OFFICIALLY.
REALLY? THAT'S TOO BAD.
THINK ABOUT IT THIS WAY, YOU WANT TO MAKE SURE THAT THE PEOPLE YOU'RE MEETING ON THE NET ARE WHO THEY SAY THEY ARE, RIGHT?
01
02
I SUPPOSE YOU'RE RIGHT. I HADN'T THOUGHT ABOUT THAT.
BUT I KNOW THIS GUY...
...IF YOU'RE REALLY INTERESTED, HE CAN MAKE YOU LOOK LIKE WHOEVER YOU WANT. MARLON BRANDO EVEN. BUT HE'S NOT CHEAP...
SOUNDS SHADY. SEE YA!

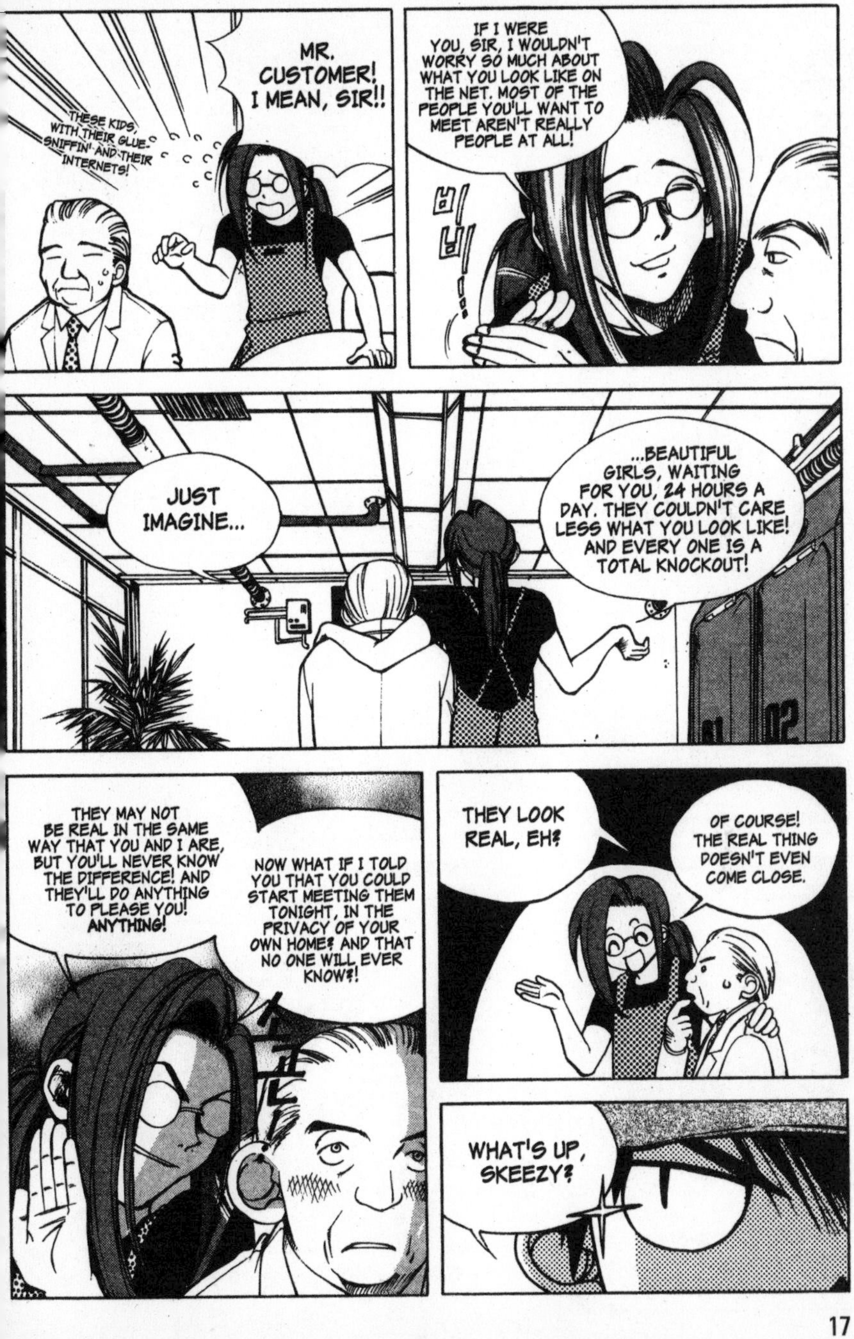
MR. CUSTOMER! I MEAN, SIR!!
THESE KIDS, WITH THEIR GLUE-SNIFFIN' AND THEIR INTERNETS!
IF I WERE YOU, SIR, I WOULDN'T WORRY SO MUCH ABOUT WHAT YOU LOOK LIKE ON THE NET. MOST OF THE PEOPLE YOU'LL WANT TO MEET AREN'T REALLY PEOPLE AT ALL!
JUST IMAGINE...
...BEAUTIFUL GIRLS, WAITING FOR YOU, 24 HOURS A DAY. THEY COULDN'T CARE LESS WHAT YOU LOOK LIKE! AND EVERY ONE IS A TOTAL KNOCKOUT!
THEY MAY NOT BE REAL IN THE SAME WAY THAT YOU AND I ARE, BUT YOU'LL NEVER KNOW THE DIFFERENCE! AND THEY'LL DO ANYTHING TO PLEASE YOU! ANYTHING!
NOW WHAT IF I TOLD YOU THAT YOU COULD START MEETING THEM TONIGHT, IN THE PRIVACY OF YOUR OWN HOME? AND THAT NO ONE WILL EVER KNOW?!
THEY LOOK REAL, EH?
OF COURSE! THE REAL THING DOESN'T EVEN COME CLOSE.
WHAT'S UP, SKEEZY?

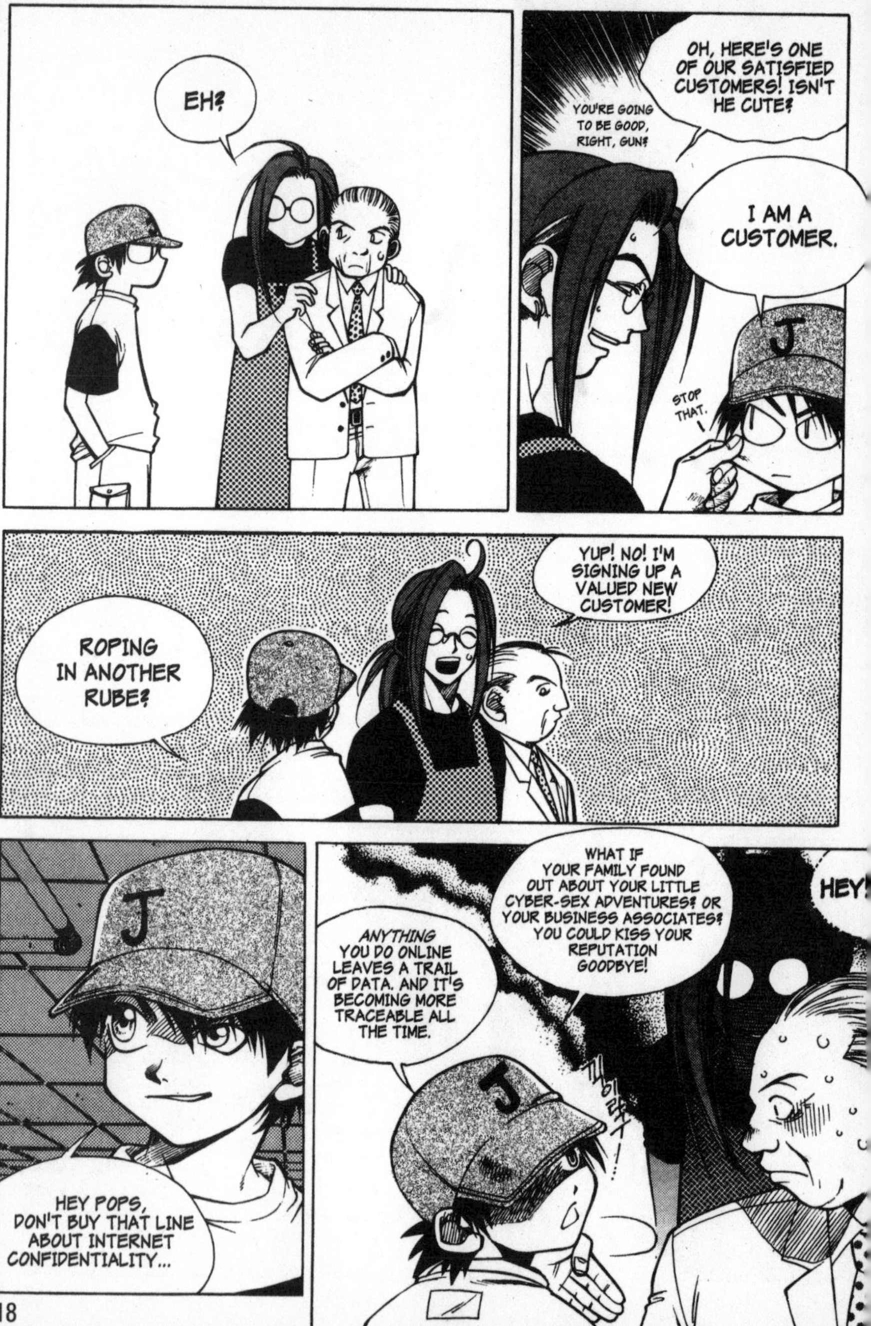
EH?
YOU'RE GOING TO BE GOOD, RIGHT, GUN?
OH, HERE'S ONE OF OUR SATISFIED CUSTOMERS! ISN'T HE CUTE?
I AM A CUSTOMER.
STOP THAT.
ROPING IN ANOTHER RUBE?
YUP! NO! I'M SIGNING UP A VALUED NEW CUSTOMER!
HEY POPS, DON'T BUY THAT LINE ABOUT INTERNET CONFIDENTIALITY...
ANYTHING YOU DO ONLINE LEAVES A TRAIL OF DATA. AND IT'S BECOMING MORE TRACEABLE ALL THE TIME.
WHAT IF YOUR FAMILY FOUND OUT ABOUT YOUR LITTLE CYBER-SEX ADVENTURES? OR YOUR BUSINESS ASSOCIATES? YOU COULD KISS YOUR REPUTATION GOODBYE!
HEY!

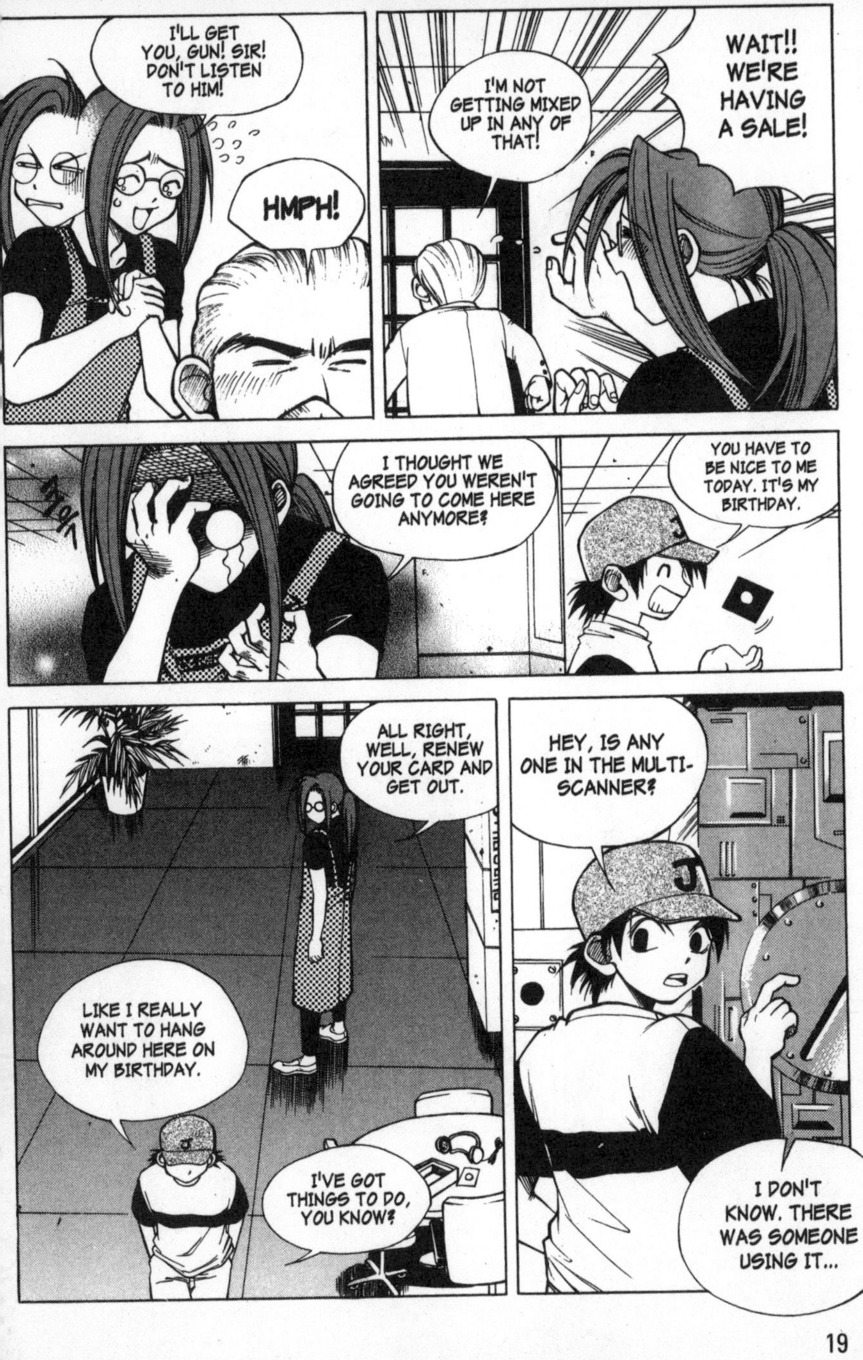
I'LL GET YOU, GUN! SIR! DON'T LISTEN TO HIM!
HMPH!
I'M NOT GETTING MIXED UP IN ANY OF THAT!
WAIT!! WE'RE HAVING A SALE!
I THOUGHT WE AGREED YOU WEREN'T GOING TO COME HERE ANYMORE?
YOU HAVE TO BE NICE TO ME TODAY. IT'S MY BIRTHDAY.
ALL RIGHT, WELL, RENEW YOUR CARD AND GET OUT.
LIKE I REALLY WANT TO HANG AROUND HERE ON MY BIRTHDAY.
I'VE GOT THINGS TO DO, YOU KNOW?
HEY, IS ANY ONE IN THE MULTI-SCANNER?
I DON'T KNOW. THERE WAS SOMEONE USING IT...

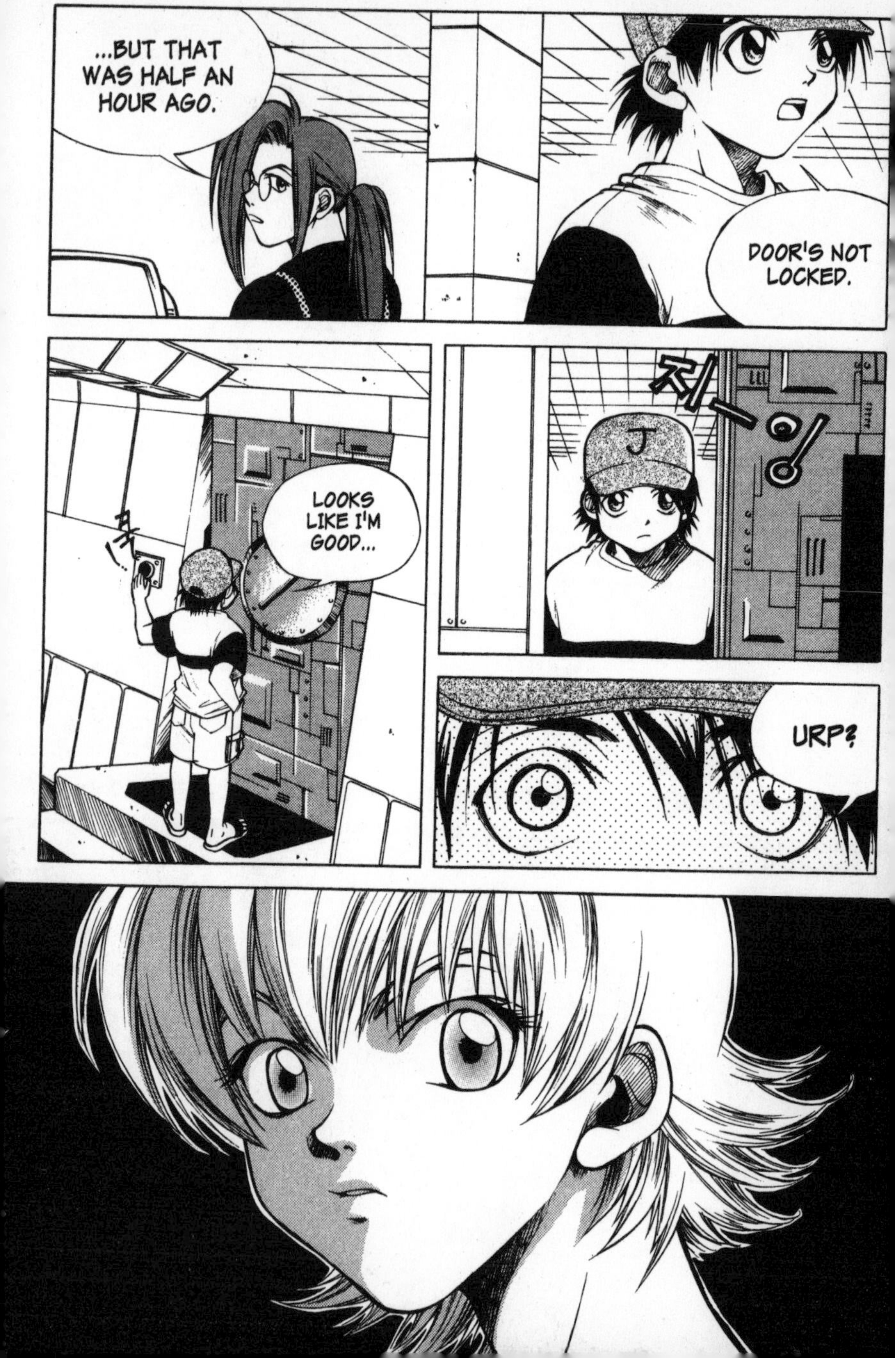
...BUT THAT WAS HALF AN HOUR AGO.
DOOR'S NOT LOCKED.
LOOKS LIKE I'M GOOD...
URP?

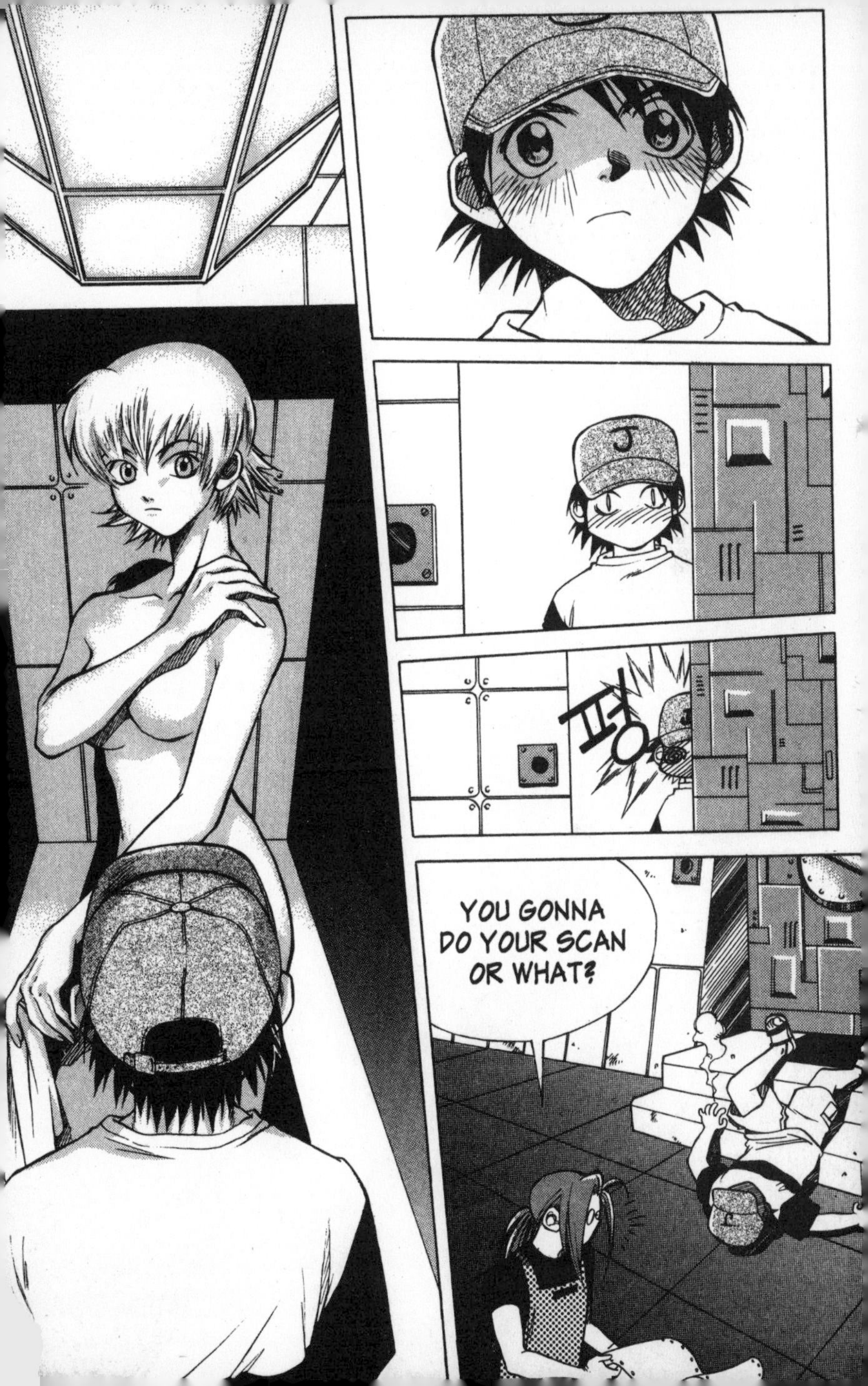
펑
YOU GONNA DO YOUR SCAN OR WHAT?

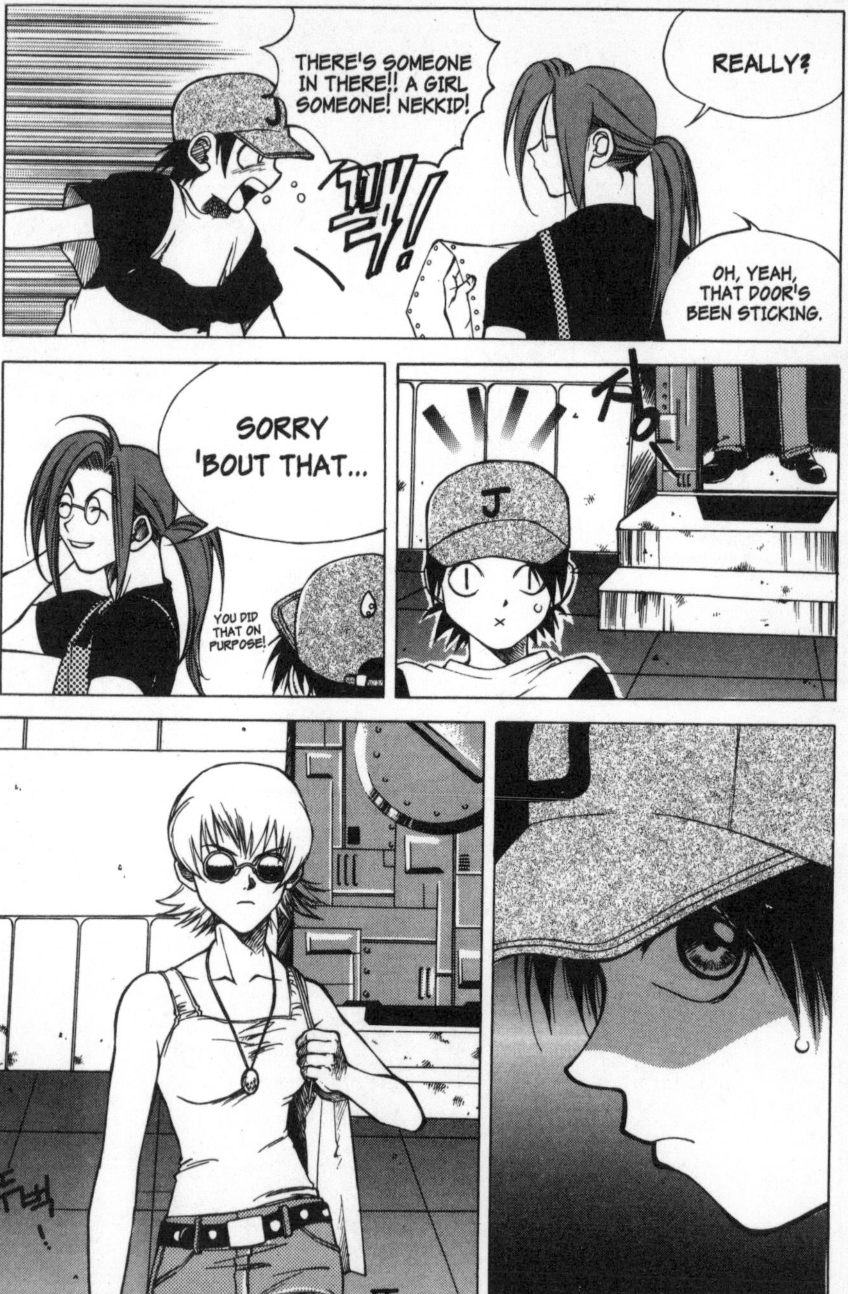
THERE'S SOMEONE IN THERE!! A GIRL SOMEONE! NEKKID!
REALLY?
OH, YEAH, THAT DOOR'S BEEN STICKING.
SORRY 'BOUT THAT...
YOU DID THAT ON PURPOSE!
뚜벅
뚜벅

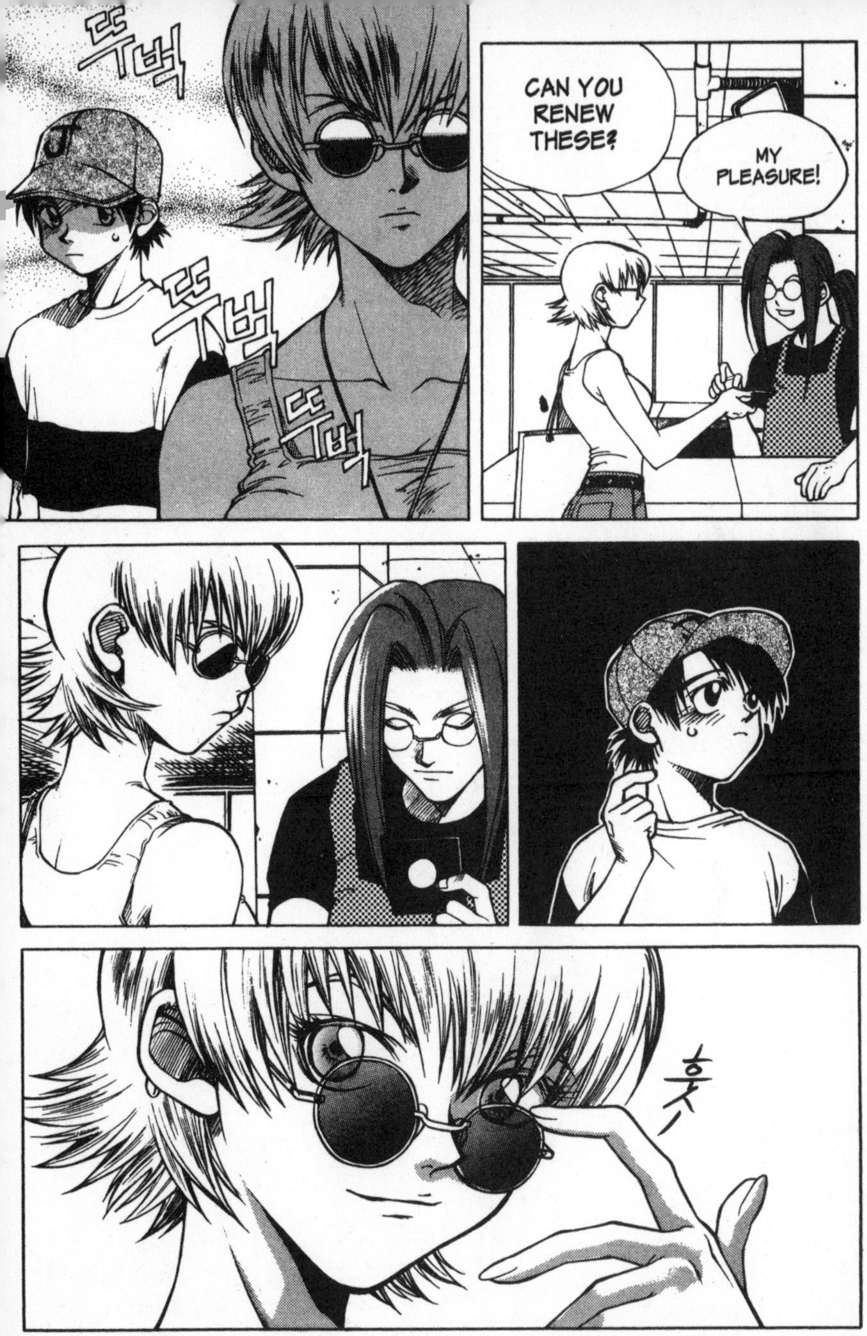
뚜벅
뚜벅
뚜벅
CAN YOU RENEW THESE?
MY PLEASURE!
훗

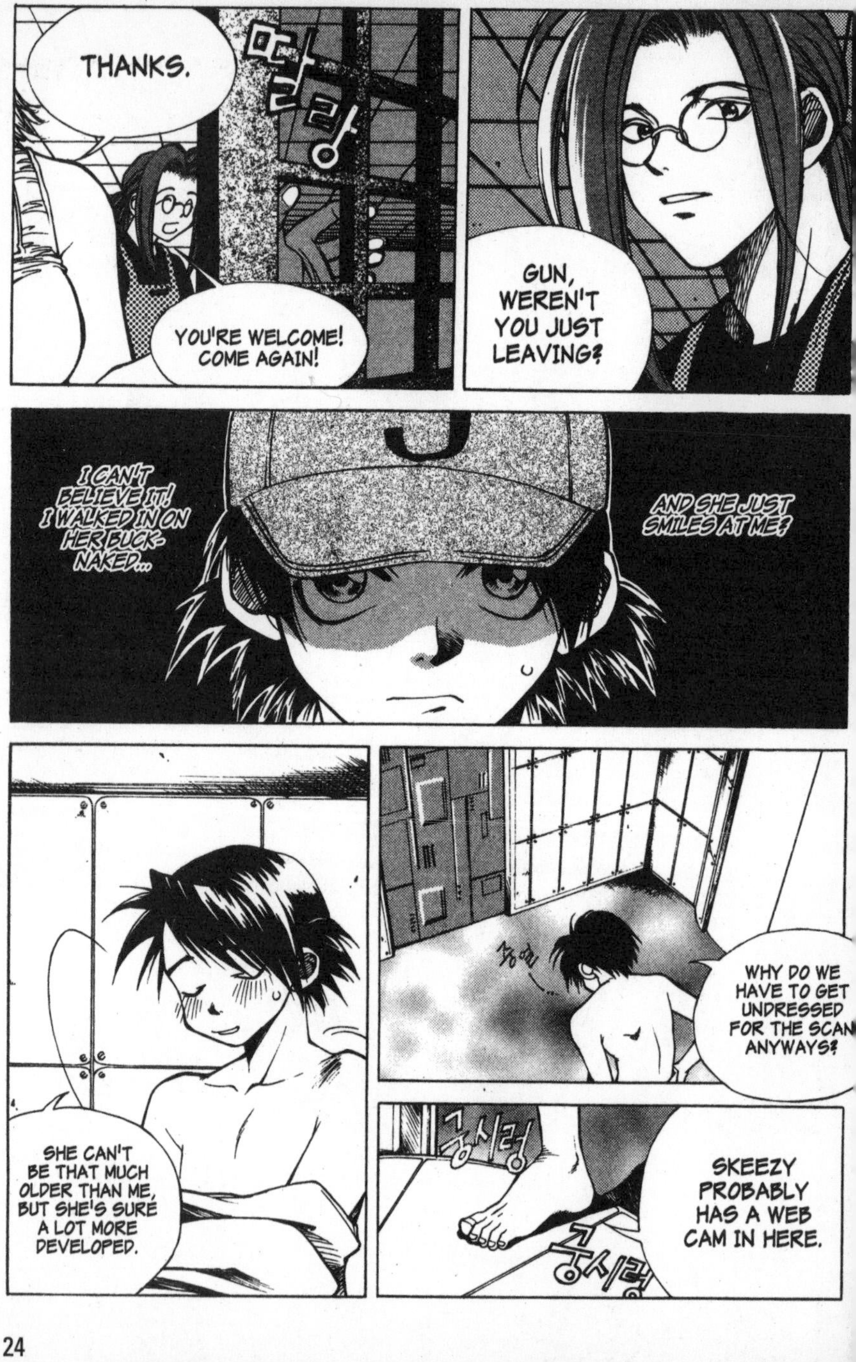
THANKS.
딸랑
YOU'RE WELCOME! COME AGAIN!
GUN, WEREN'T YOU JUST LEAVING?
I CAN'T BELIEVE IT! I WALKED IN ON HER BUCK-NAKED...
AND SHE JUST SMILES AT ME?
SHE CAN'T BE THAT MUCH OLDER THAN ME, BUT SHE'S SURE A LOT MORE DEVELOPED.
중얼...
WHY DO WE HAVE TO GET UNDRESSED FOR THE SCAN ANYWAYS?
궁시렁
SKEEZY PROBABLY HAS A WEB CAM IN HERE.
궁시렁

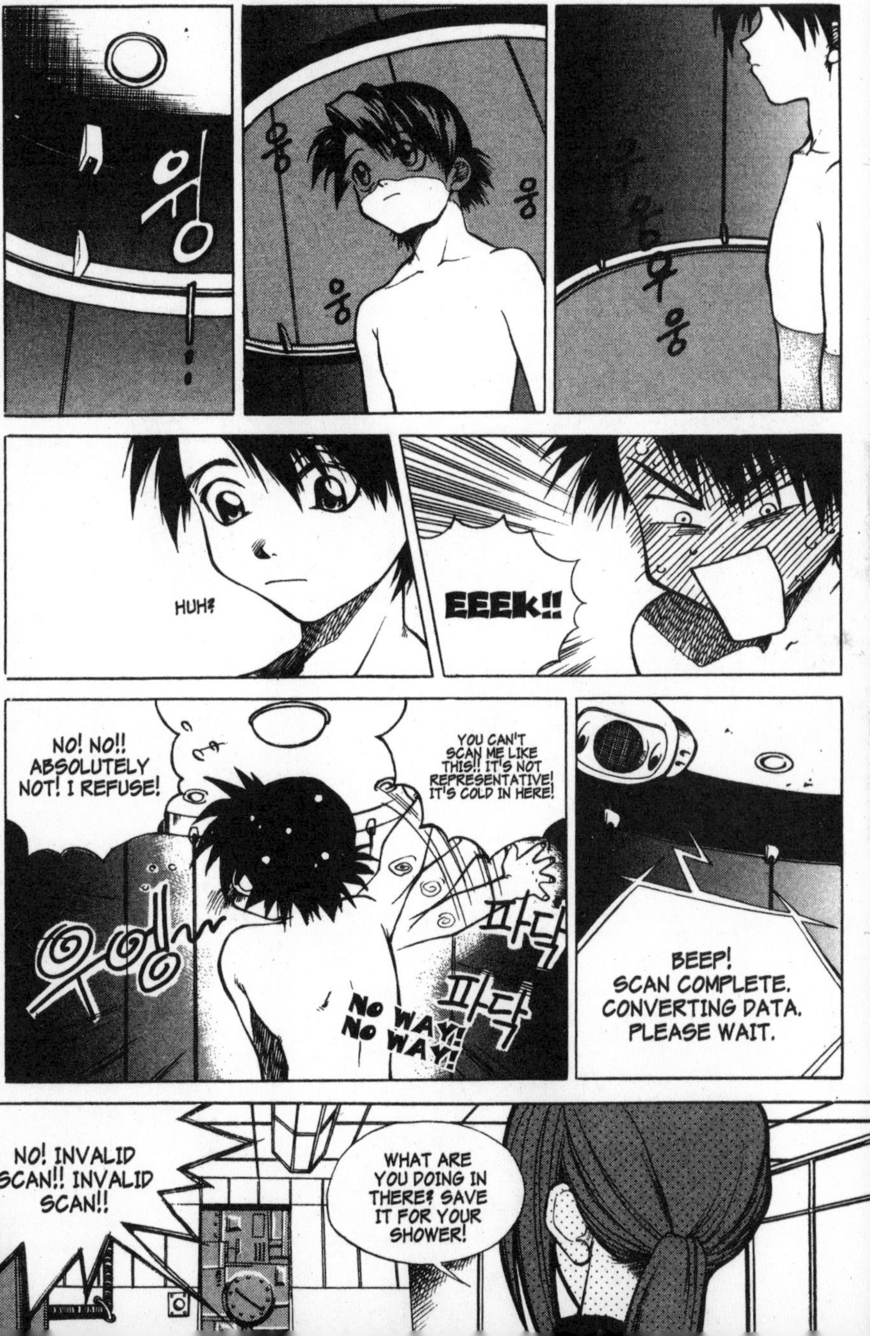

웅
웅
웅
웅
웅
HUH?
EEEK!!
NO! NO!! ABSOLUTELY NOT! I REFUSE!
YOU CAN'T SCAN ME LIKE THIS!! IT'S NOT REPRESENTATIVE! IT'S COLD IN HERE!
파닥
파닥
NO WAY! NO WAY!
BEEP! SCAN COMPLETE. CONVERTING DATA. PLEASE WAIT.
NO! INVALID SCAN!! INVALID SCAN!!
WHAT ARE YOU DOING IN THERE? SAVE IT FOR YOUR SHOWER!

IT'S NOT WORKING. I'LL JUST HAVE COME BACK LATER AND RE-SCAN.

SKEEZY'S GOING TO CHARGE ME TWICE, I'M SURE.

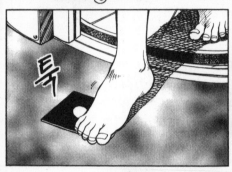

THIS ISN'T MINE.

SHE MUST HAVE DROPPED IT.

HUH?

YUREKA?

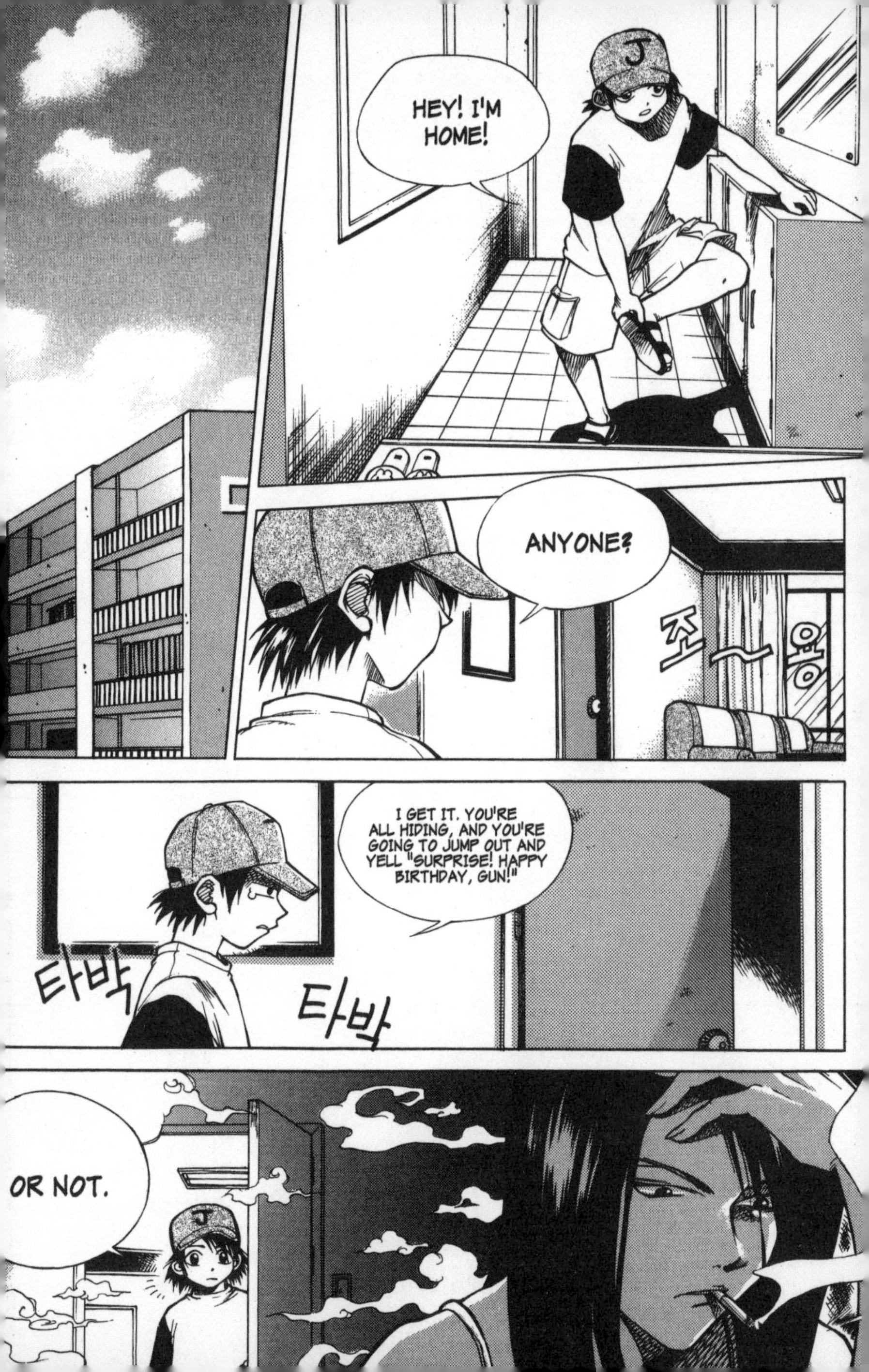
HEY! I'M HOME!
ANYONE?
조~용
I GET IT. YOU'RE ALL HIDING, AND YOU'RE GOING TO JUMP OUT AND YELL "SURPRISE! HAPPY BIRTHDAY, GUN!"
타박
타박
OR NOT.

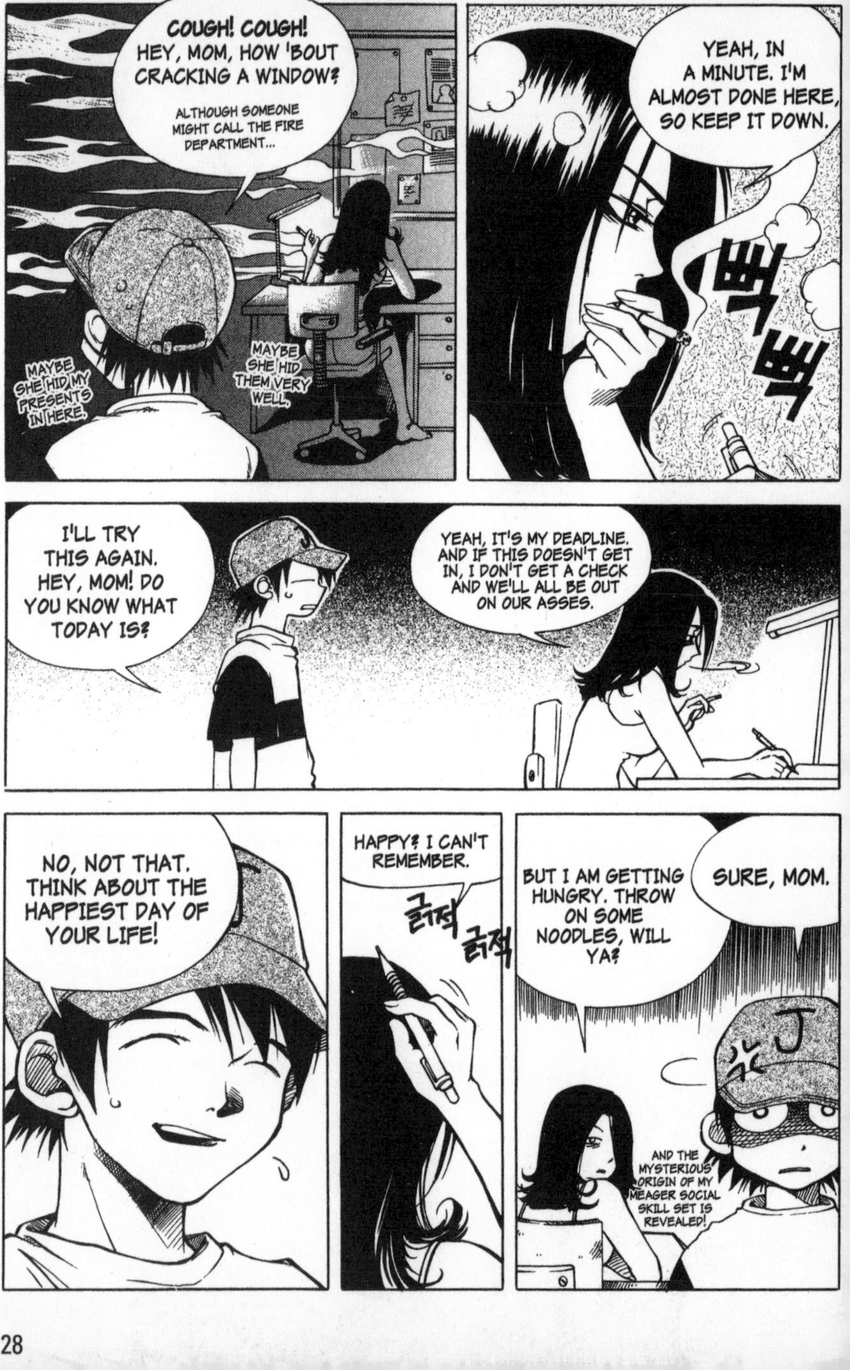
COUGH! COUGH! HEY, MOM, HOW 'BOUT CRACKING A WINDOW?
ALTHOUGH SOMEONE MIGHT CALL THE FIRE DEPARTMENT...
MAYBE SHE HID MY PRESENTS IN HERE.
MAYBE SHE HID THEM VERY WELL.
YEAH, IN A MINUTE. I'M ALMOST DONE HERE, SO KEEP IT DOWN.
뻑
뻑
I'LL TRY THIS AGAIN. HEY, MOM! DO YOU KNOW WHAT TODAY IS?
YEAH, IT'S MY DEADLINE. AND IF THIS DOESN'T GET IN, I DON'T GET A CHECK AND WE'LL ALL BE OUT ON OUR ASSES.
NO, NOT THAT. THINK ABOUT THE HAPPIEST DAY OF YOUR LIFE!
HAPPY? I CAN'T REMEMBER.
긁적
긁적
BUT I AM GETTING HUNGRY. THROW ON SOME NOODLES, WILL YA?
SURE, MOM.
AND THE MYSTERIOUS ORIGIN OF MY MEAGER SOCIAL SKILL SET IS REVEALED!

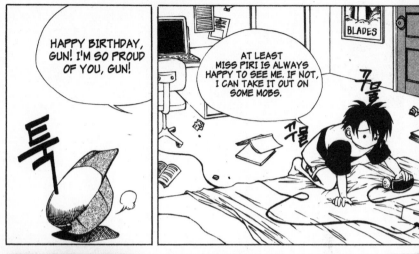

HAPPY BIRTHDAY, GUN! I'M SO PROUD OF YOU, GUN!

AT LEAST MISS PIRI IS ALWAYS HAPPY TO SEE ME. IF NOT, I CAN TAKE IT OUT ON SOME MOBS.

IT'S NOT LIKE I EVER GET ANY BIGGER.

WHY DO I EVEN HAVE TO BOTHER GETTING SCANNED?

TALLER. I MEANT TALLER.

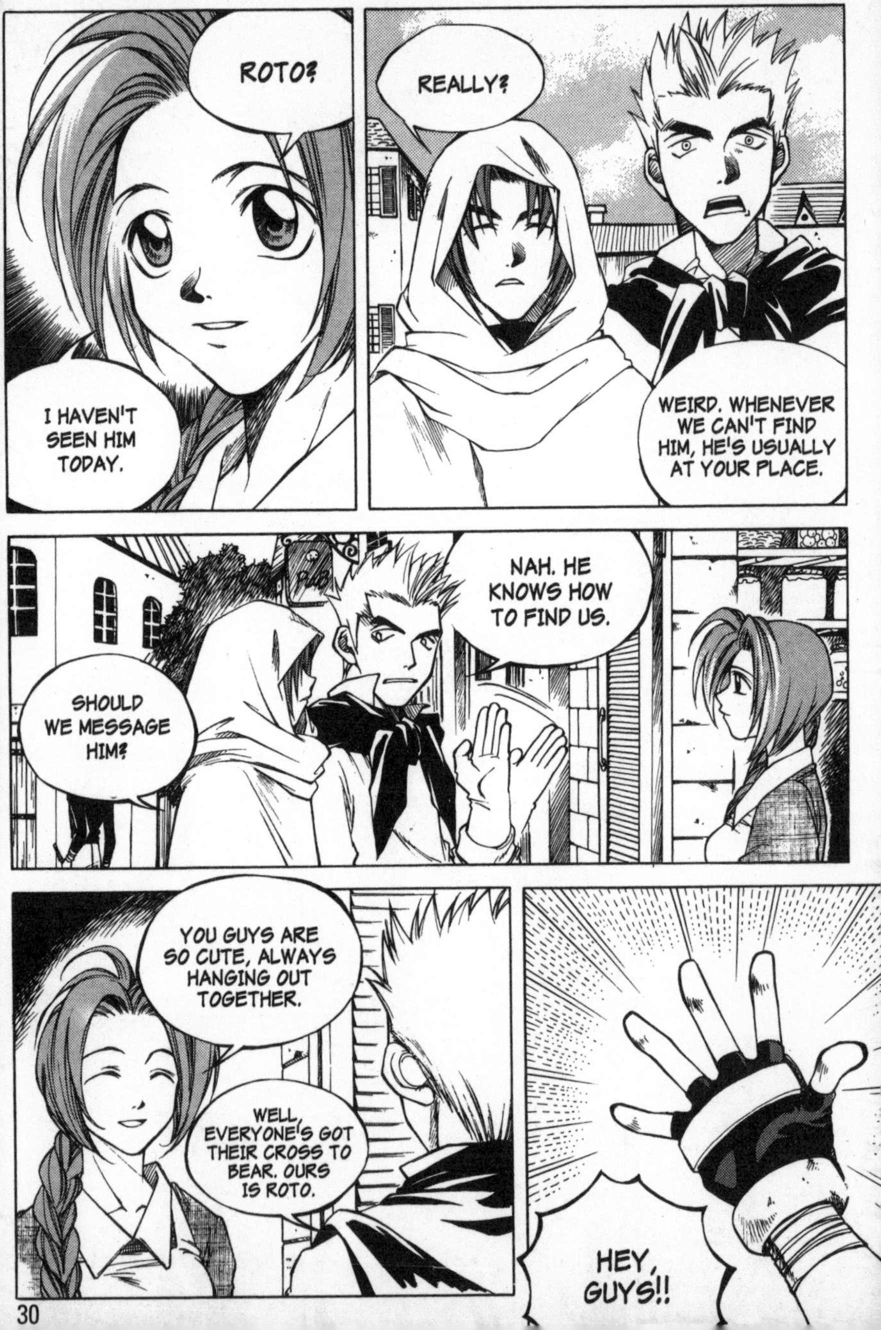
ROTO?
I HAVEN'T SEEN HIM TODAY.
REALLY?
WEIRD. WHENEVER WE CAN'T FIND HIM, HE'S USUALLY AT YOUR PLACE.
SHOULD WE MESSAGE HIM?
NAH. HE KNOWS HOW TO FIND US.
YOU GUYS ARE SO CUTE, ALWAYS HANGING OUT TOGETHER.
WELL, EVERYONE'S GOT THEIR CROSS TO BEAR. OURS IS ROTO.
HEY, GUYS!!

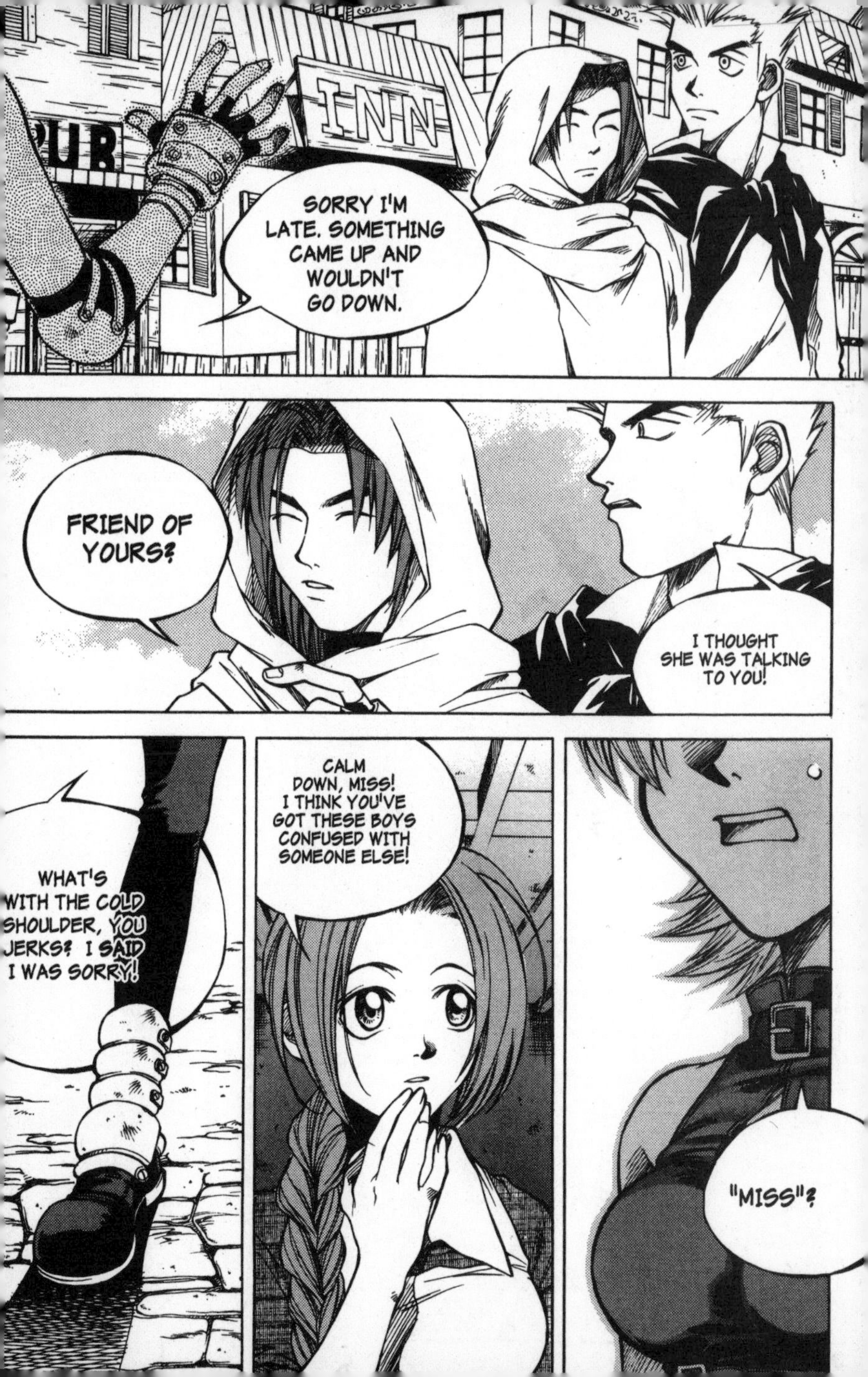

INN
SORRY I'M LATE. SOMETHING CAME UP AND WOULDN'T GO DOWN.
FRIEND OF YOURS?
I THOUGHT SHE WAS TALKING TO YOU!
WHAT'S WITH THE COLD SHOULDER, YOU JERKS? I SAID I WAS SORRY!
CALM DOWN, MISS! I THINK YOU'VE GOT THESE BOYS CONFUSED WITH SOMEONE ELSE!
"MISS"?

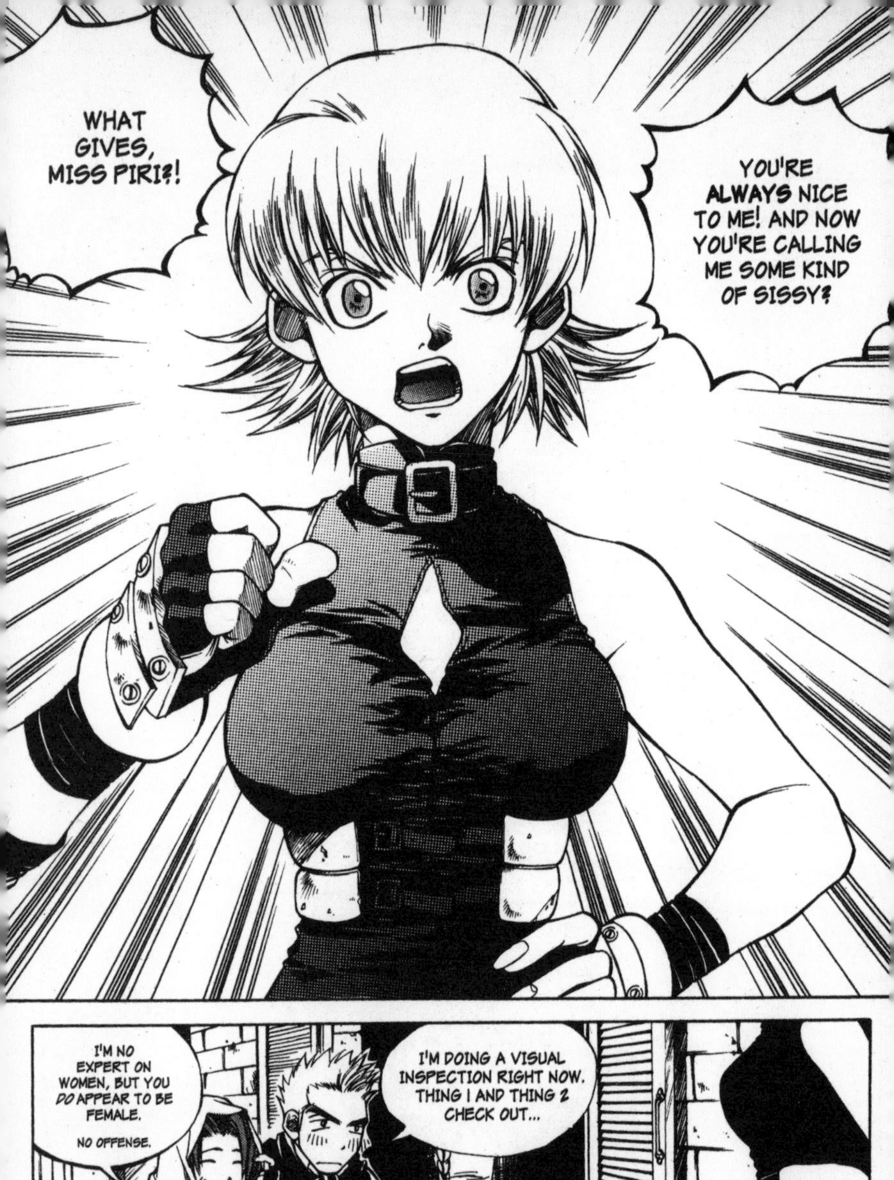
WHAT GIVES, MISS PIRI?!
YOU'RE ALWAYS NICE TO ME! AND NOW YOU'RE CALLING ME SOME KIND OF SISSY?

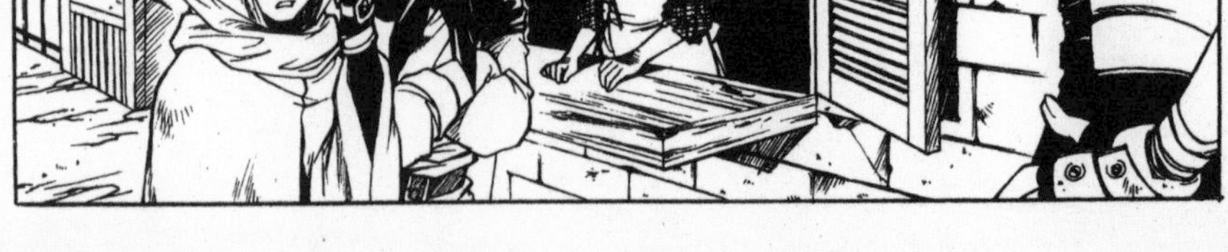
I'M NO EXPERT ON WOMEN, BUT YOU DO APPEAR TO BE FEMALE.
NO OFFENSE.
I'M DOING A VISUAL INSPECTION RIGHT NOW. THING 1 AND THING 2 CHECK OUT...

WHAT ARE YOU TALKING ABOUT?

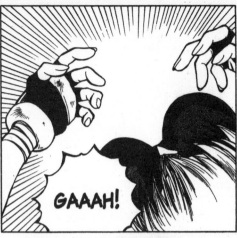

GAAAH!

THEY'RE GINORMOUS!

I'VE HEARD BLONDES AREN'T TOO BRIGHT...BUT SHE SHOULD AT LEAST KNOW SHE'S A GIRL, RIGHT?

THAT GETS COVERED PRETTY EARLY ON. YOU'D THINK SHE'D HAVE THAT DOWN BY NOW.

HEH.

IF YOU KNOW HER, I'D LIKE AN INTRODUCTION!

YOU SURE WE HAVEN'T MET HER SOMEWHERE BEFORE?

HA HA HA.

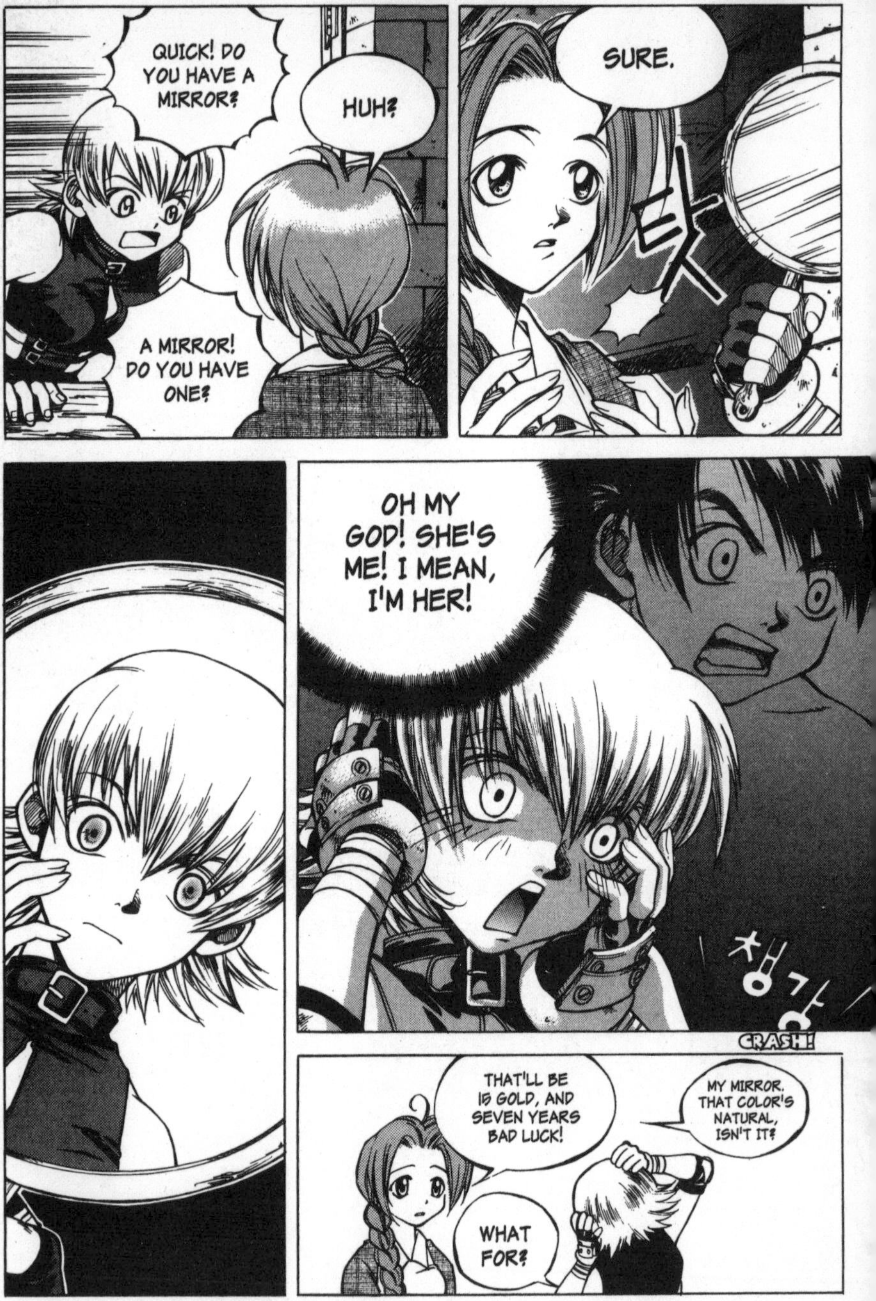
QUICK! DO YOU HAVE A MIRROR?
HUH?
A MIRROR! DO YOU HAVE ONE?
SURE.
OH MY GOD! SHE'S ME! I MEAN, I'M HER!
CRASH!
THAT'LL BE 15 GOLD, AND SEVEN YEARS BAD LUCK!
MY MIRROR. THAT COLOR'S NATURAL, ISN'T IT?
WHAT FOR?

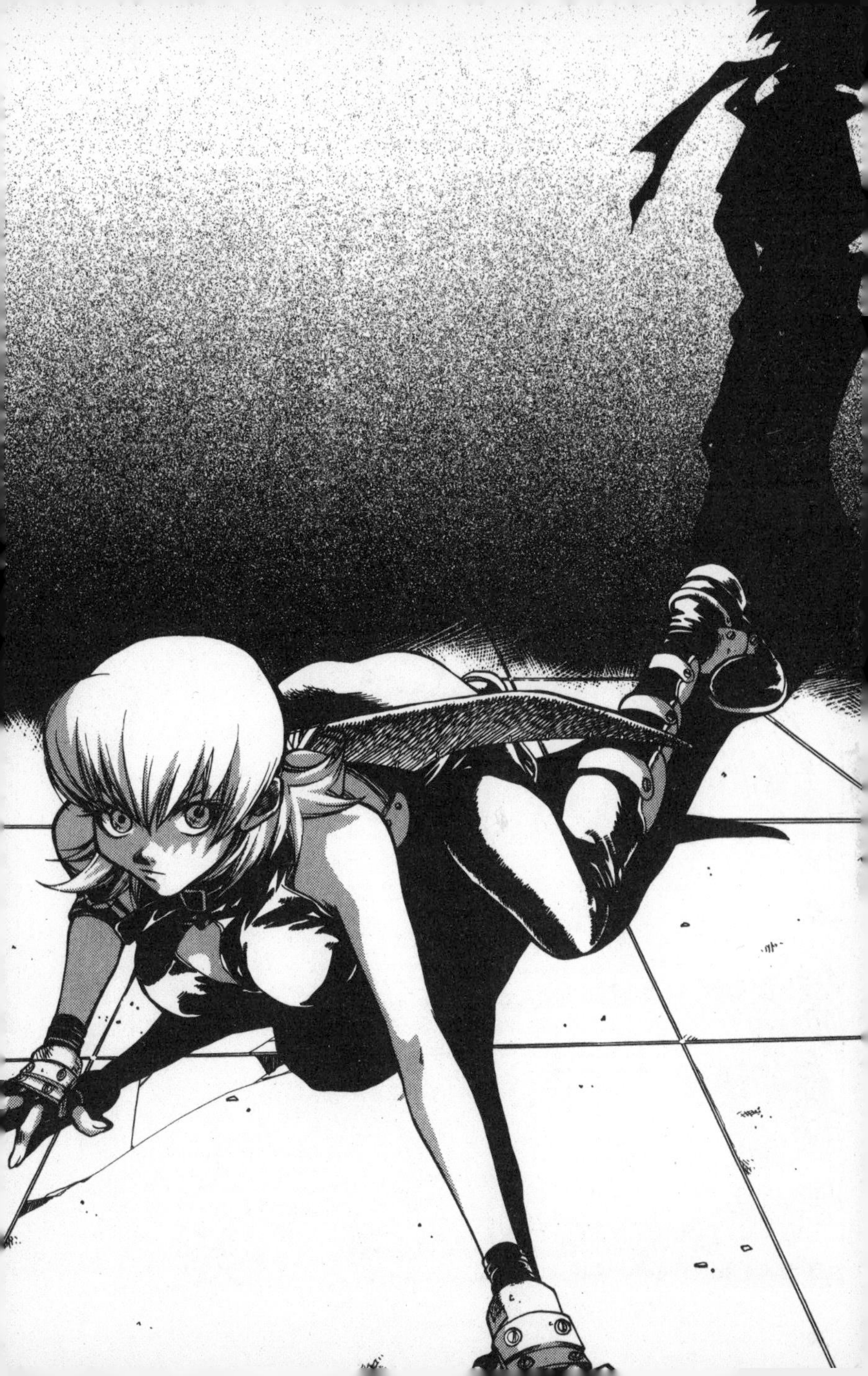

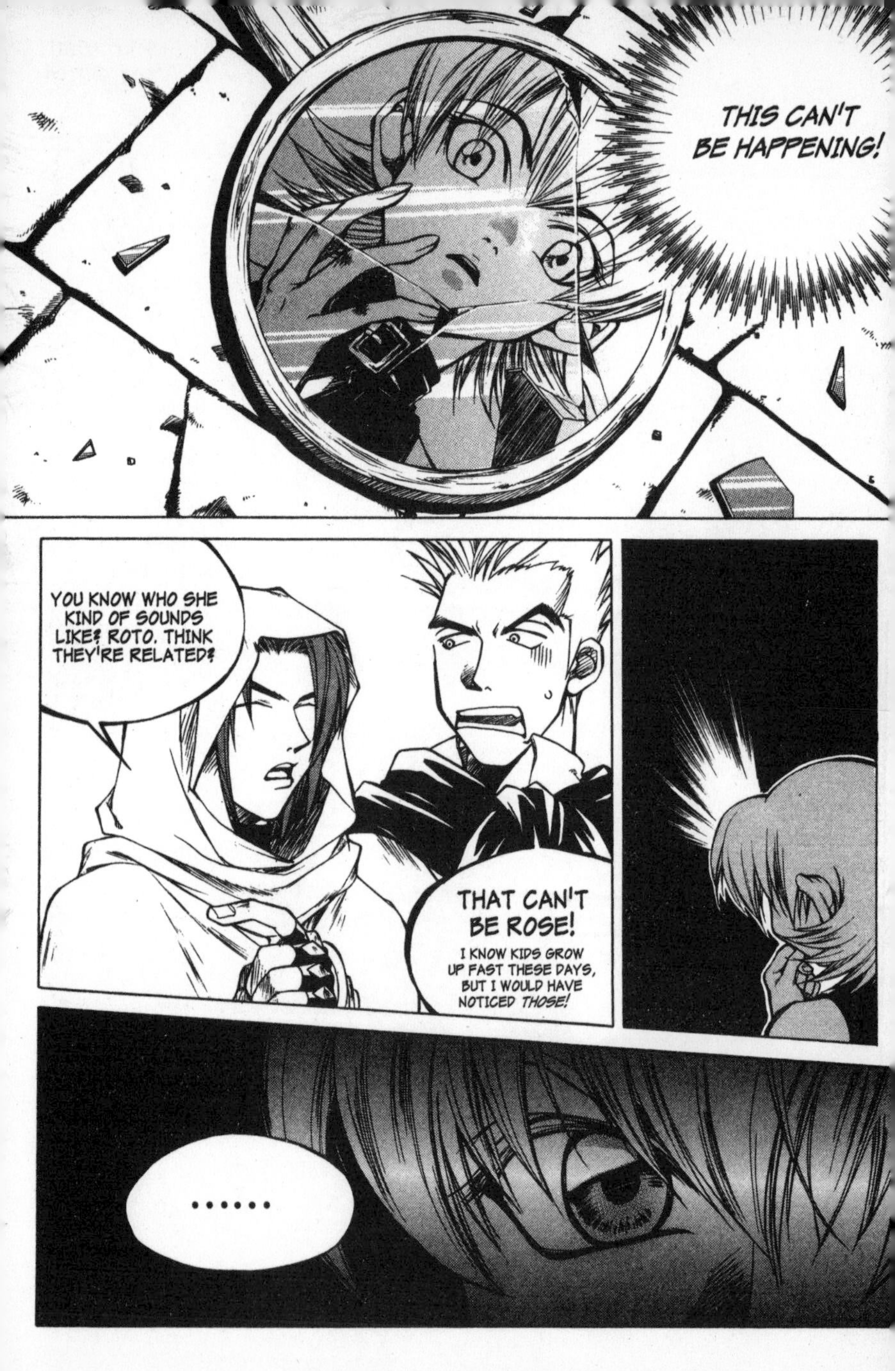

THIS CAN'T BE HAPPENING!
YOU KNOW WHO SHE KIND OF SOUNDS LIKE? ROTO. THINK THEY'RE RELATED?
THAT CAN'T BE ROSE!
I KNOW KIDS GROW UP FAST THESE DAYS, BUT I WOULD HAVE NOTICED *THOSE!*
......

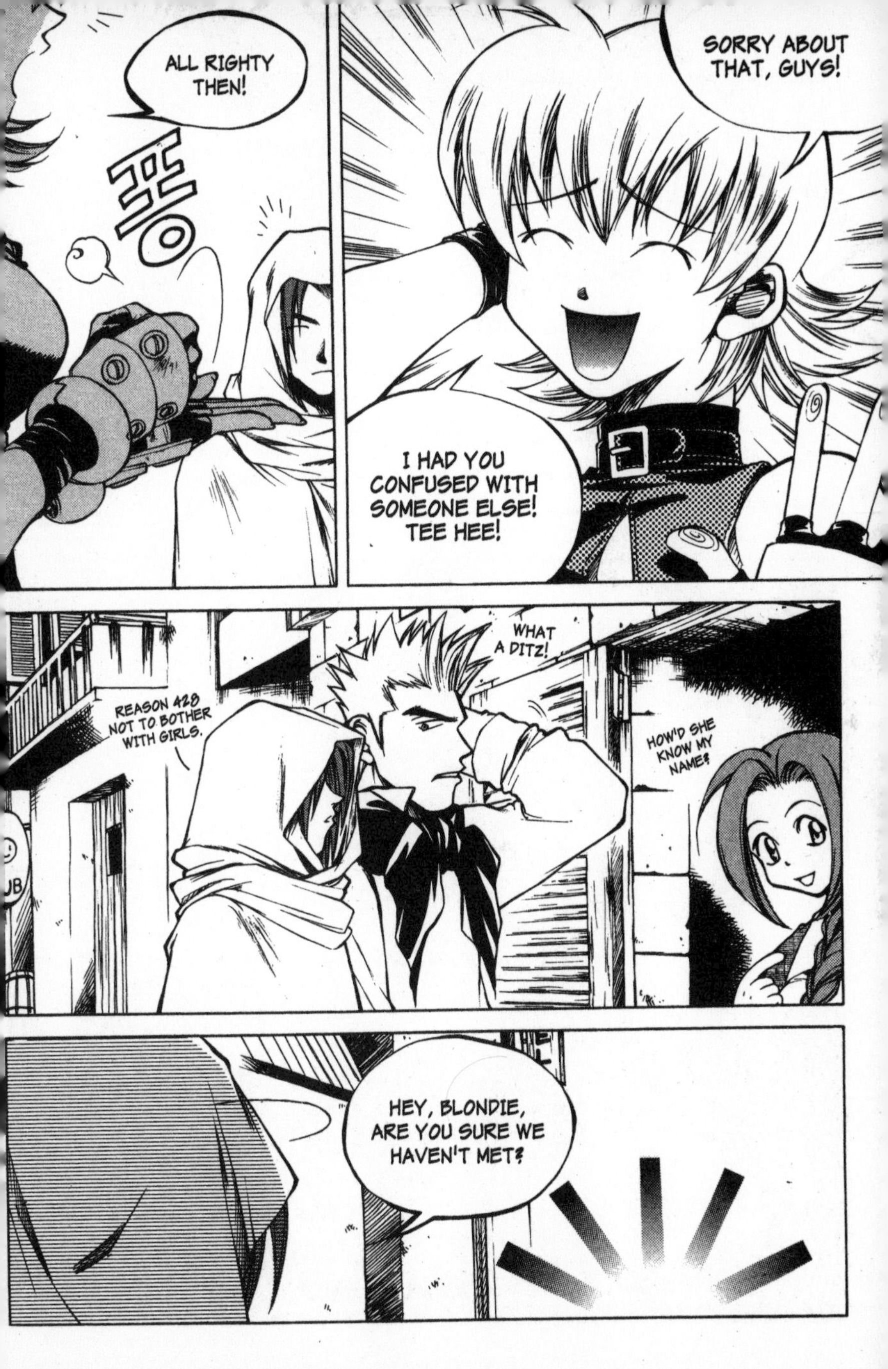
ALL RIGHTY THEN!
SORRY ABOUT THAT, GUYS!
I HAD YOU CONFUSED WITH SOMEONE ELSE! TEE HEE!
REASON 428 NOT TO BOTHER WITH GIRLS.
WHAT A DITZ!
HOW'D SHE KNOW MY NAME?
HEY, BLONDIE, ARE YOU SURE WE HAVEN'T MET?

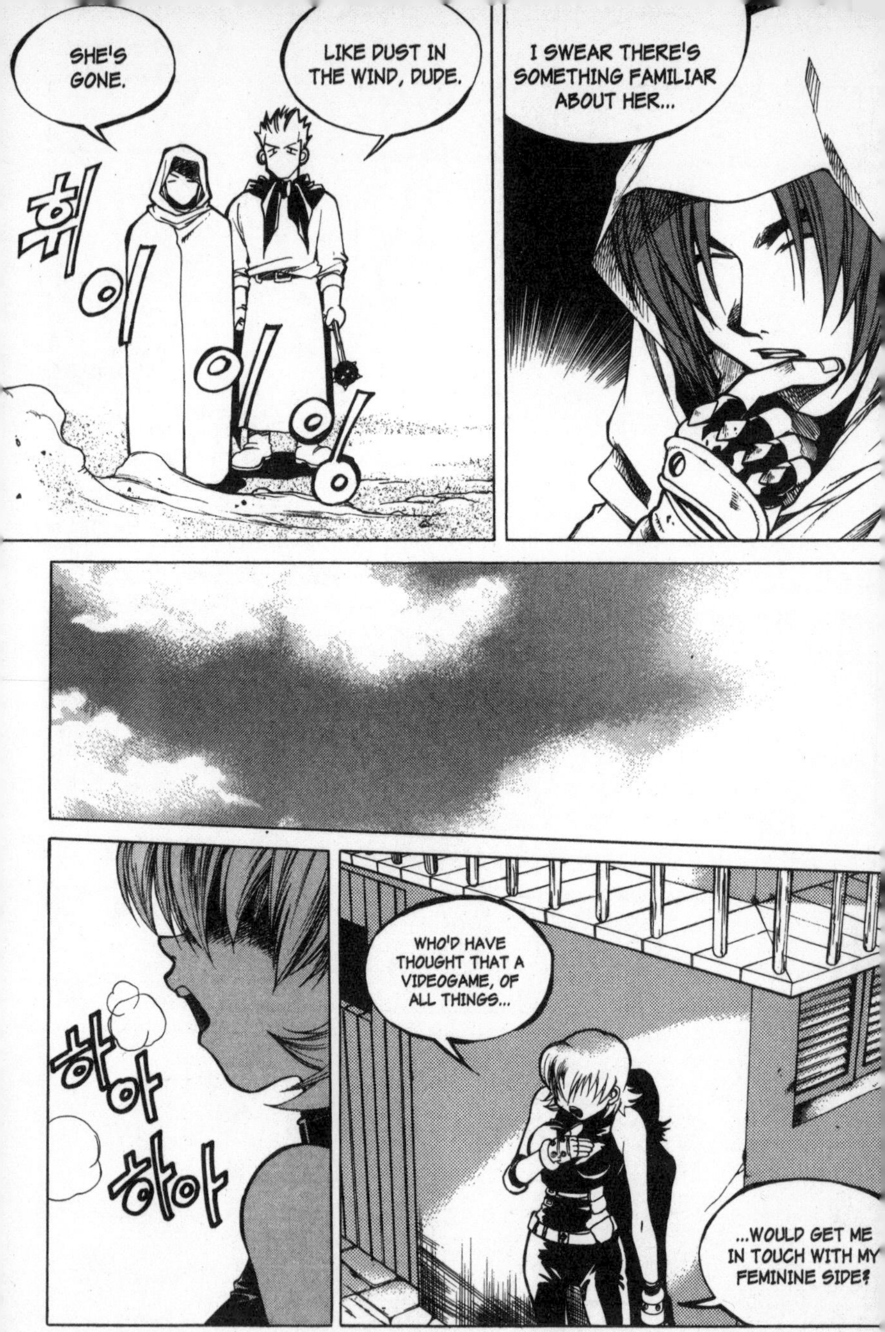
SHE'S GONE.
LIKE DUST IN THE WIND, DUDE.
휘이이잉
I SWEAR THERE'S SOMETHING FAMILIAR ABOUT HER...
하아 하아
WHO'D HAVE THOUGHT THAT A VIDEOGAME, OF ALL THINGS...
...WOULD GET ME IN TOUCH WITH MY FEMININE SIDE?

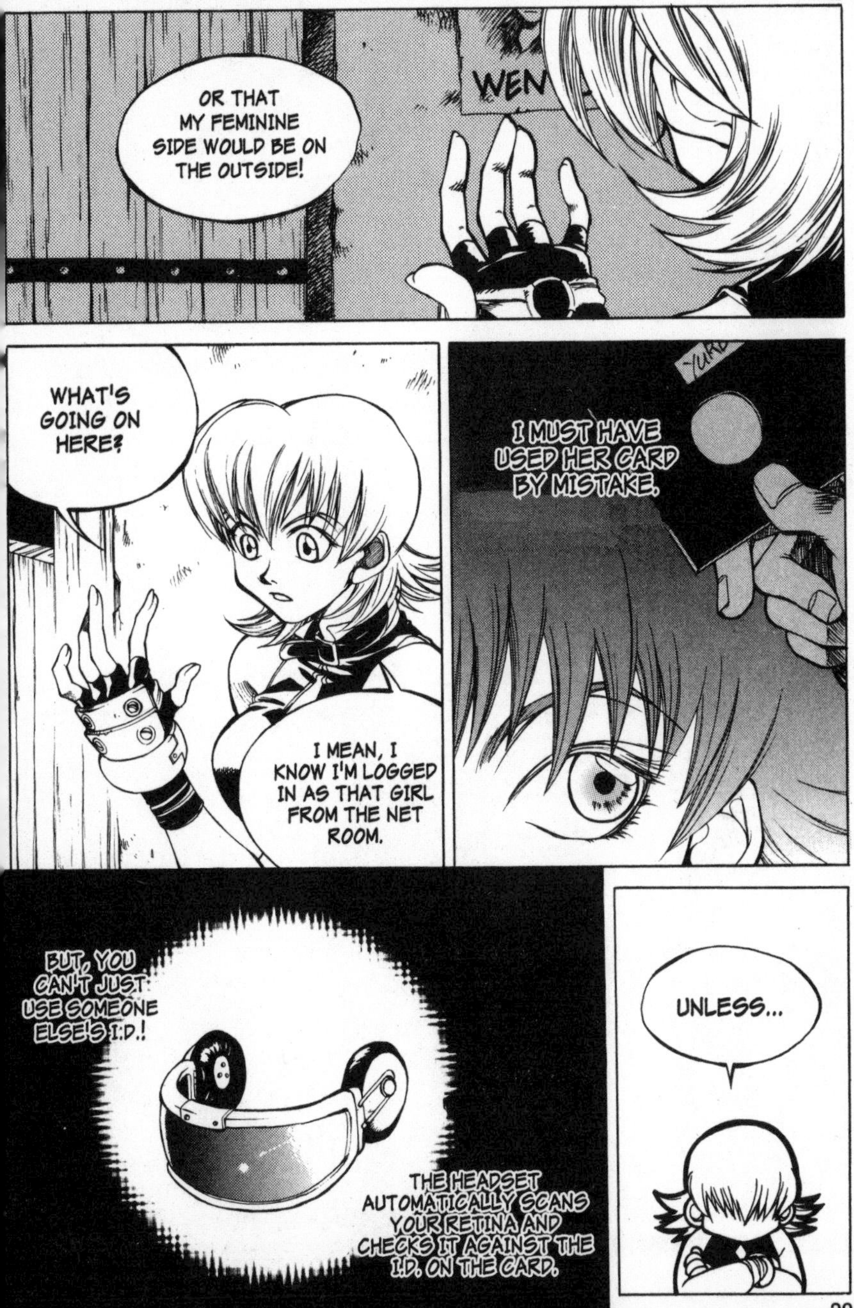
WEN
OR THAT MY FEMININE SIDE WOULD BE ON THE OUTSIDE!
WHAT'S GOING ON HERE?
I MEAN, I KNOW I'M LOGGED IN AS THAT GIRL FROM THE NET ROOM.
I MUST HAVE USED HER CARD BY MISTAKE.
BUT, YOU CAN'T JUST USE SOMEONE ELSE'S I.D.!
THE HEADSET AUTOMATICALLY SCANS YOUR RETINA AND CHECKS IT AGAINST THE I.D. ON THE CARD.
UNLESS...

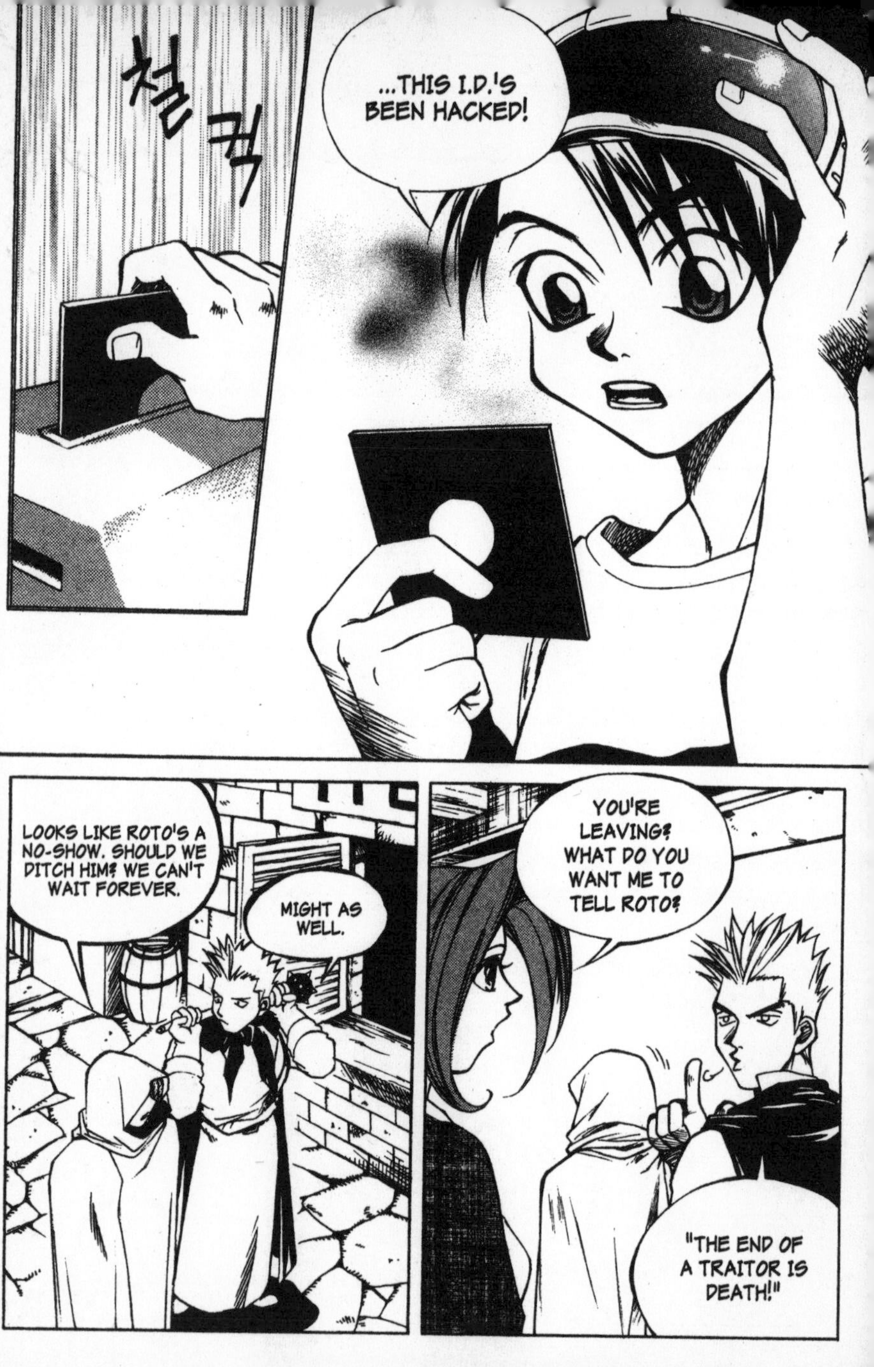
철컥
...THIS I.D.'S BEEN HACKED!
LOOKS LIKE ROTO'S A NO-SHOW. SHOULD WE DITCH HIM? WE CAN'T WAIT FOREVER.
MIGHT AS WELL.
YOU'RE LEAVING? WHAT DO YOU WANT ME TO TELL ROTO?
"THE END OF A TRAITOR IS DEATH!"

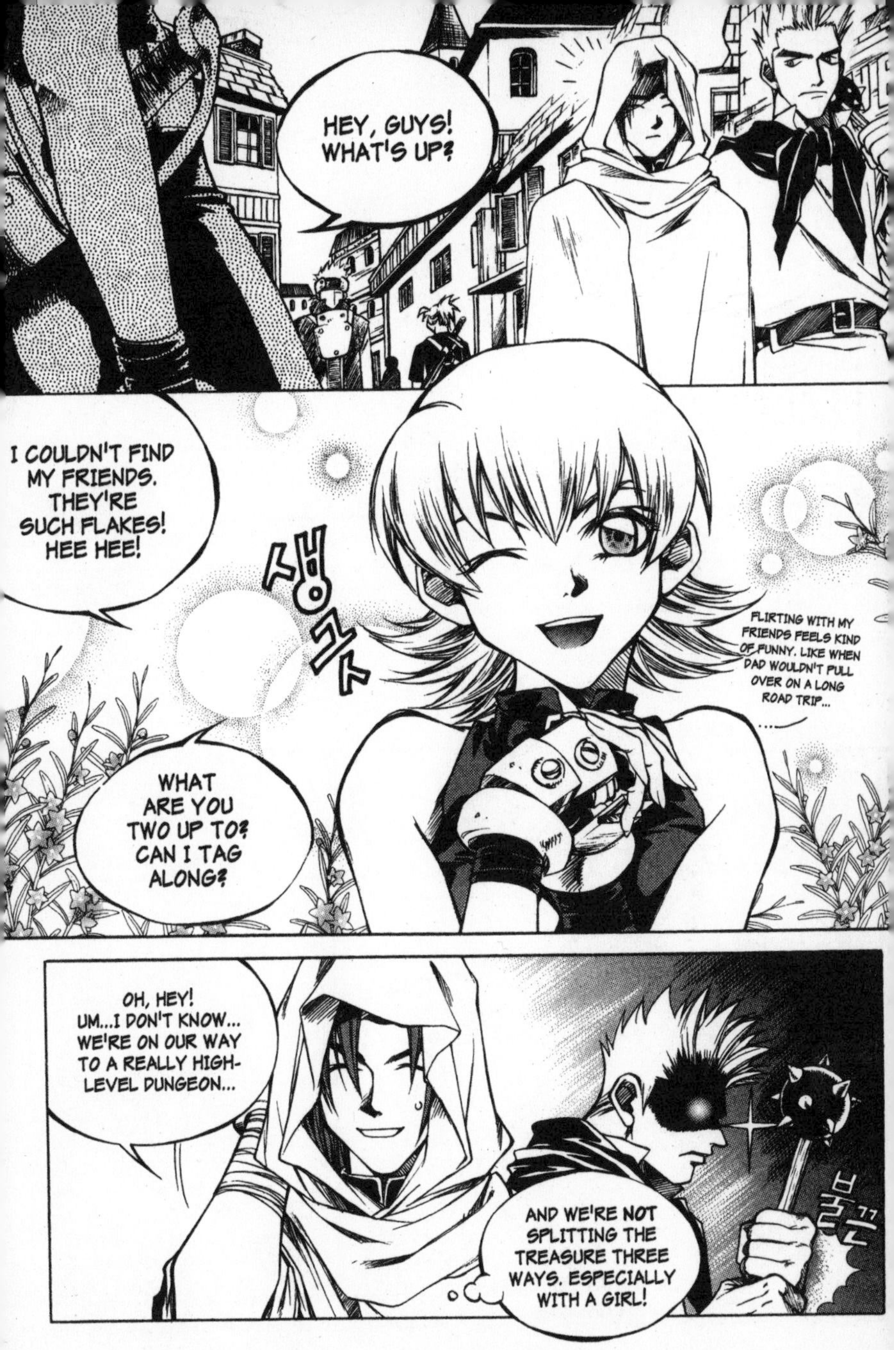
HEY, GUYS! WHAT'S UP?
I COULDN'T FIND MY FRIENDS. THEY'RE SUCH FLAKES! HEE HEE!
FLIRTING WITH MY FRIENDS FEELS KIND OF FUNNY. LIKE WHEN DAD WOULDN'T PULL OVER ON A LONG ROAD TRIP...
...
WHAT ARE YOU TWO UP TO? CAN I TAG ALONG?
OH, HEY! UM...I DON'T KNOW... WE'RE ON OUR WAY TO A REALLY HIGH-LEVEL DUNGEON...
AND WE'RE NOT SPLITTING THE TREASURE THREE WAYS. ESPECIALLY WITH A GIRL!

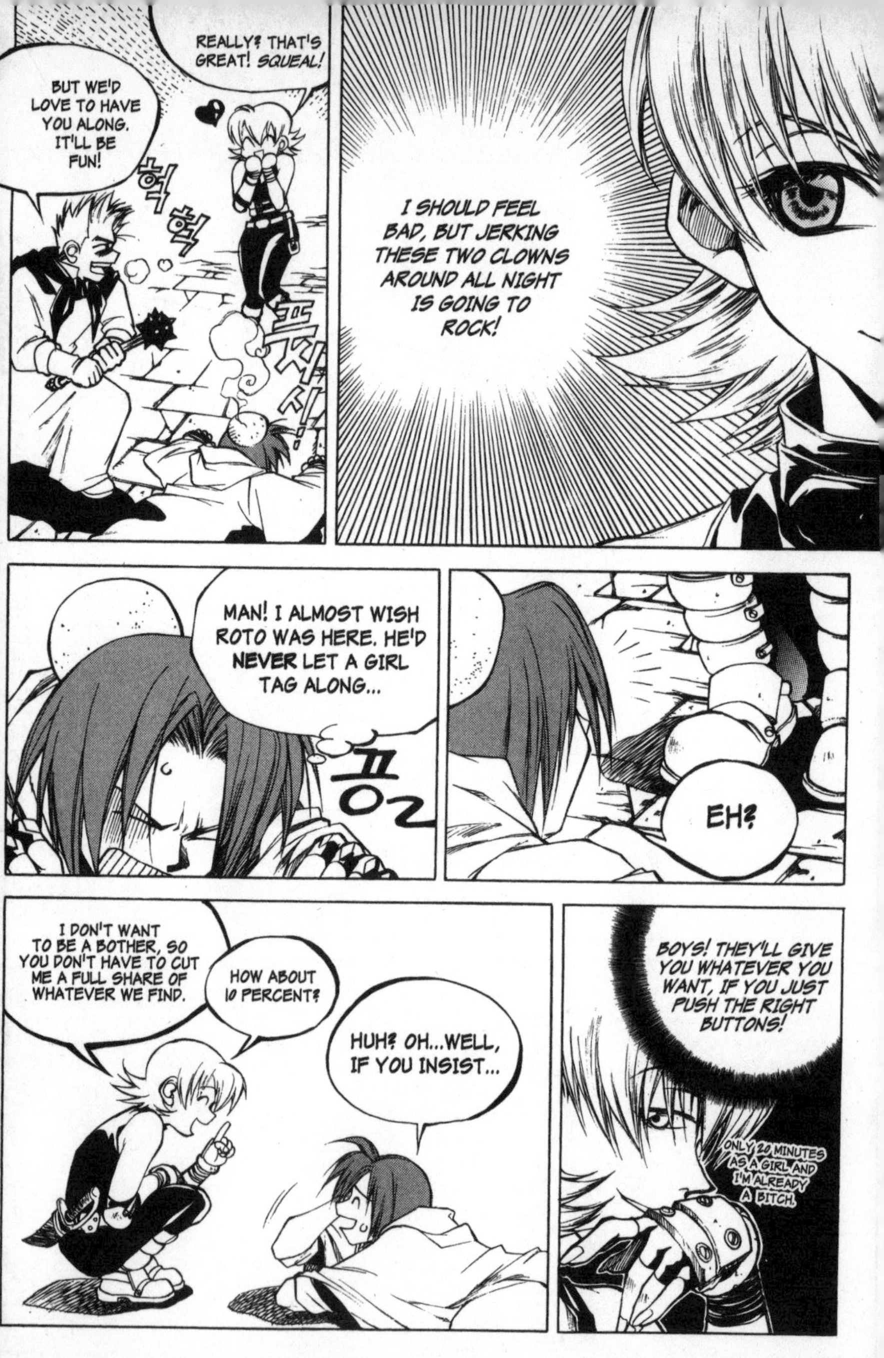
BUT WE'D LOVE TO HAVE YOU ALONG. IT'LL BE FUN!
REALLY? THAT'S GREAT! SQUEAL!
헉 헉
I SHOULD FEEL BAD, BUT JERKING THESE TWO CLOWNS AROUND ALL NIGHT IS GOING TO ROCK!
MAN! I ALMOST WISH ROTO WAS HERE. HE'D NEVER LET A GIRL TAG ALONG...
EH?
I DON'T WANT TO BE A BOTHER, SO YOU DON'T HAVE TO CUT ME A FULL SHARE OF WHATEVER WE FIND.
HOW ABOUT 10 PERCENT?
HUH? OH...WELL, IF YOU INSIST...
BOYS! THEY'LL GIVE YOU WHATEVER YOU WANT, IF YOU JUST PUSH THE RIGHT BUTTONS!
ONLY 20 MINUTES AS A GIRL AND I'M ALREADY A BITCH.

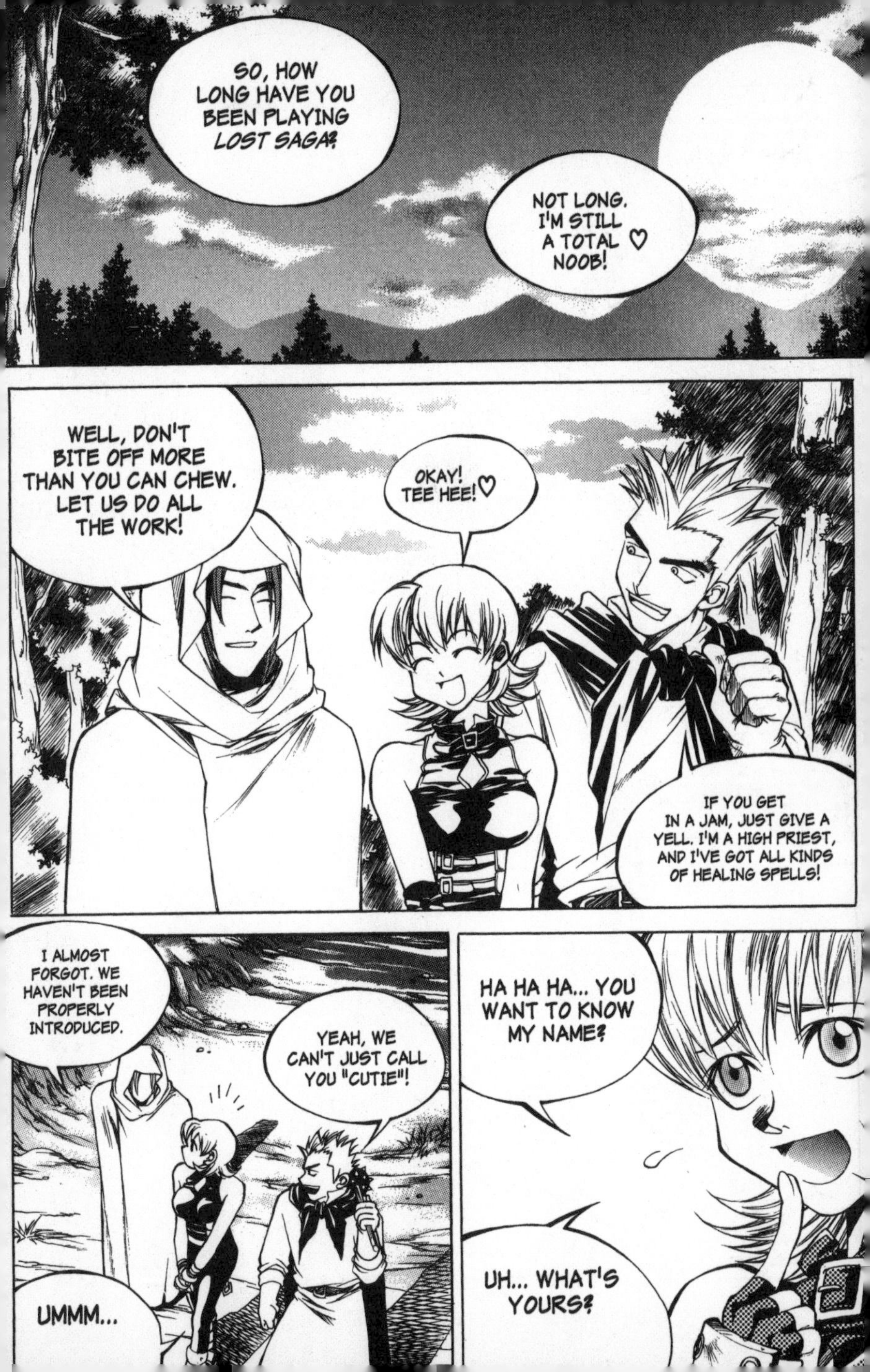
SO, HOW LONG HAVE YOU BEEN PLAYING LOST SAGA?
NOT LONG. I'M STILL A TOTAL NOOB! ♡
WELL, DON'T BITE OFF MORE THAN YOU CAN CHEW. LET US DO ALL THE WORK!
OKAY! TEE HEE! ♡
IF YOU GET IN A JAM, JUST GIVE A YELL. I'M A HIGH PRIEST, AND I'VE GOT ALL KINDS OF HEALING SPELLS!
I ALMOST FORGOT. WE HAVEN'T BEEN PROPERLY INTRODUCED.
YEAH, WE CAN'T JUST CALL YOU "CUTIE"!
UMMM...
HA HA HA... YOU WANT TO KNOW MY NAME?
UH... WHAT'S YOURS?

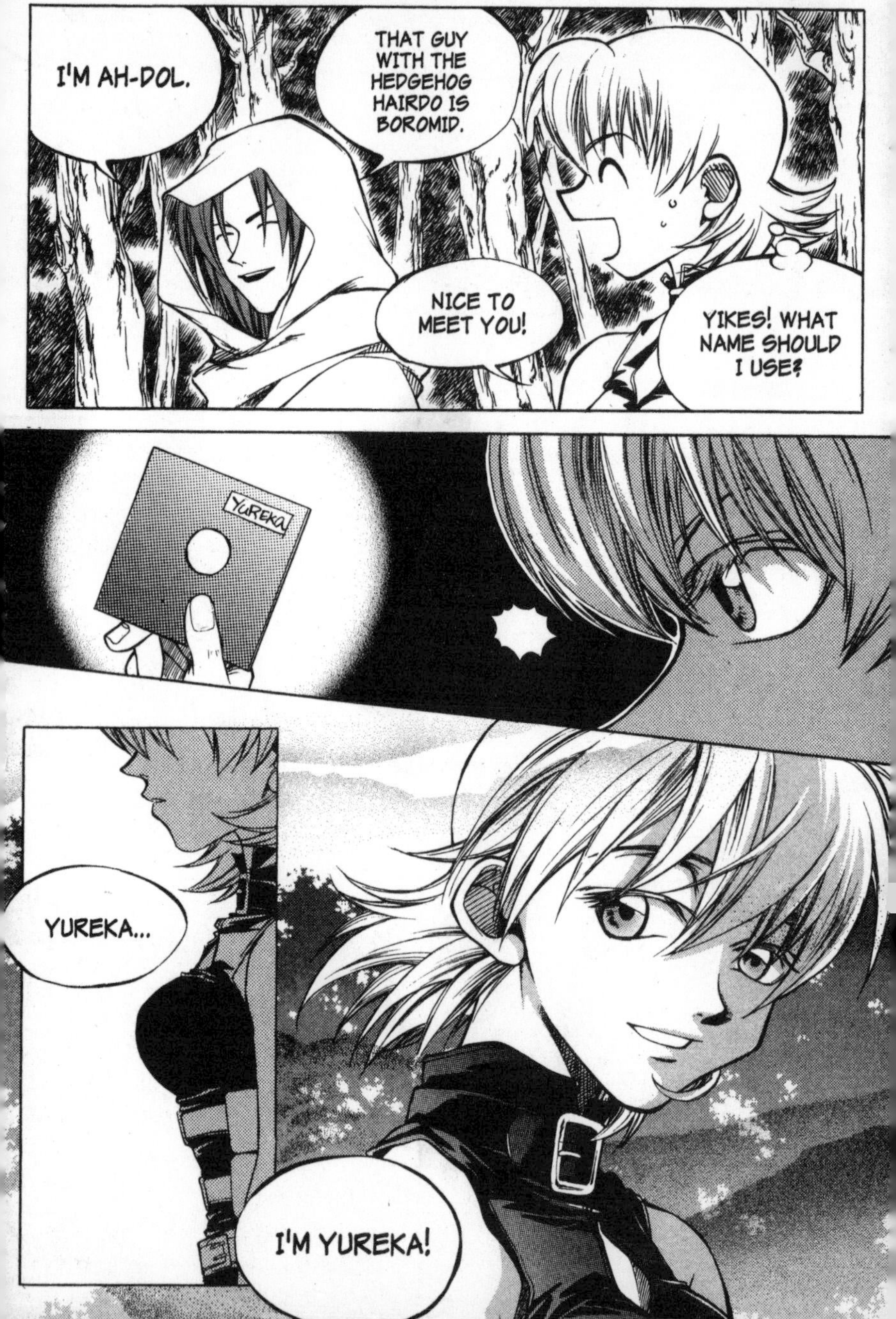
I'M AH-DOL.
THAT GUY WITH THE HEDGEHOG HAIRDO IS BOROMID.
NICE TO MEET YOU!
YIKES! WHAT NAME SHOULD I USE?
YuReka
YUREKA...
I'M YUREKA!

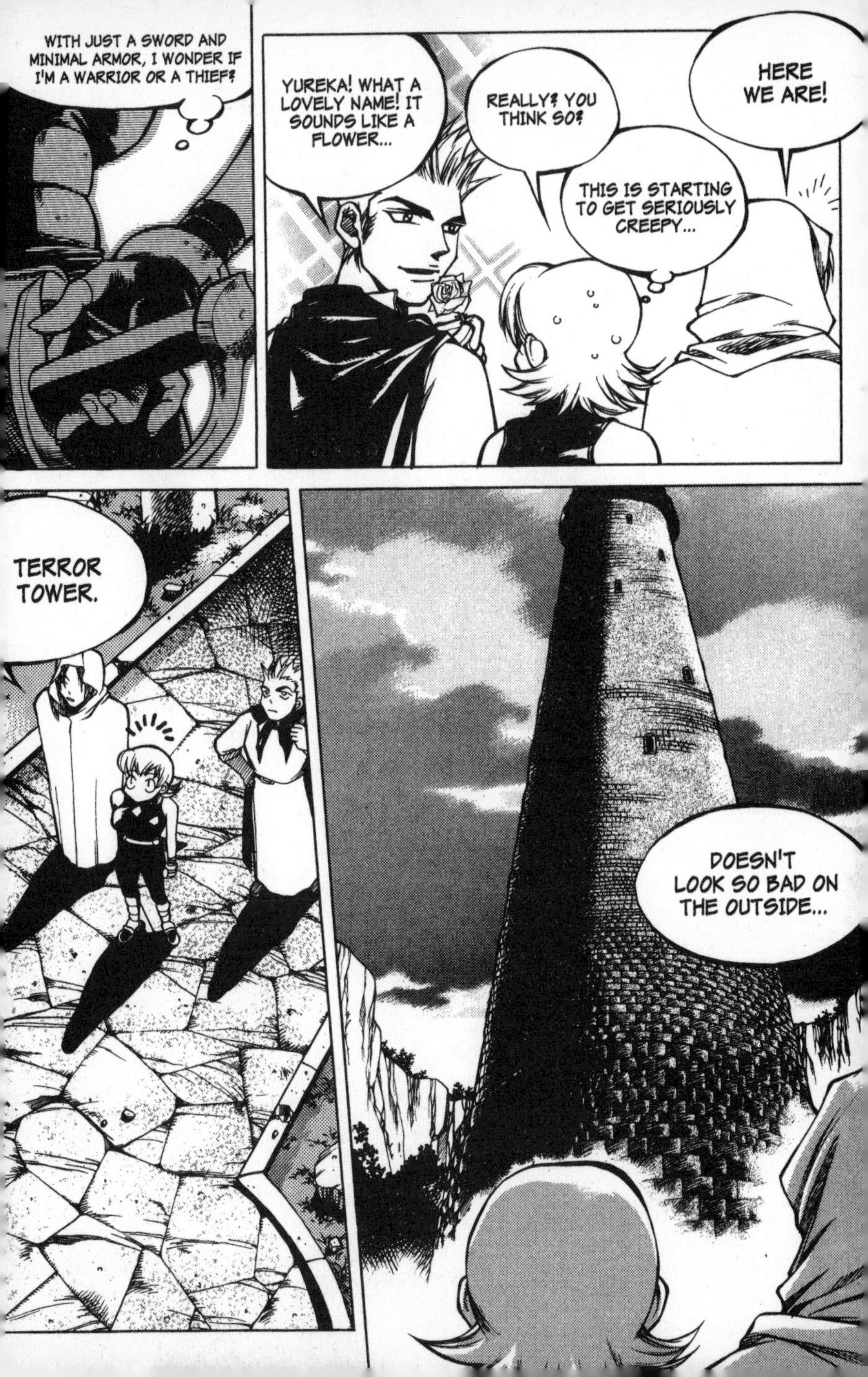

WITH JUST A SWORD AND MINIMAL ARMOR, I WONDER IF I'M A WARRIOR OR A THIEF?
YUREKA! WHAT A LOVELY NAME! IT SOUNDS LIKE A FLOWER...
REALLY? YOU THINK SO?
THIS IS STARTING TO GET SERIOUSLY CREEPY...
HERE WE ARE!
TERROR TOWER.
DOESN'T LOOK SO BAD ON THE OUTSIDE...

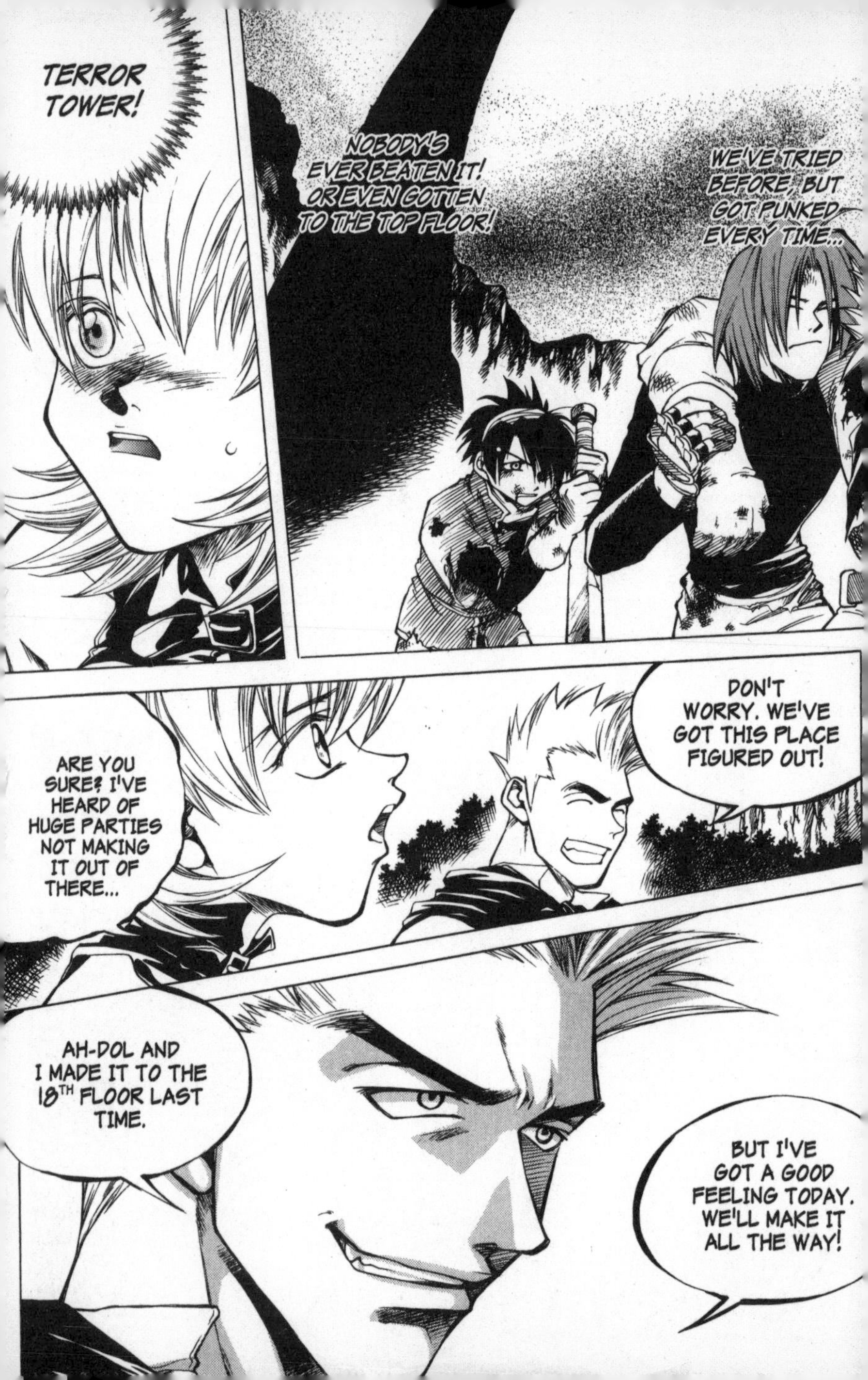
TERROR TOWER!
NOBODY'S EVER BEATEN IT! OR EVEN GOTTEN TO THE TOP FLOOR!
WE'VE TRIED BEFORE, BUT GOT PUNKED EVERY TIME...
ARE YOU SURE? I'VE HEARD OF HUGE PARTIES NOT MAKING IT OUT OF THERE...
DON'T WORRY. WE'VE GOT THIS PLACE FIGURED OUT!
AH-DOL AND I MADE IT TO THE 18TH FLOOR LAST TIME.
BUT I'VE GOT A GOOD FEELING TODAY. WE'LL MAKE IT ALL THE WAY!

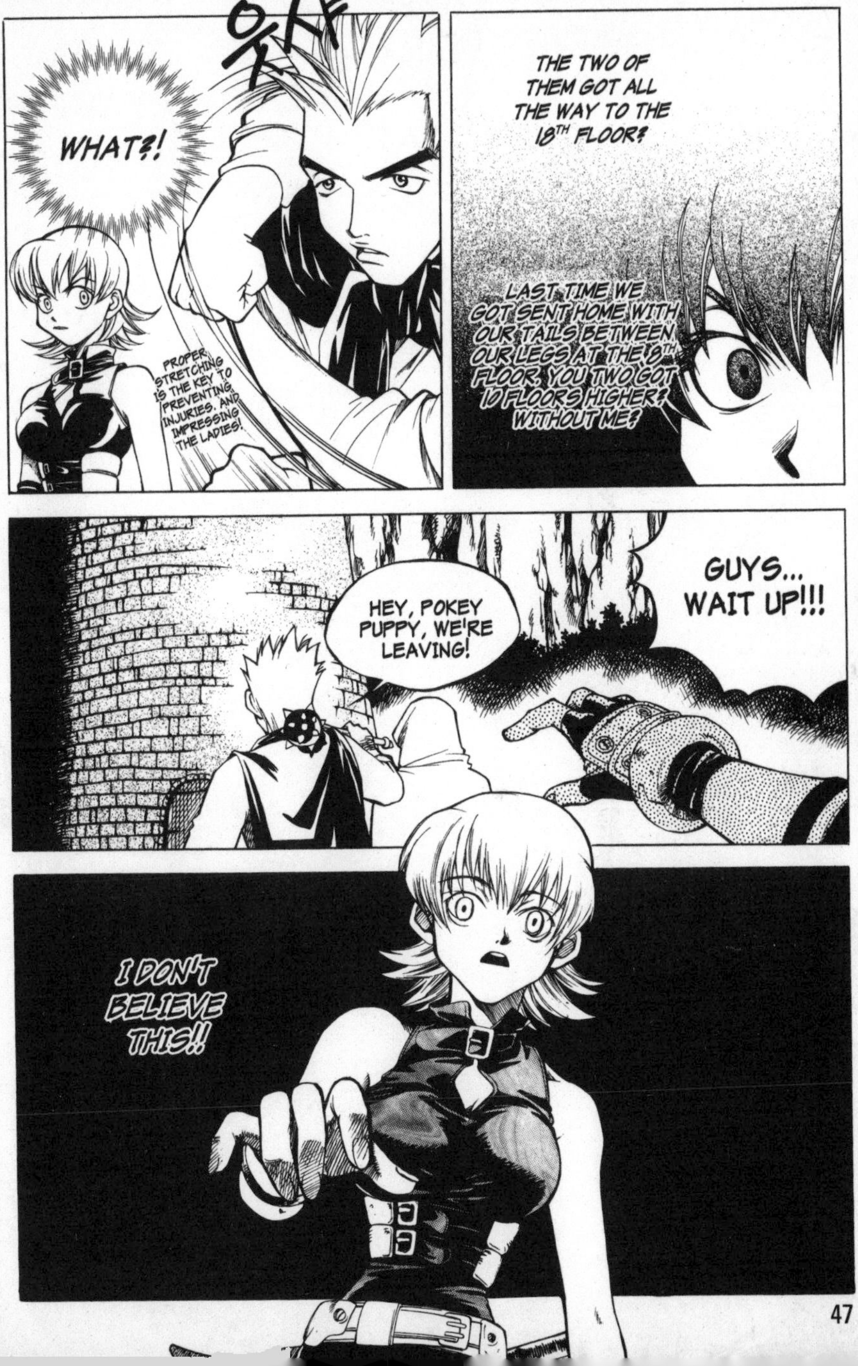
WHAT?!
PROPER STRETCHING IS THE KEY TO PREVENTING INJURIES, AND IMPRESSING THE LADIES!
THE TWO OF THEM GOT ALL THE WAY TO THE 18TH FLOOR?
LAST TIME WE GOT SENT HOME WITH OUR TAILS BETWEEN OUR LEGS AT THE 8TH FLOOR. YOU TWO GOT 10 FLOORS HIGHER? WITHOUT ME?
HEY, POKEY PUPPY, WE'RE LEAVING!
GUYS... WAIT UP!!!
I DON'T BELIEVE THIS!!

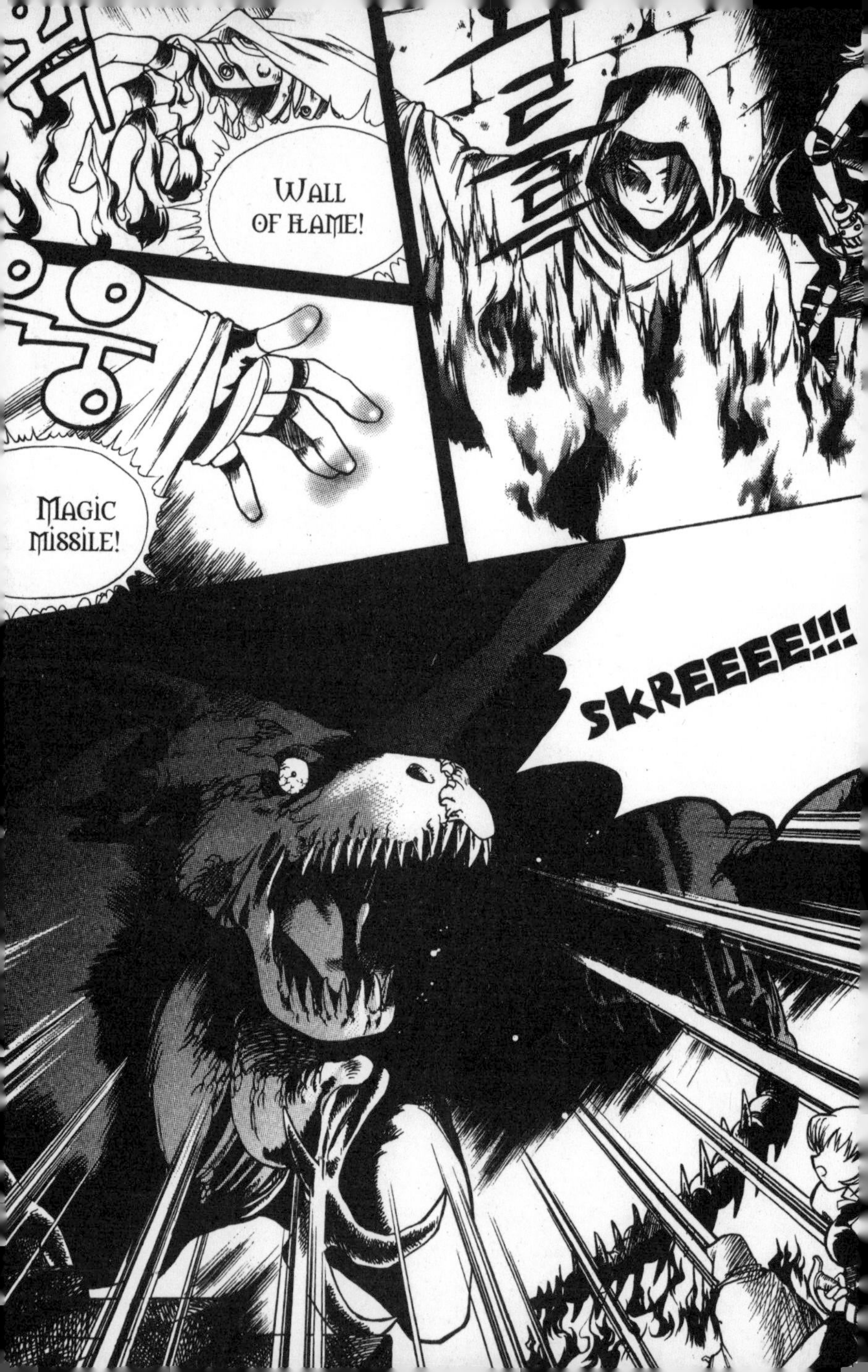
WALL OF FLAME!
MAGIC MISSILE!
SKREEEEE!!!

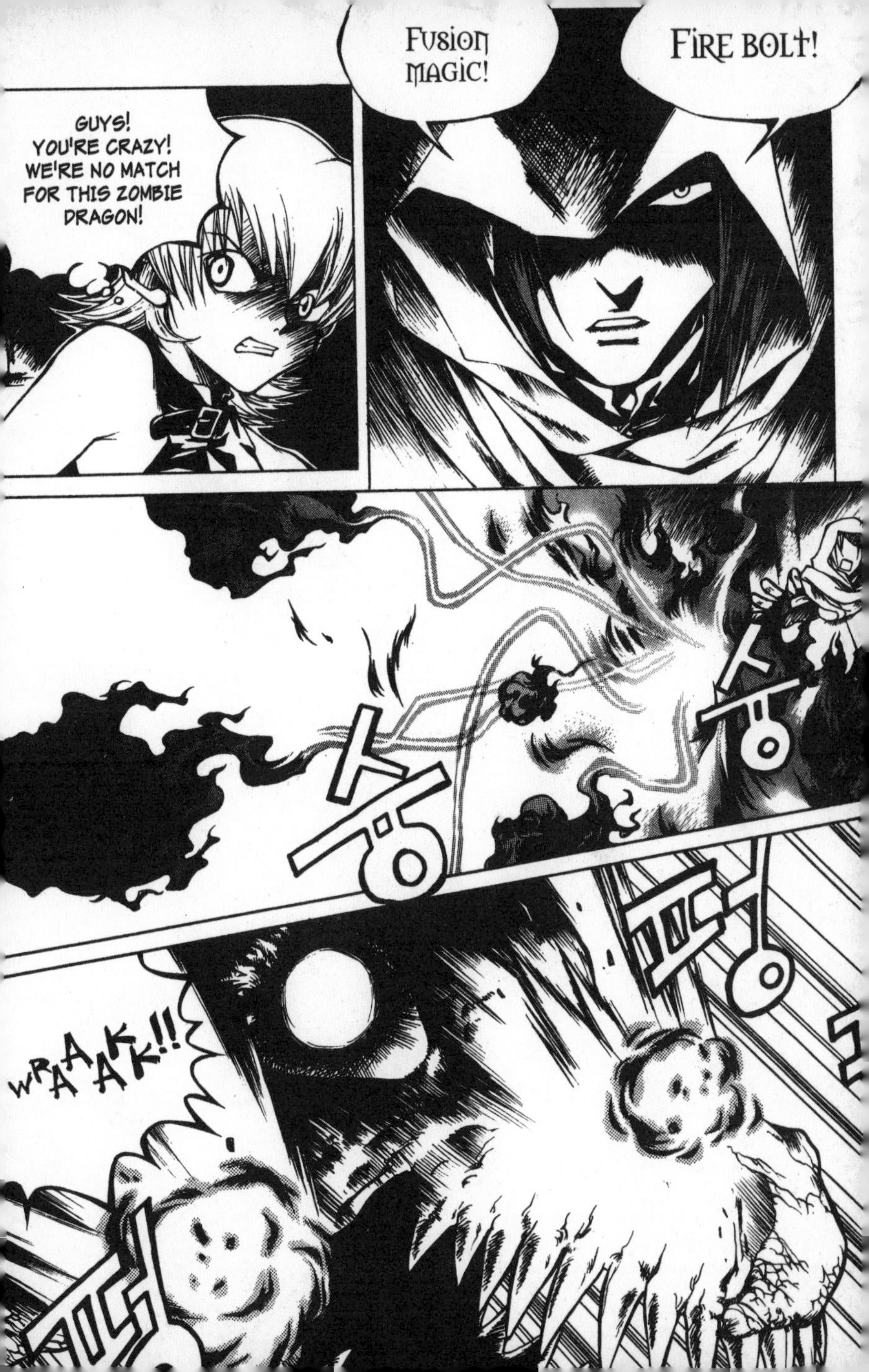
GUYS! YOU'RE CRAZY! WE'RE NO MATCH FOR THIS ZOMBIE DRAGON!
FUSION MAGIC!
FIRE BOLT!
WRAAAKK!!

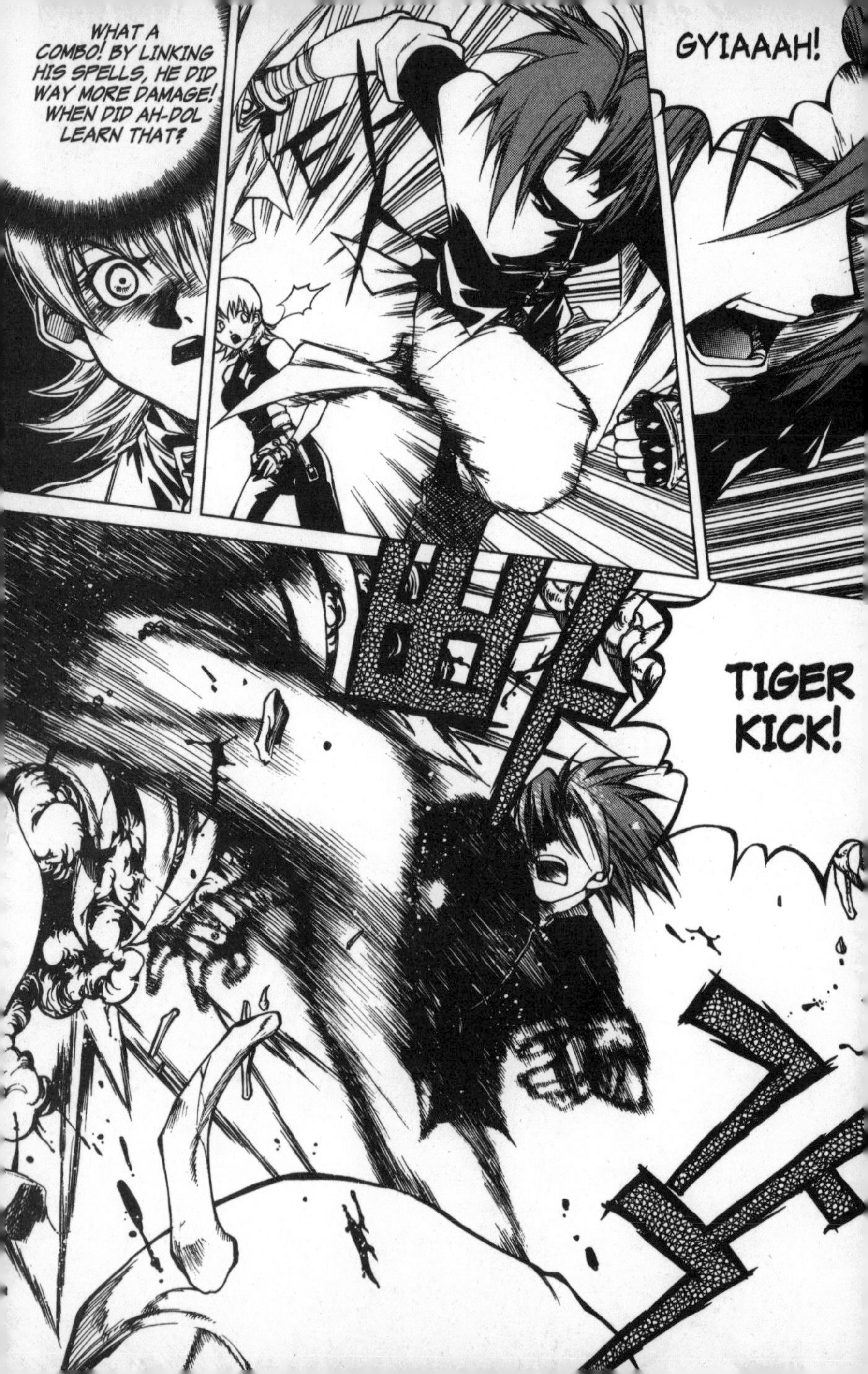
WHAT A COMBO! BY LINKING HIS SPELLS, HE DID WAY MORE DAMAGE! WHEN DID AH-DOL LEARN THAT?
GYIAAAH!
TIGER KICK!

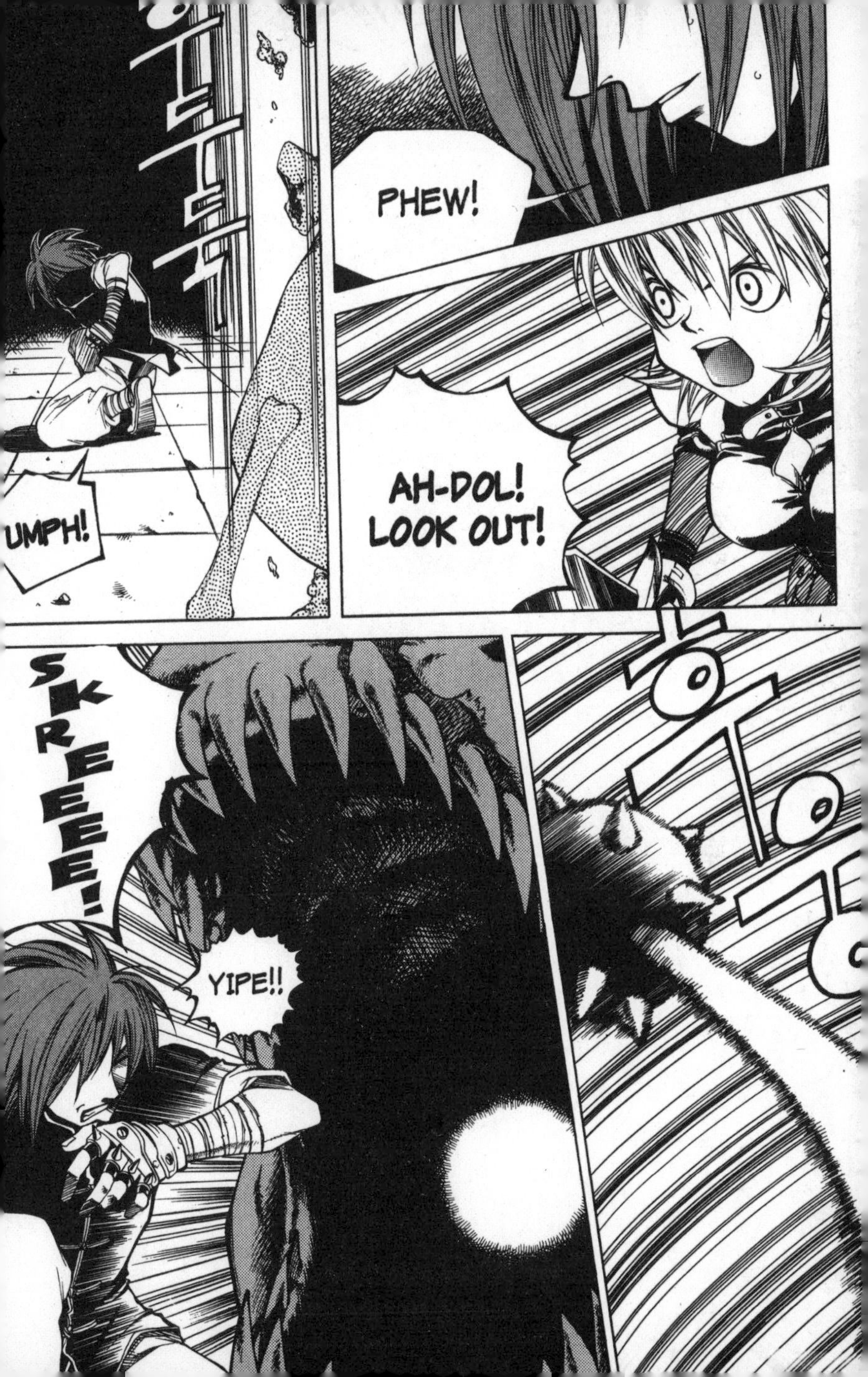
UMPH!
PHEW!
AH-DOL! LOOK OUT!
SKREEEE!!
YIPE!!

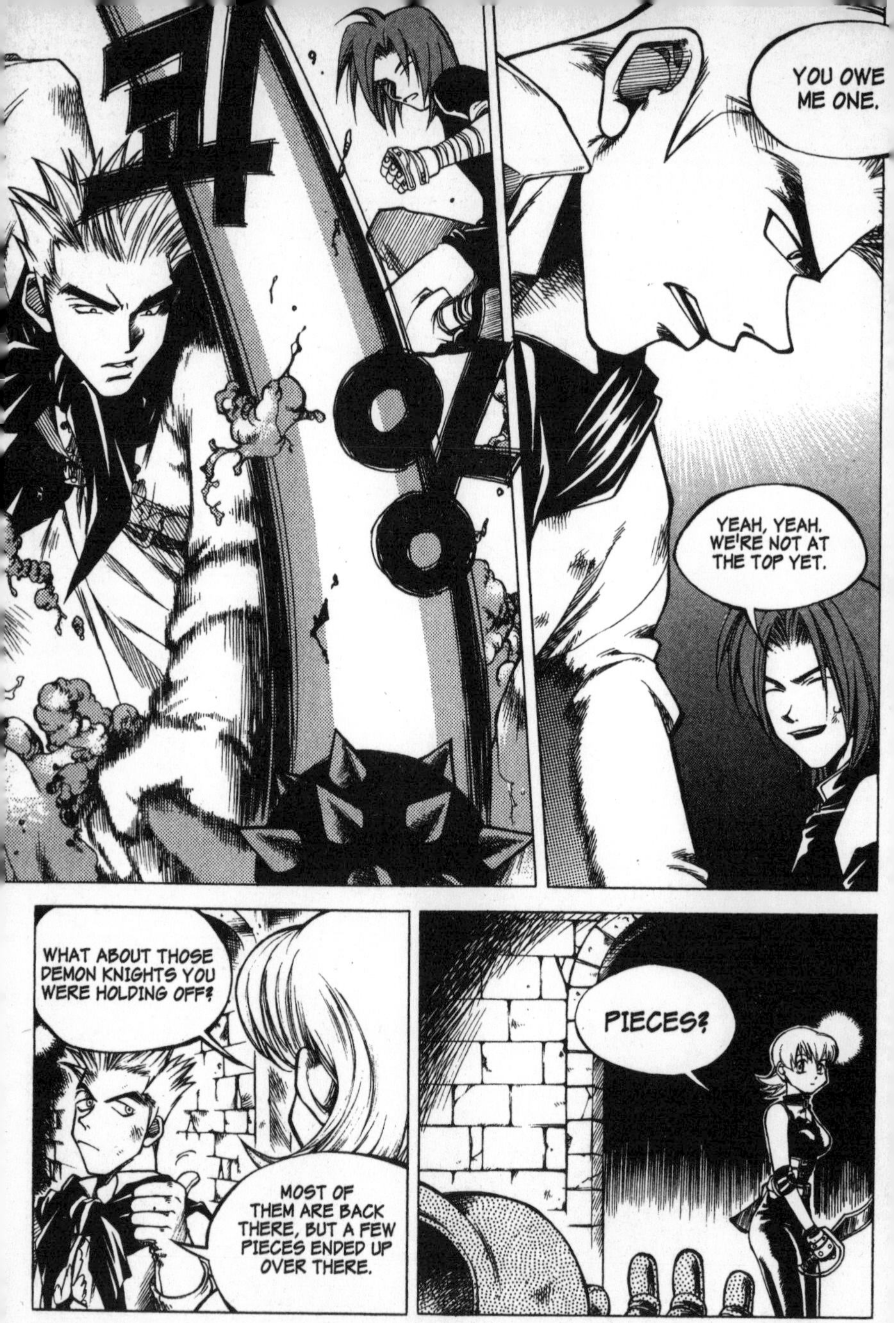
YOU OWE ME ONE.
YEAH, YEAH. WE'RE NOT AT THE TOP YET.
WHAT ABOUT THOSE DEMON KNIGHTS YOU WERE HOLDING OFF?
MOST OF THEM ARE BACK THERE, BUT A FEW PIECES ENDED UP OVER THERE.
PIECES?

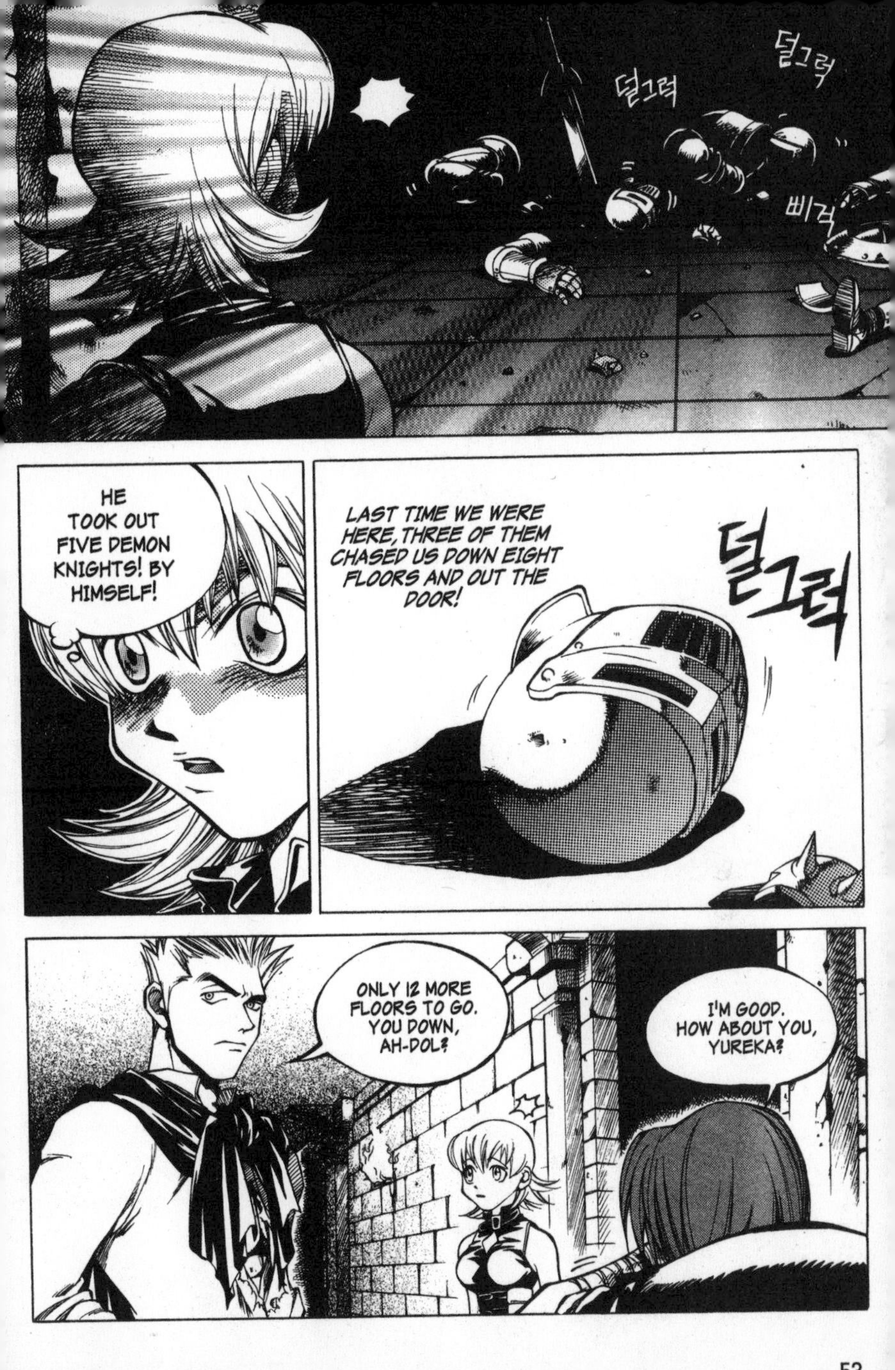
덜그럭
덜그럭
삐걱
HE TOOK OUT FIVE DEMON KNIGHTS! BY HIMSELF!
LAST TIME WE WERE HERE, THREE OF THEM CHASED US DOWN EIGHT FLOORS AND OUT THE DOOR!
덜그럭
ONLY 12 MORE FLOORS TO GO. YOU DOWN, AH-DOL?
I'M GOOD. HOW ABOUT YOU, YUREKA?

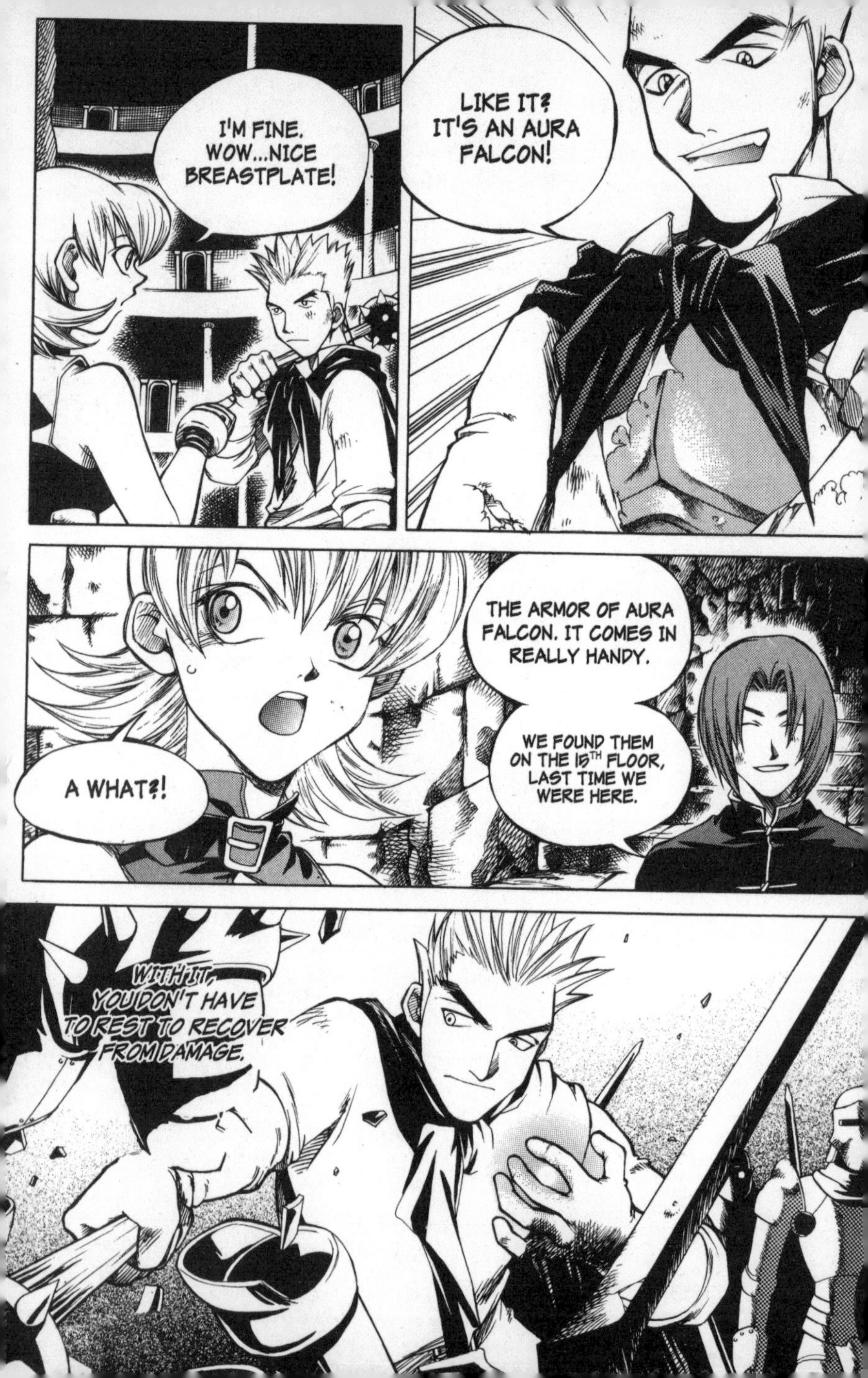
I'M FINE. WOW...NICE BREASTPLATE!
LIKE IT? IT'S AN AURA FALCON!
A WHAT?!
THE ARMOR OF AURA FALCON. IT COMES IN REALLY HANDY.
WE FOUND THEM ON THE 15TH FLOOR, LAST TIME WE WERE HERE.
WITH IT, YOU DON'T HAVE TO REST TO RECOVER FROM DAMAGE.

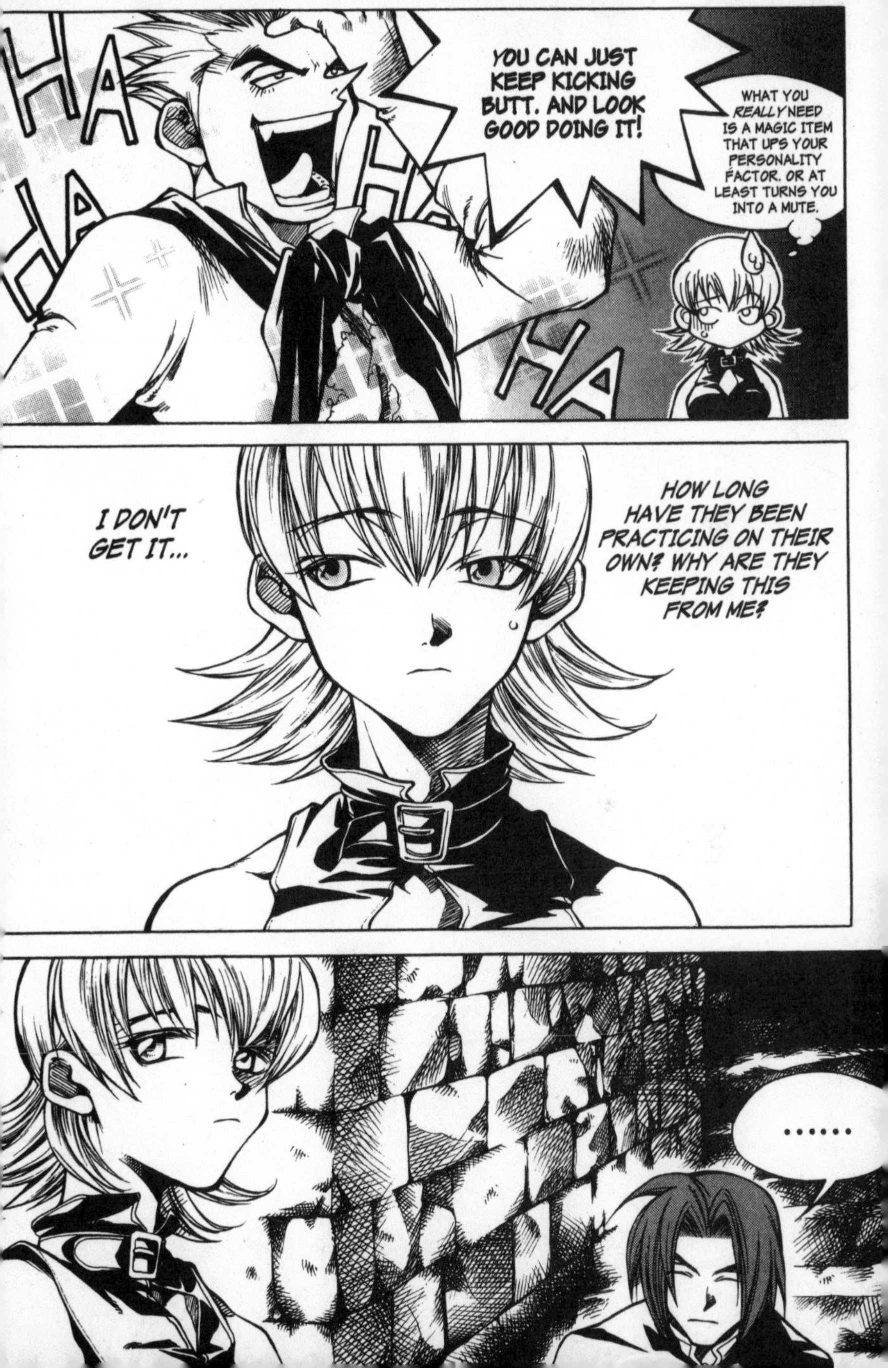
HA HA
HA HA
YOU CAN JUST KEEP KICKING BUTT. AND LOOK GOOD DOING IT!
HA HA
WHAT YOU REALLY NEED IS A MAGIC ITEM THAT UPS YOUR PERSONALITY FACTOR. OR AT LEAST TURNS YOU INTO A MUTE.
I DON'T GET IT...
HOW LONG HAVE THEY BEEN PRACTICING ON THEIR OWN? WHY ARE THEY KEEPING THIS FROM ME?
......

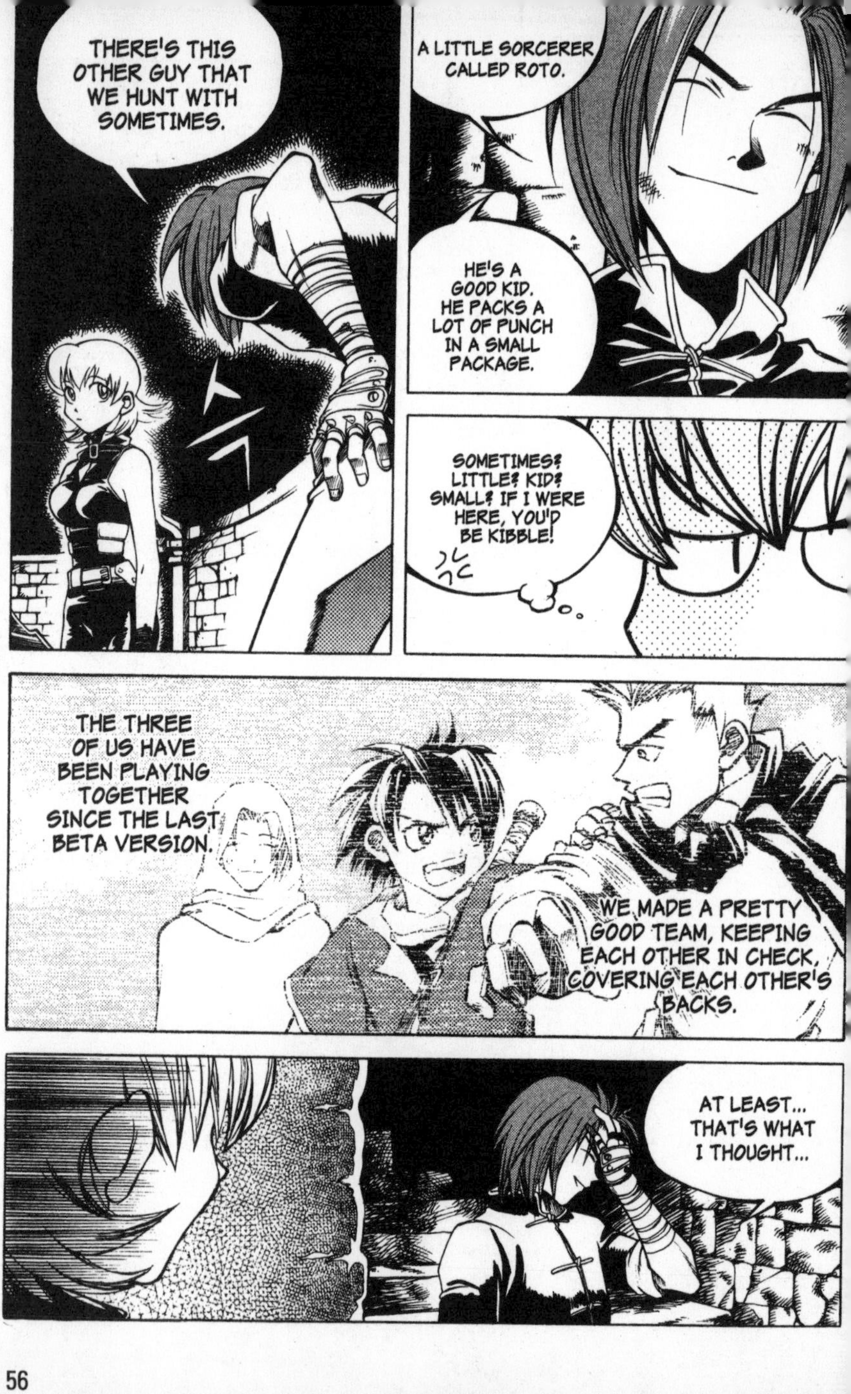
THERE'S THIS OTHER GUY THAT WE HUNT WITH SOMETIMES.
A LITTLE SORCERER CALLED ROTO.
HE'S A GOOD KID. HE PACKS A LOT OF PUNCH IN A SMALL PACKAGE.
SOMETIMES? LITTLE? KID? SMALL? IF I WERE HERE, YOU'D BE KIBBLE!
THE THREE OF US HAVE BEEN PLAYING TOGETHER SINCE THE LAST BETA VERSION.
WE MADE A PRETTY GOOD TEAM, KEEPING EACH OTHER IN CHECK, COVERING EACH OTHER'S BACKS.
AT LEAST... THAT'S WHAT I THOUGHT...

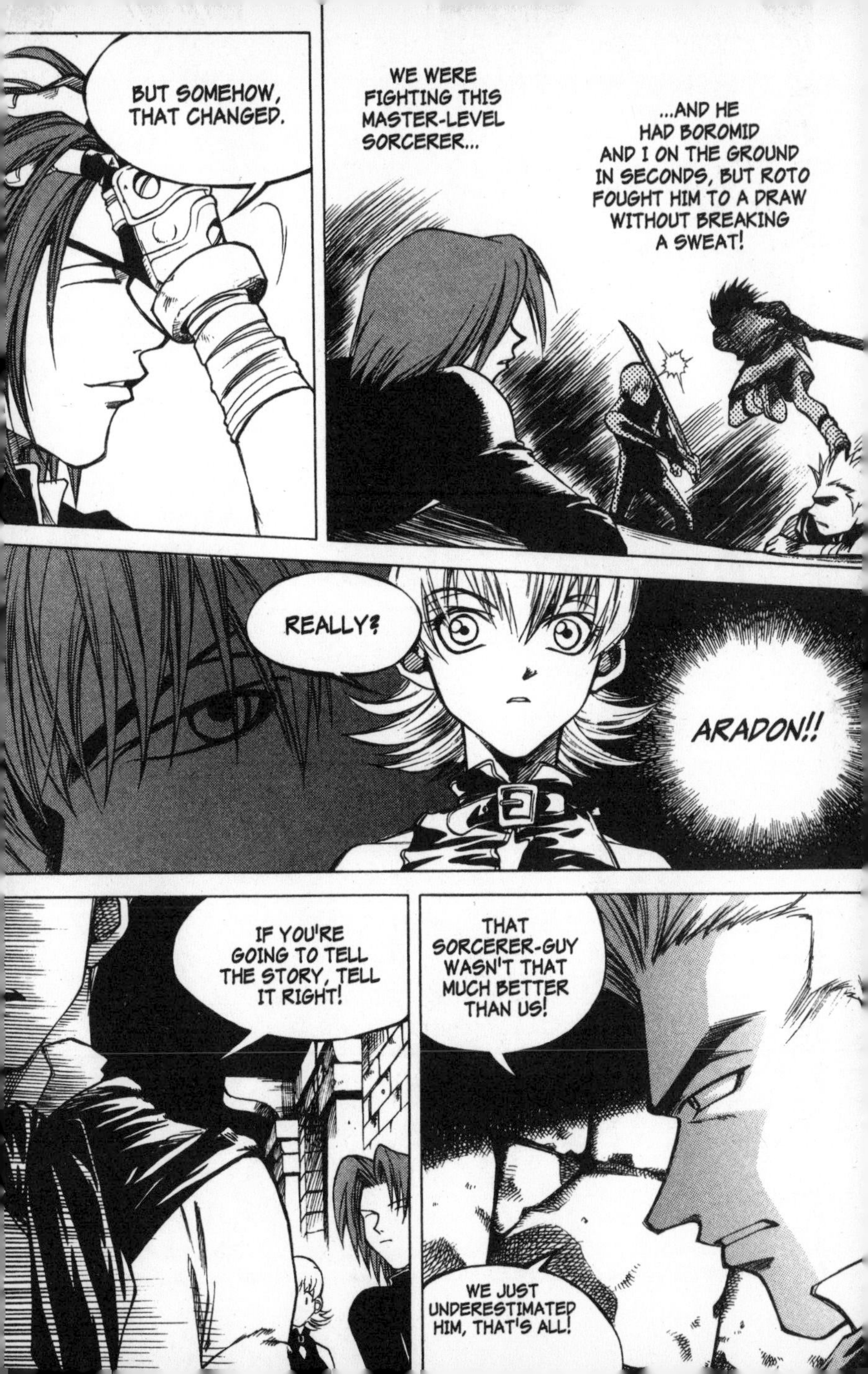
BUT SOMEHOW, THAT CHANGED.
WE WERE FIGHTING THIS MASTER-LEVEL SORCERER...
...AND HE HAD BOROMID AND I ON THE GROUND IN SECONDS, BUT ROTO FOUGHT HIM TO A DRAW WITHOUT BREAKING A SWEAT!
REALLY?
ARADON!!
IF YOU'RE GOING TO TELL THE STORY, TELL IT RIGHT!
THAT SORCERER-GUY WASN'T THAT MUCH BETTER THAN US!
WE JUST UNDERESTIMATED HIM, THAT'S ALL!

REALLY? THEN WHY ARE WE SNEAKING AROUND BEHIND ROTO'S BACK LIKE THIS?

ANYWAYS, WE FIGURED THAT...

...IF ROTO GOT ANY MORE POWERFUL, HE WOULDN'T NEED US ANYMORE.

AND THAT WOULD BE THE END OF TEAM TRIPLE THREAT.

ENOUGH WITH THE TALKY-TALKY! THERE'S MOBS THAT NEED SMASHING UP THERE!

BASTARDS!

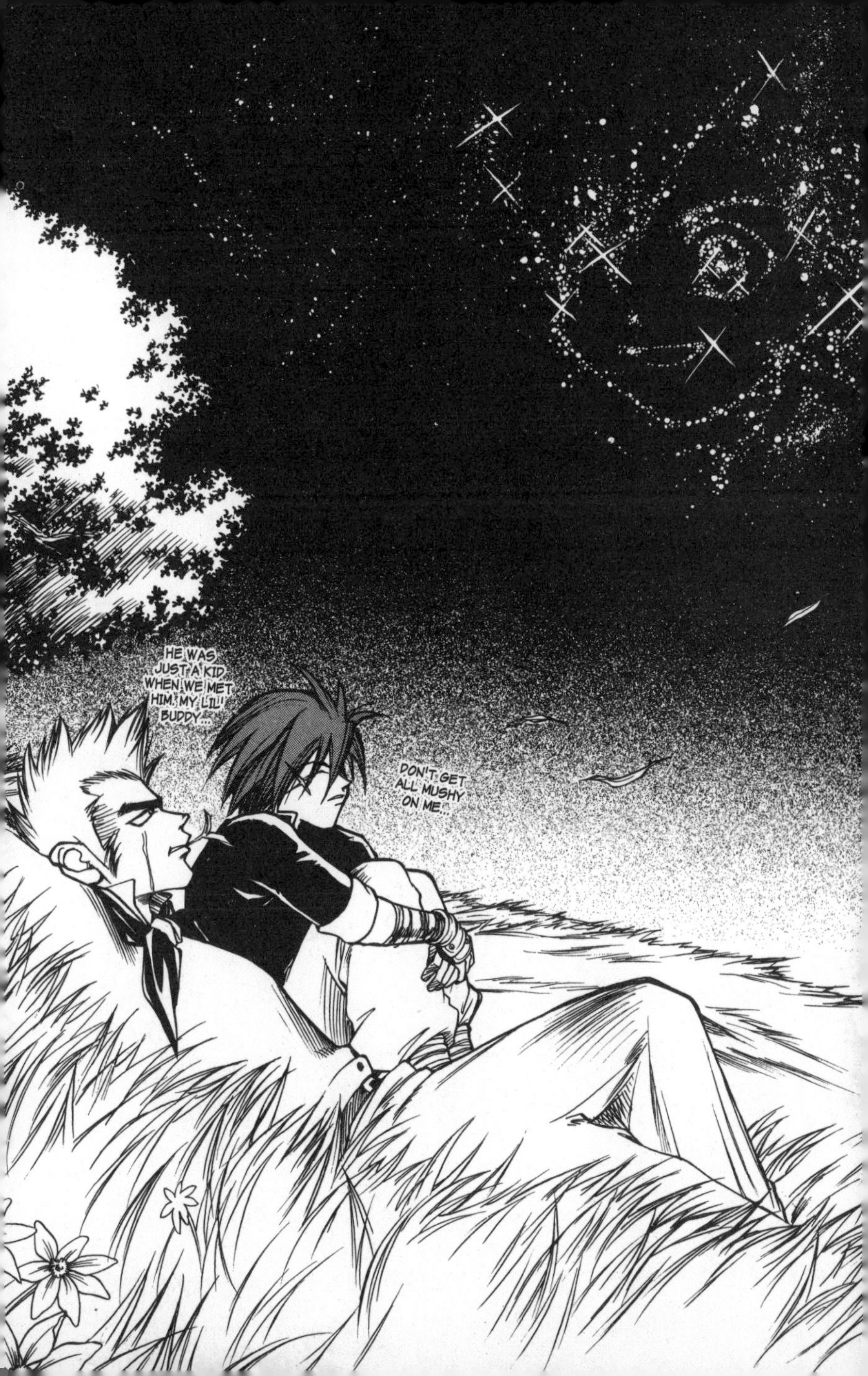
HE WAS JUST A KID WHEN WE MET HIM, MY LIL' BUDDY...
DON'T GET ALL MUSHY ON ME...

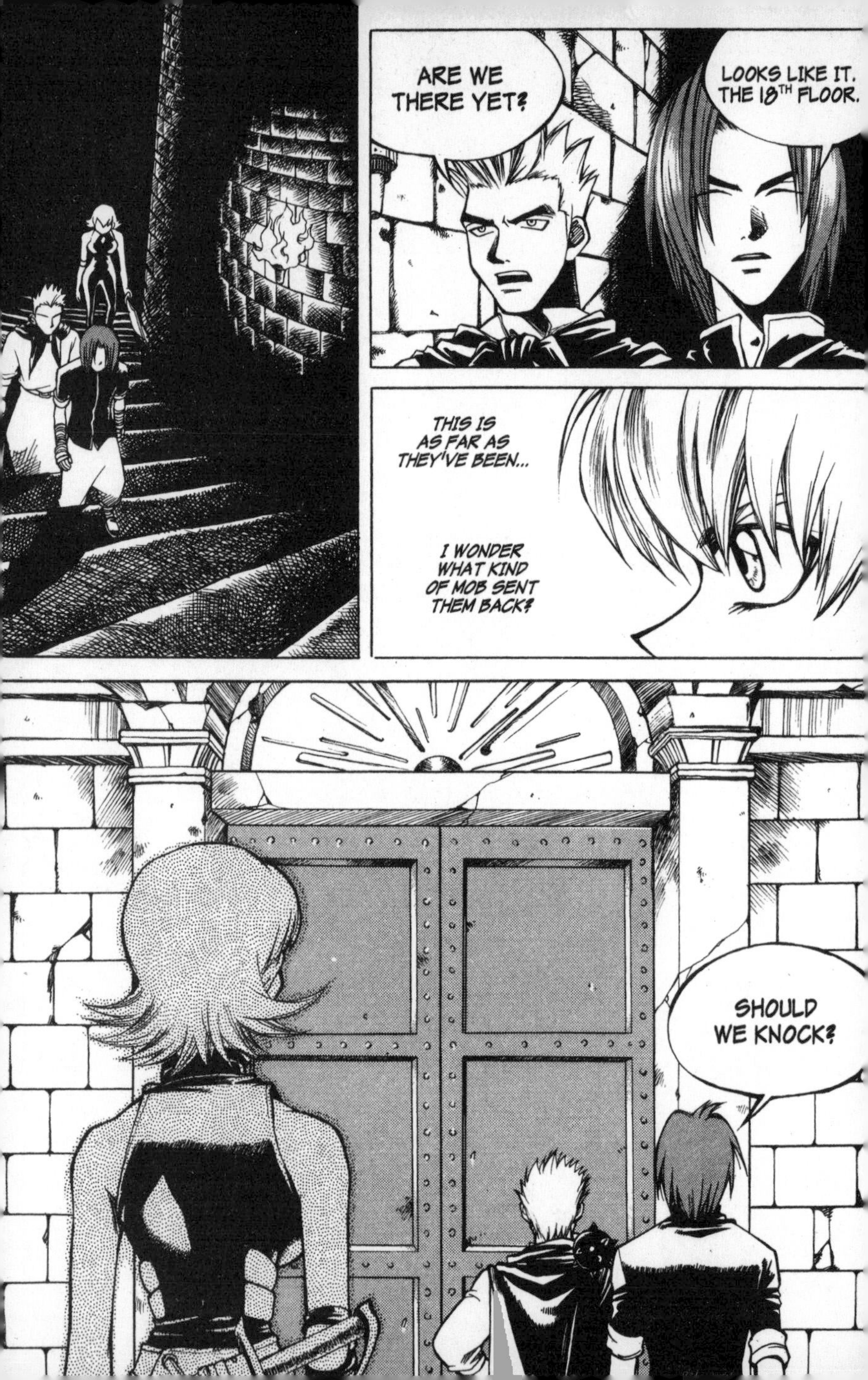
ARE WE THERE YET?
LOOKS LIKE IT. THE 18TH FLOOR.
THIS IS AS FAR AS THEY'VE BEEN...
I WONDER WHAT KIND OF MOB SENT THEM BACK?
SHOULD WE KNOCK?

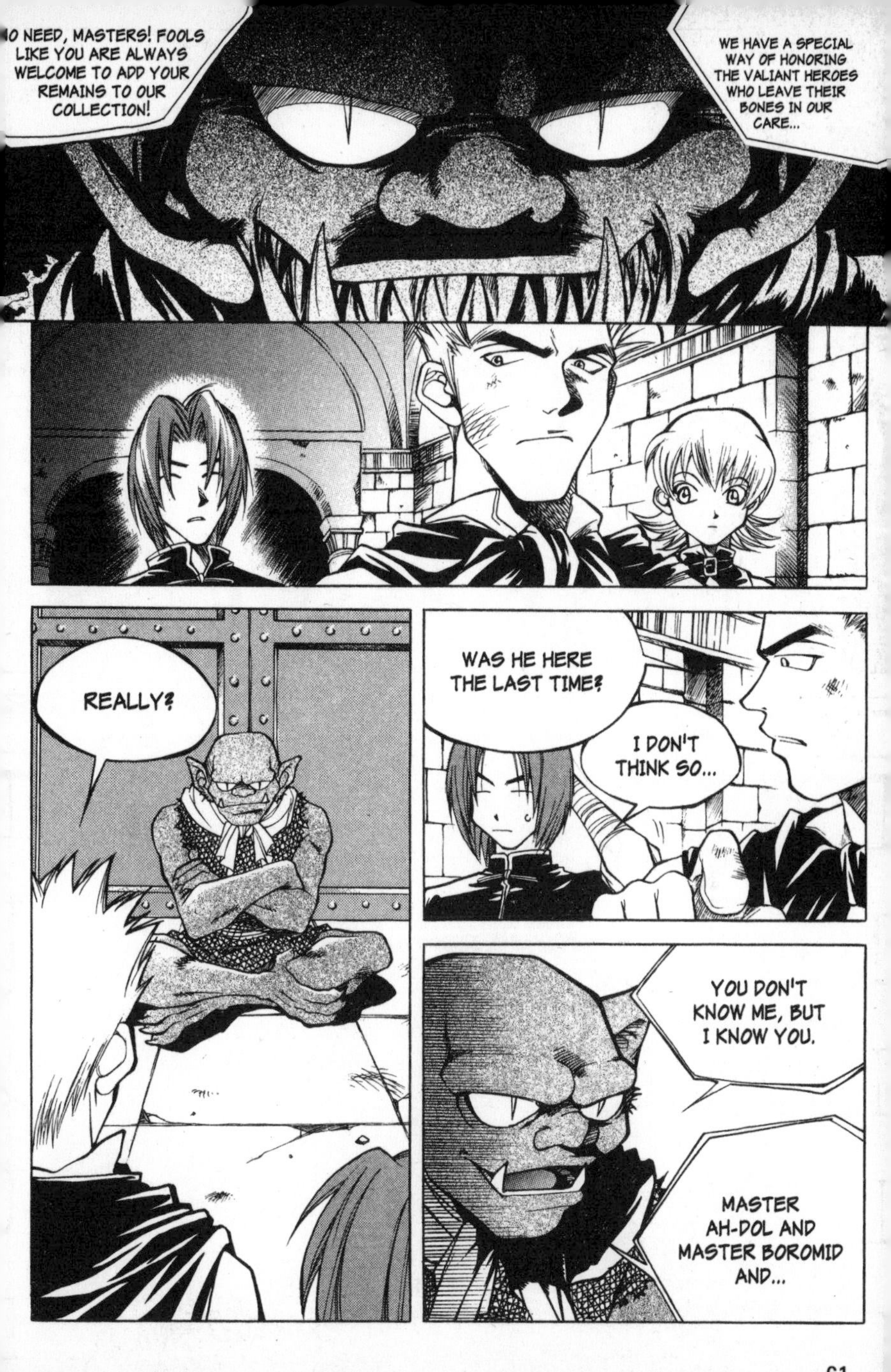
O NEED, MASTERS! FOOLS LIKE YOU ARE ALWAYS WELCOME TO ADD YOUR REMAINS TO OUR COLLECTION!
WE HAVE A SPECIAL WAY OF HONORING THE VALIANT HEROES WHO LEAVE THEIR BONES IN OUR CARE...
REALLY?
WAS HE HERE THE LAST TIME?
I DON'T THINK SO...
YOU DON'T KNOW ME, BUT I KNOW YOU.
MASTER AH-DOL AND MASTER BOROMID AND...

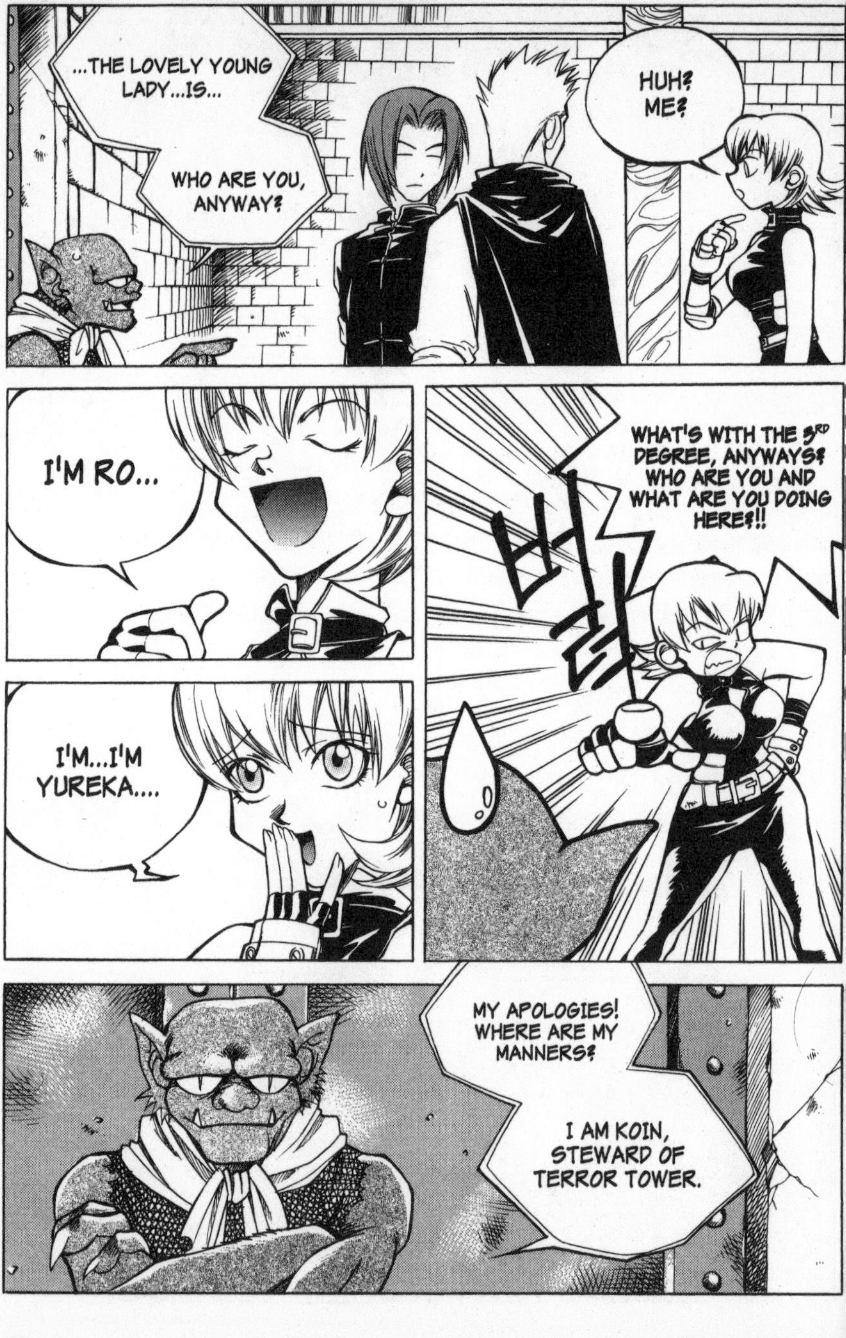

...THE LOVELY YOUNG LADY...IS...
WHO ARE YOU, ANYWAY?
HUH? ME?
I'M RO...
I'M...I'M YUREKA....
WHAT'S WITH THE 3RD DEGREE, ANYWAYS? WHO ARE YOU AND WHAT ARE YOU DOING HERE?!!
MY APOLOGIES! WHERE ARE MY MANNERS?
I AM KOIN, STEWARD OF TERROR TOWER.

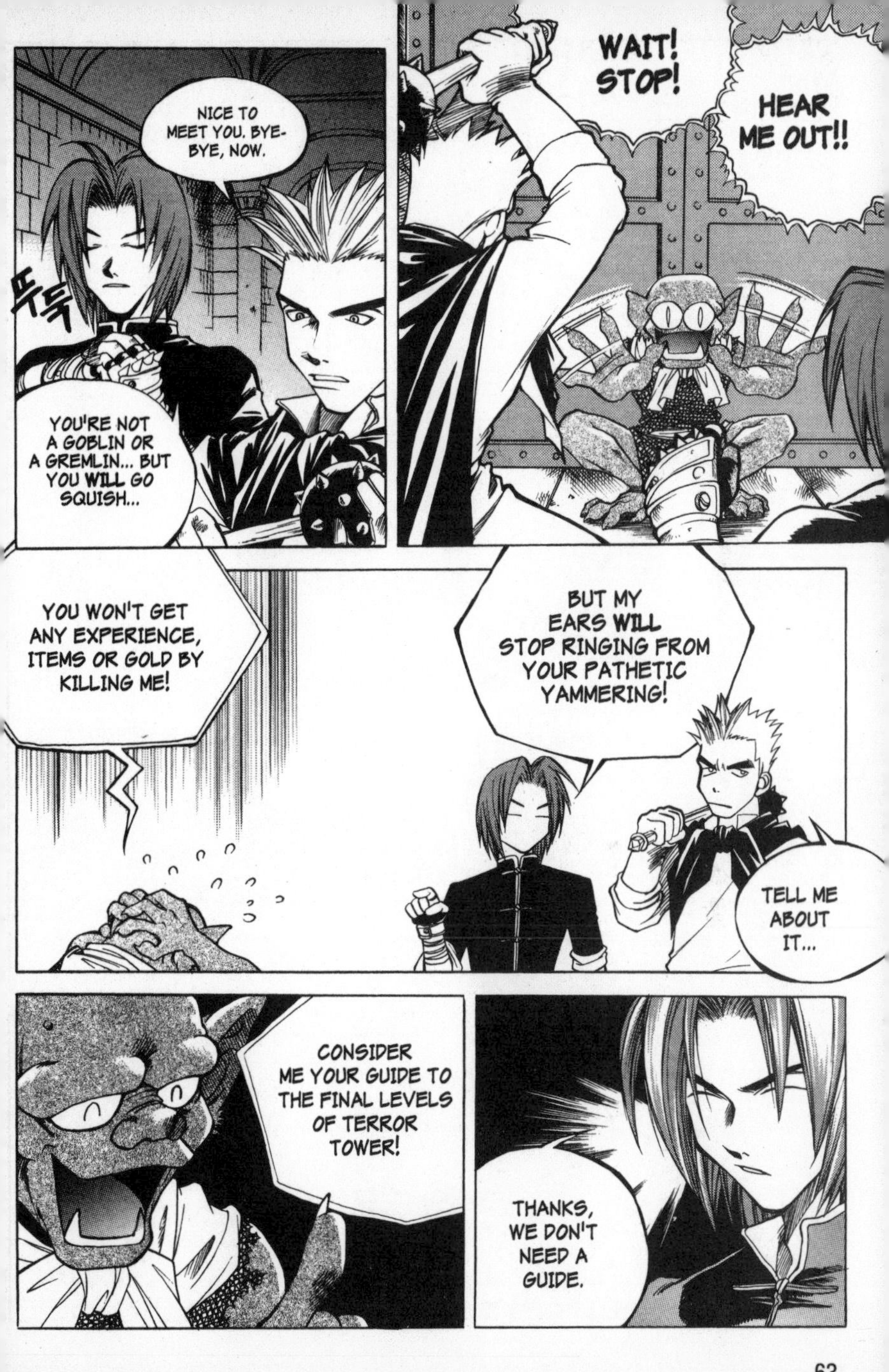

NICE TO MEET YOU. BYE-BYE, NOW.
뚜둑
YOU'RE NOT A GOBLIN OR A GREMLIN... BUT YOU WILL GO SQUISH...
WAIT! STOP!
HEAR ME OUT!!
YOU WON'T GET ANY EXPERIENCE, ITEMS OR GOLD BY KILLING ME!
BUT MY EARS WILL STOP RINGING FROM YOUR PATHETIC YAMMERING!
TELL ME ABOUT IT...
CONSIDER ME YOUR GUIDE TO THE FINAL LEVELS OF TERROR TOWER!
THANKS, WE DON'T NEED A GUIDE.

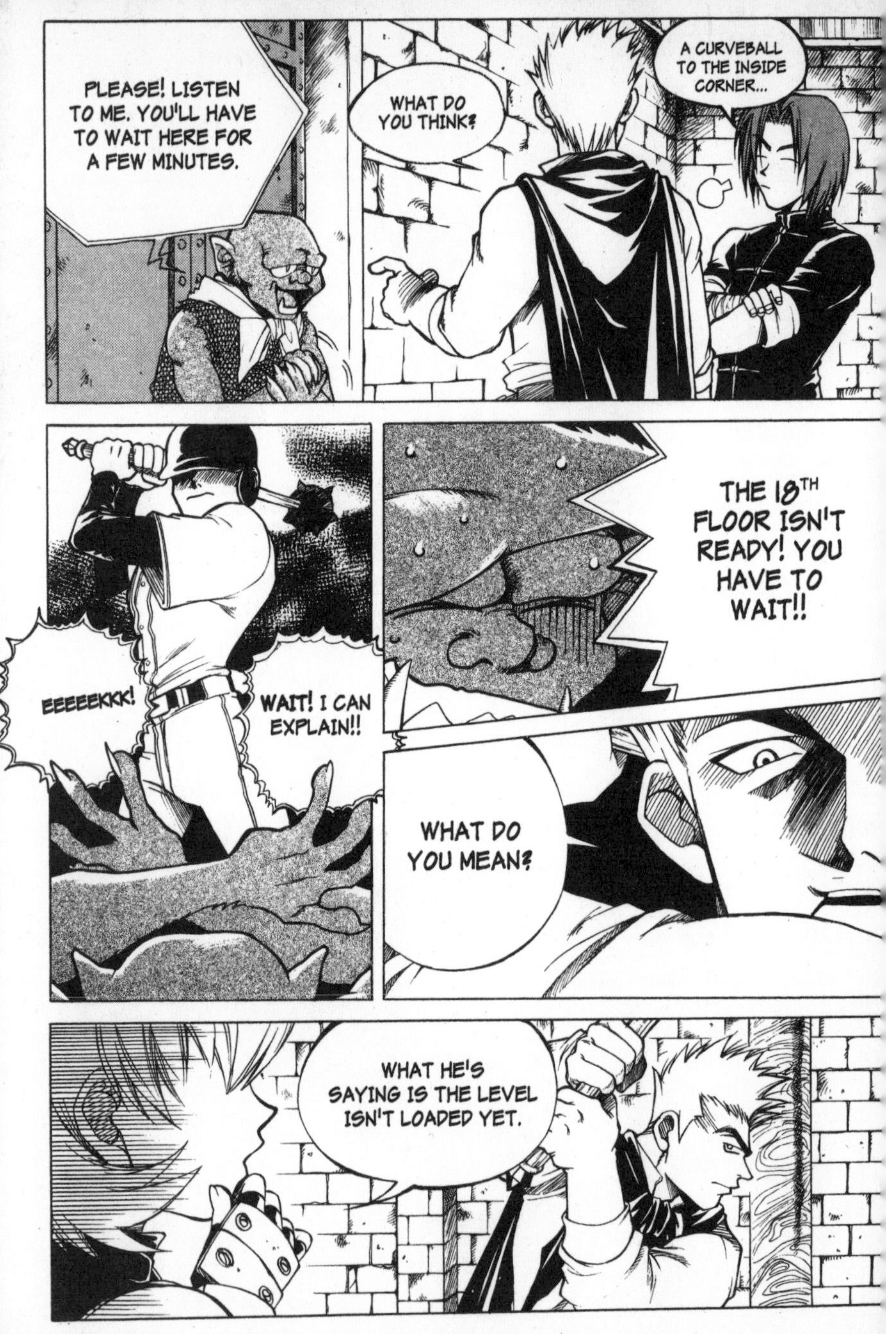
PLEASE! LISTEN TO ME. YOU'LL HAVE TO WAIT HERE FOR A FEW MINUTES.
WHAT DO YOU THINK?
A CURVEBALL TO THE INSIDE CORNER...
EEEEEKKK!
WAIT! I CAN EXPLAIN!!
THE 18TH FLOOR ISN'T READY! YOU HAVE TO WAIT!!
WHAT DO YOU MEAN?
WHAT HE'S SAYING IS THE LEVEL ISN'T LOADED YET.

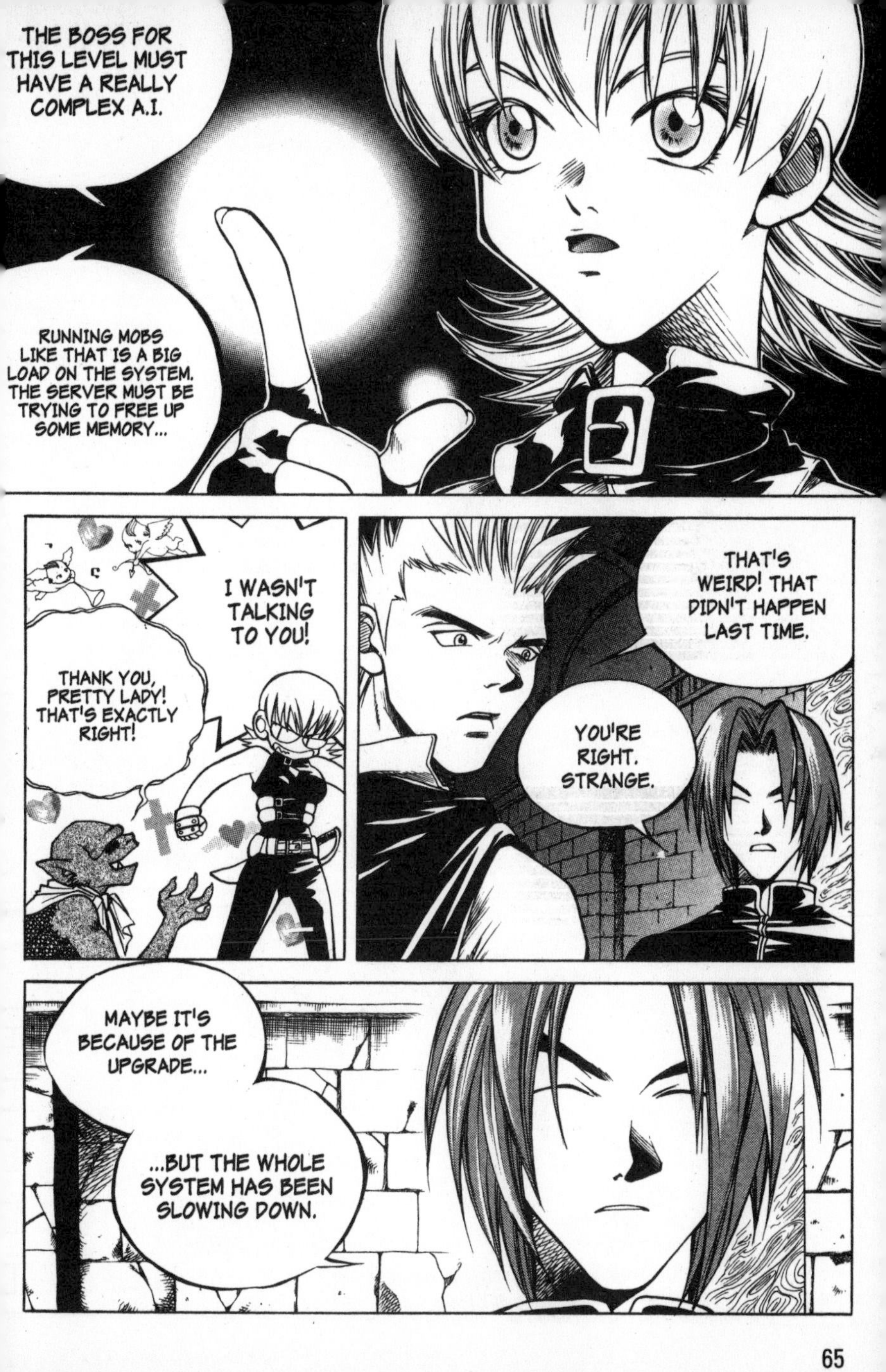
THE BOSS FOR THIS LEVEL MUST HAVE A REALLY COMPLEX A.I.
RUNNING MOBS LIKE THAT IS A BIG LOAD ON THE SYSTEM. THE SERVER MUST BE TRYING TO FREE UP SOME MEMORY...
THANK YOU, PRETTY LADY! THAT'S EXACTLY RIGHT!
I WASN'T TALKING TO YOU!
THAT'S WEIRD! THAT DIDN'T HAPPEN LAST TIME.
YOU'RE RIGHT. STRANGE.
MAYBE IT'S BECAUSE OF THE UPGRADE...
...BUT THE WHOLE SYSTEM HAS BEEN SLOWING DOWN.

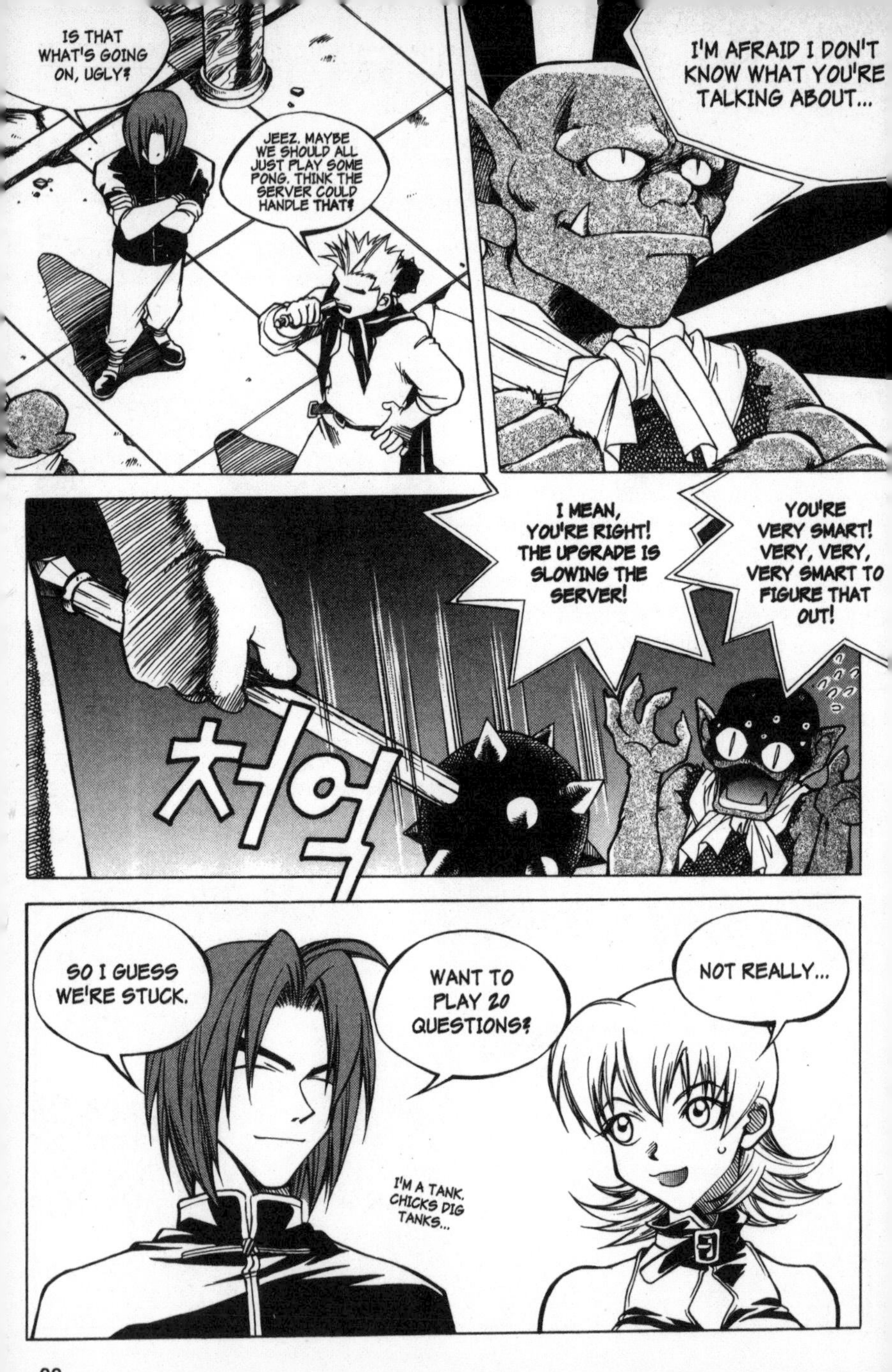
IS THAT WHAT'S GOING ON, UGLY?
JEEZ. MAYBE WE SHOULD ALL JUST PLAY SOME PONG. THINK THE SERVER COULD HANDLE THAT?
I'M AFRAID I DON'T KNOW WHAT YOU'RE TALKING ABOUT...
처억
I MEAN, YOU'RE RIGHT! THE UPGRADE IS SLOWING THE SERVER!
YOU'RE VERY SMART! VERY, VERY, VERY SMART TO FIGURE THAT OUT!
SO I GUESS WE'RE STUCK.
WANT TO PLAY 20 QUESTIONS?
NOT REALLY...
I'M A TANK. CHICKS DIG TANKS...

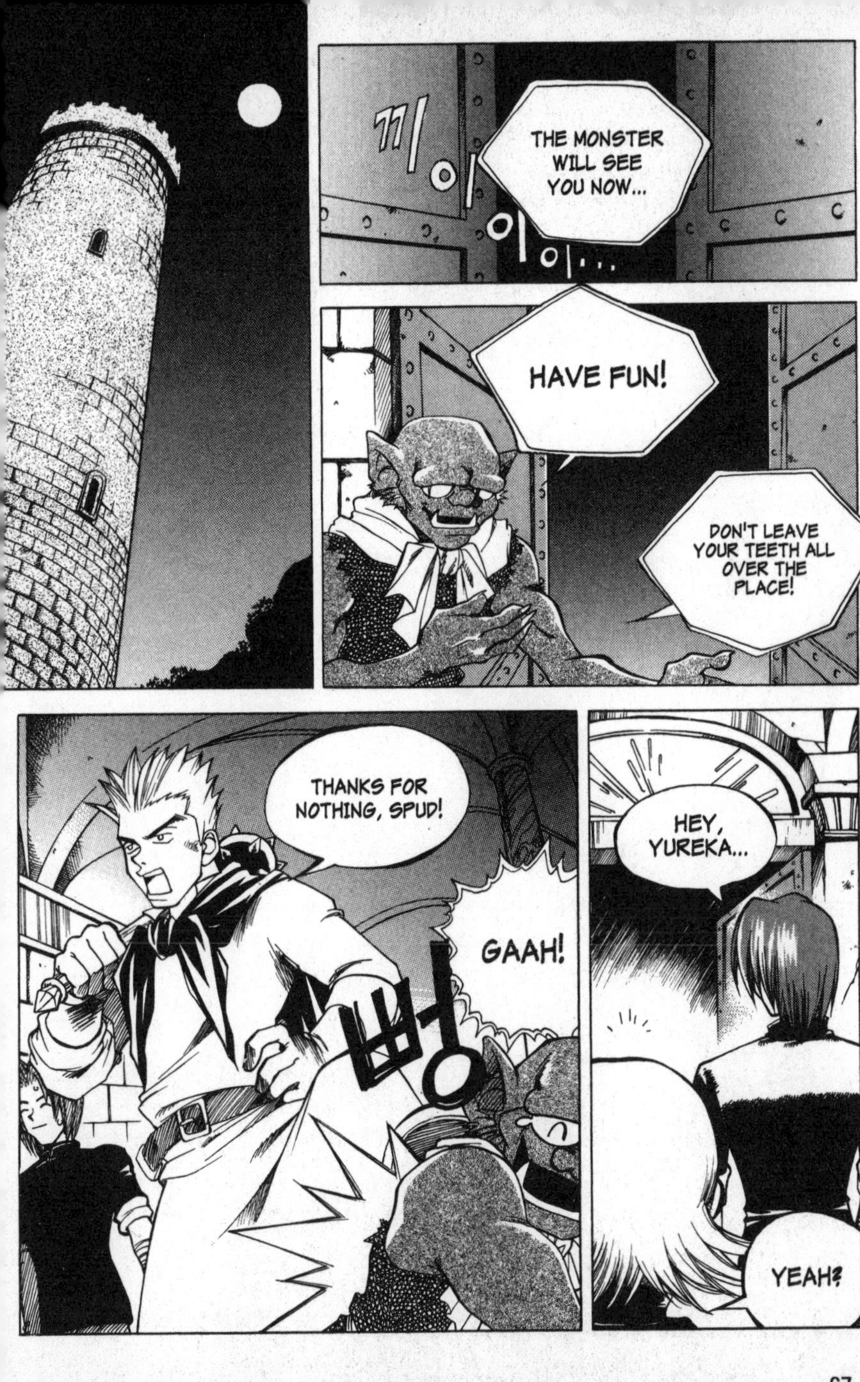
THE MONSTER WILL SEE YOU NOW...
HAVE FUN!
DON'T LEAVE YOUR TEETH ALL OVER THE PLACE!
THANKS FOR NOTHING, SPUD!
GAAH!
HEY, YUREKA...
YEAH?

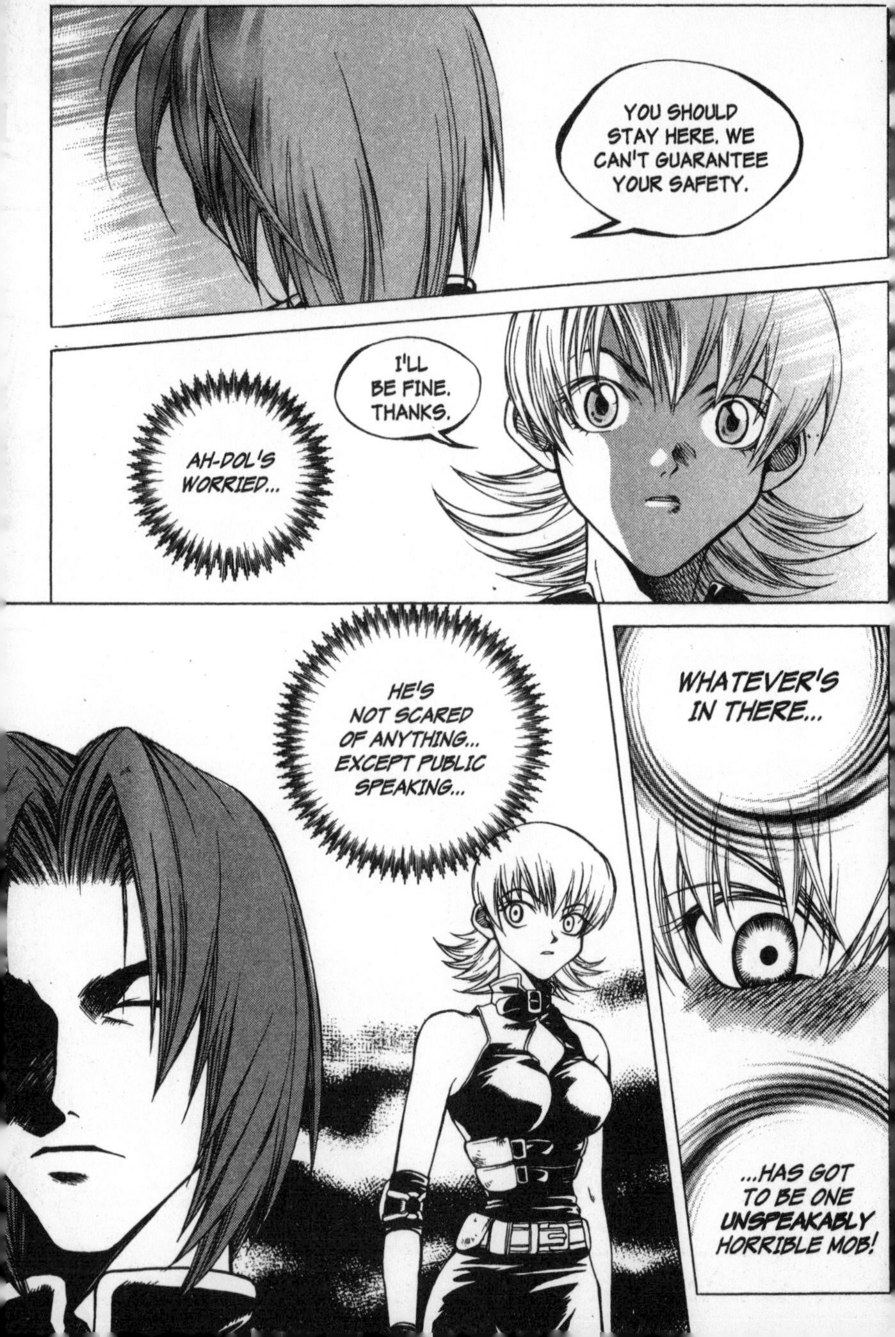
YOU SHOULD STAY HERE. WE CAN'T GUARANTEE YOUR SAFETY.
AH-DOL'S WORRIED...
I'LL BE FINE. THANKS.
HE'S NOT SCARED OF ANYTHING... EXCEPT PUBLIC SPEAKING...
WHATEVER'S IN THERE...
...HAS GOT TO BE ONE UNSPEAKABLY HORRIBLE MOB!

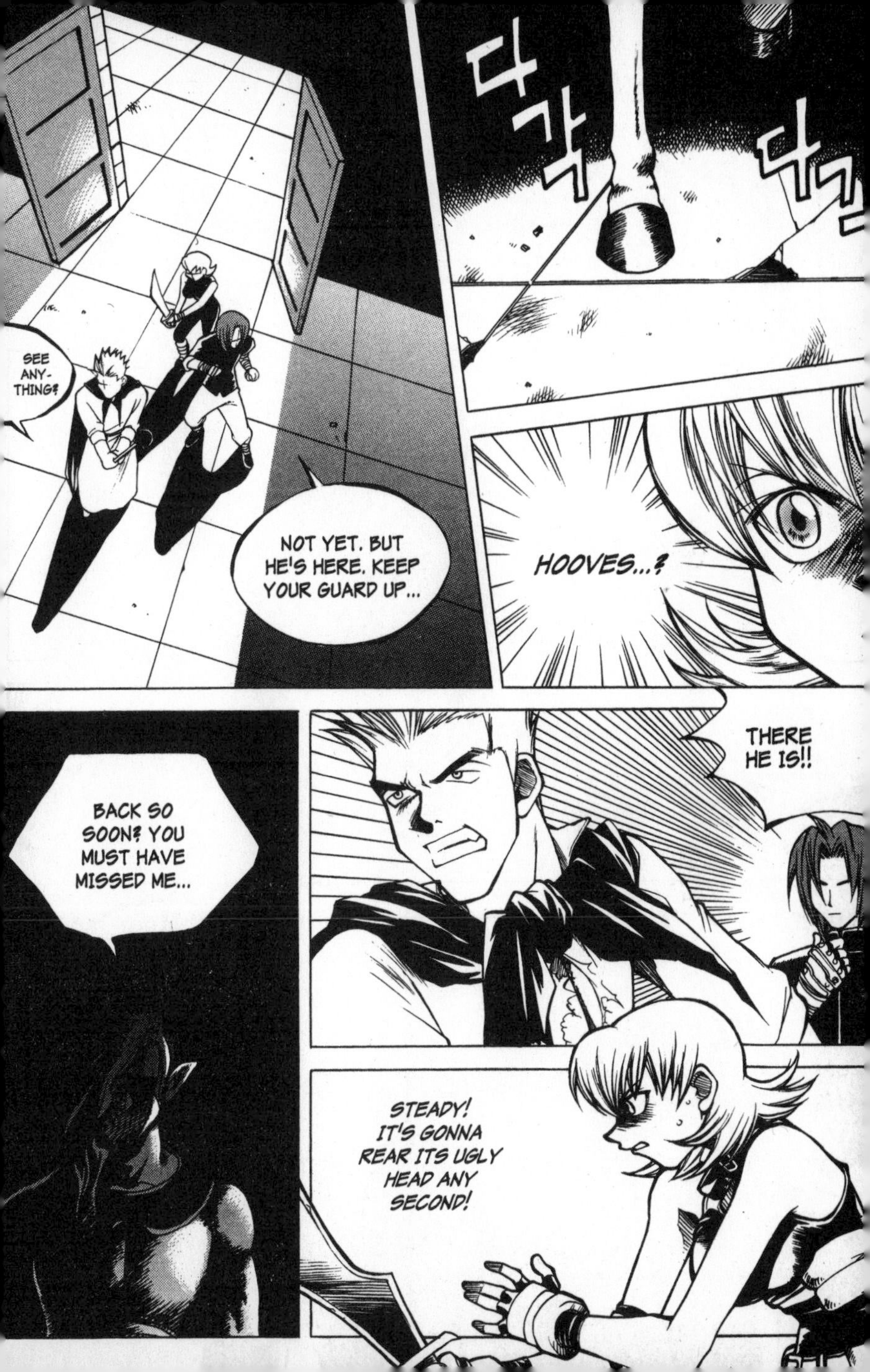
SEE ANY-THING?
NOT YET. BUT HE'S HERE. KEEP YOUR GUARD UP...
다각
다
HOOVES...?
BACK SO SOON? YOU MUST HAVE MISSED ME...
THERE HE IS!!
STEADY! IT'S GONNA REAR ITS UGLY HEAD ANY SECOND!

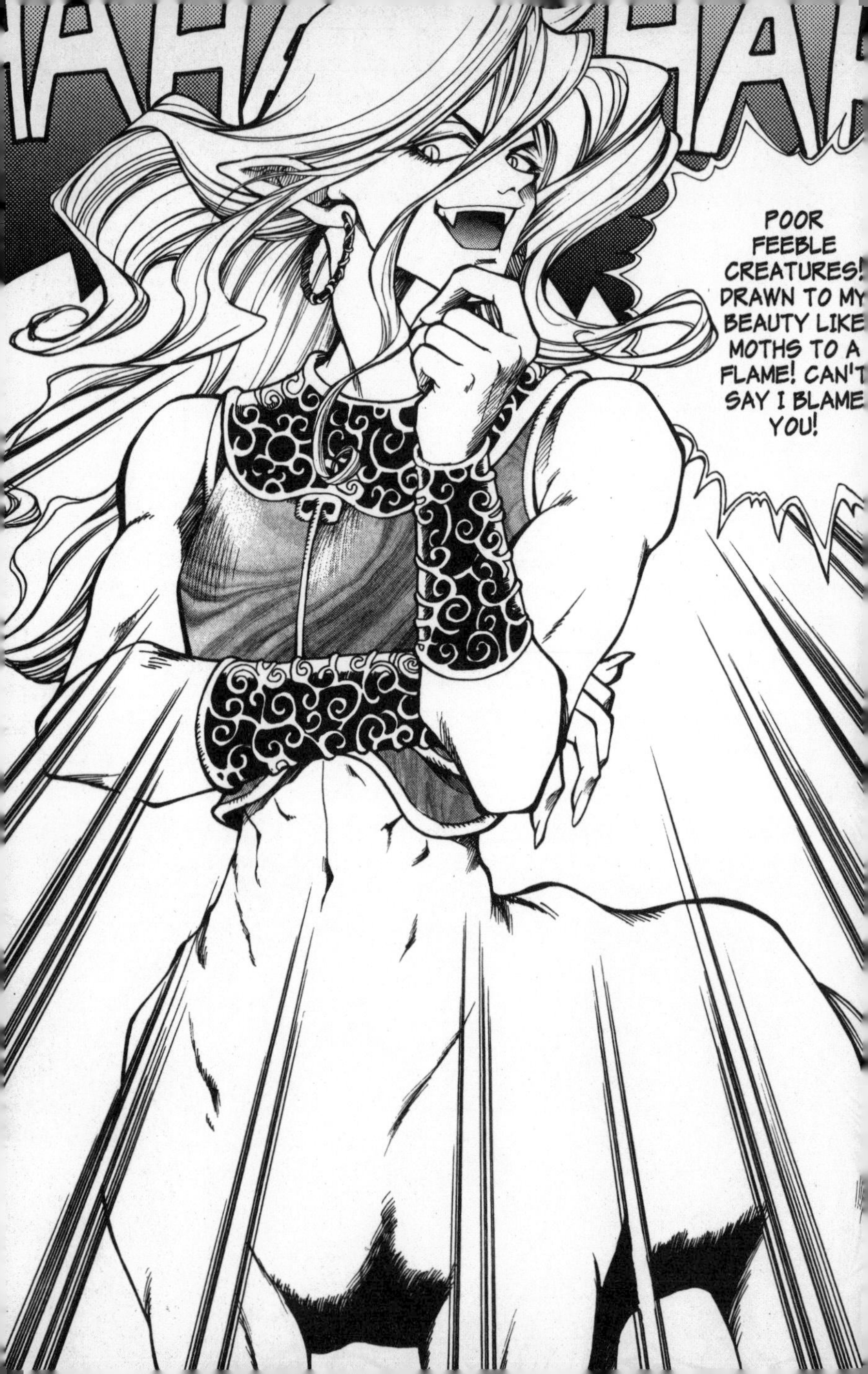

POOR FEEBLE CREATURES! DRAWN TO MY BEAUTY LIKE MOTHS TO A FLAME! CAN'T SAY I BLAME YOU!

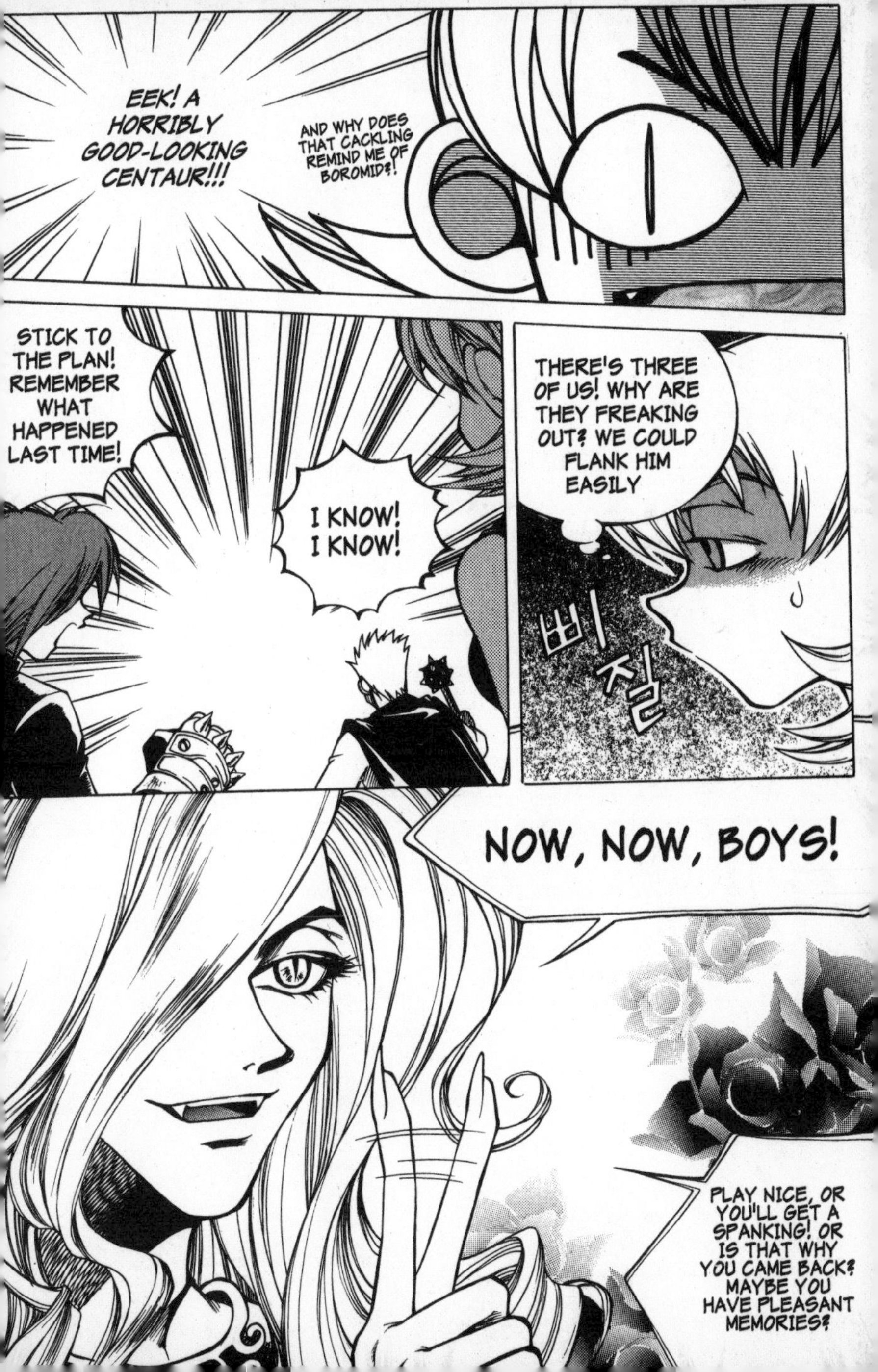
EEK! A HORRIBLY GOOD-LOOKING CENTAUR!!!
AND WHY DOES THAT CACKLING REMIND ME OF BOROMID?!
STICK TO THE PLAN! REMEMBER WHAT HAPPENED LAST TIME!
I KNOW! I KNOW!
THERE'S THREE OF US! WHY ARE THEY FREAKING OUT? WE COULD FLANK HIM EASILY
삐질
NOW, NOW, BOYS!
PLAY NICE, OR YOU'LL GET A SPANKING! OR IS THAT WHY YOU CAME BACK? MAYBE YOU HAVE PLEASANT MEMORIES?

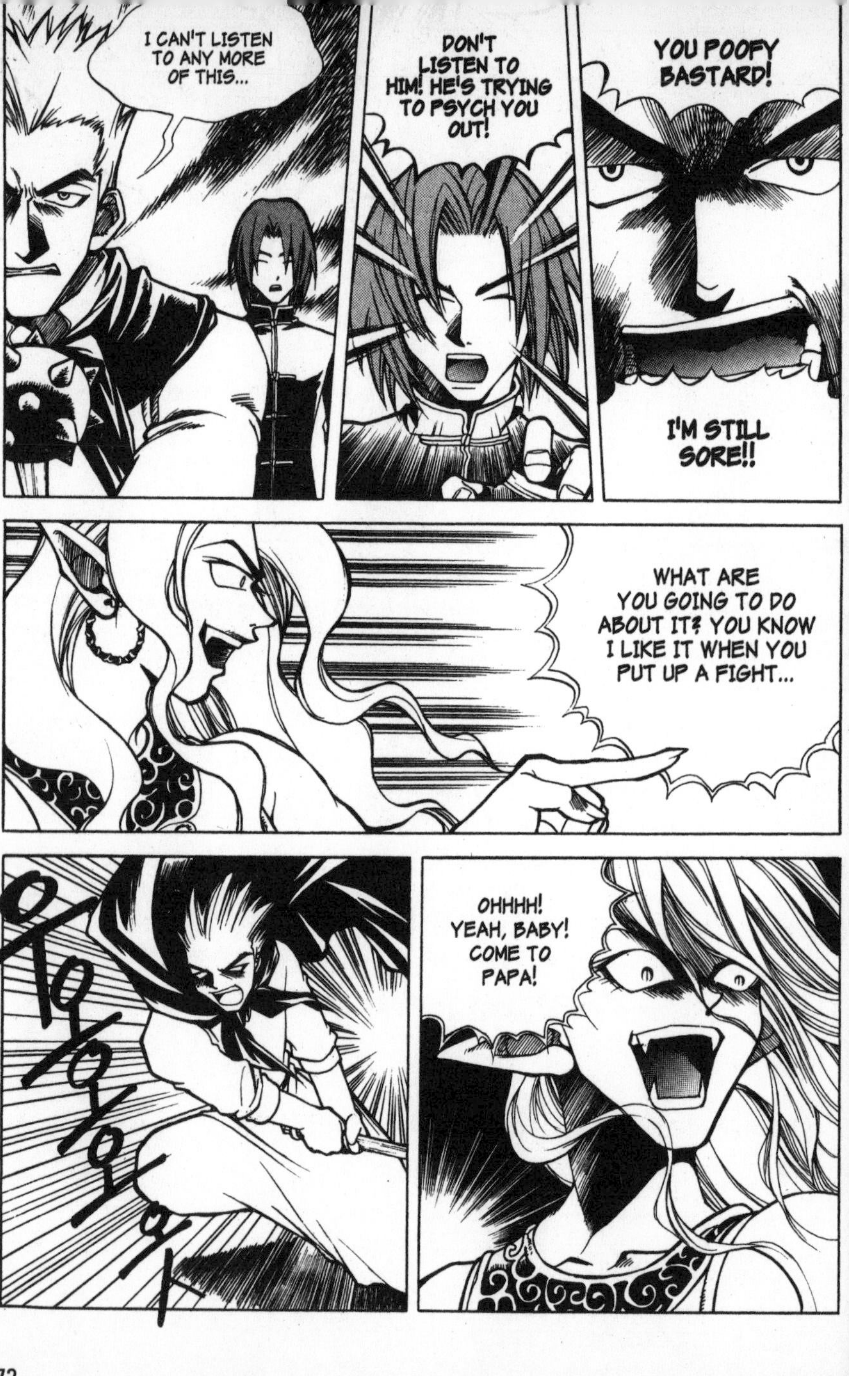
I CAN'T LISTEN TO ANY MORE OF THIS...
DON'T LISTEN TO HIM! HE'S TRYING TO PSYCH YOU OUT!
YOU POOFY BASTARD!
I'M STILL SORE!!
WHAT ARE YOU GOING TO DO ABOUT IT? YOU KNOW I LIKE IT WHEN YOU PUT UP A FIGHT...
OHHHH! YEAH, BABY! COME TO PAPA!

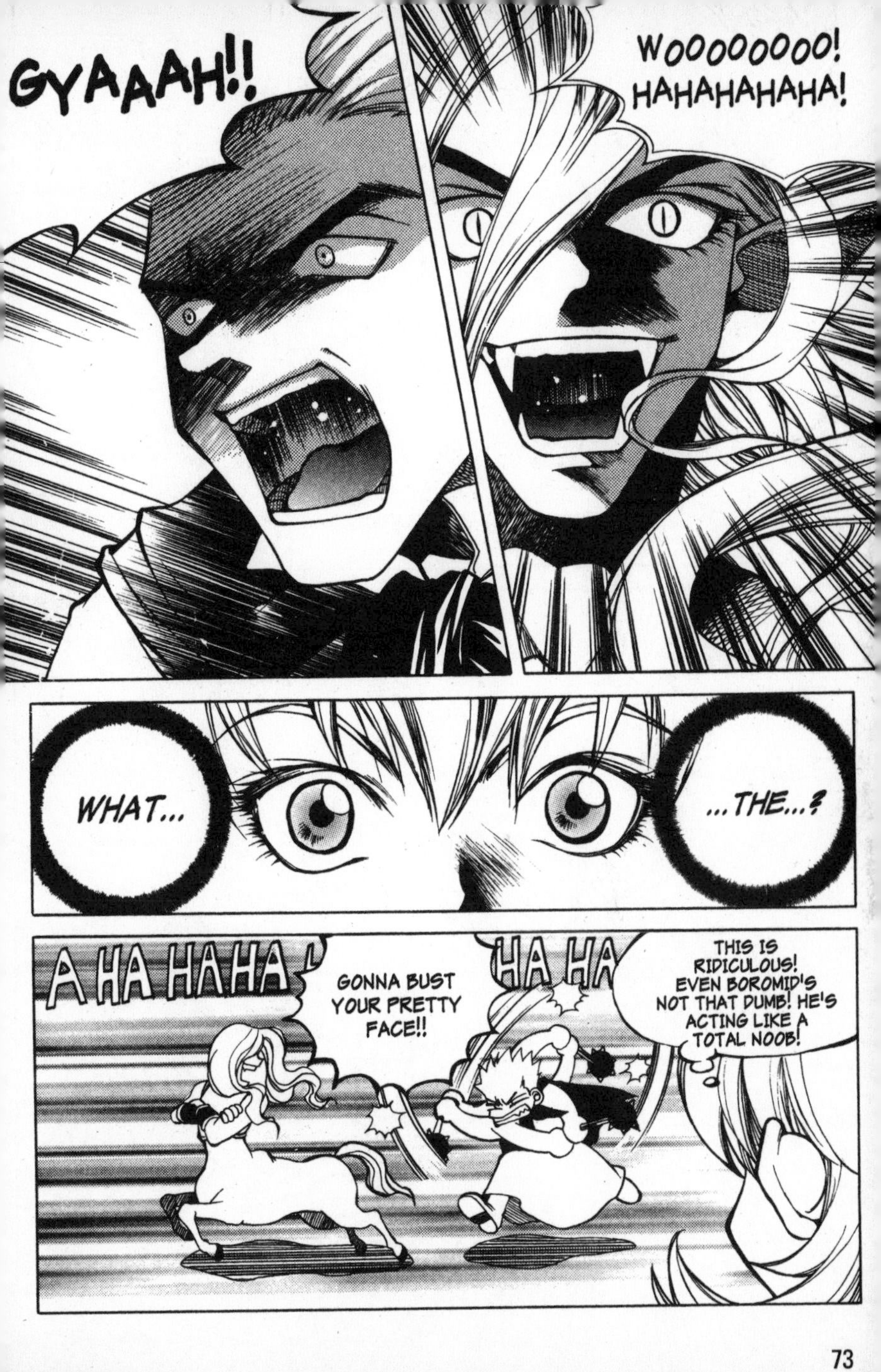
GYAAAH!!
WOOOOOOOO! HAHAHAHAHA!
WHAT...
...THE...?
A HA HAHA
GONNA BUST YOUR PRETTY FACE!!
HA HA
THIS IS RIDICULOUS! EVEN BOROMID'S NOT THAT DUMB! HE'S ACTING LIKE A TOTAL NOOB!

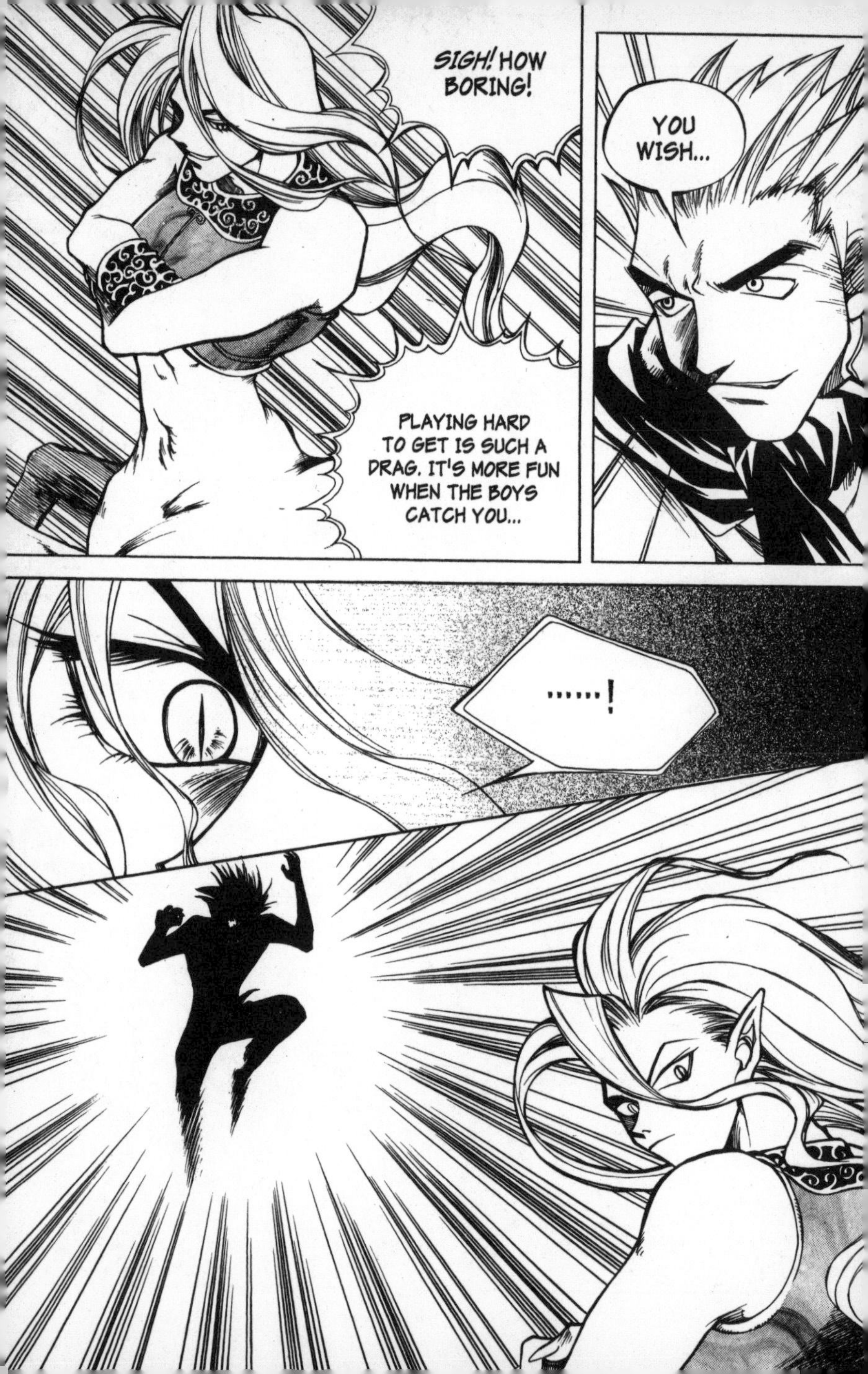
SIGH! HOW BORING!
PLAYING HARD TO GET IS SUCH A DRAG. IT'S MORE FUN WHEN THE BOYS CATCH YOU...
YOU WISH...
......!

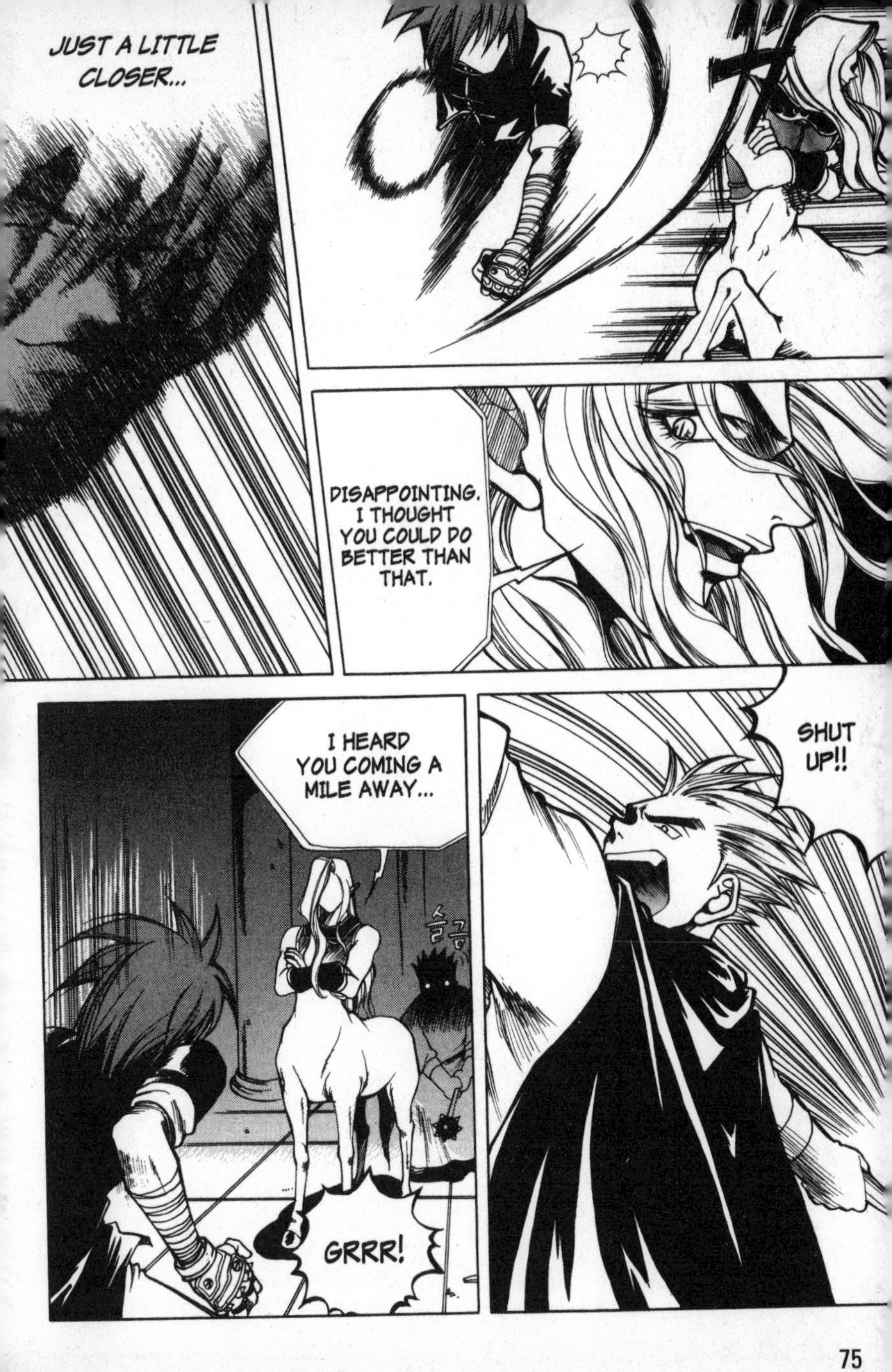

JUST A LITTLE CLOSER...
DISAPPOINTING. I THOUGHT YOU COULD DO BETTER THAN THAT.
I HEARD YOU COMING A MILE AWAY...
슬금
GRRR!
SHUT UP!!

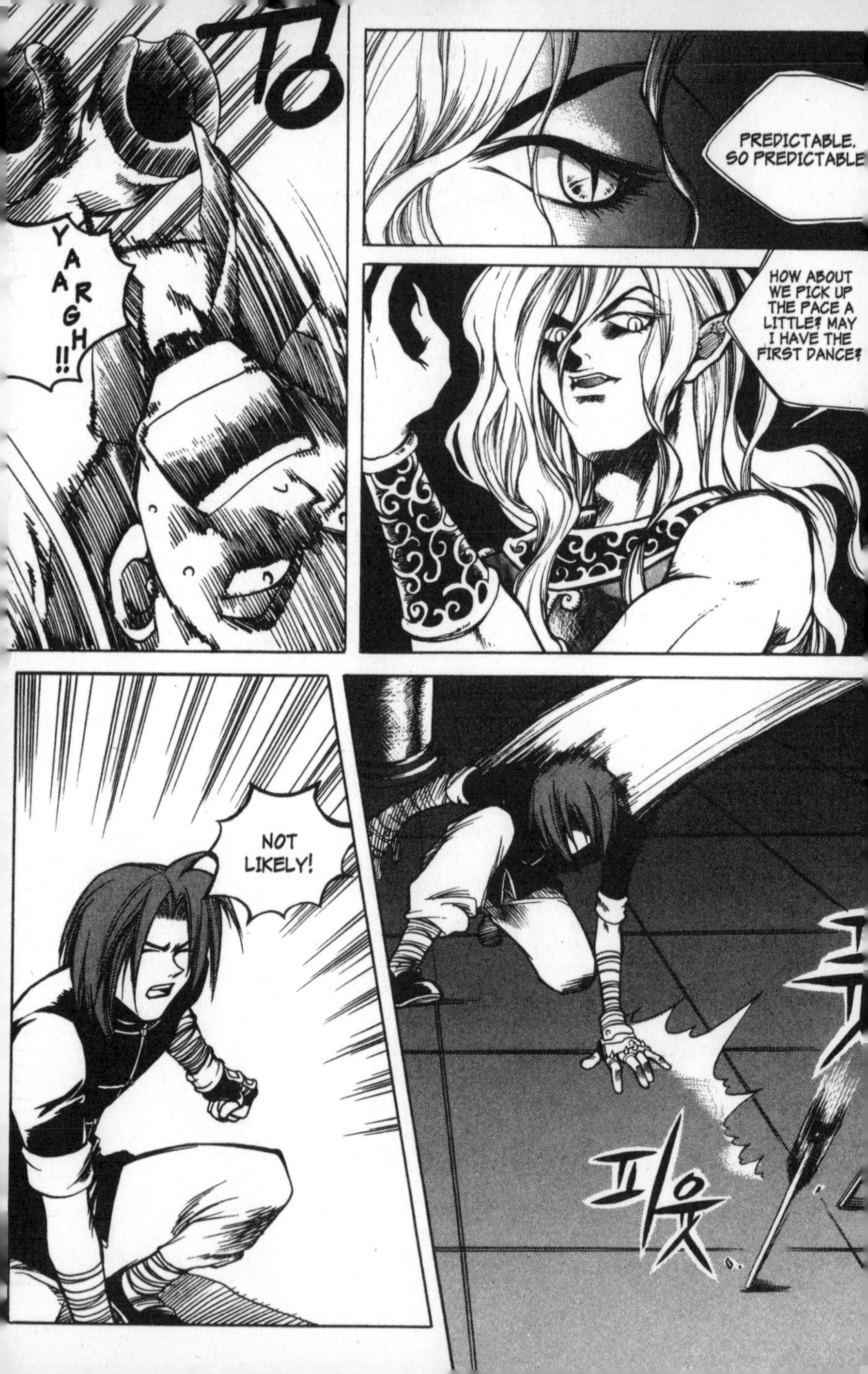
YAARGH!!
PREDICTABLE. SO PREDICTABLE.
HOW ABOUT WE PICK UP THE PACE A LITTLE? MAY I HAVE THE FIRST DANCE?
NOT LIKELY!

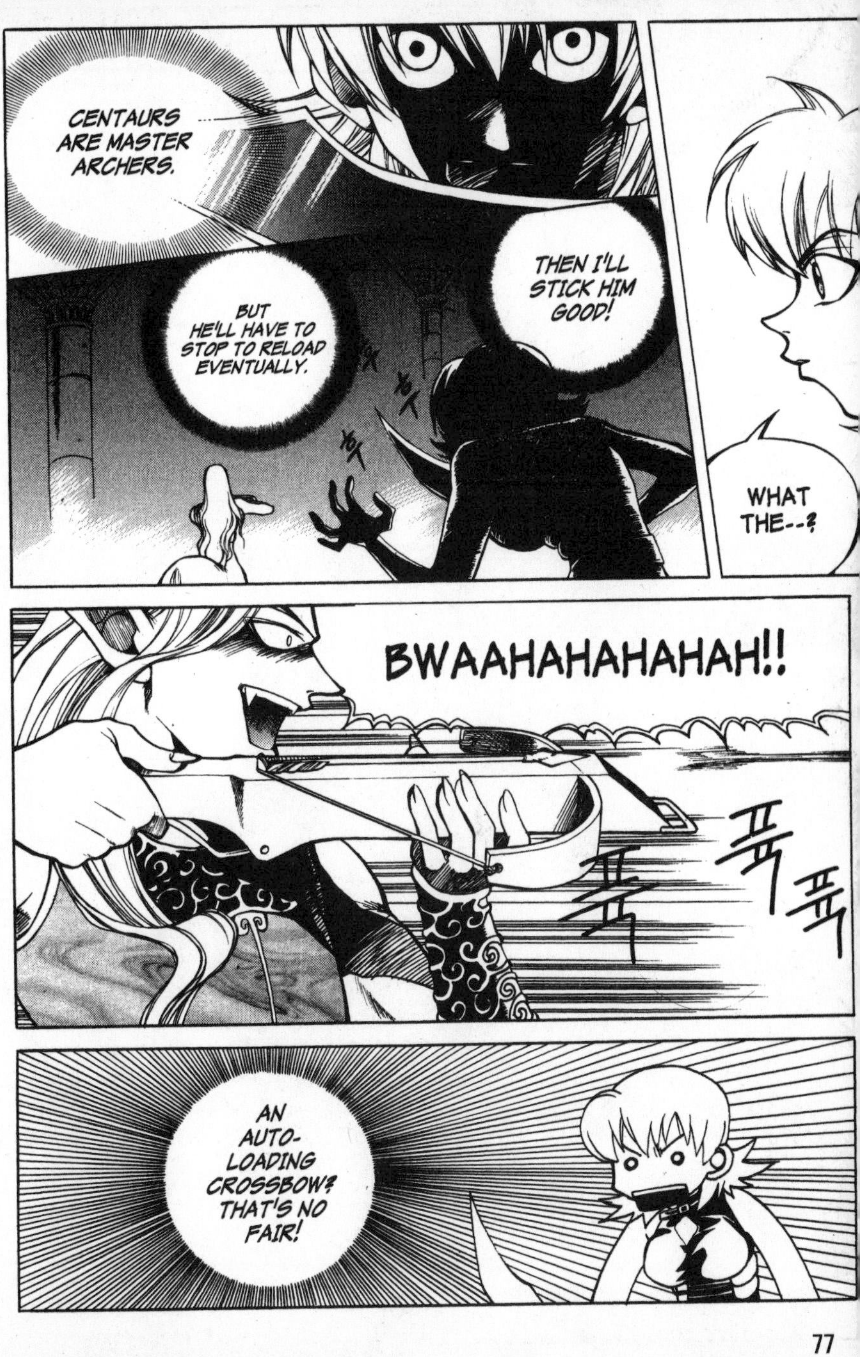
CENTAURS ARE MASTER ARCHERS.
BUT HE'LL HAVE TO STOP TO RELOAD EVENTUALLY.
THEN I'LL STICK HIM GOOD!
WHAT THE--?
BWAAHAHAHAHAH!!
퓩
퓩 퓩
AN AUTO-LOADING CROSSBOW? THAT'S NO FAIR!

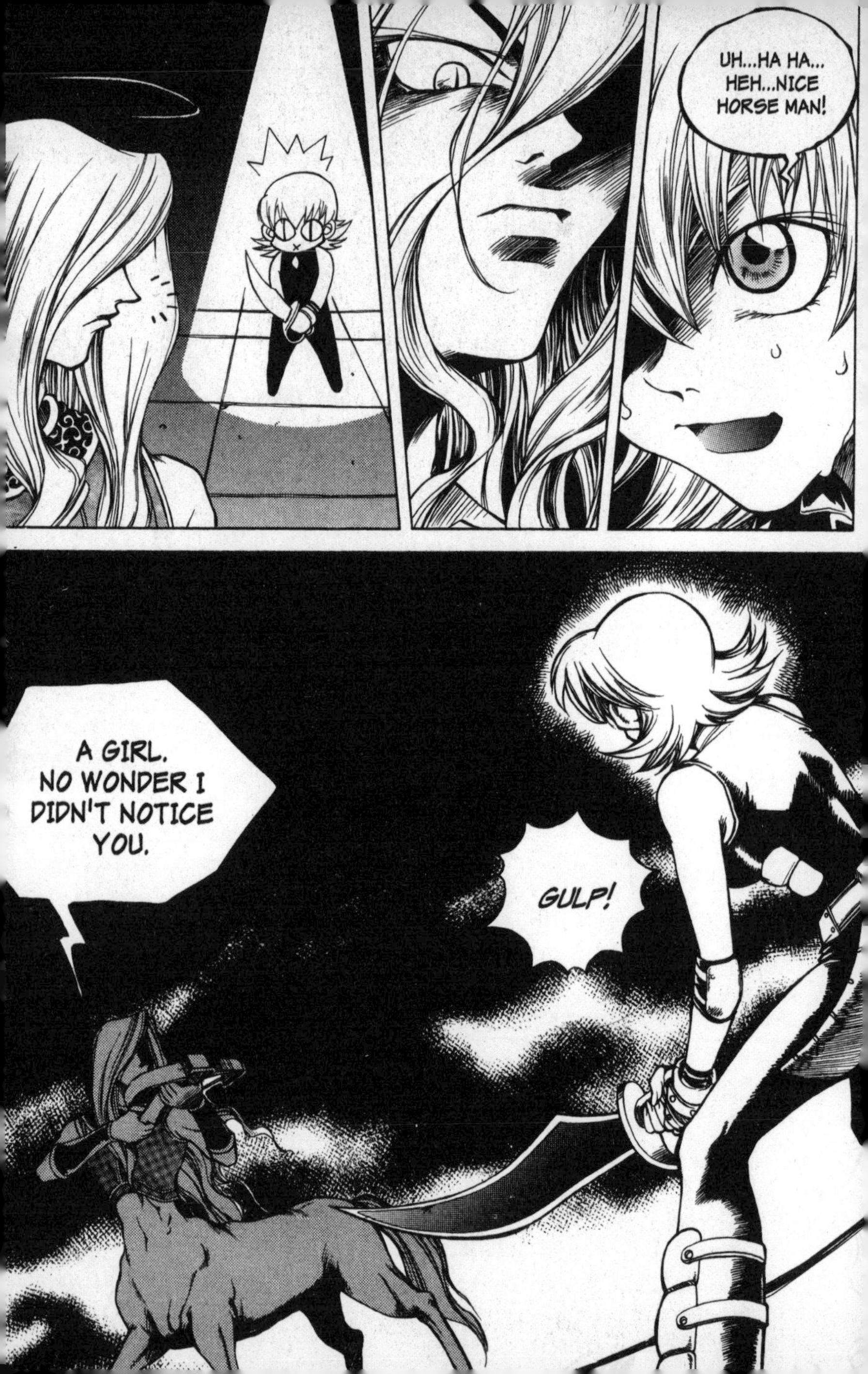
UH...HA HA... HEH...NICE HORSE MAN!
A GIRL. NO WONDER I DIDN'T NOTICE YOU.
GULP!

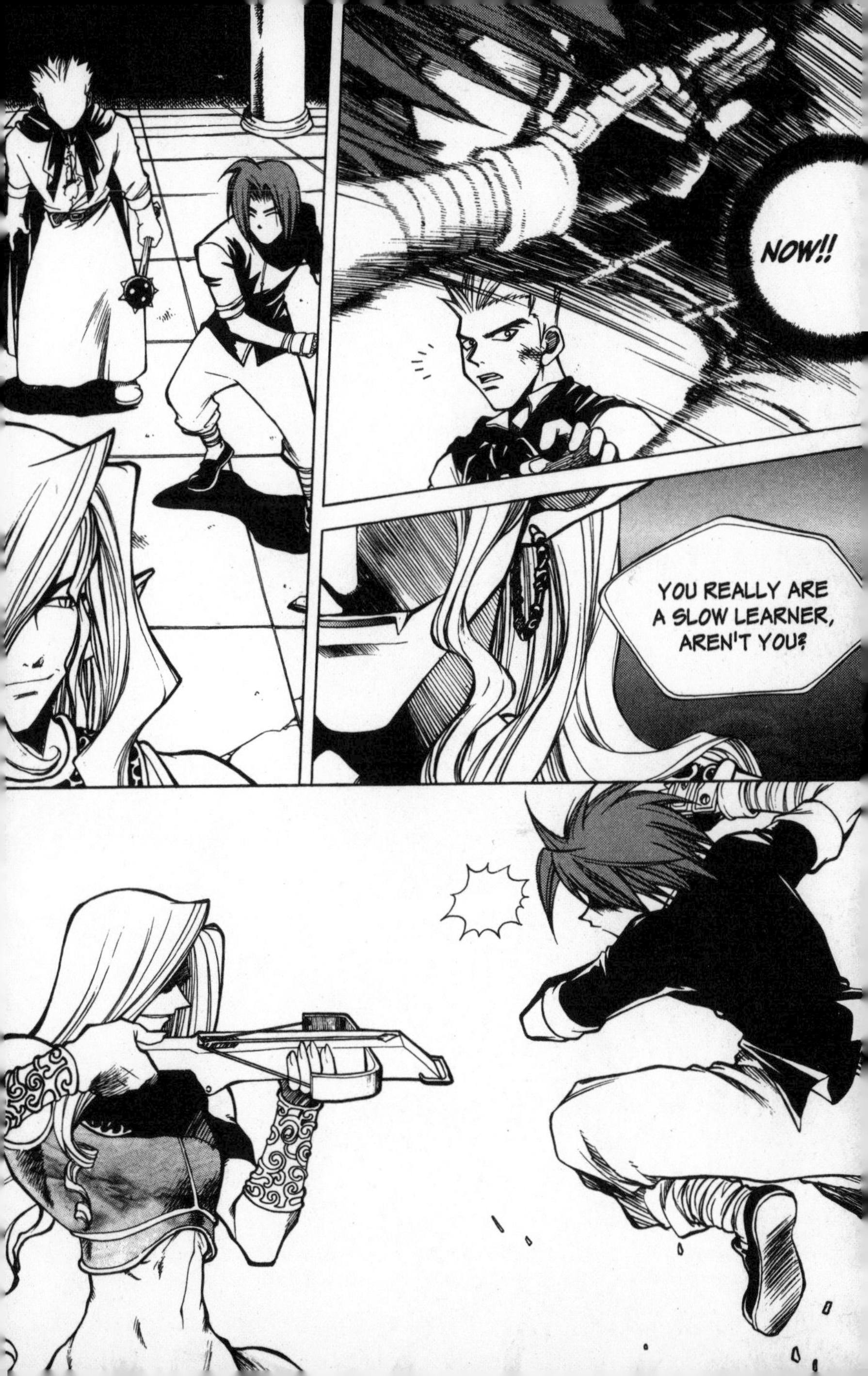
NOW!!
YOU REALLY ARE A SLOW LEARNER, AREN'T YOU?

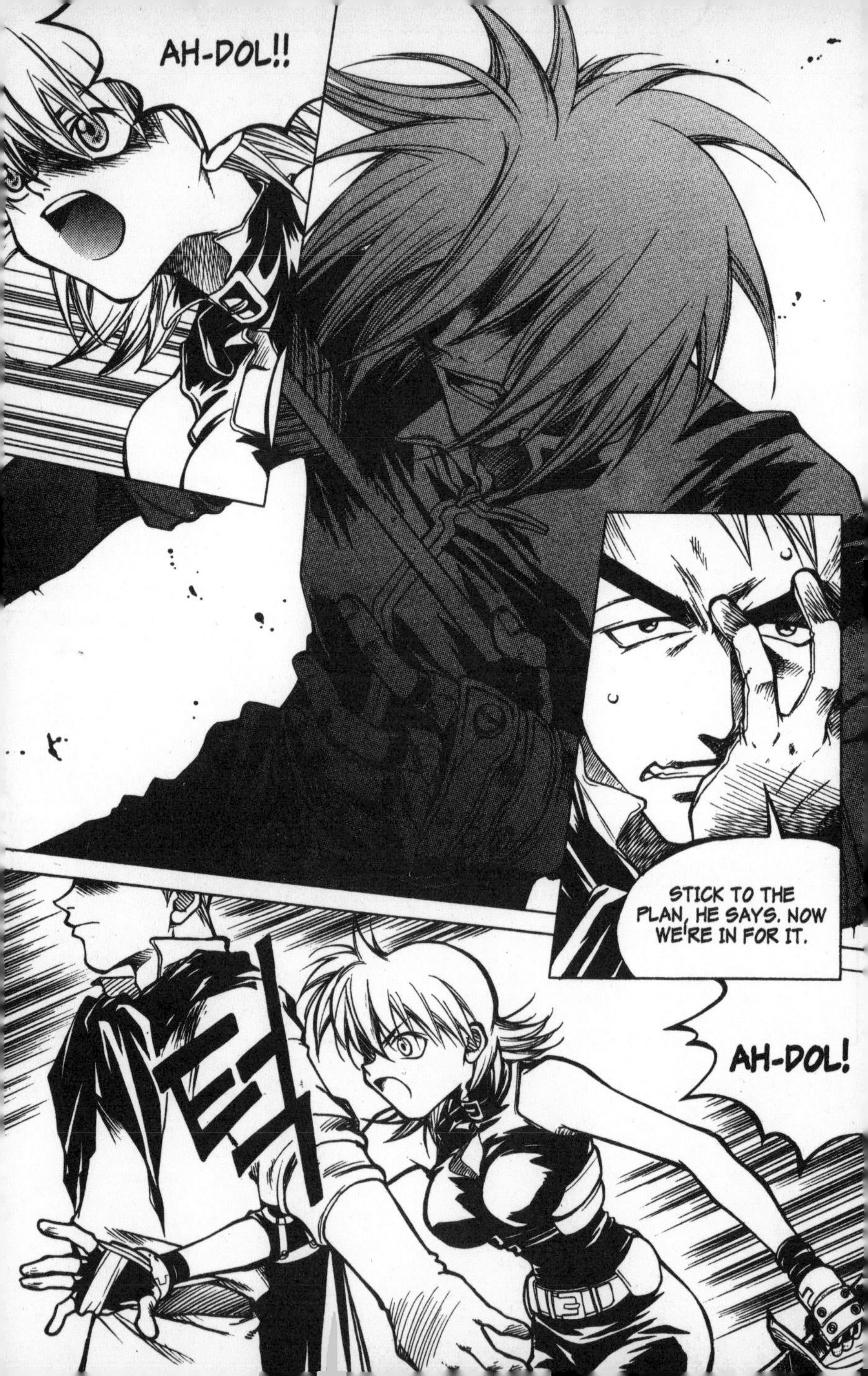
AH-DOL!!
STICK TO THE PLAN, HE SAYS. NOW WE'RE IN FOR IT.
AH-DOL!

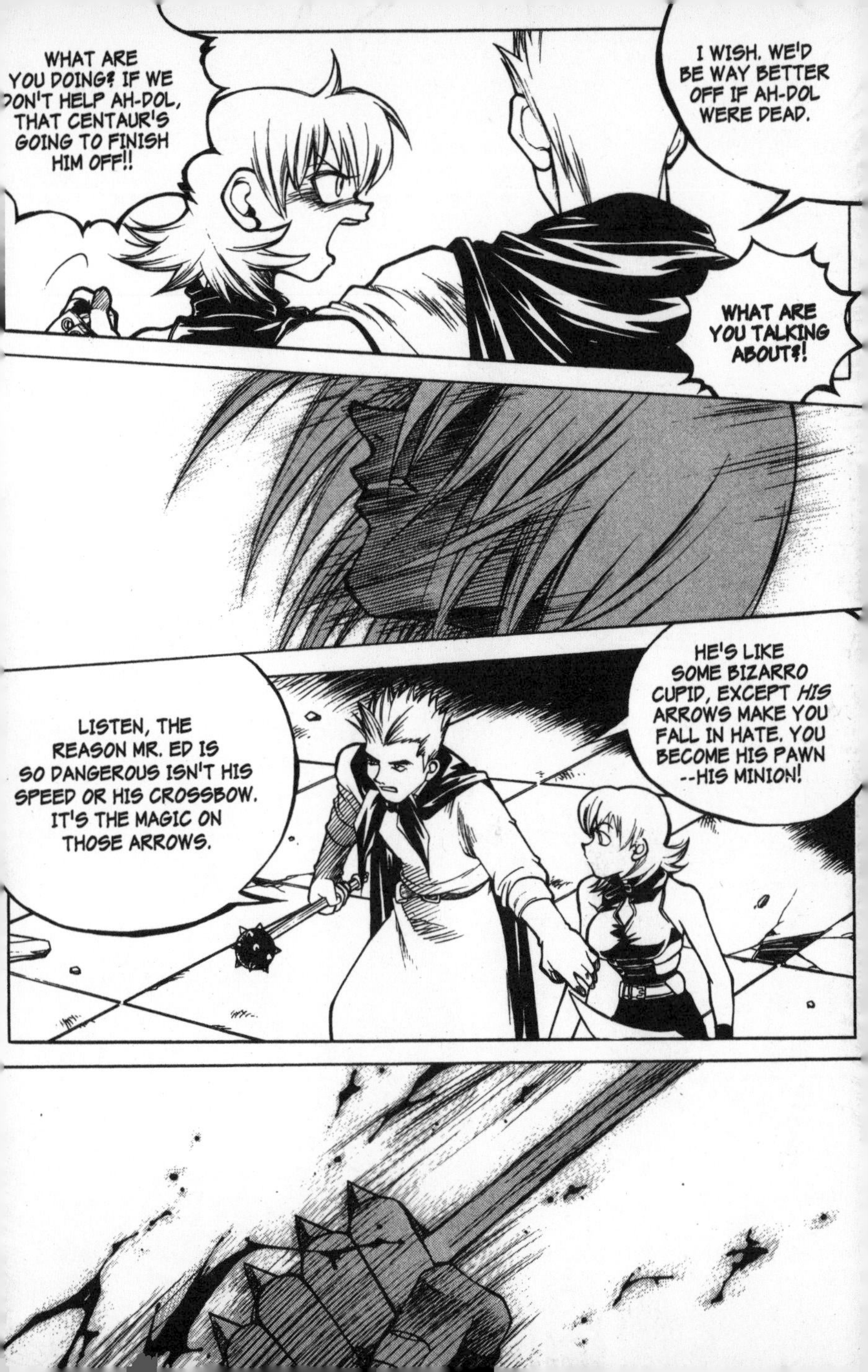
WHAT ARE YOU DOING? IF WE DON'T HELP AH-DOL, THAT CENTAUR'S GOING TO FINISH HIM OFF!!
I WISH. WE'D BE WAY BETTER OFF IF AH-DOL WERE DEAD.
WHAT ARE YOU TALKING ABOUT?!
LISTEN, THE REASON MR. ED IS SO DANGEROUS ISN'T HIS SPEED OR HIS CROSSBOW. IT'S THE MAGIC ON THOSE ARROWS.
HE'S LIKE SOME BIZARRO CUPID, EXCEPT *HIS* ARROWS MAKE YOU FALL IN HATE. YOU BECOME HIS PAWN --HIS MINION!

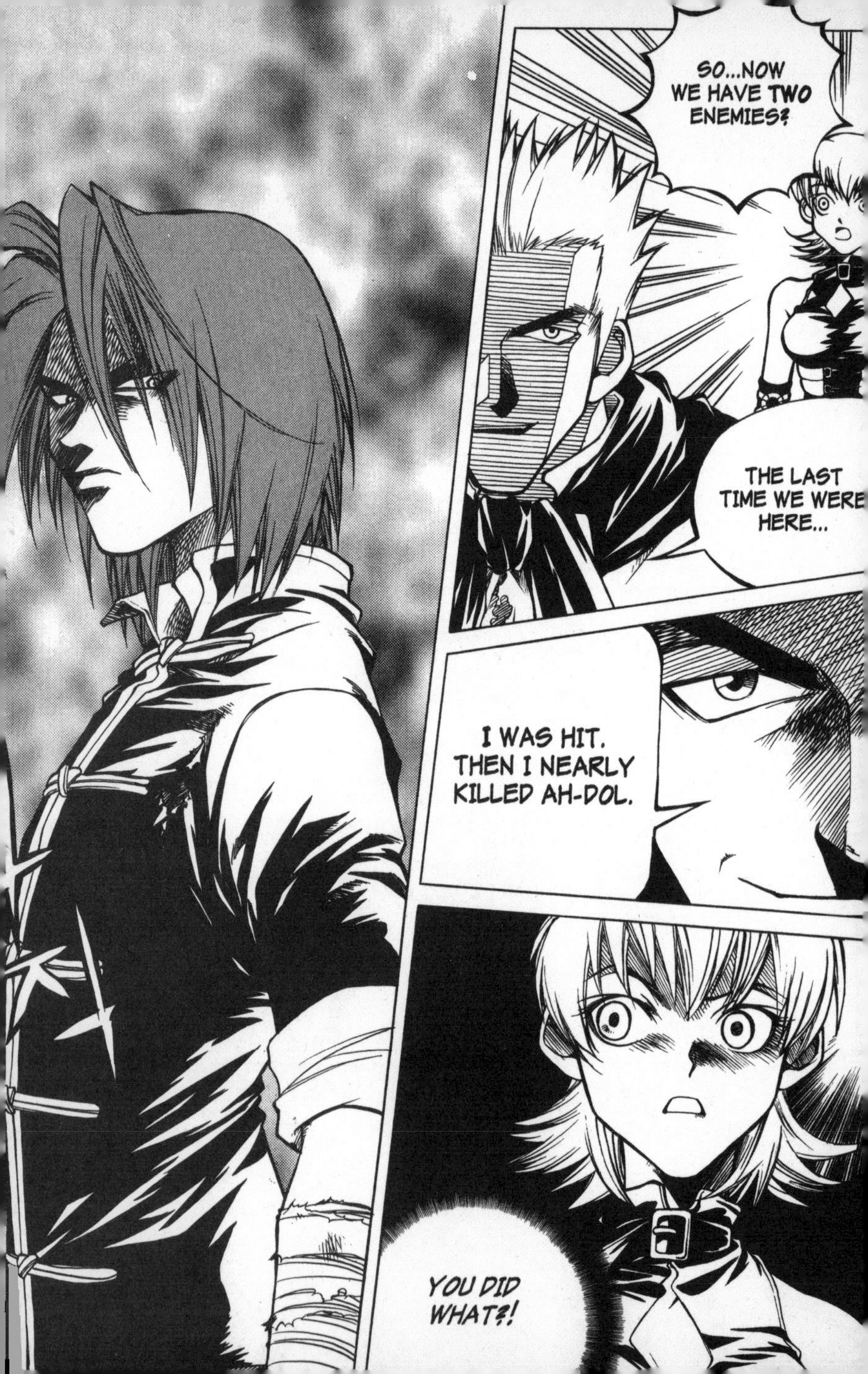
SO...NOW WE HAVE TWO ENEMIES?
THE LAST TIME WE WERE HERE...
I WAS HIT. THEN I NEARLY KILLED AH-DOL.
YOU DID WHAT?!

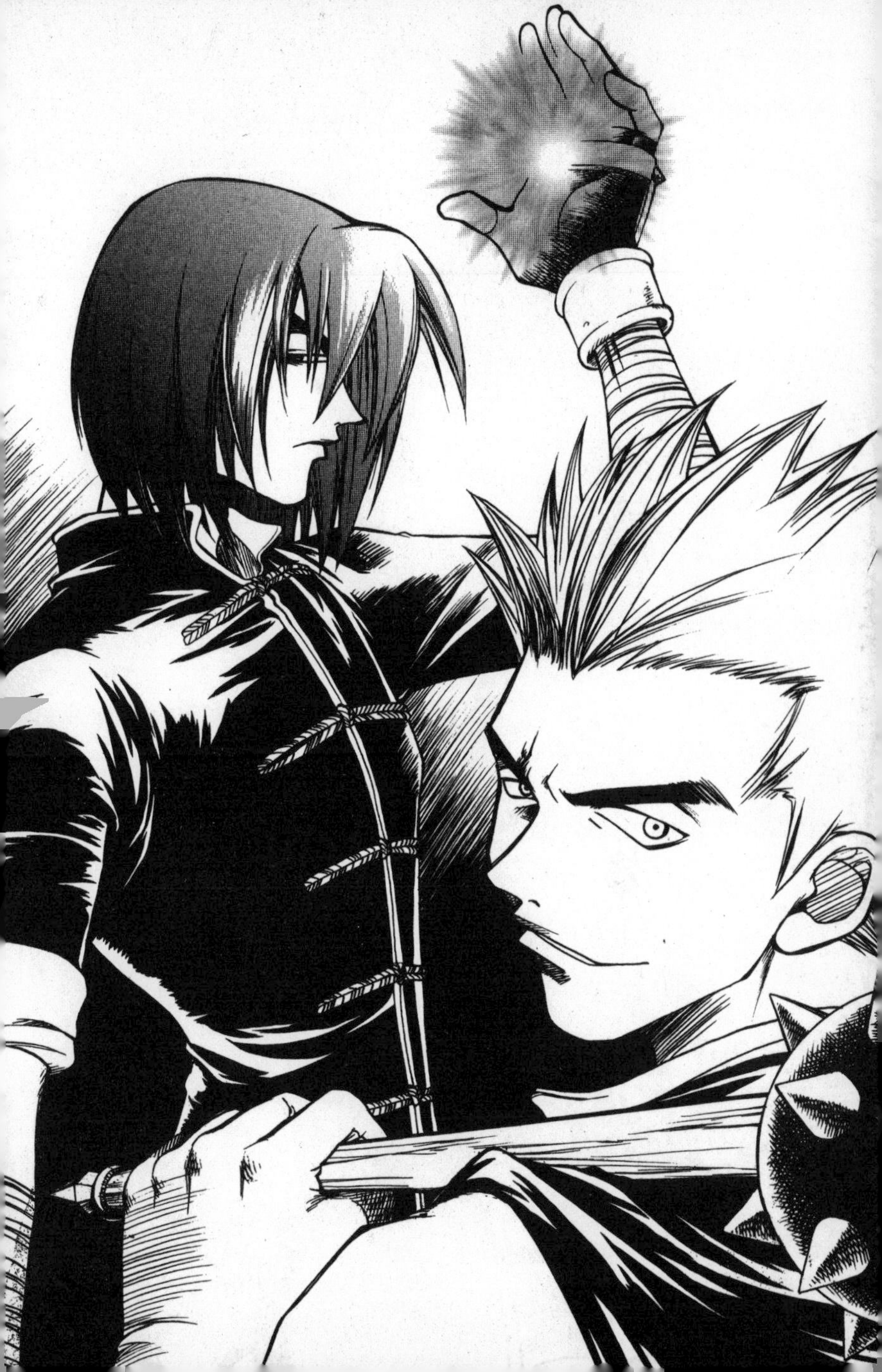

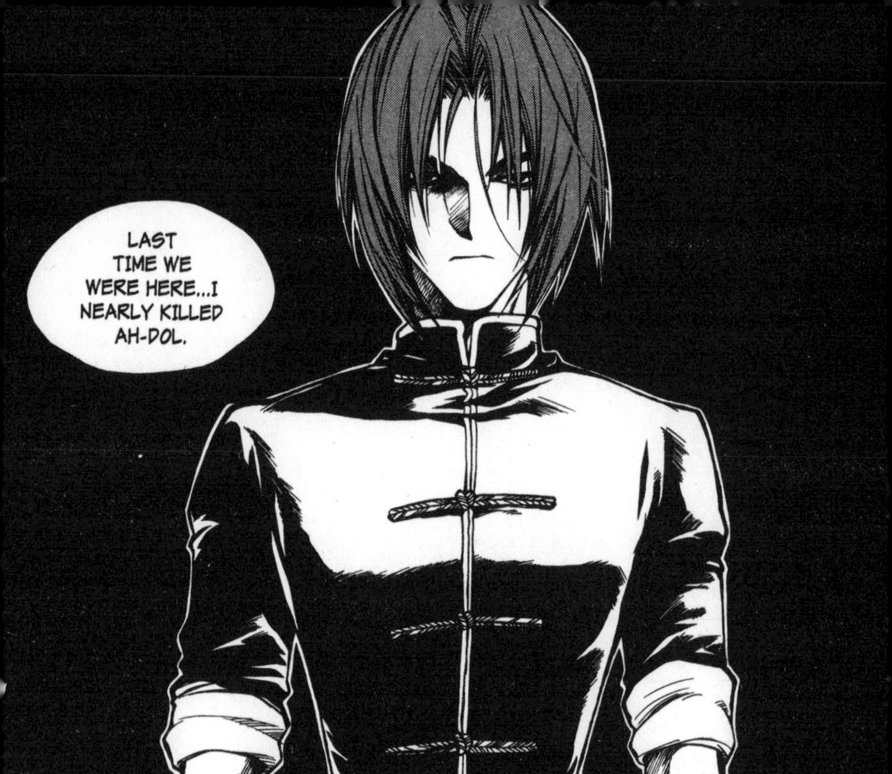
LAST TIME WE WERE HERE...I NEARLY KILLED AH-DOL.

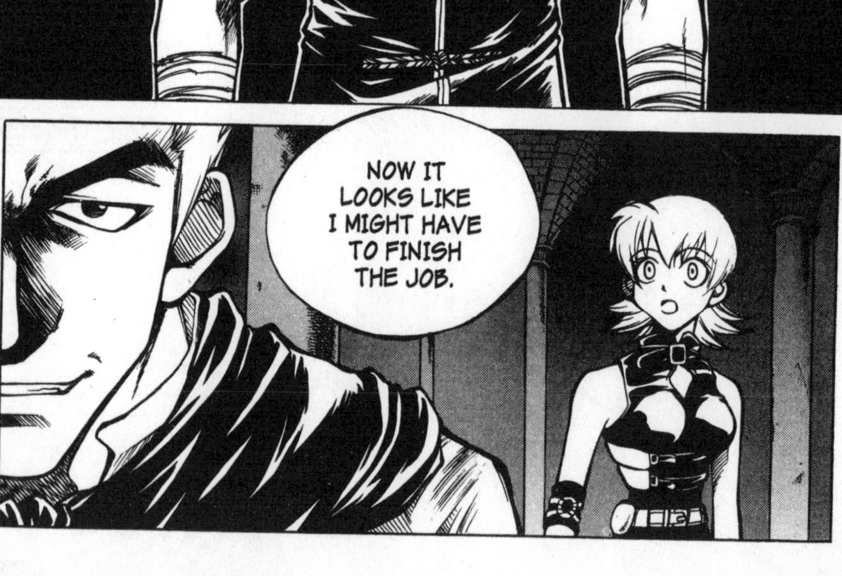
NOW IT LOOKS LIKE I MIGHT HAVE TO FINISH THE JOB.

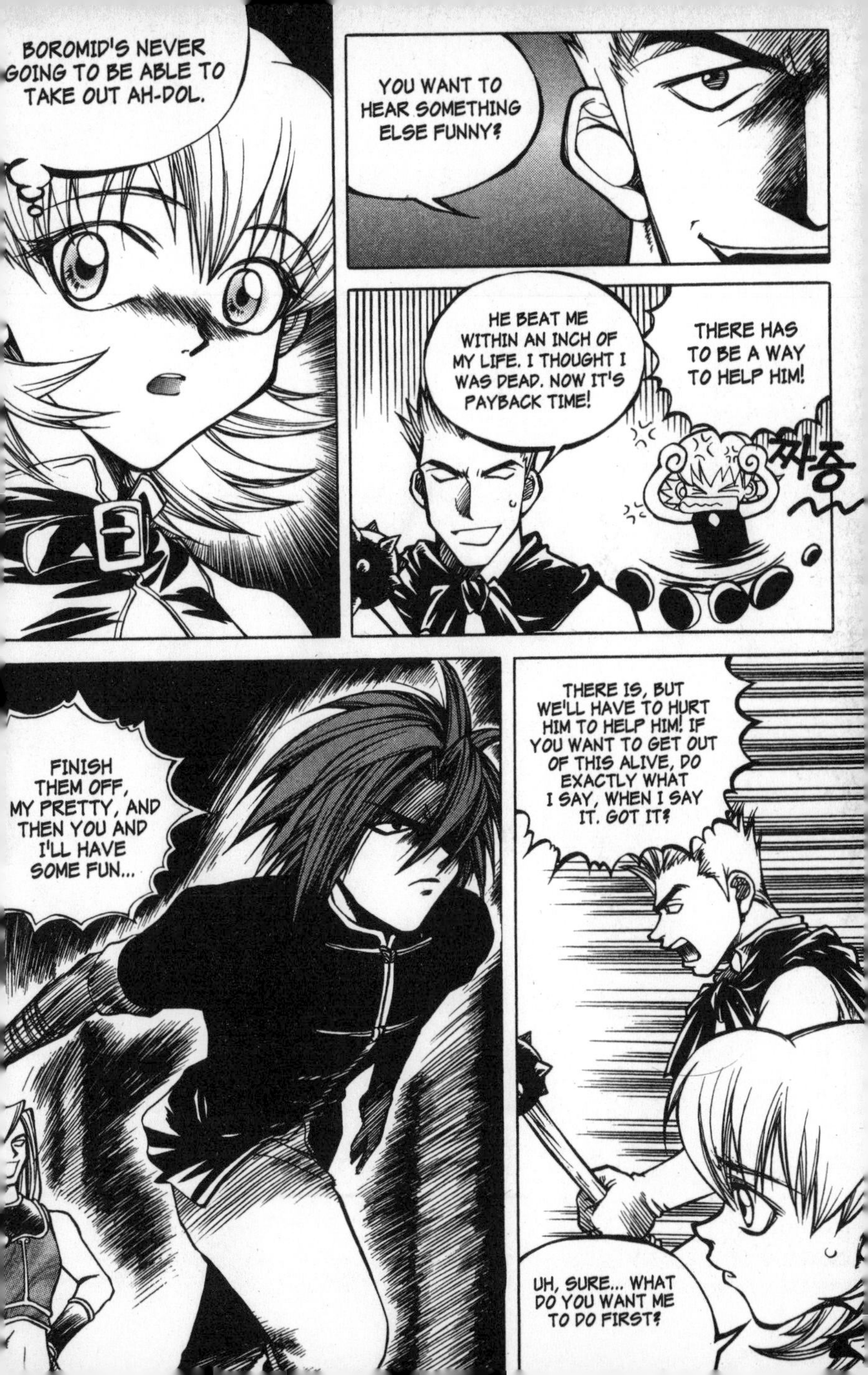
BOROMID'S NEVER GOING TO BE ABLE TO TAKE OUT AH-DOL.
YOU WANT TO HEAR SOMETHING ELSE FUNNY?
HE BEAT ME WITHIN AN INCH OF MY LIFE. I THOUGHT I WAS DEAD. NOW IT'S PAYBACK TIME!
THERE HAS TO BE A WAY TO HELP HIM!
짜증
FINISH THEM OFF, MY PRETTY, AND THEN YOU AND I'LL HAVE SOME FUN...
THERE IS, BUT WE'LL HAVE TO HURT HIM TO HELP HIM! IF YOU WANT TO GET OUT OF THIS ALIVE, DO EXACTLY WHAT I SAY, WHEN I SAY IT. GOT IT?
UH, SURE... WHAT DO YOU WANT ME TO DO FIRST?

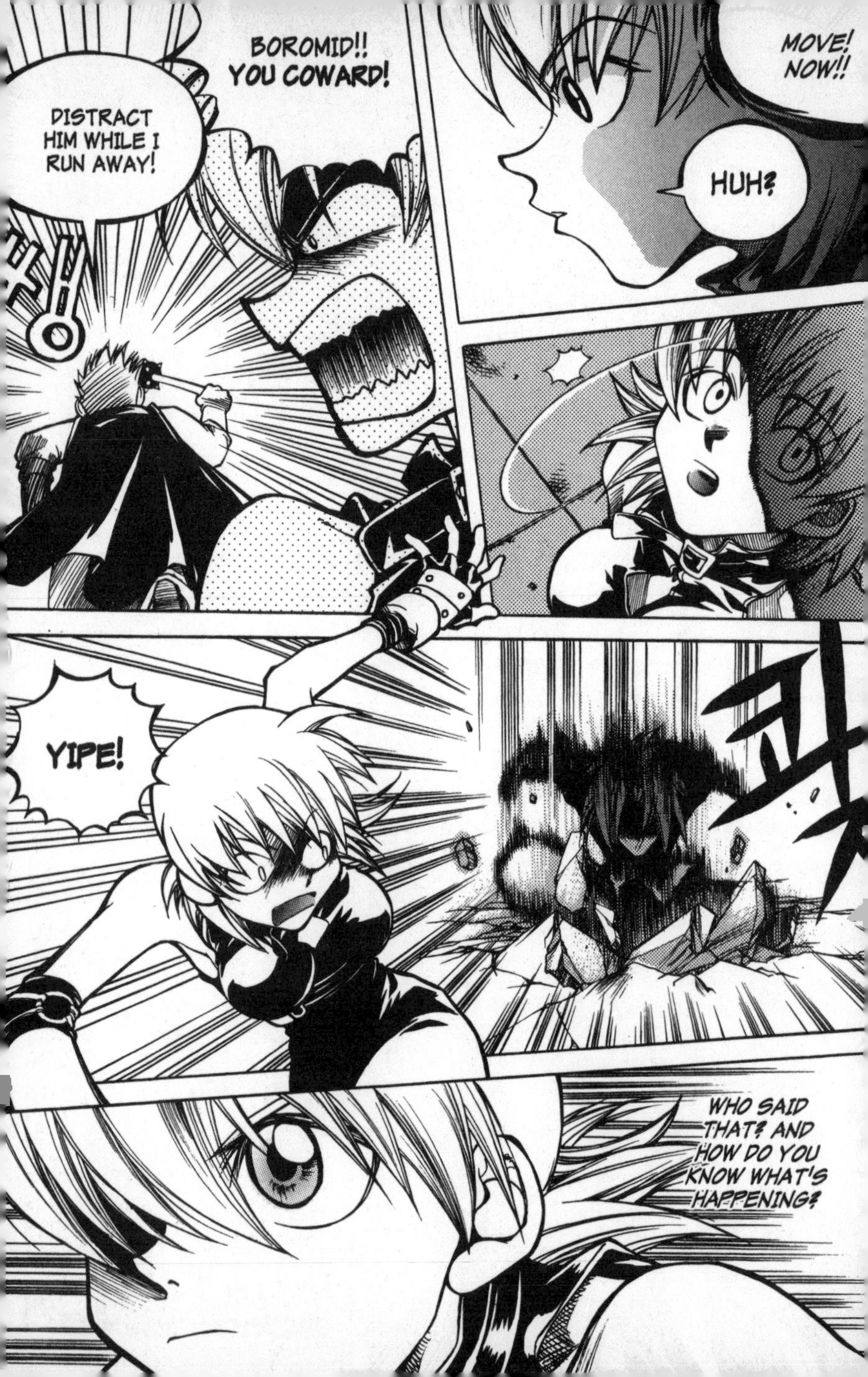
DISTRACT HIM WHILE I RUN AWAY!
BOROMID!! YOU COWARD!
MOVE! NOW!!
HUH?
YIPE!
WHO SAID THAT? AND HOW DO YOU KNOW WHAT'S HAPPENING?

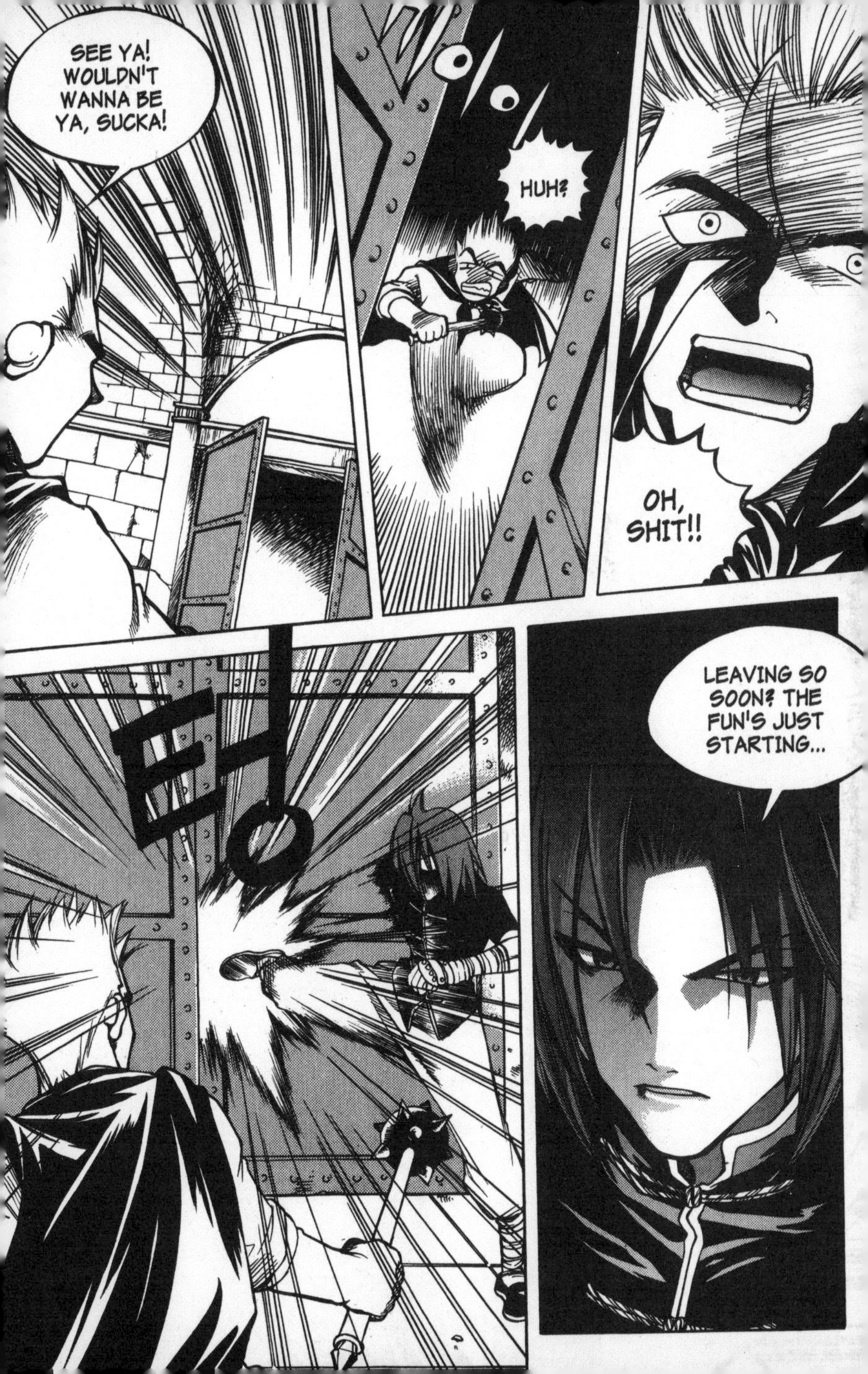
SEE YA! WOULDN'T WANNA BE YA, SUCKA!
HUH?
OH, SHIT!!
LEAVING SO SOON? THE FUN'S JUST STARTING...

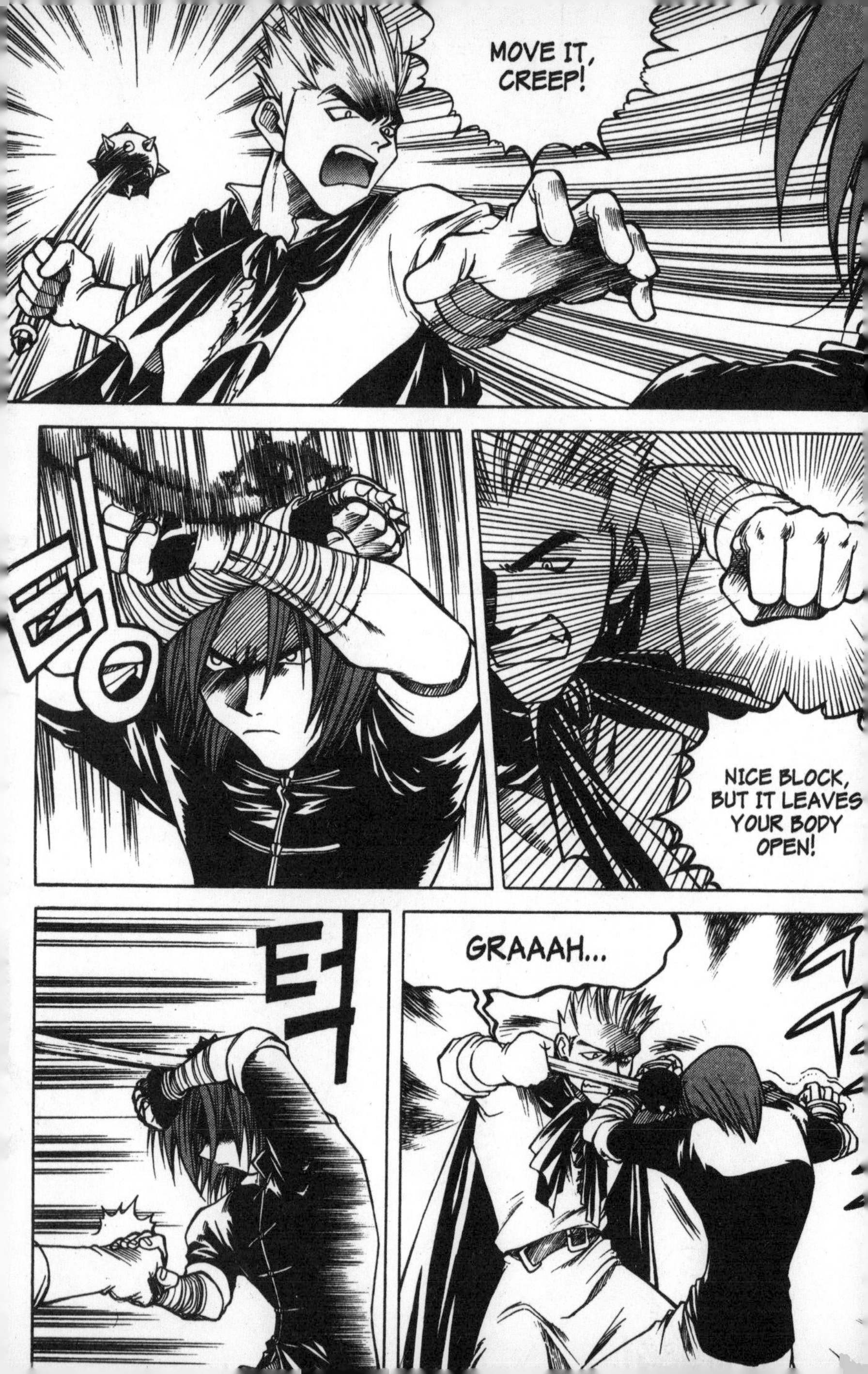
MOVE IT, CREEP!
NICE BLOCK, BUT IT LEAVES YOUR BODY OPEN!
GRAAAH...

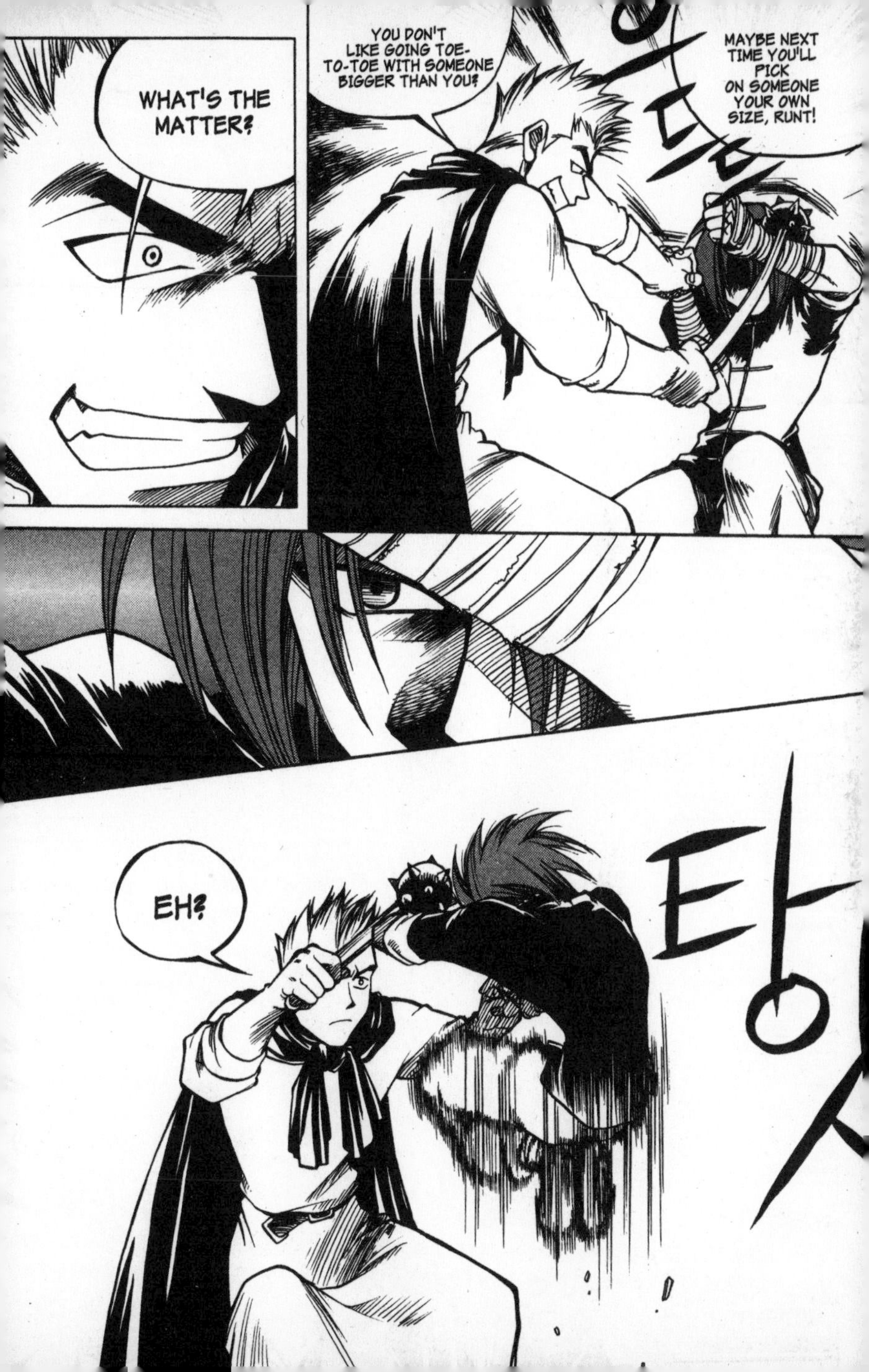
WHAT'S THE MATTER?
YOU DON'T LIKE GOING TOE-TO-TOE WITH SOMEONE BIGGER THAN YOU?
MAYBE NEXT TIME YOU'LL PICK ON SOMEONE YOUR OWN SIZE, RUNT!
EH?

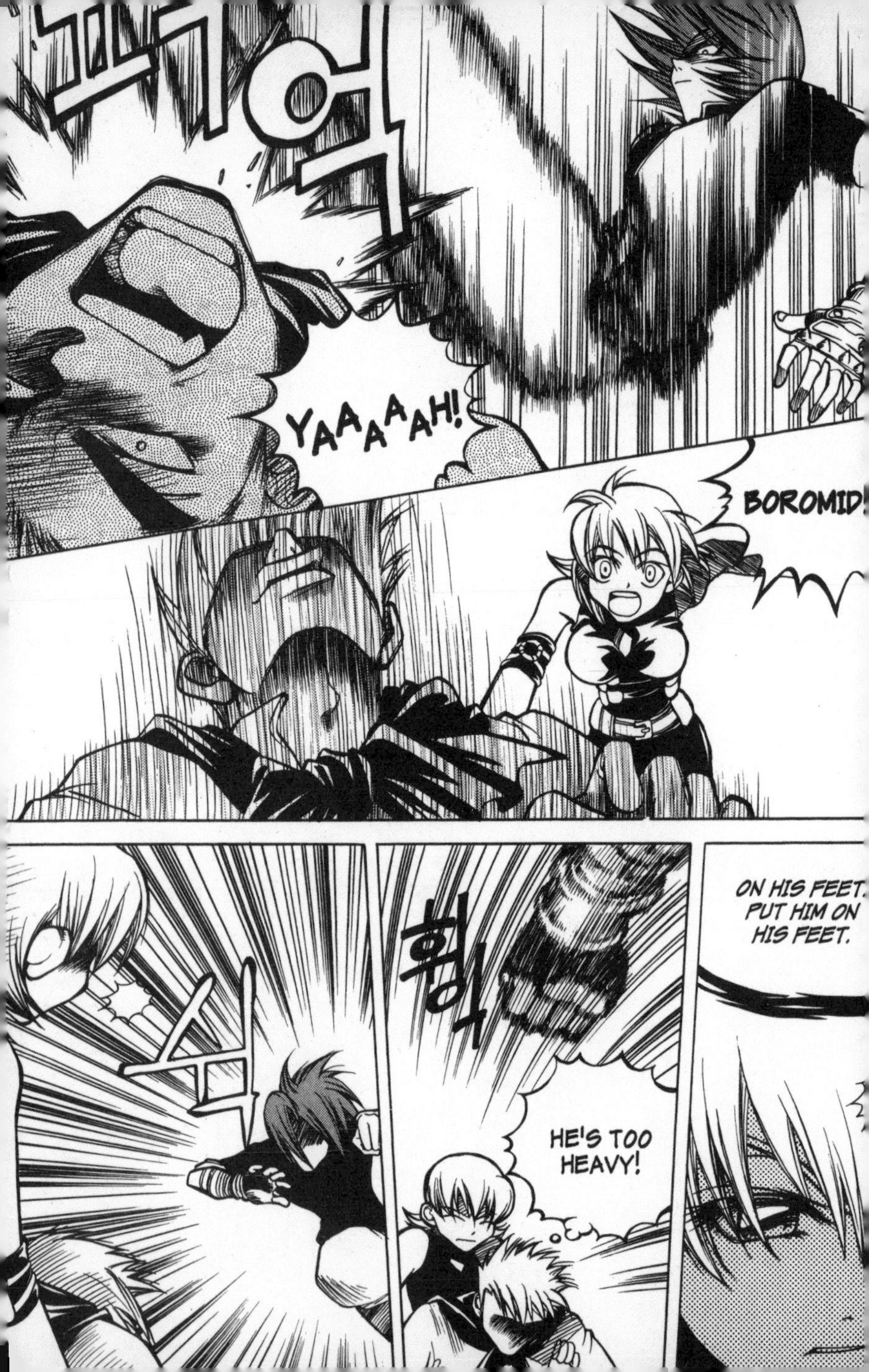
YAAAAAH!
BOROMID!
HE'S TOO HEAVY!
ON HIS FEET. PUT HIM ON HIS FEET.

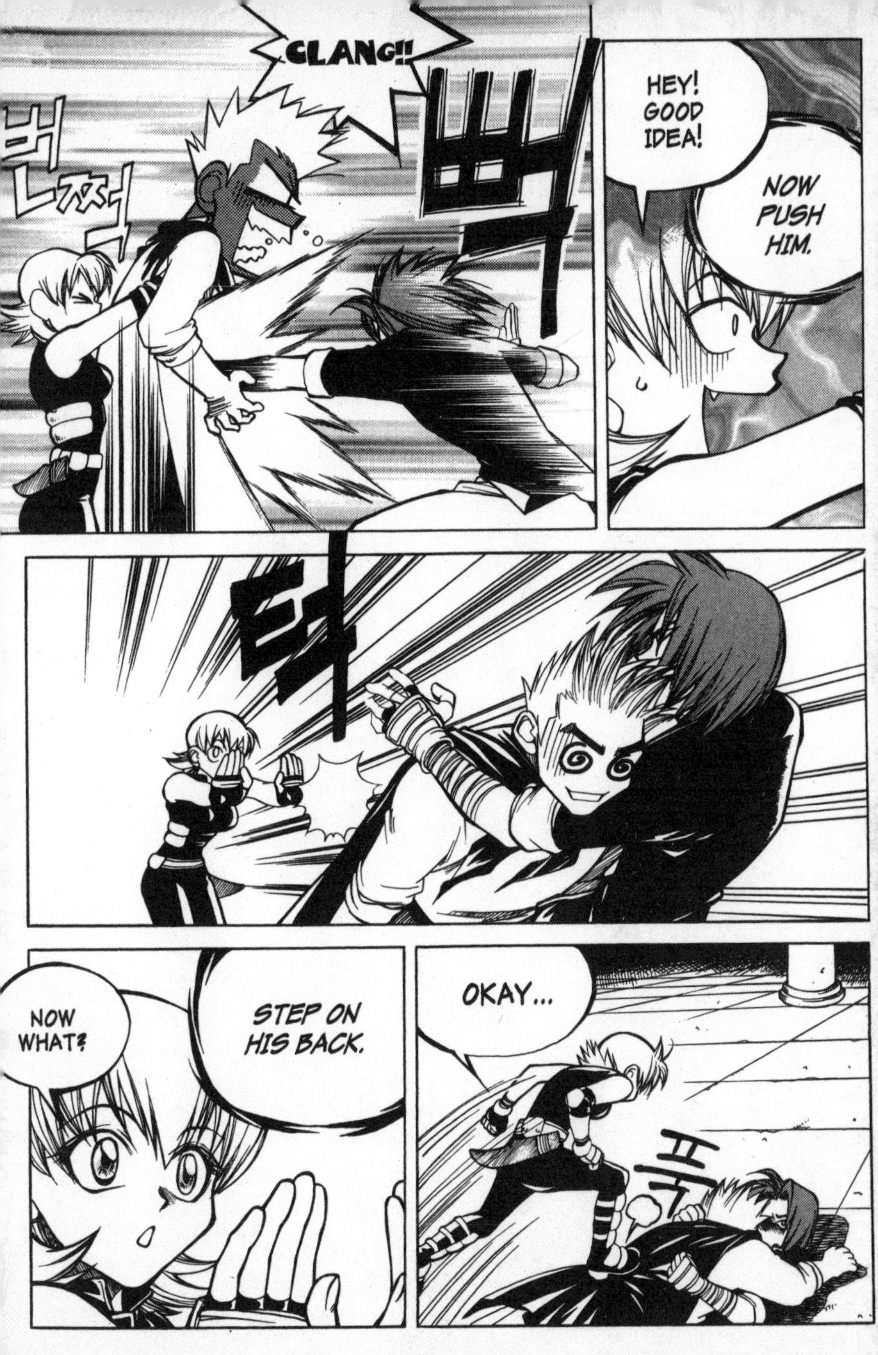
CLANG!!
HEY! GOOD IDEA!
NOW PUSH HIM.
NOW WHAT?
STEP ON HIS BACK.
OKAY...

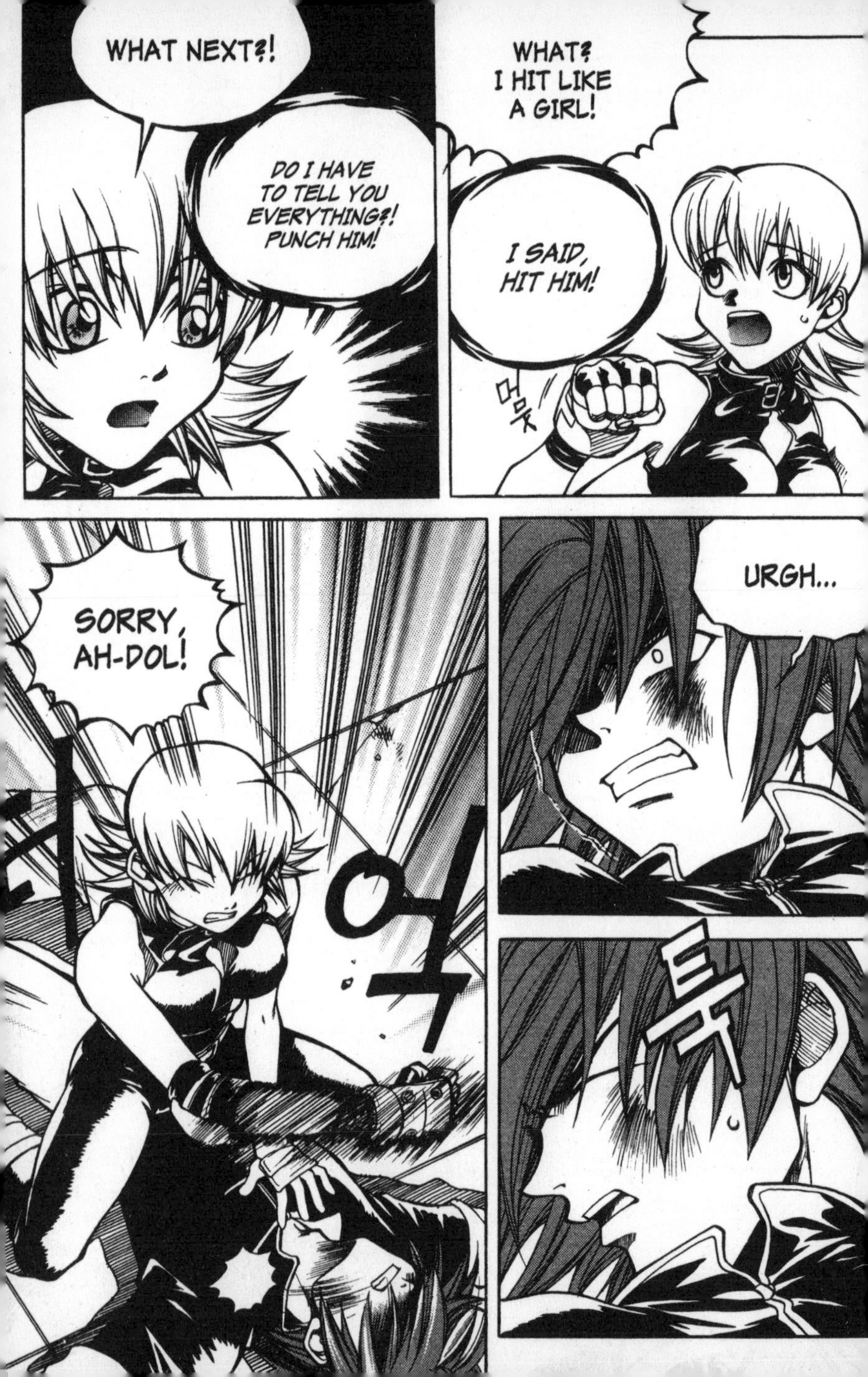
WHAT NEXT?!
DO I HAVE TO TELL YOU EVERYTHING?! PUNCH HIM!
WHAT? I HIT LIKE A GIRL!
I SAID, HIT HIM!
머뭇
SORRY, AH-DOL!
URGH...
턱

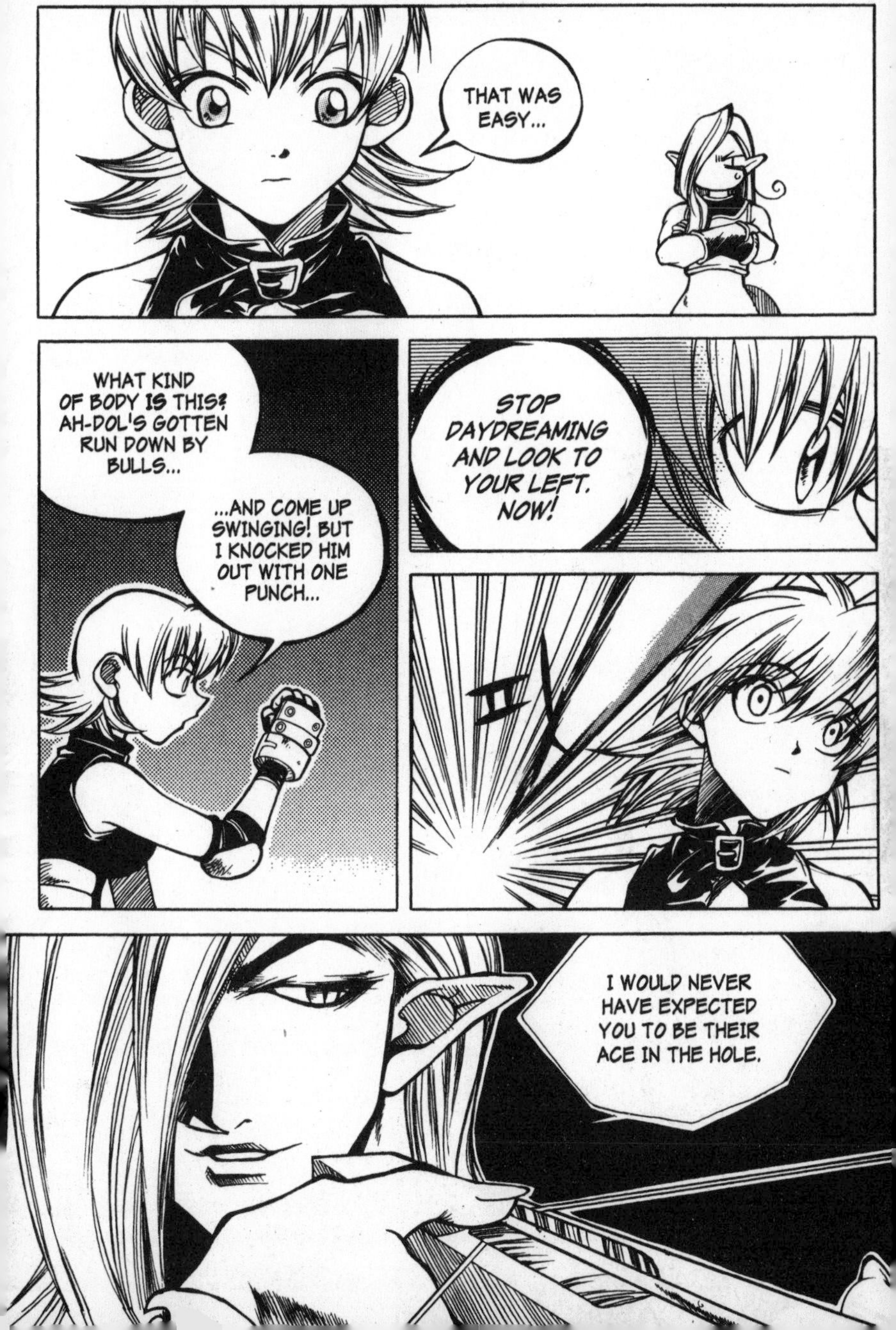
THAT WAS EASY...
WHAT KIND OF BODY IS THIS? AH-DOL'S GOTTEN RUN DOWN BY BULLS...
...AND COME UP SWINGING! BUT I KNOCKED HIM OUT WITH ONE PUNCH...
STOP DAYDREAMING AND LOOK TO YOUR LEFT. NOW!
I WOULD NEVER HAVE EXPECTED YOU TO BE THEIR ACE IN THE HOLE.

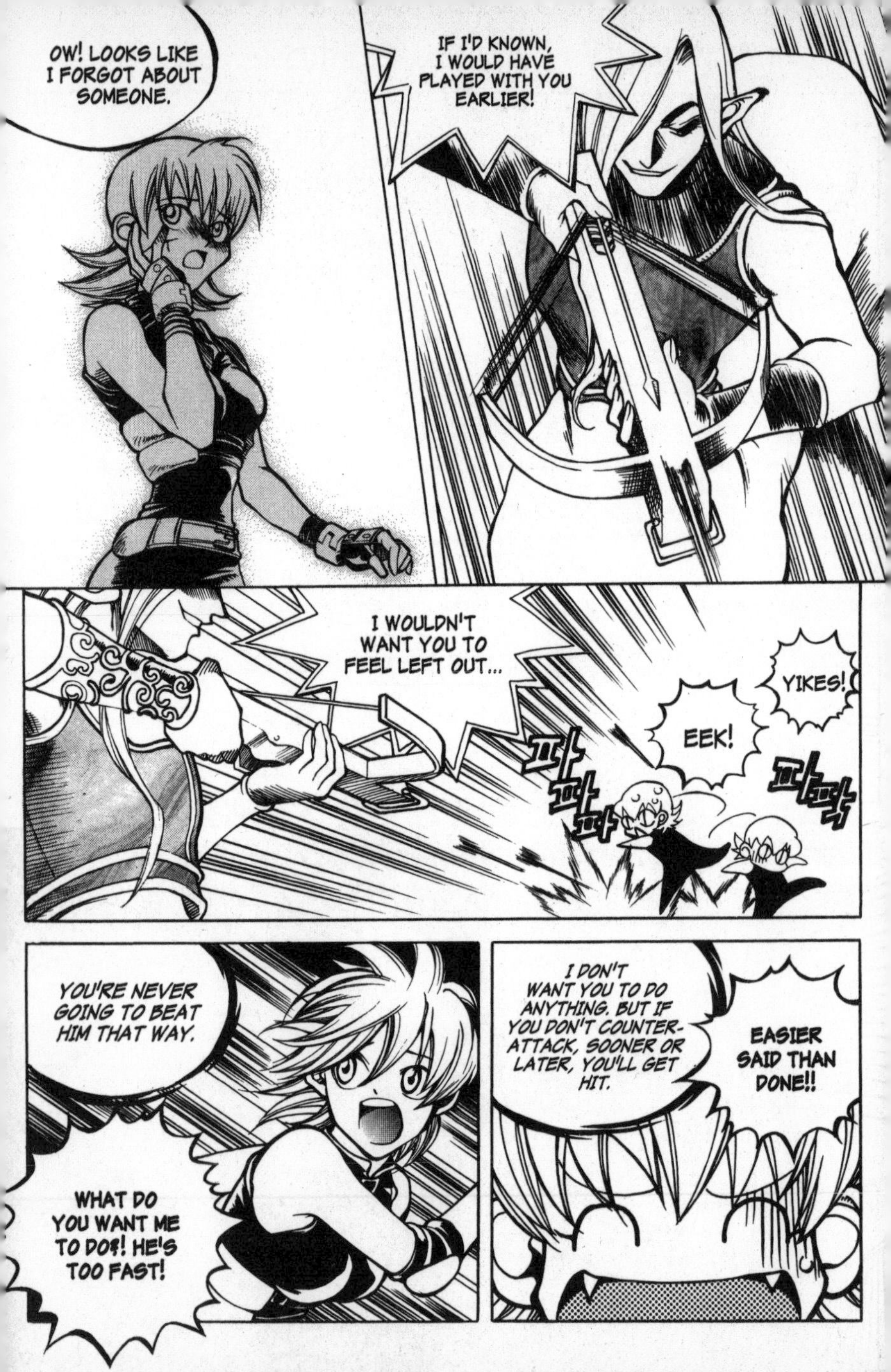
OW! LOOKS LIKE I FORGOT ABOUT SOMEONE.
IF I'D KNOWN, I WOULD HAVE PLAYED WITH YOU EARLIER!
I WOULDN'T WANT YOU TO FEEL LEFT OUT...
EEK!
YIKES!
YOU'RE NEVER GOING TO BEAT HIM THAT WAY.
WHAT DO YOU WANT ME TO DO?! HE'S TOO FAST!
I DON'T WANT YOU TO DO ANYTHING. BUT IF YOU DON'T COUNTER-ATTACK, SOONER OR LATER, YOU'LL GET HIT.
EASIER SAID THAN DONE!!

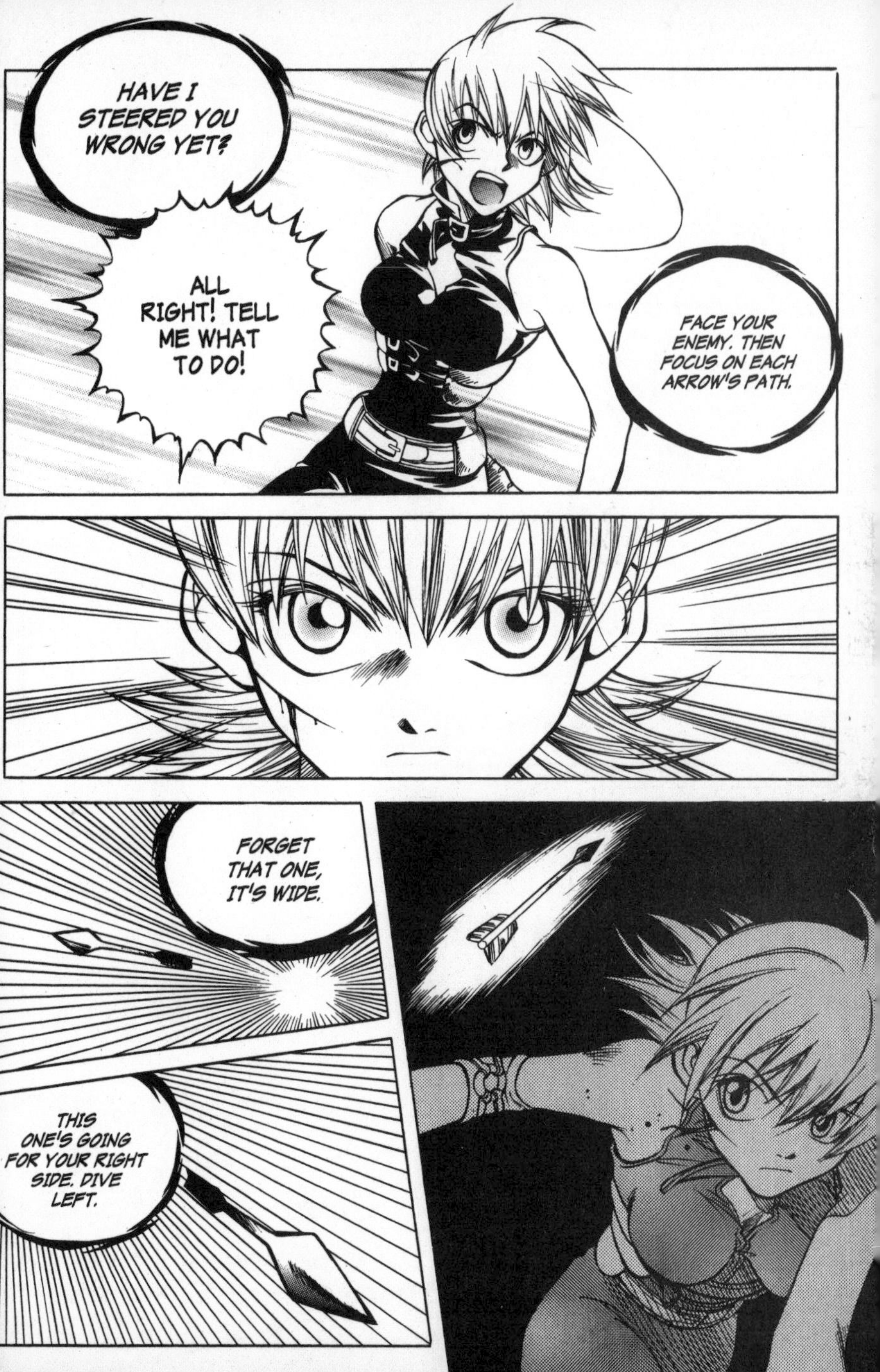
HAVE I STEERED YOU WRONG YET?
ALL RIGHT! TELL ME WHAT TO DO!
FACE YOUR ENEMY. THEN FOCUS ON EACH ARROW'S PATH.
FORGET THAT ONE, IT'S WIDE.
THIS ONE'S GOING FOR YOUR RIGHT SIDE. DIVE LEFT.

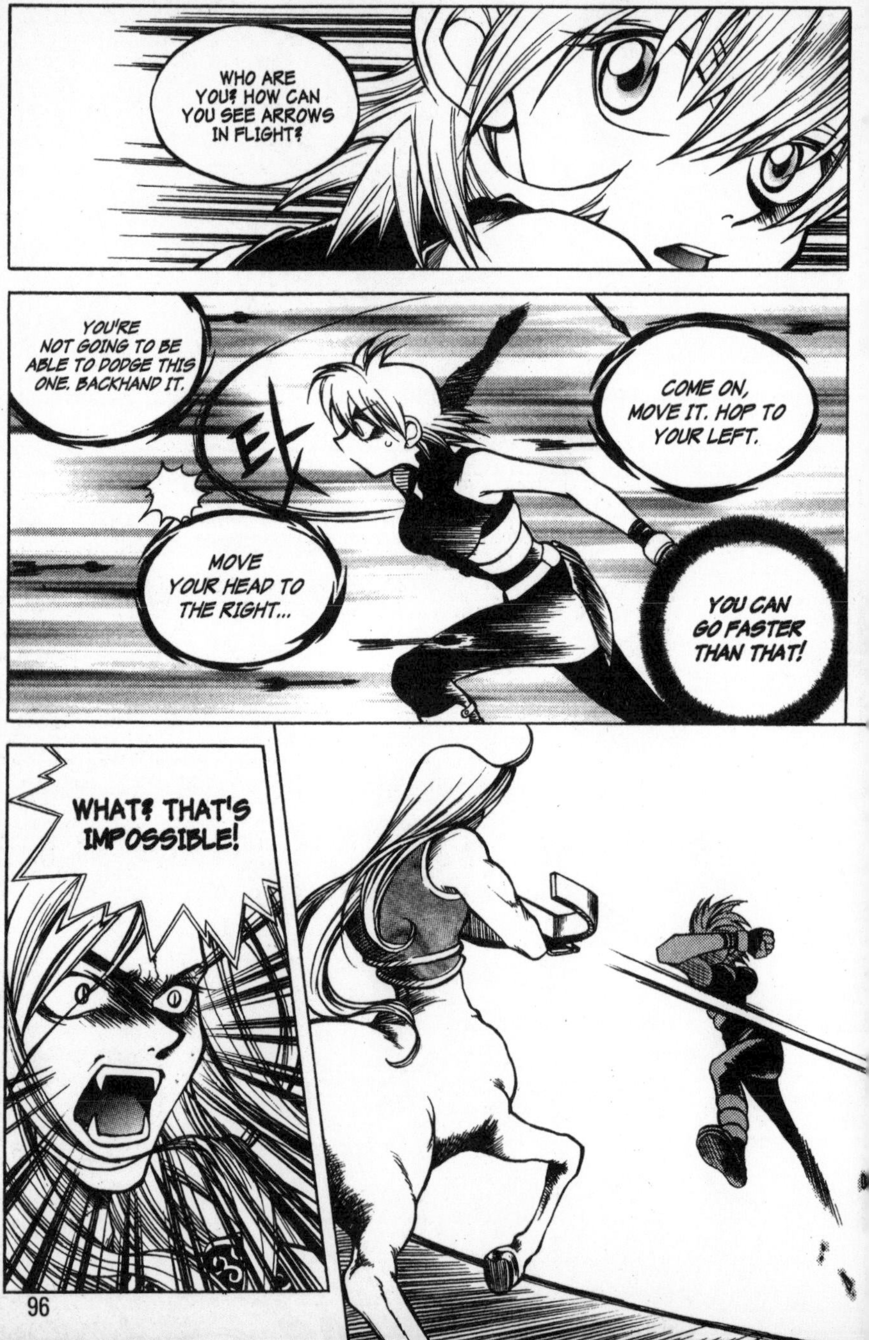
WHO ARE YOU? HOW CAN YOU SEE ARROWS IN FLIGHT?
YOU'RE NOT GOING TO BE ABLE TO DODGE THIS ONE. BACKHAND IT.
COME ON, MOVE IT. HOP TO YOUR LEFT.
MOVE YOUR HEAD TO THE RIGHT...
YOU CAN GO FASTER THAN THAT!
WHAT? THAT'S IMPOSSIBLE!

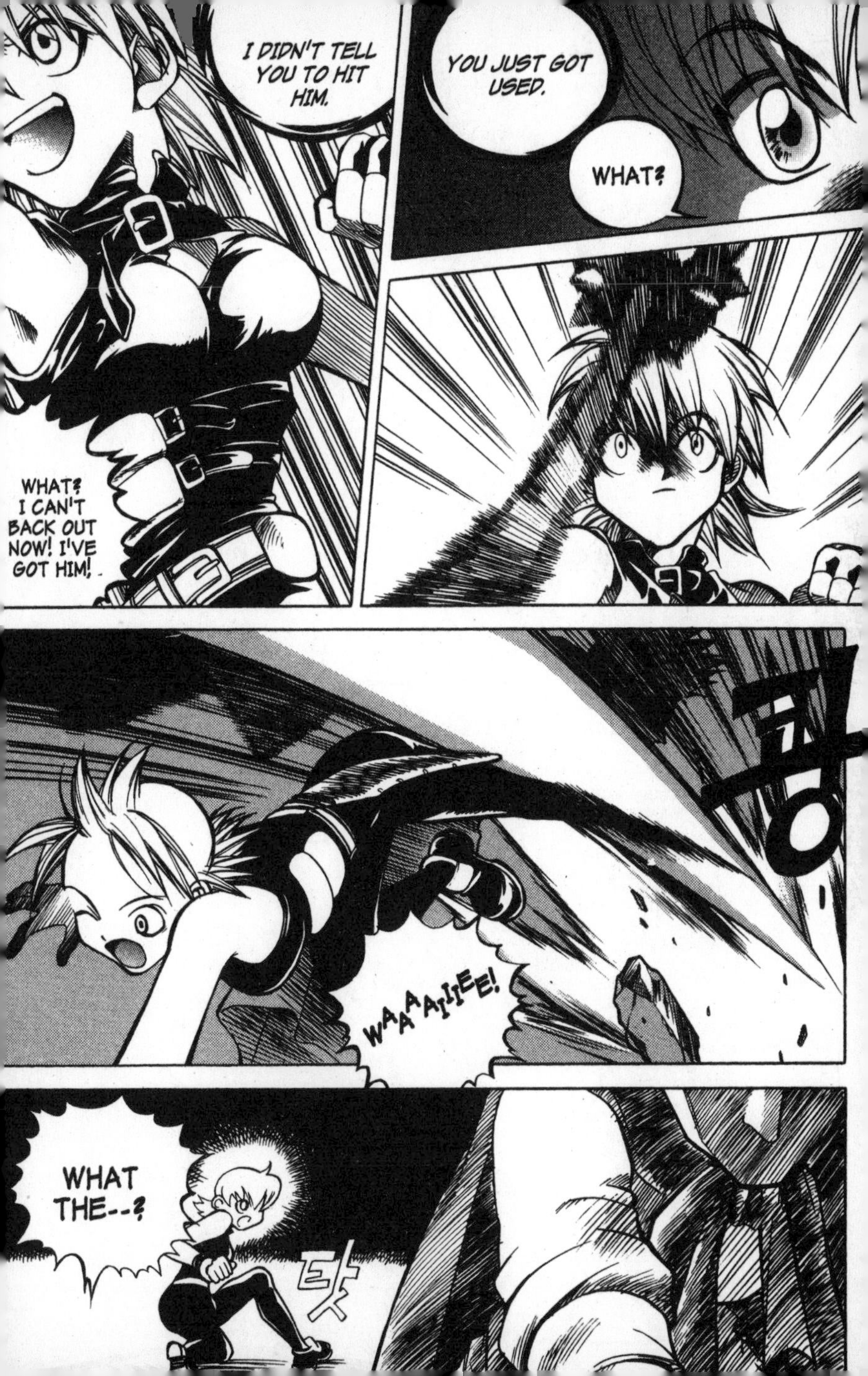
I DIDN'T TELL YOU TO HIT HIM.
WHAT? I CAN'T BACK OUT NOW! I'VE GOT HIM!
YOU JUST GOT USED.
WHAT?
쾅
WAAAAIIIEE!
WHAT THE--?
탁

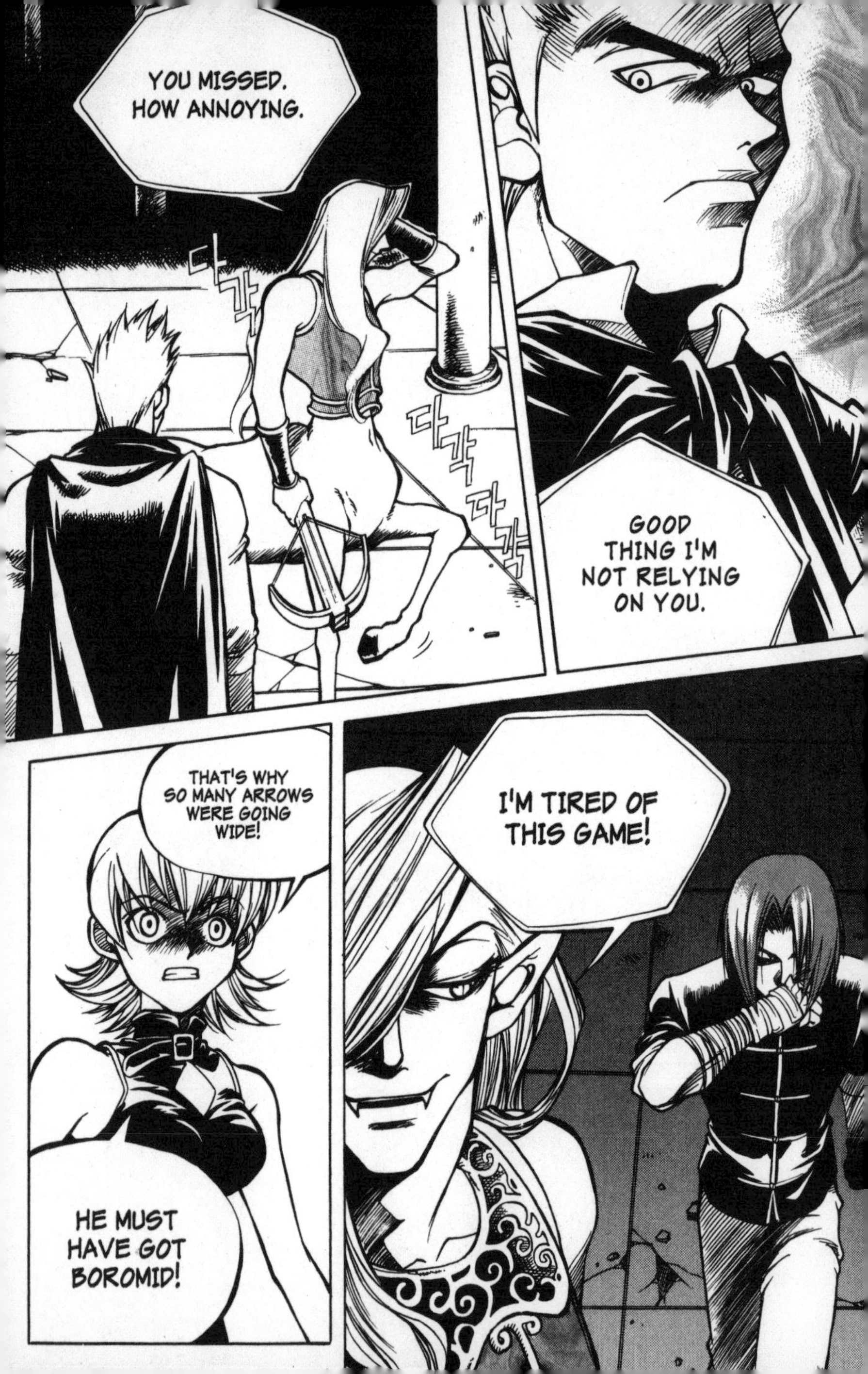
YOU MISSED. HOW ANNOYING.
다각
다각
다각
GOOD THING I'M NOT RELYING ON YOU.
THAT'S WHY SO MANY ARROWS WERE GOING WIDE!
HE MUST HAVE GOT BOROMID!
I'M TIRED OF THIS GAME!

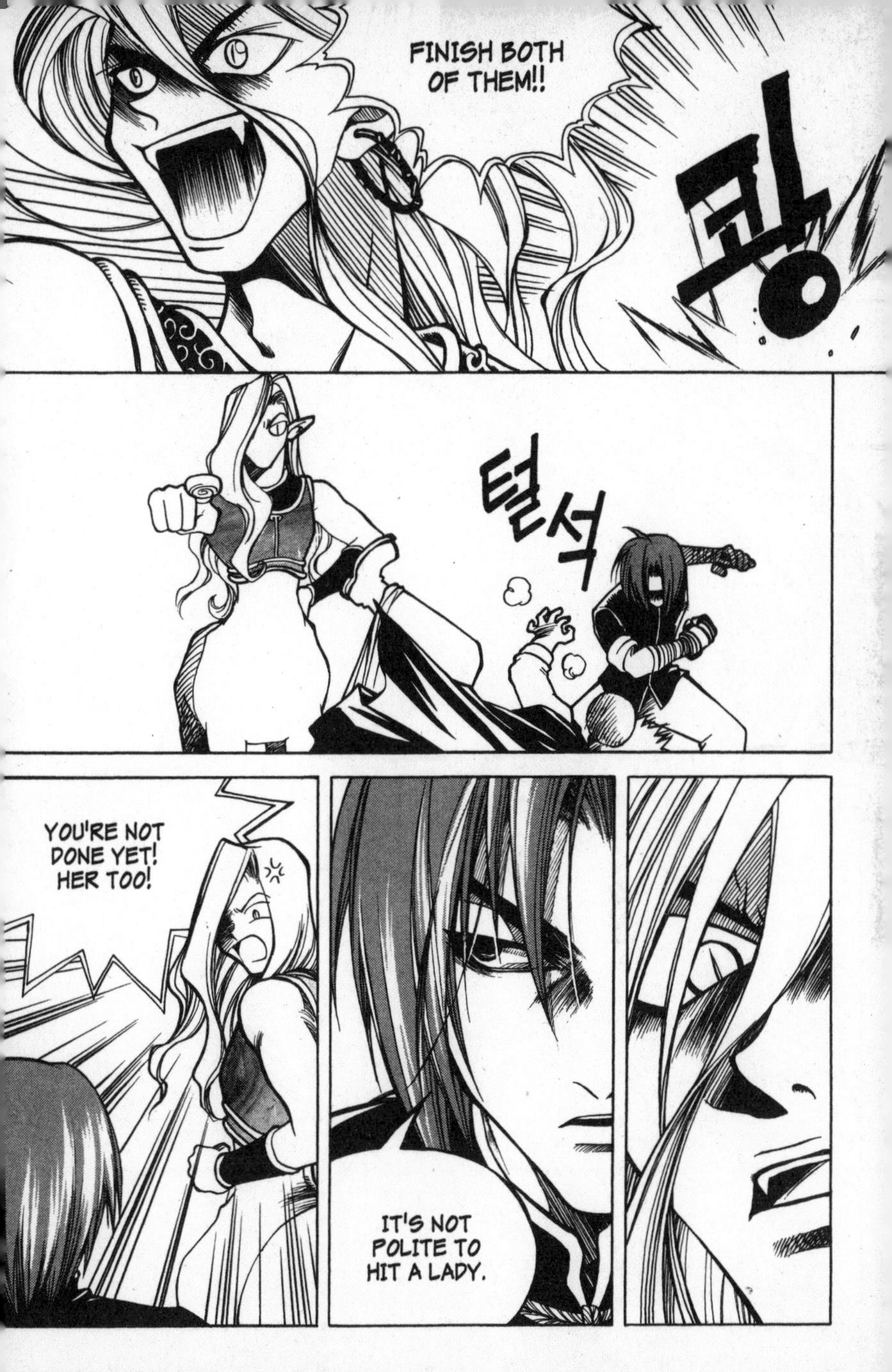
FINISH BOTH OF THEM!!
쾅
털석
YOU'RE NOT DONE YET! HER TOO!
IT'S NOT POLITE TO HIT A LADY.

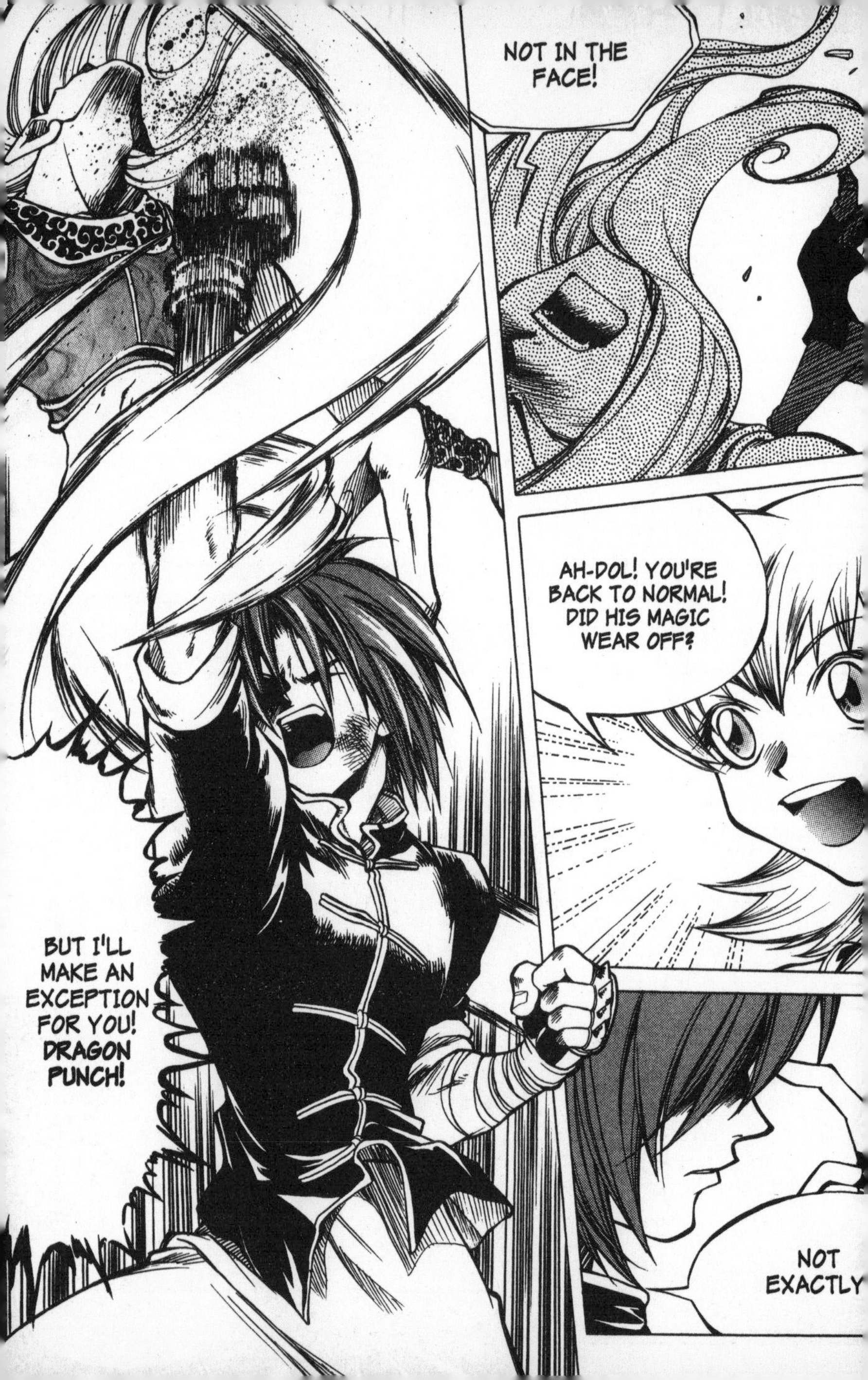
BUT I'LL MAKE AN EXCEPTION FOR YOU! DRAGON PUNCH!
NOT IN THE FACE!
AH-DOL! YOU'RE BACK TO NORMAL! DID HIS MAGIC WEAR OFF?
NOT EXACTLY

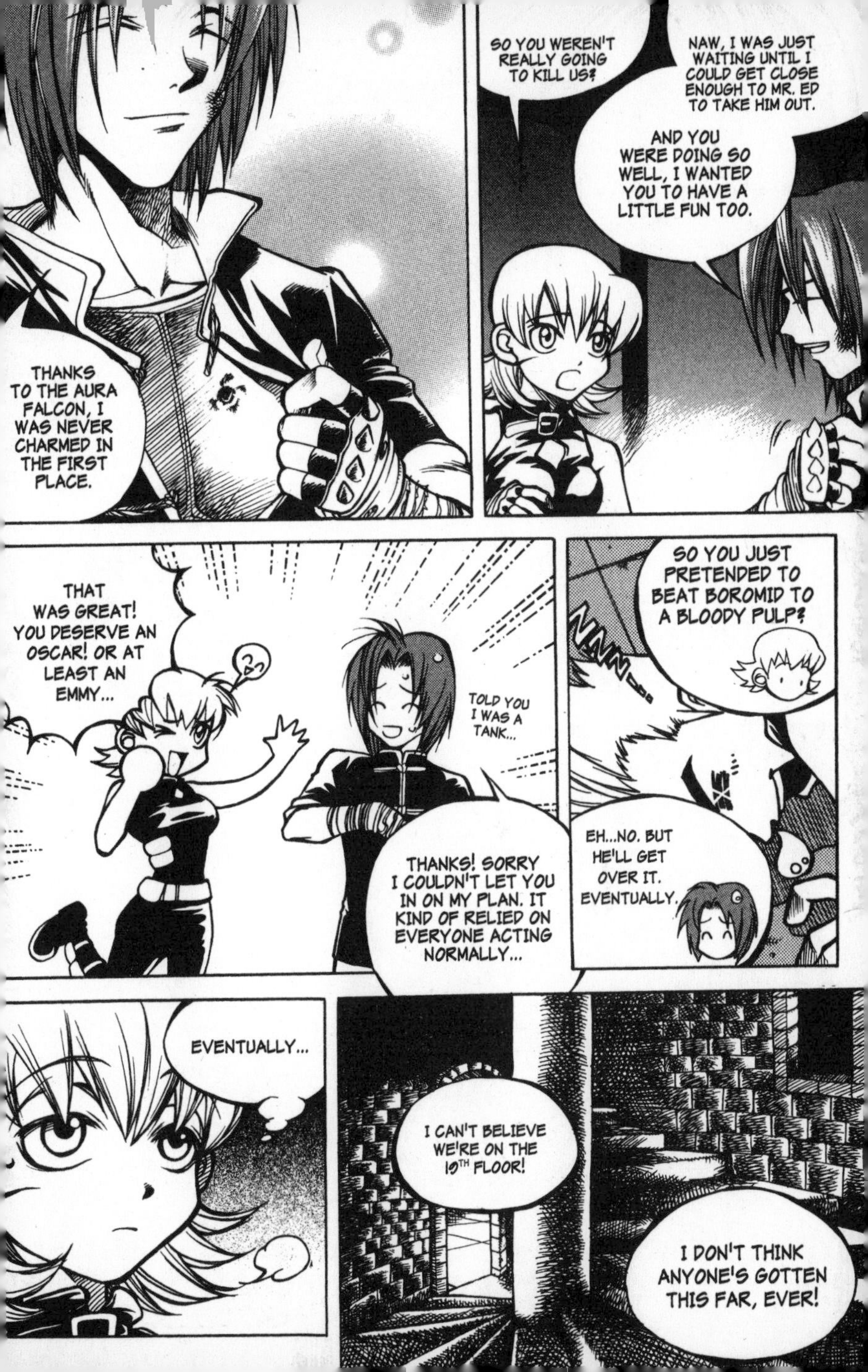
THANKS TO THE AURA FALCON, I WAS NEVER CHARMED IN THE FIRST PLACE.
SO YOU WEREN'T REALLY GOING TO KILL US?
NAW, I WAS JUST WAITING UNTIL I COULD GET CLOSE ENOUGH TO MR. ED TO TAKE HIM OUT.
AND YOU WERE DOING SO WELL, I WANTED YOU TO HAVE A LITTLE FUN TOO.
THAT WAS GREAT! YOU DESERVE AN OSCAR! OR AT LEAST AN EMMY...
TOLD YOU I WAS A TANK...
THANKS! SORRY I COULDN'T LET YOU IN ON MY PLAN. IT KIND OF RELIED ON EVERYONE ACTING NORMALLY...
SO YOU JUST PRETENDED TO BEAT BOROMID TO A BLOODY PULP?
NNNN...
EH...NO. BUT HE'LL GET OVER IT. EVENTUALLY.
EVENTUALLY...
I CAN'T BELIEVE WE'RE ON THE 19TH FLOOR!
I DON'T THINK ANYONE'S GOTTEN THIS FAR, EVER!

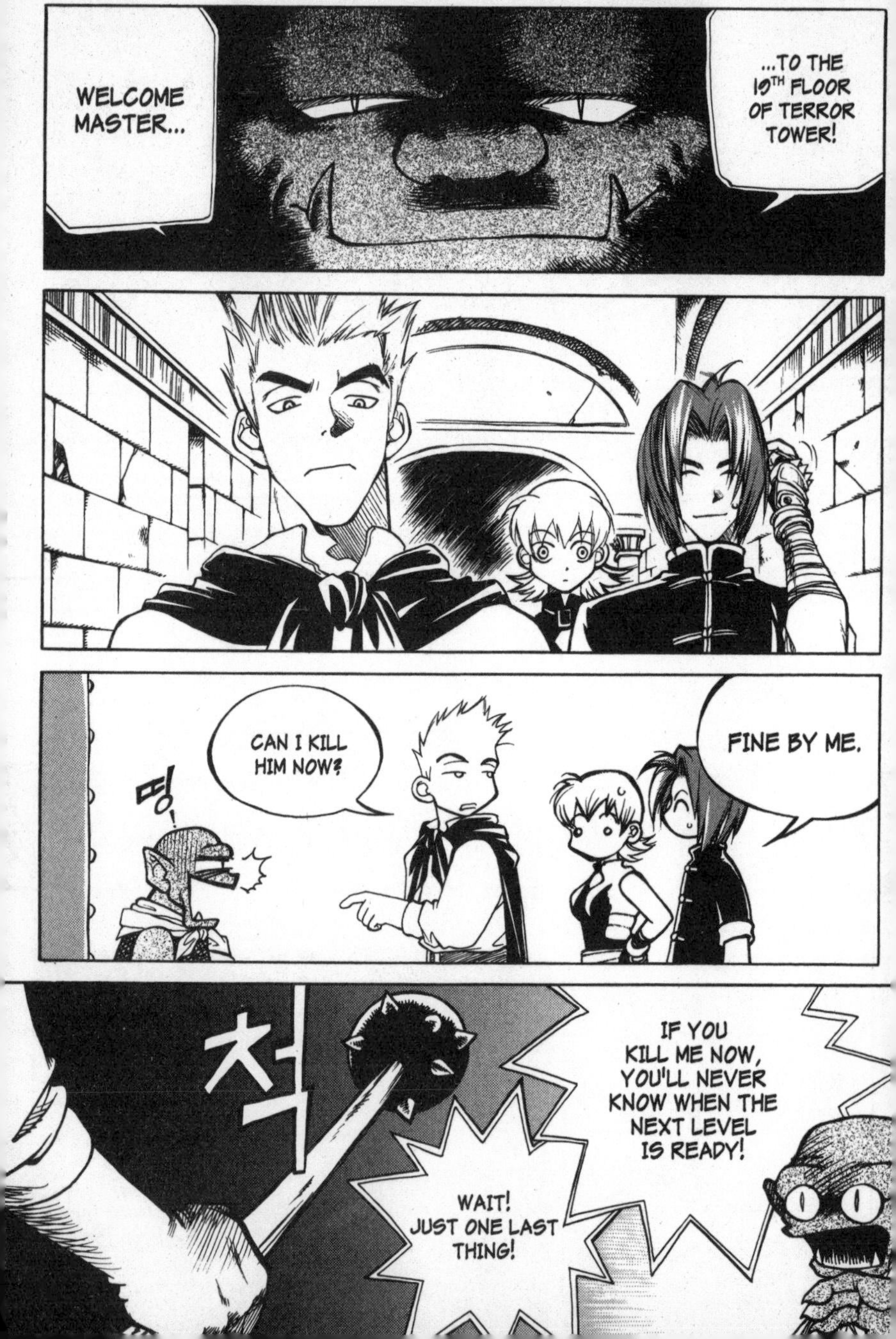
WELCOME MASTER...
...TO THE 19TH FLOOR OF TERROR TOWER!
CAN I KILL HIM NOW?
FINE BY ME.
IF YOU KILL ME NOW, YOU'LL NEVER KNOW WHEN THE NEXT LEVEL IS READY!
WAIT! JUST ONE LAST THING!

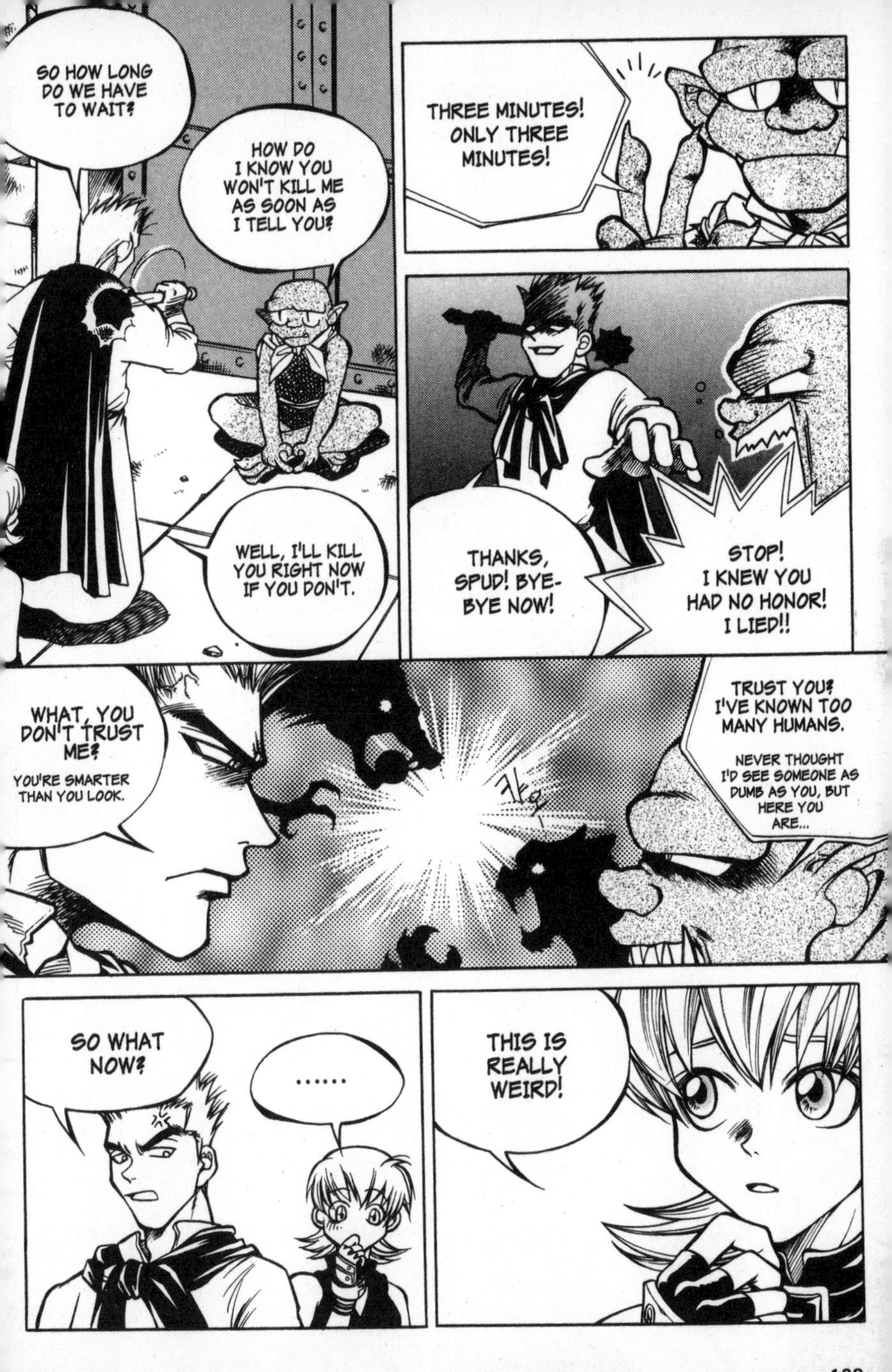
SO HOW LONG DO WE HAVE TO WAIT?
HOW DO I KNOW YOU WON'T KILL ME AS SOON AS I TELL YOU?
WELL, I'LL KILL YOU RIGHT NOW IF YOU DON'T.
THREE MINUTES! ONLY THREE MINUTES!
THANKS, SPUD! BYE-BYE NOW!
STOP! I KNEW YOU HAD NO HONOR! I LIED!!
WHAT, YOU DON'T TRUST ME?
YOU'RE SMARTER THAN YOU LOOK.
TRUST YOU? I'VE KNOWN TOO MANY HUMANS.
NEVER THOUGHT I'D SEE SOMEONE AS DUMB AS YOU, BUT HERE YOU ARE...
SO WHAT NOW?
......
THIS IS REALLY WEIRD!

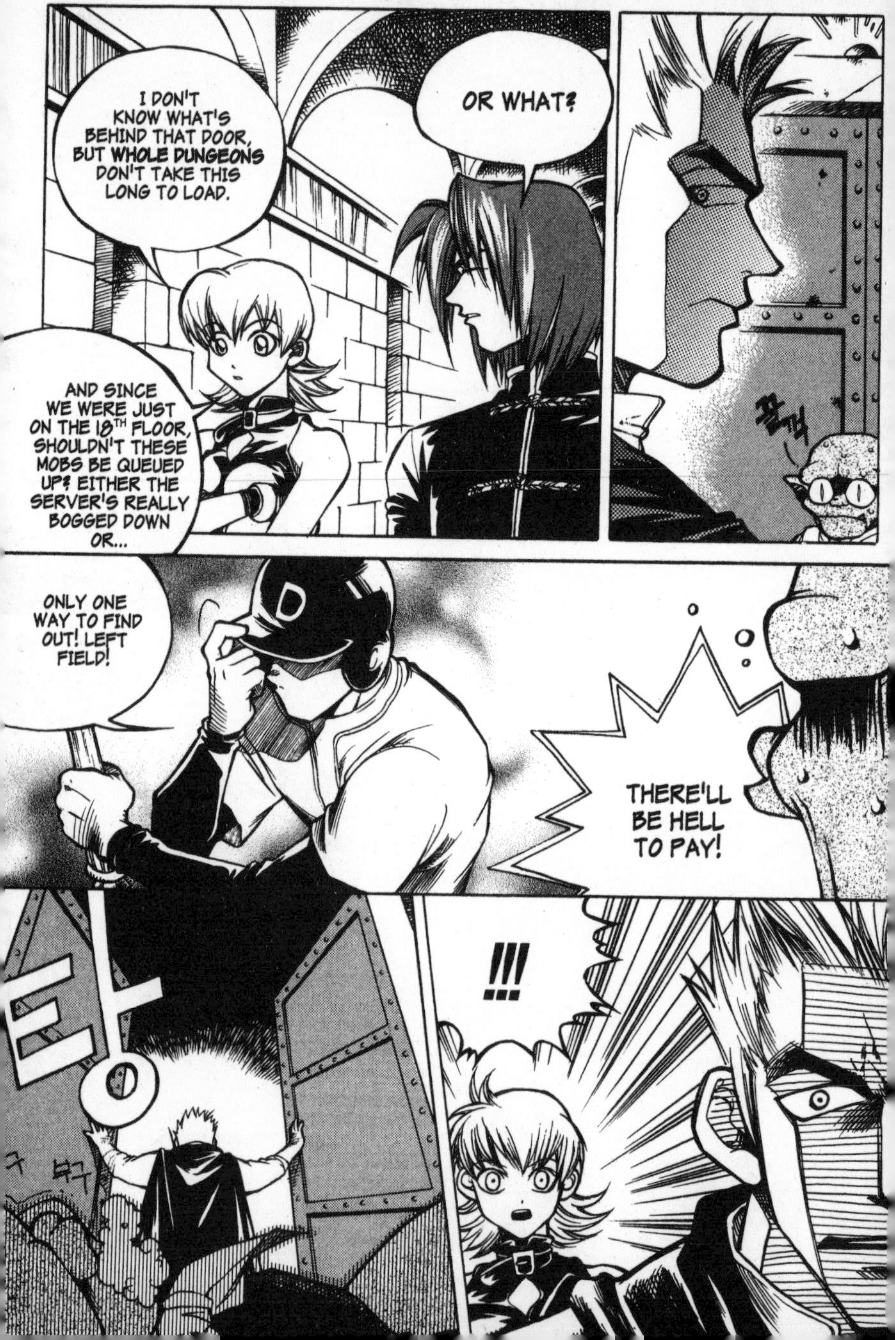
I DON'T KNOW WHAT'S BEHIND THAT DOOR, BUT WHOLE DUNGEONS DON'T TAKE THIS LONG TO LOAD.
AND SINCE WE WERE JUST ON THE 18TH FLOOR, SHOULDN'T THESE MOBS BE QUEUED UP? EITHER THE SERVER'S REALLY BOGGED DOWN OR...
OR WHAT?
ONLY ONE WAY TO FIND OUT! LEFT FIELD!
THERE'LL BE HELL TO PAY!
!!!

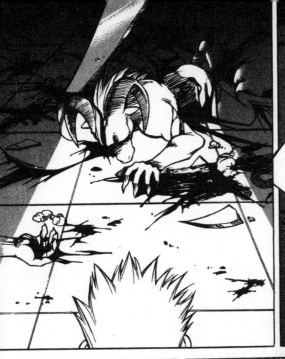

WHAT HAPPENED?! IT LOOKS LIKE THEY WERE PUT THROUGH A BLENDER!

SOMEONE MUST HAVE GOTTEN HERE FIRST!

THEY MUST BE JUST AHEAD OF US.

THAT MAKES SENSE.

IT EXPLAINS WHY WE COULDN'T ENTER. THE MOBS NEEDED TIME TO RE-SPAWN!

MAYBE WE CAN CATCH THEM!

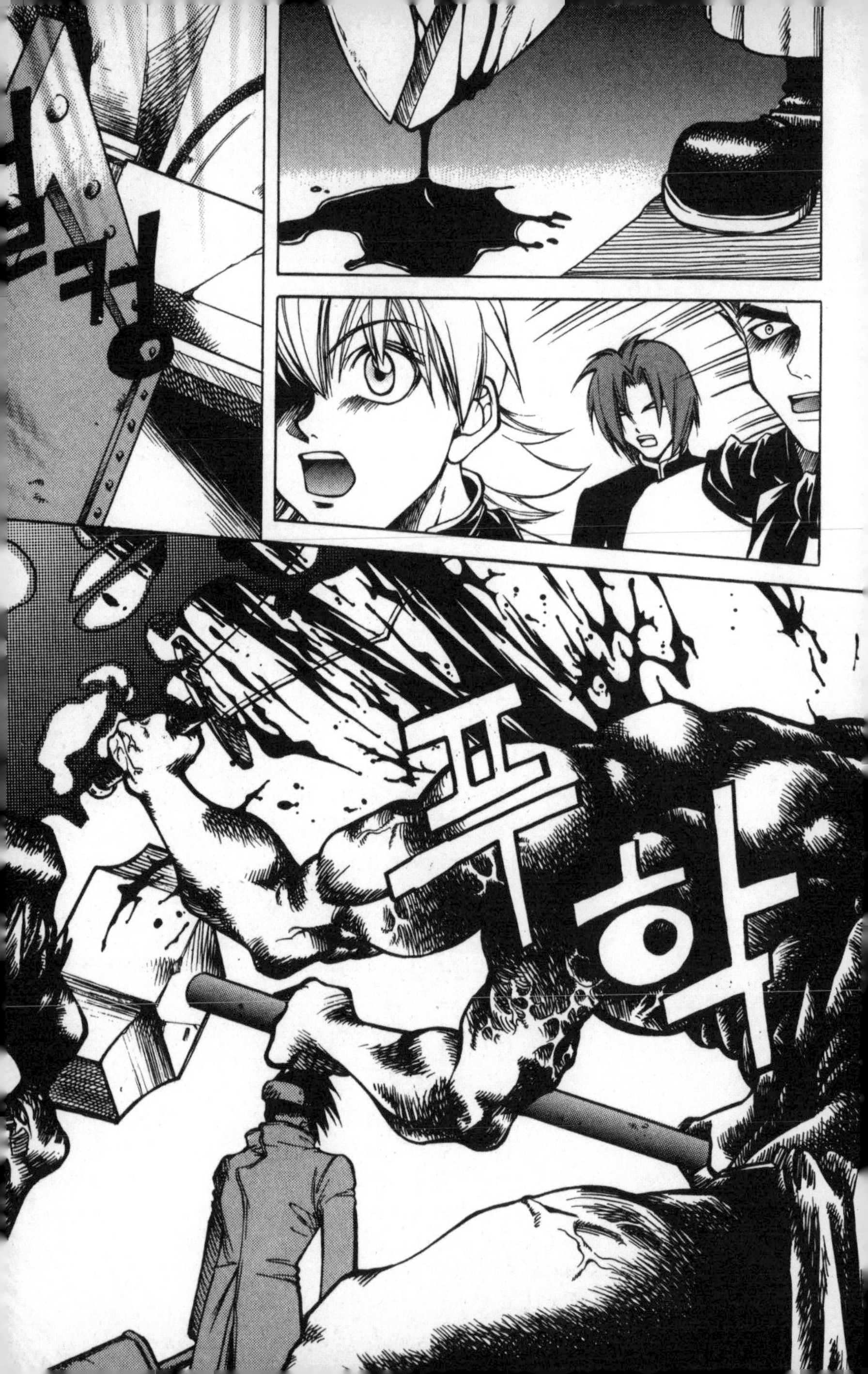
푸하

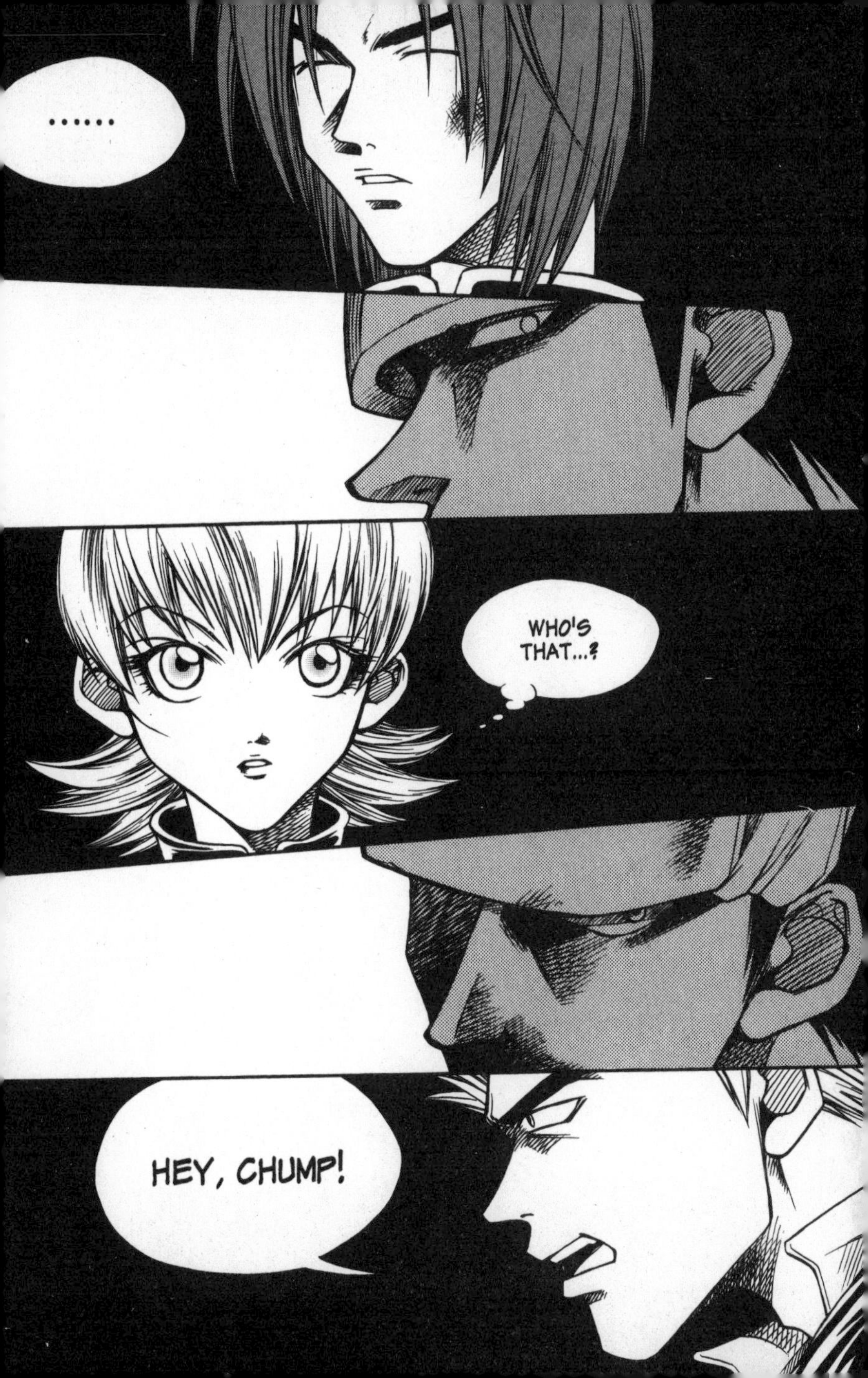
......
WHO'S THAT...?
HEY, CHUMP!

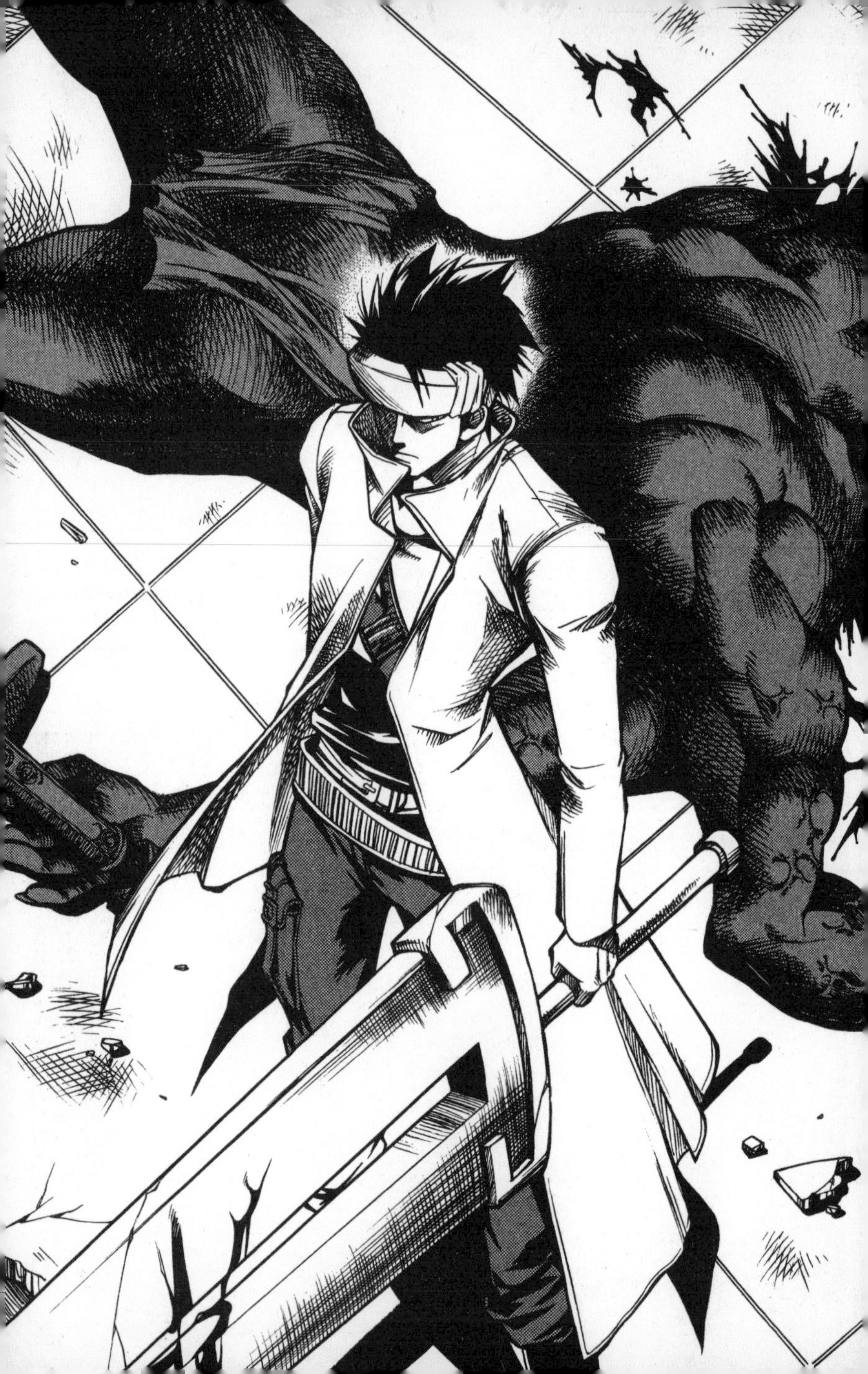

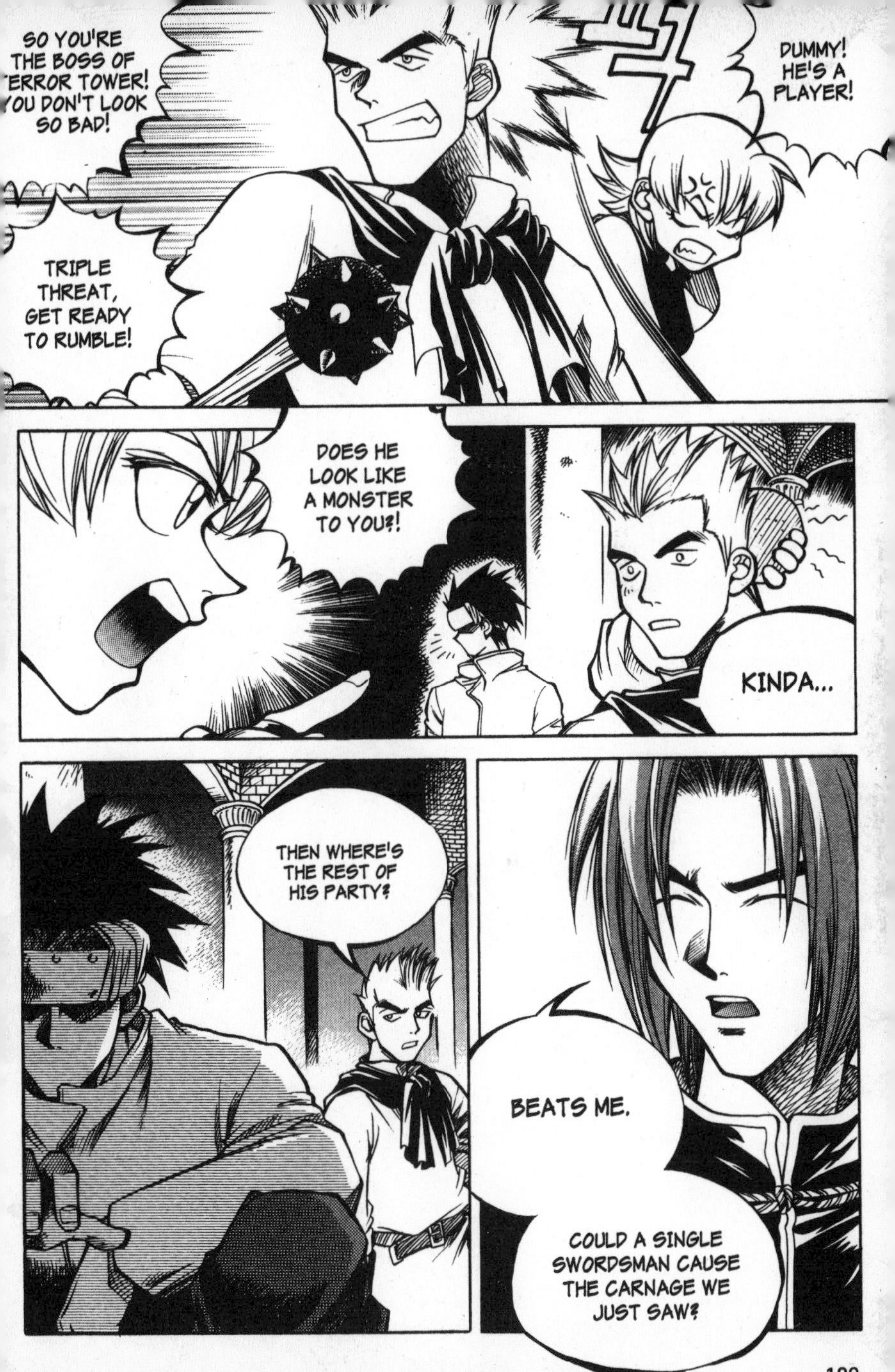
SO YOU'RE THE BOSS OF TERROR TOWER! YOU DON'T LOOK SO BAD!
TRIPLE THREAT, GET READY TO RUMBLE!
DUMMY! HE'S A PLAYER!
DOES HE LOOK LIKE A MONSTER TO YOU?!
KINDA...
THEN WHERE'S THE REST OF HIS PARTY?
BEATS ME.
COULD A SINGLE SWORDSMAN CAUSE THE CARNAGE WE JUST SAW?

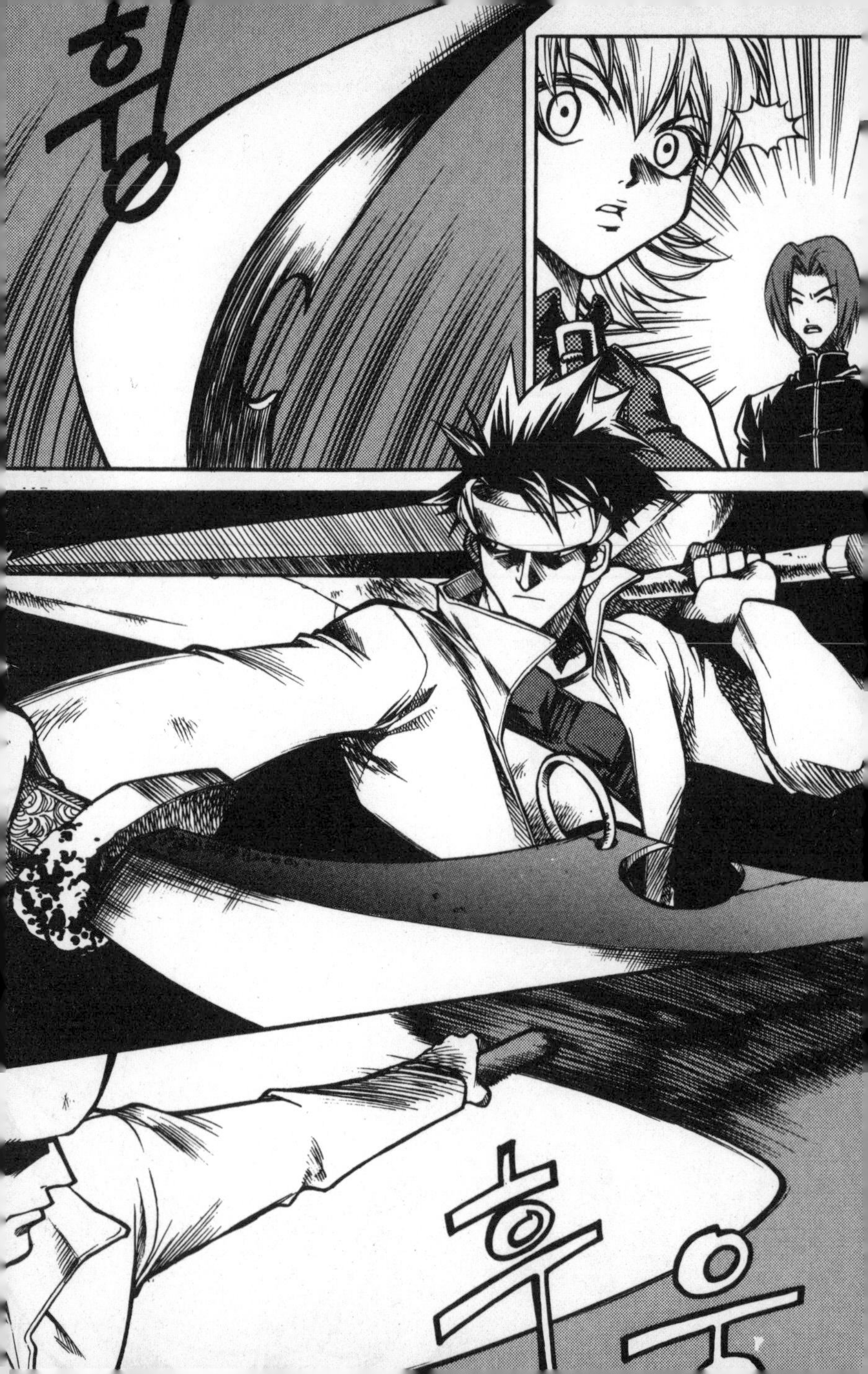
휭
후웅

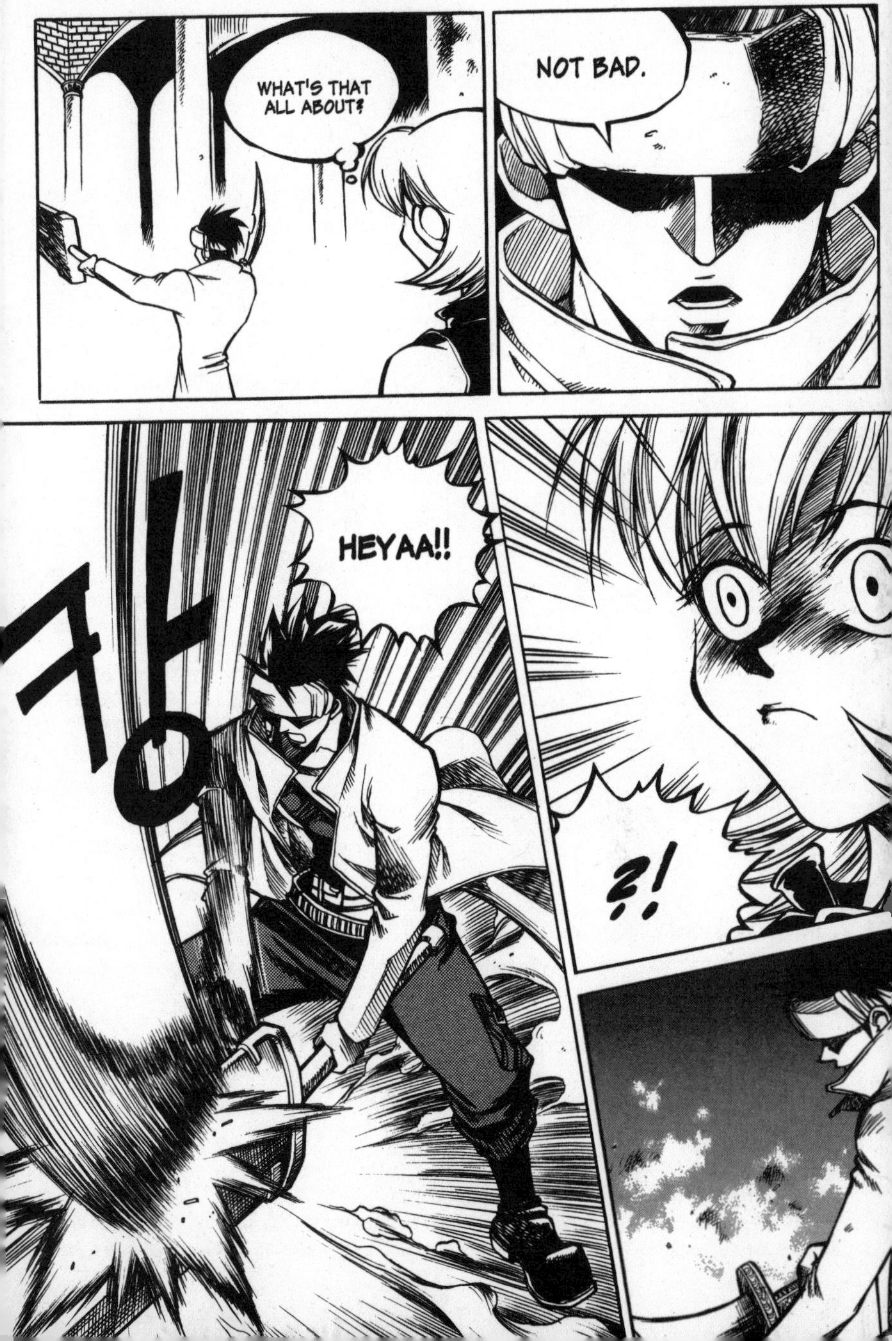
WHAT'S THAT ALL ABOUT?
NOT BAD.
HEYAA!!
?!

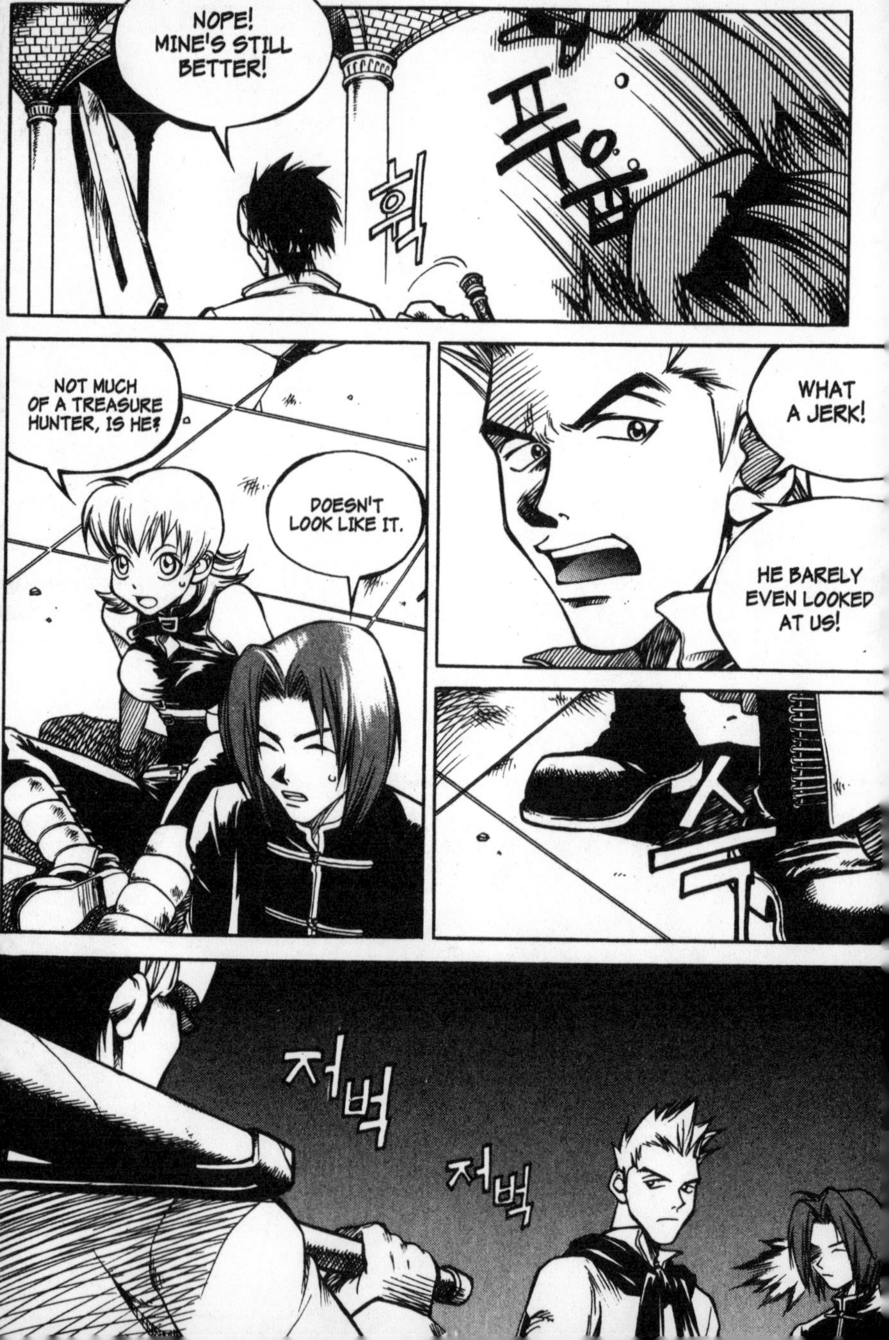
NOPE! MINE'S STILL BETTER!
NOT MUCH OF A TREASURE HUNTER, IS HE?
DOESN'T LOOK LIKE IT.
WHAT A JERK!
HE BARELY EVEN LOOKED AT US!
저벅
저벅

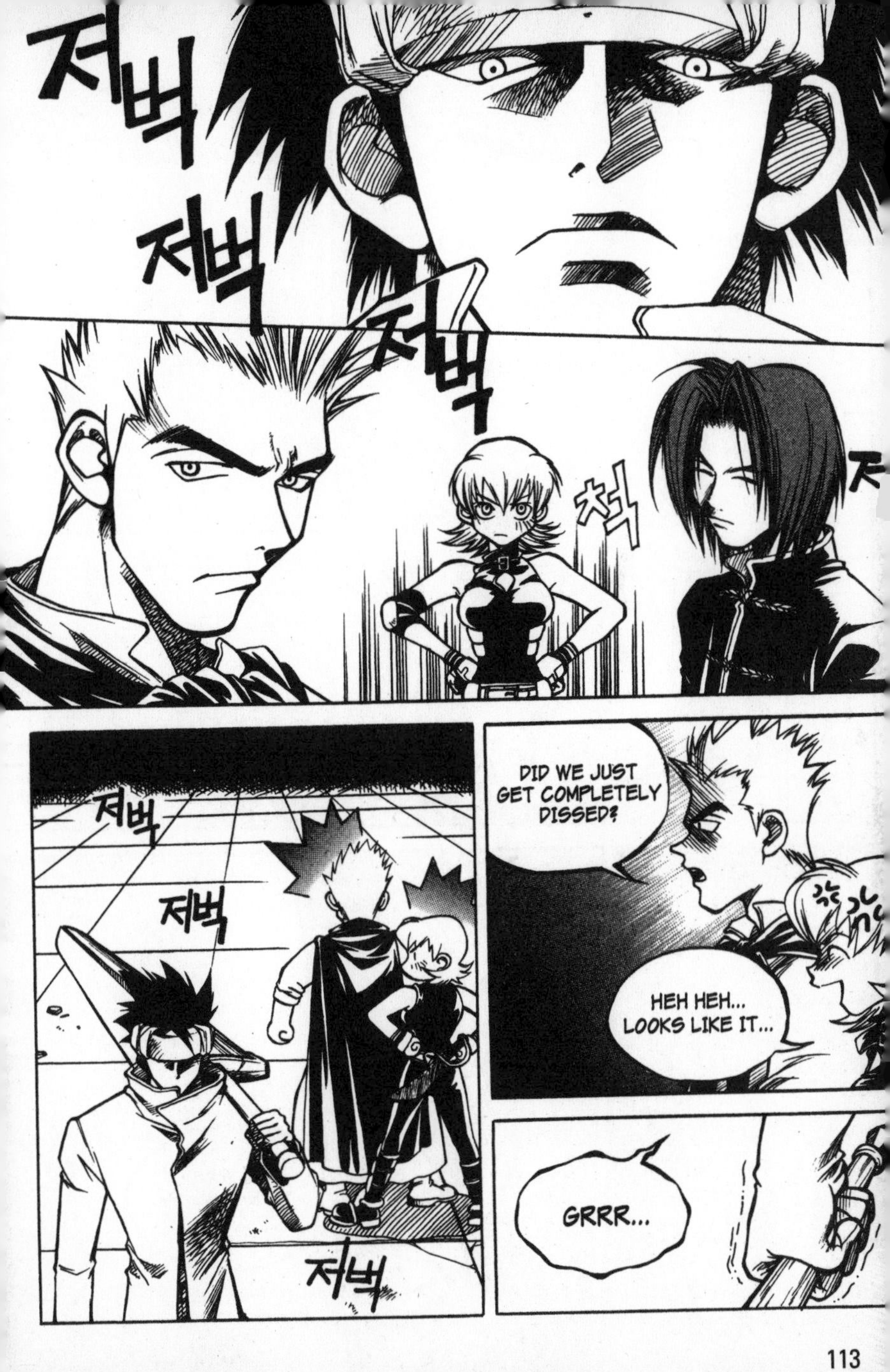
저벅
저벅
저벅
척
저벅
저벅
저벅
DID WE JUST GET COMPLETELY DISSED?
HEH HEH... LOOKS LIKE IT...
GRRR...

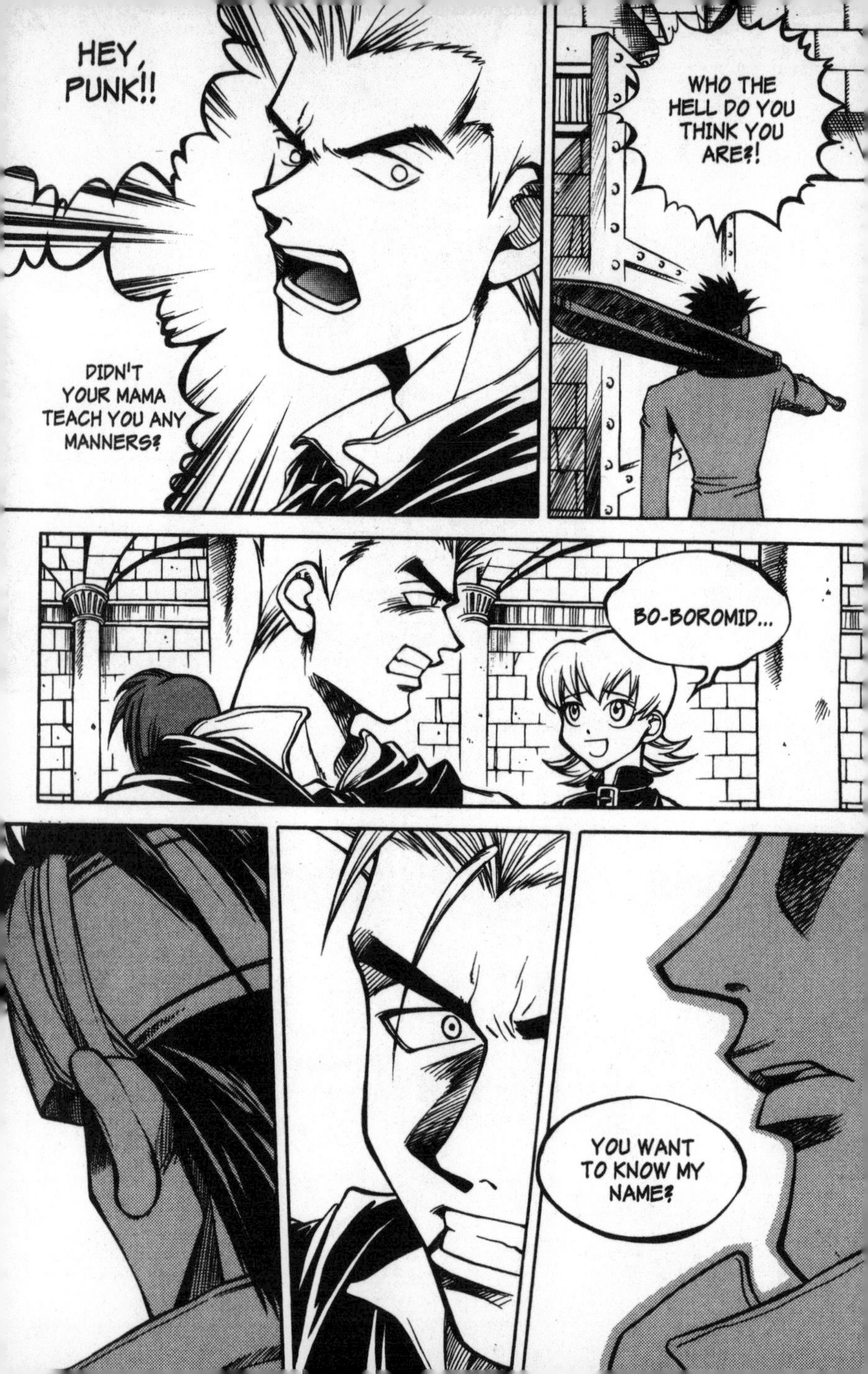
HEY, PUNK!!
DIDN'T YOUR MAMA TEACH YOU ANY MANNERS?
WHO THE HELL DO YOU THINK YOU ARE?!
BO-BOROMID...
YOU WANT TO KNOW MY NAME?

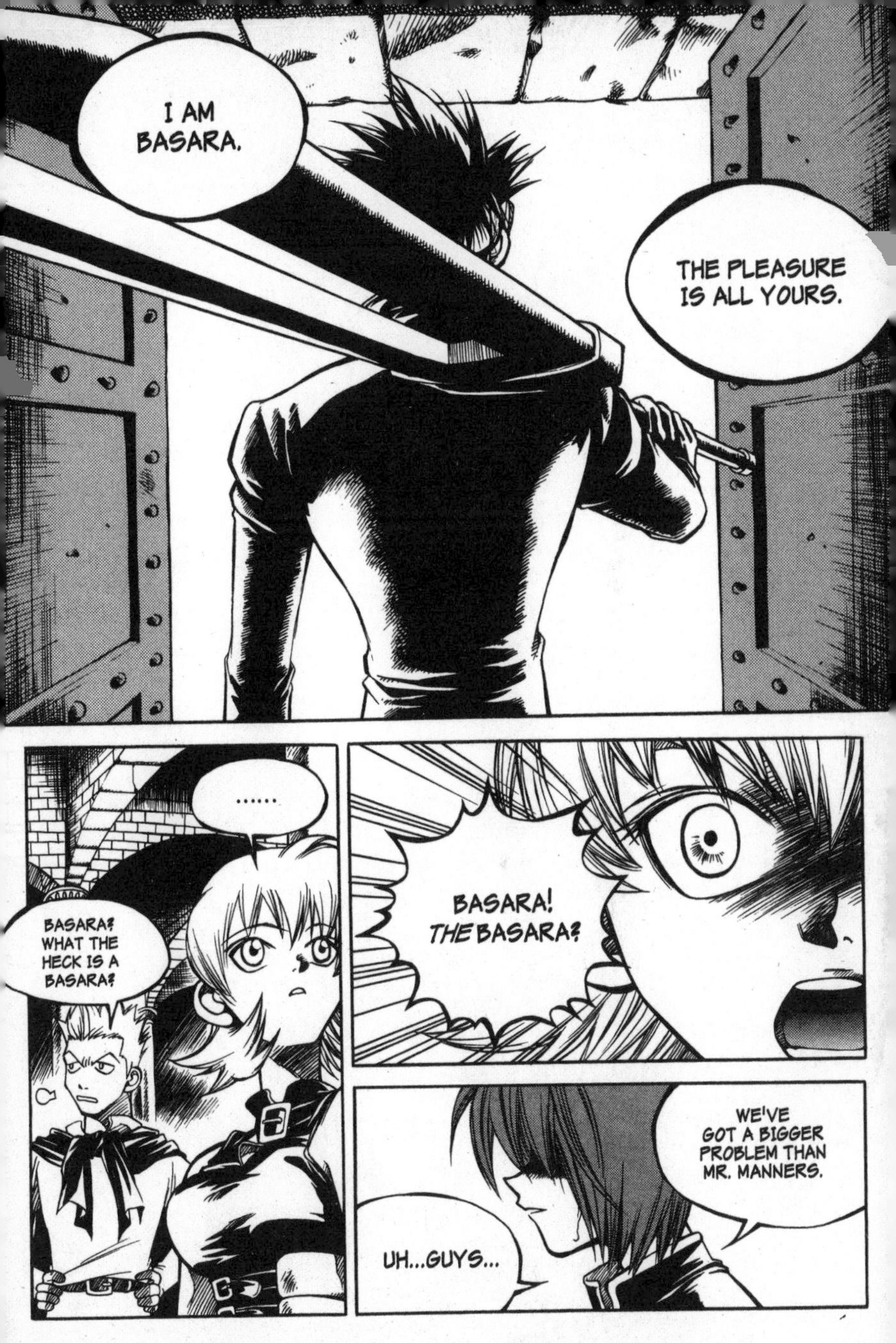
I AM BASARA.
THE PLEASURE IS ALL YOURS.
......
BASARA? WHAT THE HECK IS A BASARA?
BASARA! *THE* BASARA?
WE'VE GOT A BIGGER PROBLEM THAN MR. MANNERS.
UH...GUYS...

WHERE'D HE COME FROM?

ONCE BASARA LEFT, THE SERVER MUST HAVE FIGURED IT WAS OKAY TO RE-POP THE BOSS.

AFTER ALL THESE YEARS OF BATTLING THE ONE-EYED MONSTER...

MOMMY!

HUH?

THAT JERK! I BET HE KNEW THAT WOULD HAPPEN!

YAARGH!!

?

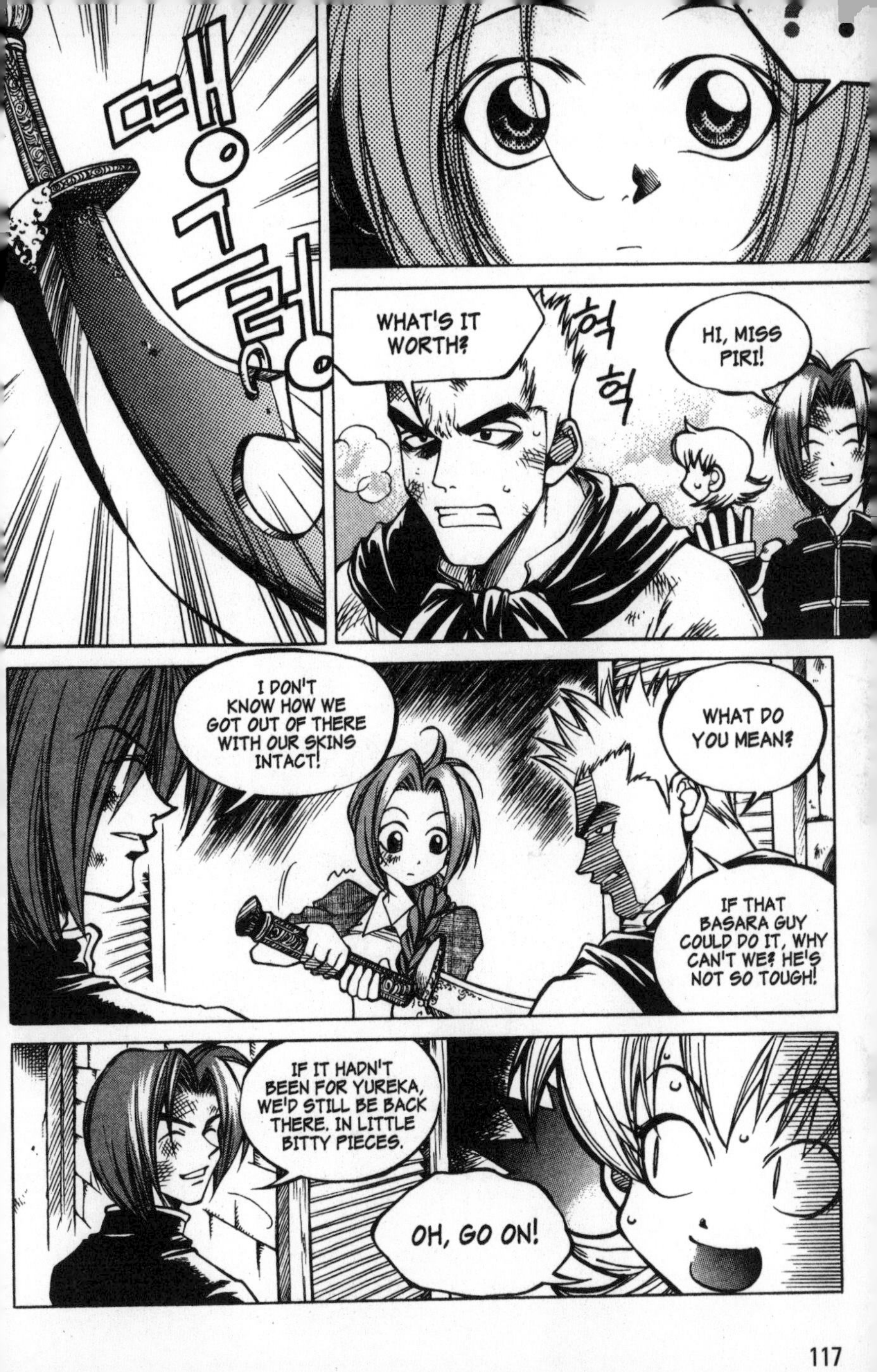

땡그렁
WHAT'S IT WORTH?
헉 헉
HI, MISS PIRI!
I DON'T KNOW HOW WE GOT OUT OF THERE WITH OUR SKINS INTACT!
WHAT DO YOU MEAN?
IF THAT BASARA GUY COULD DO IT, WHY CAN'T WE? HE'S NOT SO TOUGH!
IF IT HADN'T BEEN FOR YUREKA, WE'D STILL BE BACK THERE. IN LITTLE BITTY PIECES.
OH, GO ON!

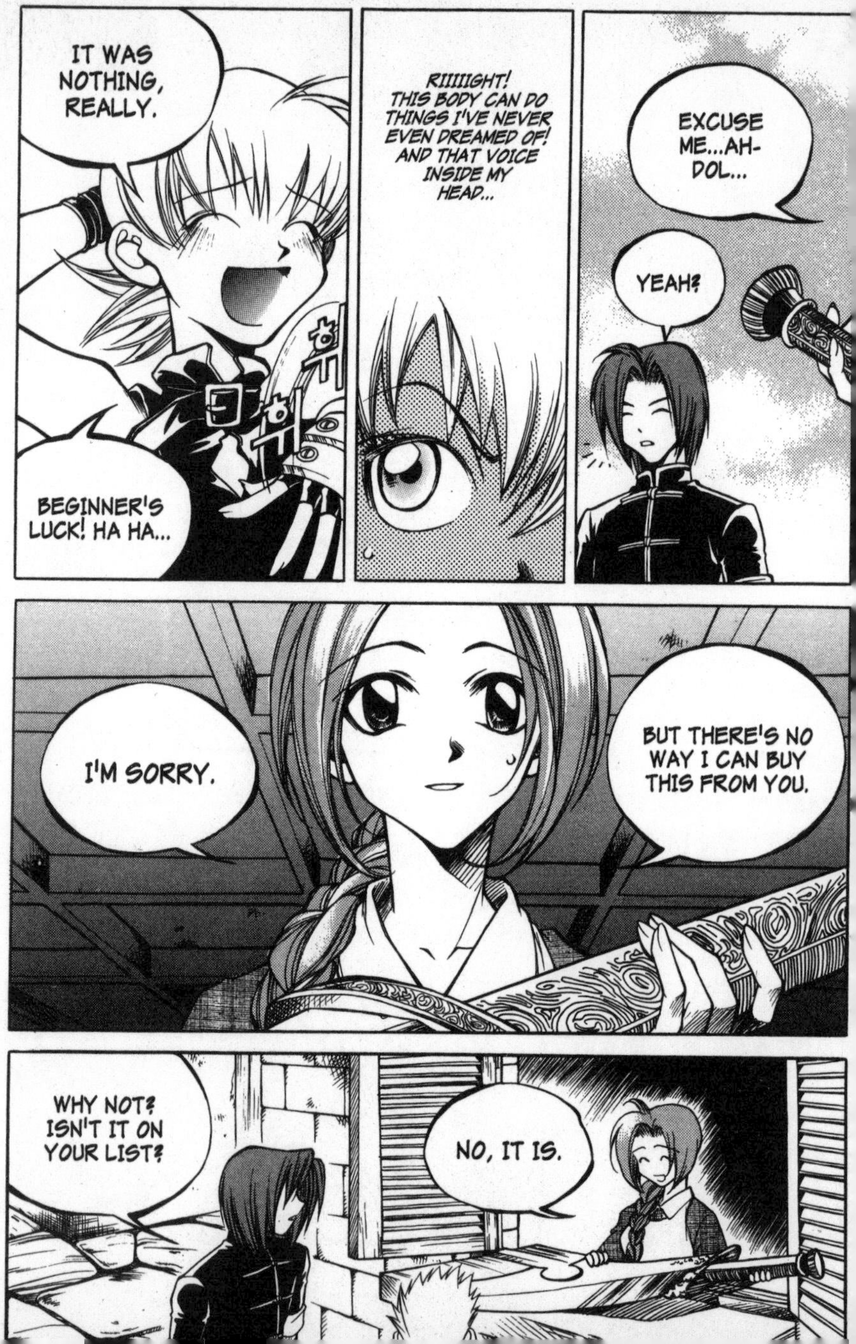
IT WAS NOTHING, REALLY.
BEGINNER'S LUCK! HA HA...
RIIIIIGHT! THIS BODY CAN DO THINGS I'VE NEVER EVEN DREAMED OF! AND THAT VOICE INSIDE MY HEAD...
EXCUSE ME...AH-DOL...
YEAH?
I'M SORRY.
BUT THERE'S NO WAY I CAN BUY THIS FROM YOU.
WHY NOT? ISN'T IT ON YOUR LIST?
NO, IT IS.

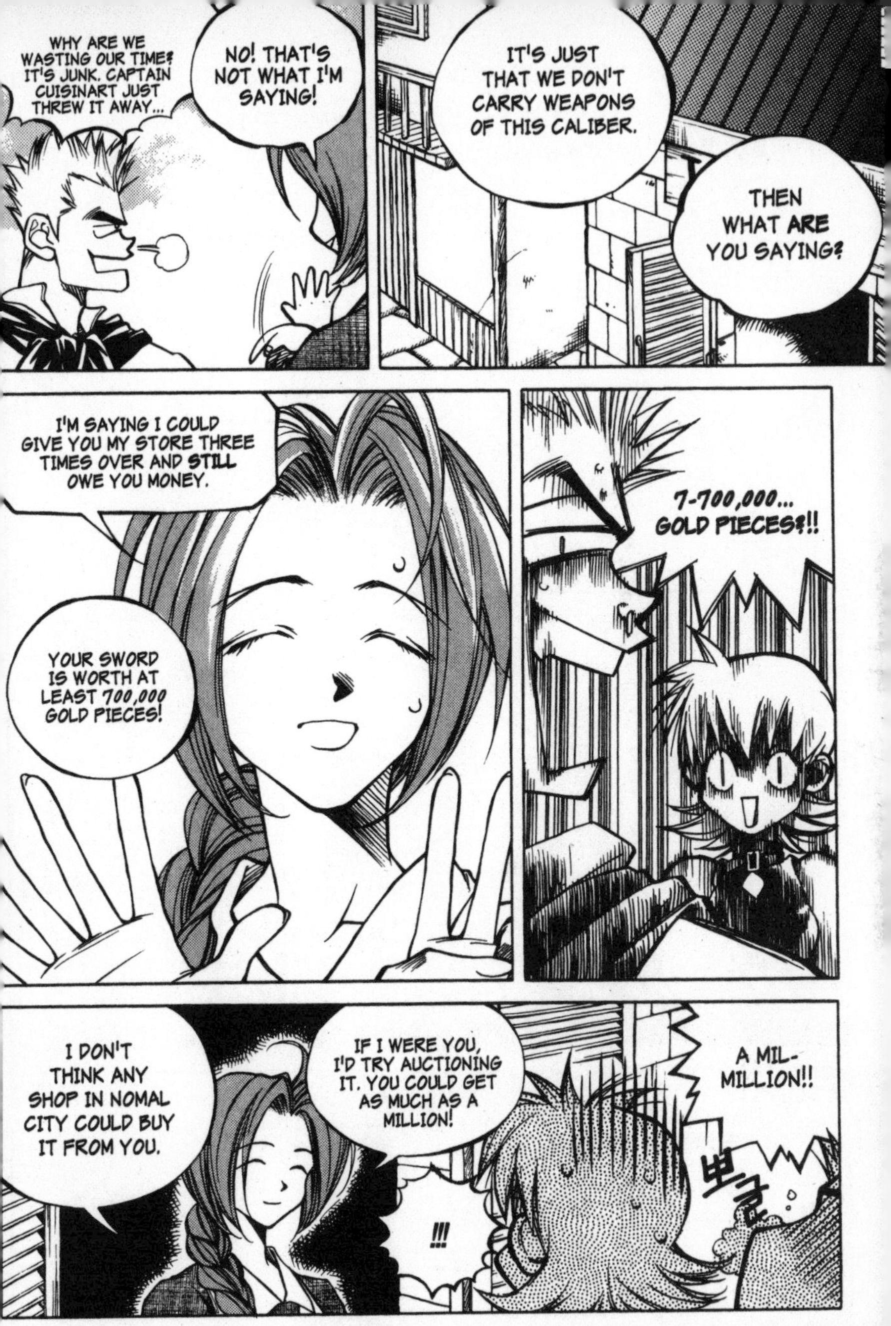
WHY ARE WE WASTING OUR TIME? IT'S JUNK. CAPTAIN CUISINART JUST THREW IT AWAY...
NO! THAT'S NOT WHAT I'M SAYING!
IT'S JUST THAT WE DON'T CARRY WEAPONS OF THIS CALIBER.
THEN WHAT ARE YOU SAYING?
I'M SAYING I COULD GIVE YOU MY STORE THREE TIMES OVER AND STILL OWE YOU MONEY.
YOUR SWORD IS WORTH AT LEAST 700,000 GOLD PIECES!
7-700,000... GOLD PIECES?!!
I DON'T THINK ANY SHOP IN NOMAL CITY COULD BUY IT FROM YOU.
IF I WERE YOU, I'D TRY AUCTIONING IT. YOU COULD GET AS MUCH AS A MILLION!
!!!
A MIL-MILLION!!

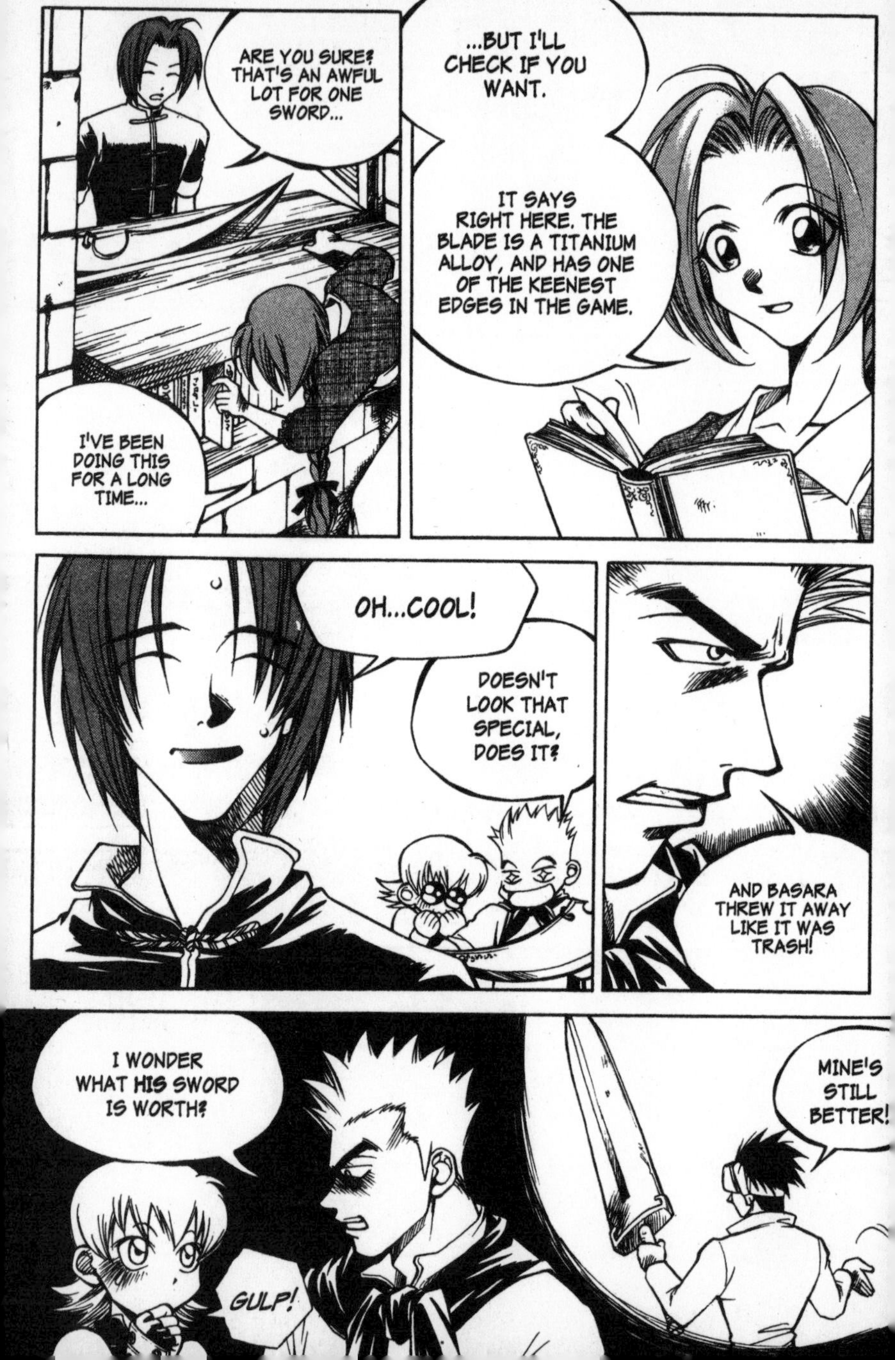
ARE YOU SURE? THAT'S AN AWFUL LOT FOR ONE SWORD...
I'VE BEEN DOING THIS FOR A LONG TIME...
...BUT I'LL CHECK IF YOU WANT.
IT SAYS RIGHT HERE. THE BLADE IS A TITANIUM ALLOY, AND HAS ONE OF THE KEENEST EDGES IN THE GAME.
OH...COOL!
DOESN'T LOOK THAT SPECIAL, DOES IT?
AND BASARA THREW IT AWAY LIKE IT WAS TRASH!
I WONDER WHAT HIS SWORD IS WORTH?
GULP!
MINE'S STILL BETTER!

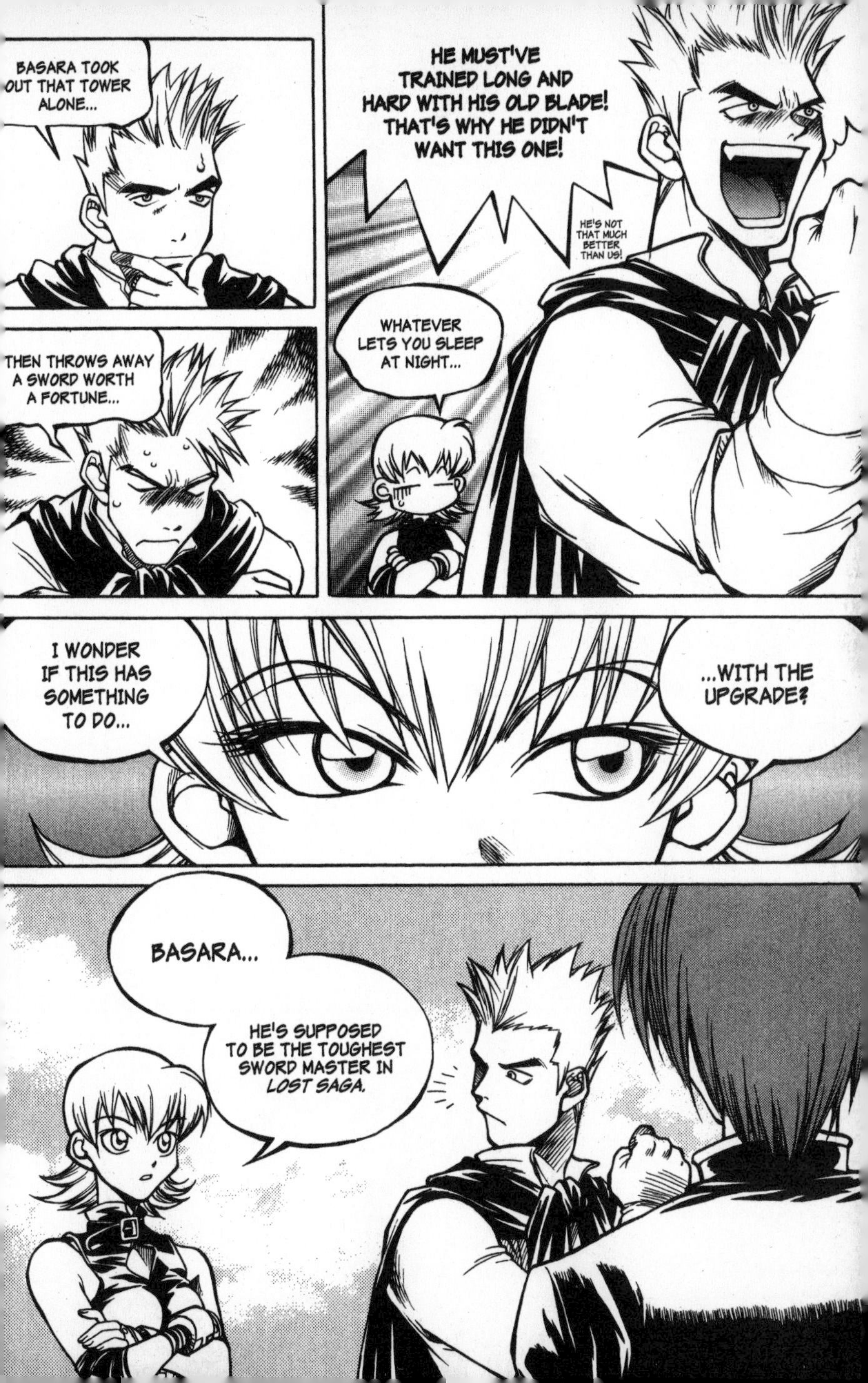
BASARA TOOK OUT THAT TOWER ALONE...
THEN THROWS AWAY A SWORD WORTH A FORTUNE...
HE MUST'VE TRAINED LONG AND HARD WITH HIS OLD BLADE! THAT'S WHY HE DIDN'T WANT THIS ONE!
HE'S NOT THAT MUCH BETTER THAN US!
WHATEVER LETS YOU SLEEP AT NIGHT...
I WONDER IF THIS HAS SOMETHING TO DO...
...WITH THE UPGRADE?
BASARA...
HE'S SUPPOSED TO BE THE TOUGHEST SWORD MASTER IN *LOST SAGA*.

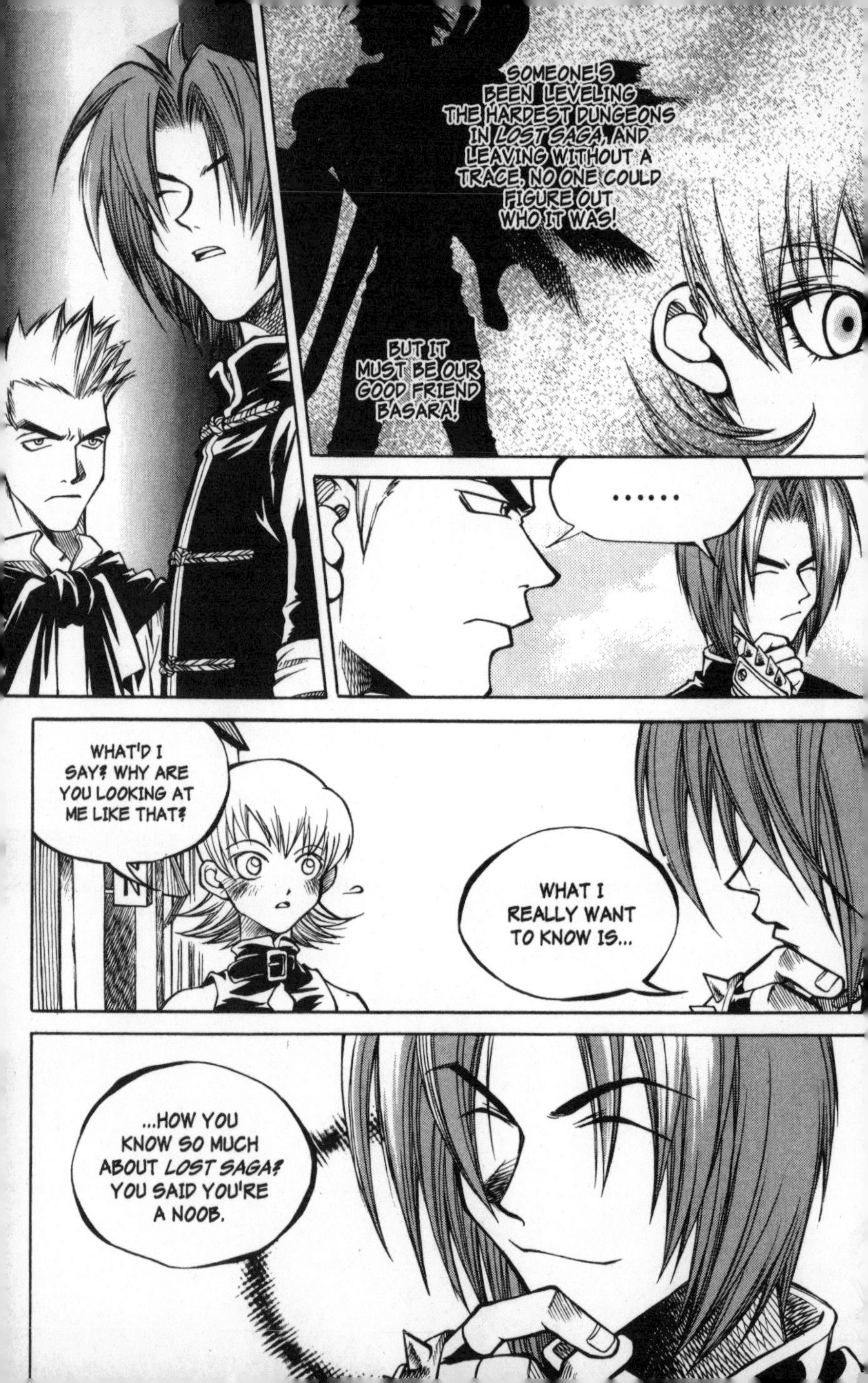
SOMEONE'S BEEN LEVELING THE HARDEST DUNGEONS IN *LOST SAGA*, AND LEAVING WITHOUT A TRACE. NO ONE COULD FIGURE OUT WHO IT WAS!
BUT IT MUST BE OUR GOOD FRIEND BASARA!
......
WHAT'D I SAY? WHY ARE YOU LOOKING AT ME LIKE THAT?
WHAT I REALLY WANT TO KNOW IS...
...HOW YOU KNOW SO MUCH ABOUT *LOST SAGA*? YOU SAID YOU'RE A NOOB.

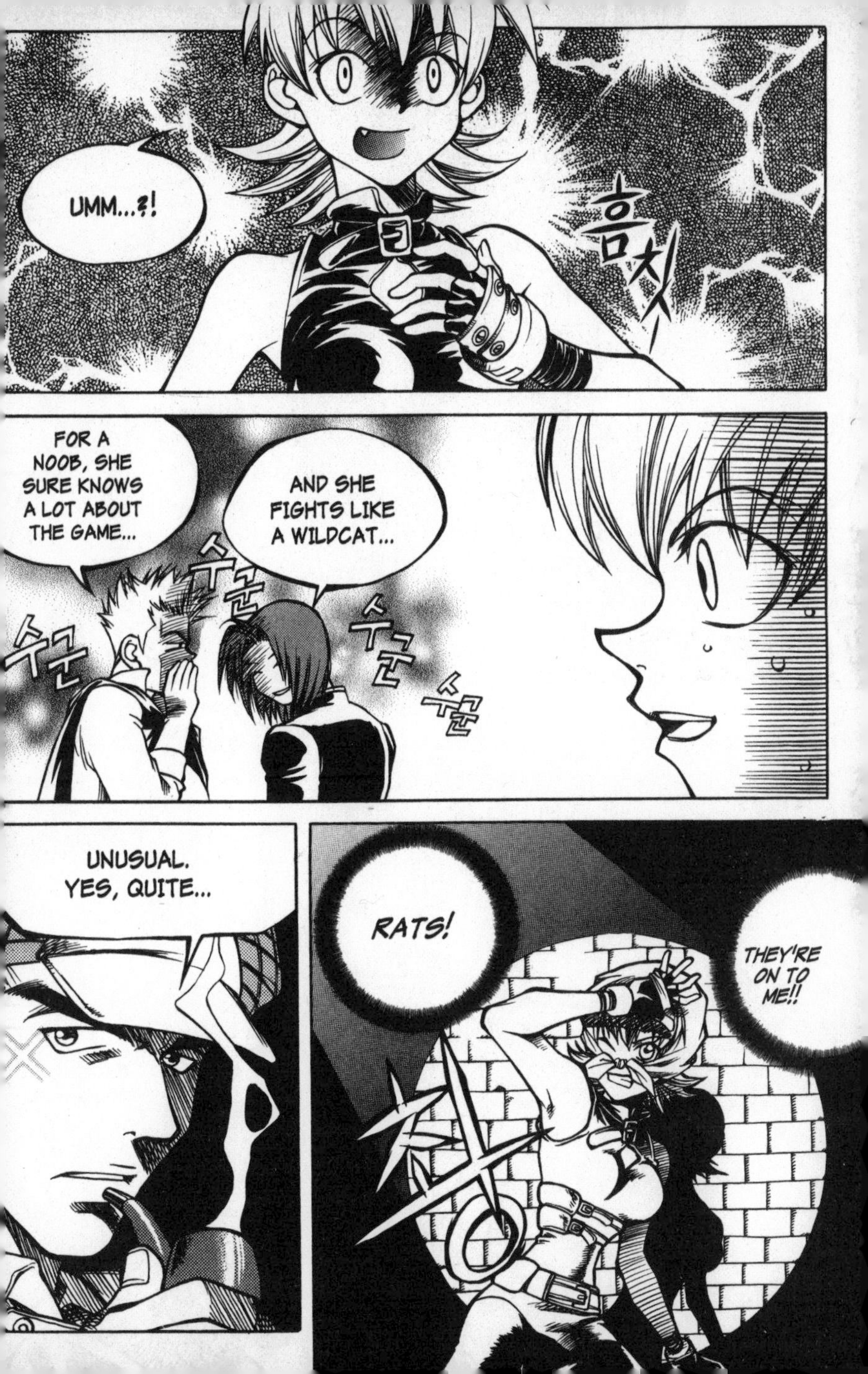
UMM...?!
흠칫
FOR A NOOB, SHE SURE KNOWS A LOT ABOUT THE GAME...
AND SHE FIGHTS LIKE A WILDCAT...
수군
수군
수군
수군
UNUSUAL. YES, QUITE...
RATS!
THEY'RE ON TO ME!!

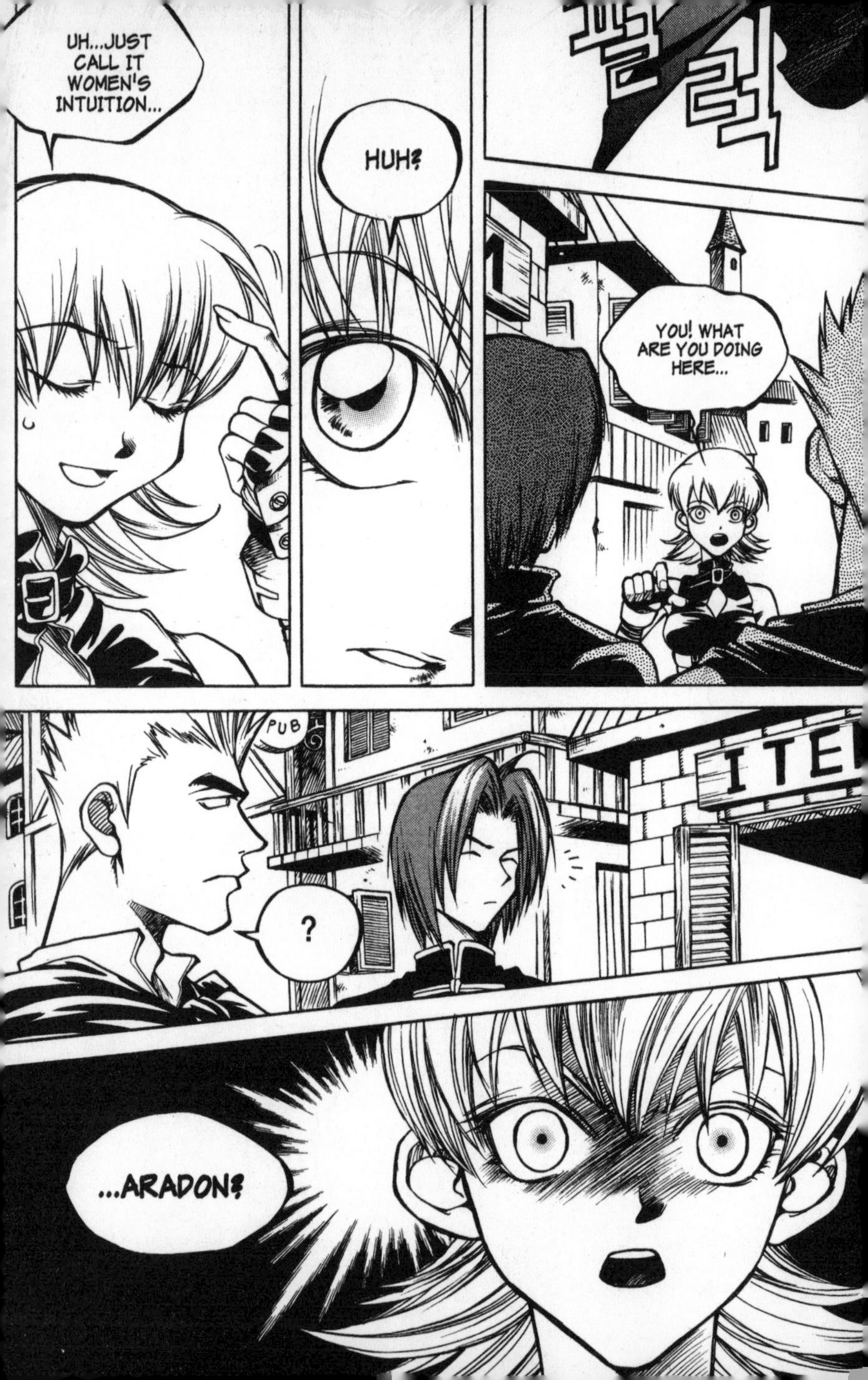
UH...JUST CALL IT WOMEN'S INTUITION...
HUH?
벌컥
YOU! WHAT ARE YOU DOING HERE...
PUB
?
...ARADON?

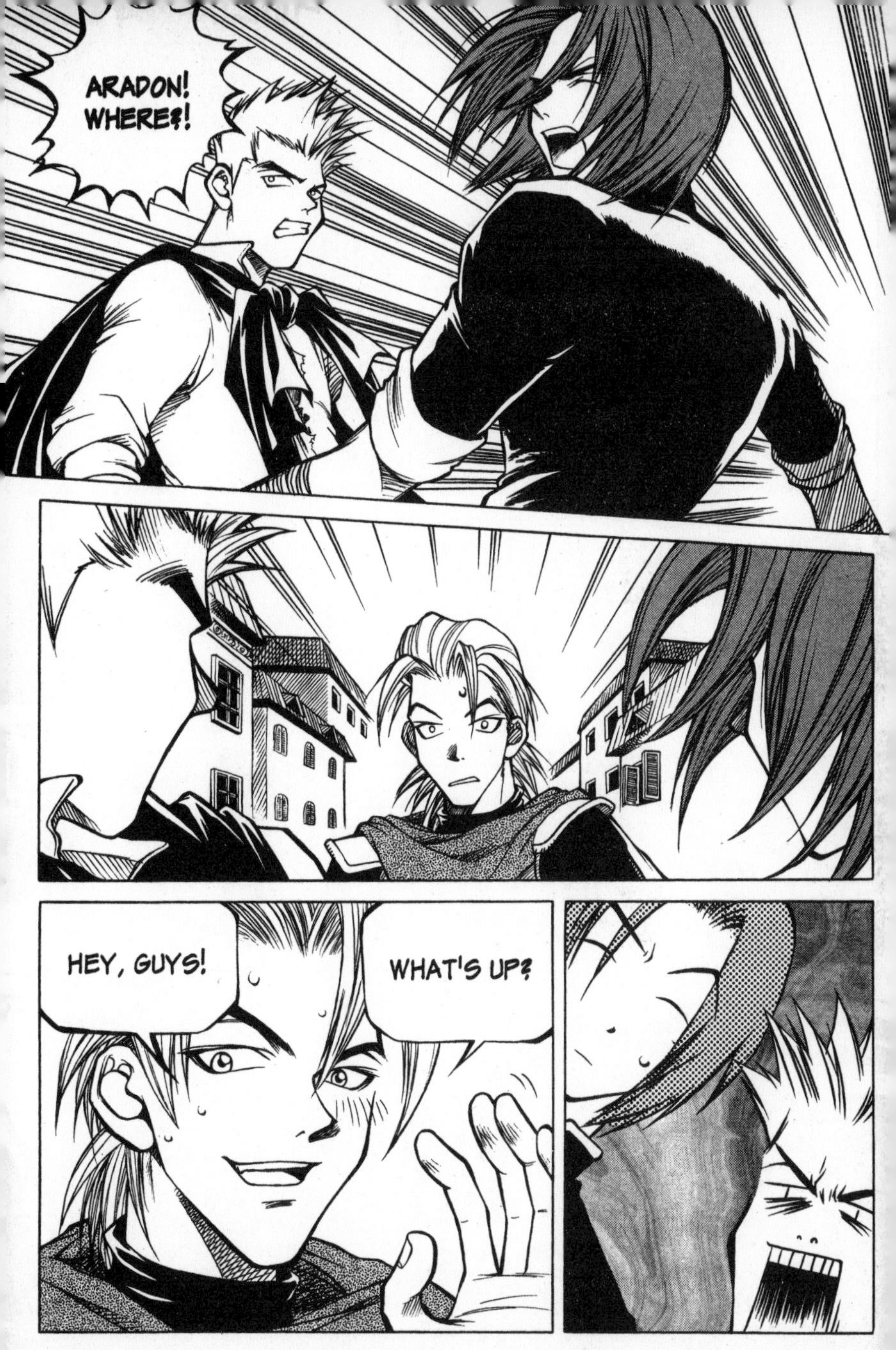
ARADON! WHERE?!
HEY, GUYS!
WHAT'S UP?

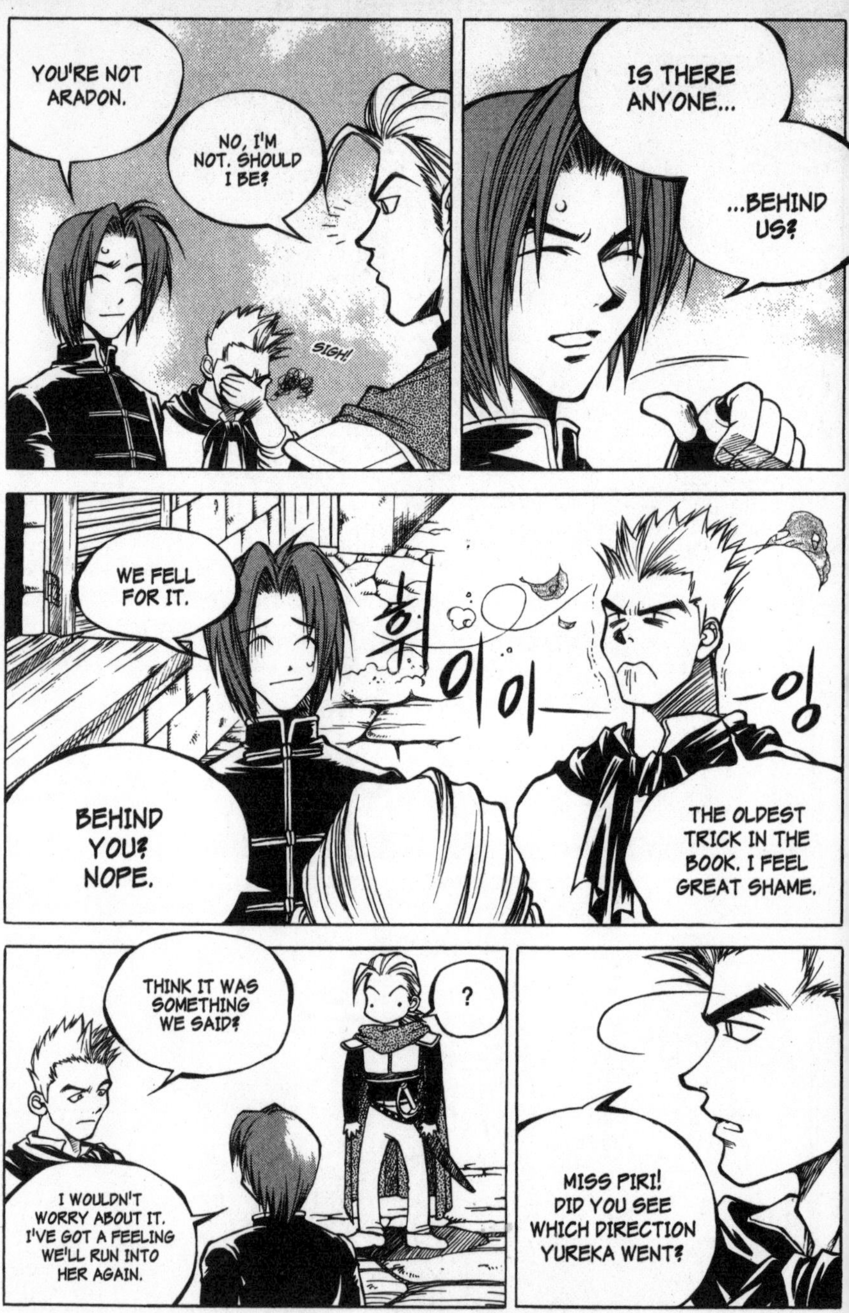
YOU'RE NOT ARADON.
NO, I'M NOT. SHOULD I BE?
SIGH!
IS THERE ANYONE...
...BEHIND US?
WE FELL FOR IT.
휘이이——잉
BEHIND YOU? NOPE.
THE OLDEST TRICK IN THE BOOK. I FEEL GREAT SHAME.
THINK IT WAS SOMETHING WE SAID?
?
I WOULDN'T WORRY ABOUT IT. I'VE GOT A FEELING WE'LL RUN INTO HER AGAIN.
MISS PIRI! DID YOU SEE WHICH DIRECTION YUREKA WENT?

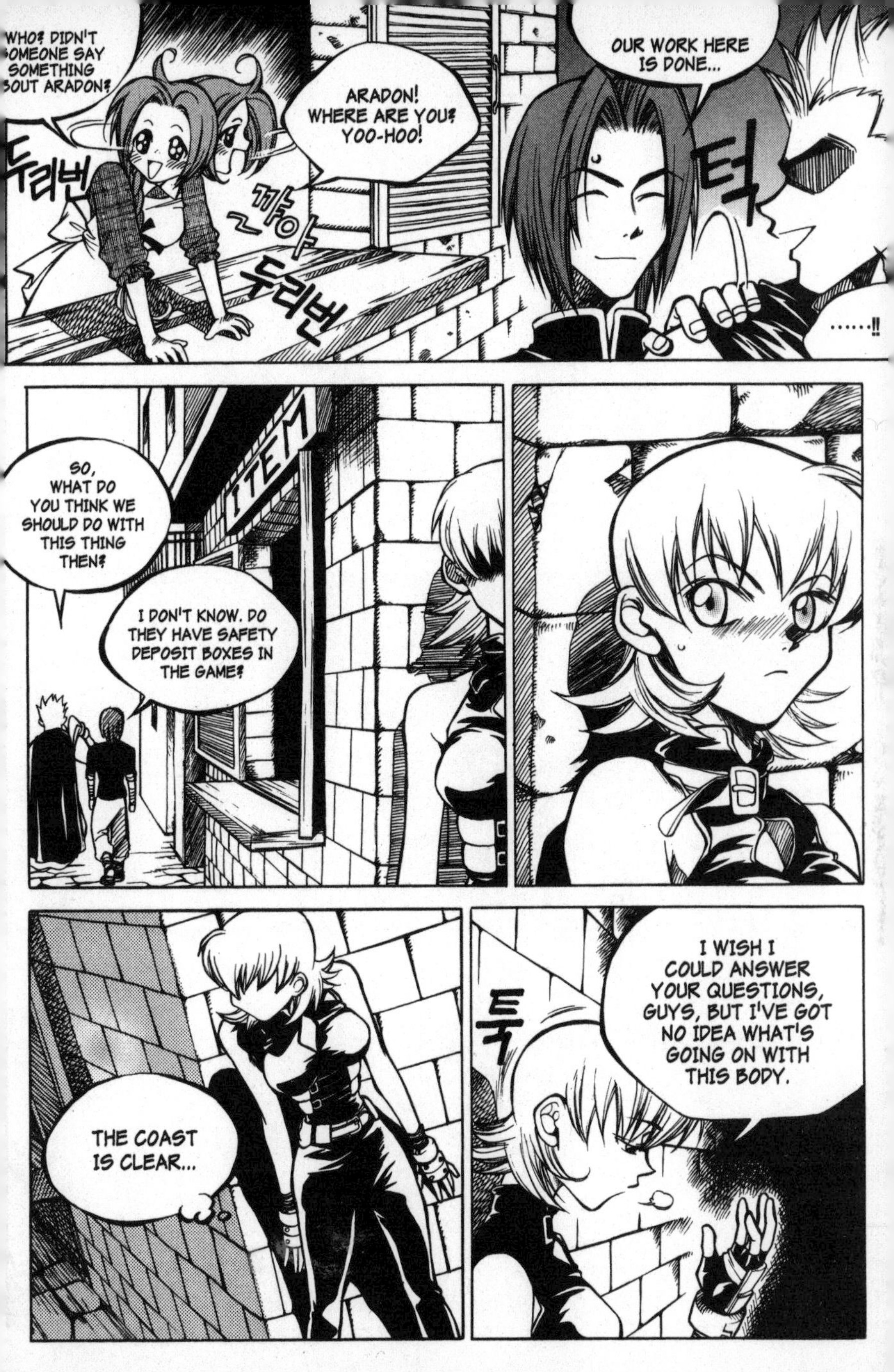
WHO? DIDN'T OMEONE SAY SOMETHING BOUT ARADON?
두리번
ARADON! WHERE ARE YOU? YOO-HOO!
두리번
OUR WORK HERE IS DONE...
턱
......!!
SO, WHAT DO YOU THINK WE SHOULD DO WITH THIS THING THEN?
ITEM
I DON'T KNOW. DO THEY HAVE SAFETY DEPOSIT BOXES IN THE GAME?
THE COAST IS CLEAR...
I WISH I COULD ANSWER YOUR QUESTIONS, GUYS, BUT I'VE GOT NO IDEA WHAT'S GOING ON WITH THIS BODY.

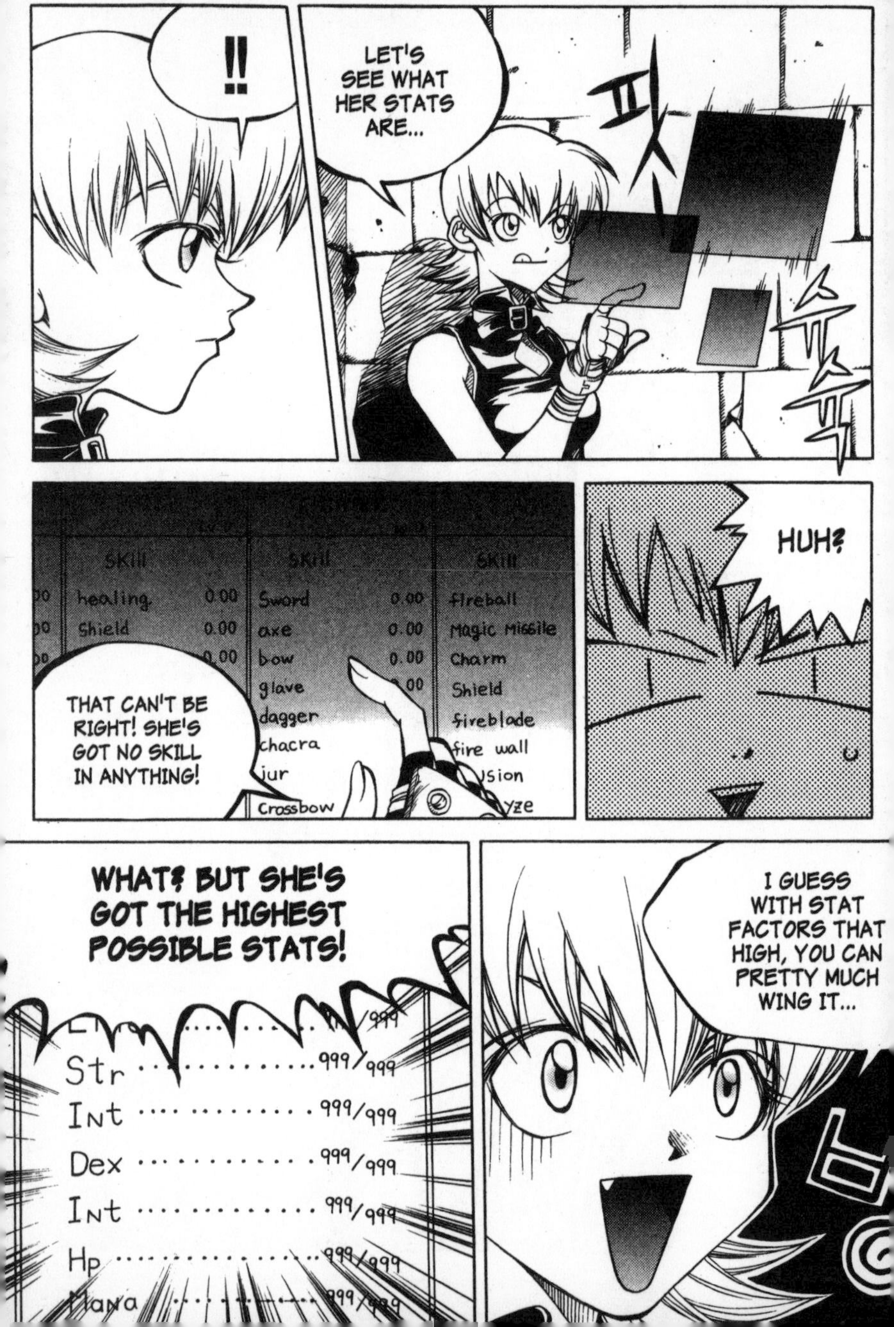
!!
LET'S SEE WHAT HER STATS ARE...
SKill
healing 0.00
Shield 0.00
SKill
Sword 0.00
axe 0.00
bow 0.00
glave
dagger
chacra
jur
Crossbow
SKill
fireball
Magic Missile
Charm
Shield
fireblade
fire wall
THAT CAN'T BE RIGHT! SHE'S GOT NO SKILL IN ANYTHING!
HUH?
WHAT? BUT SHE'S GOT THE HIGHEST POSSIBLE STATS!
Str 999/999
Int 999/999
Dex 999/999
Int 999/999
Hp 999/999
Mana 999/999
I GUESS WITH STAT FACTORS THAT HIGH, YOU CAN PRETTY MUCH WING IT...

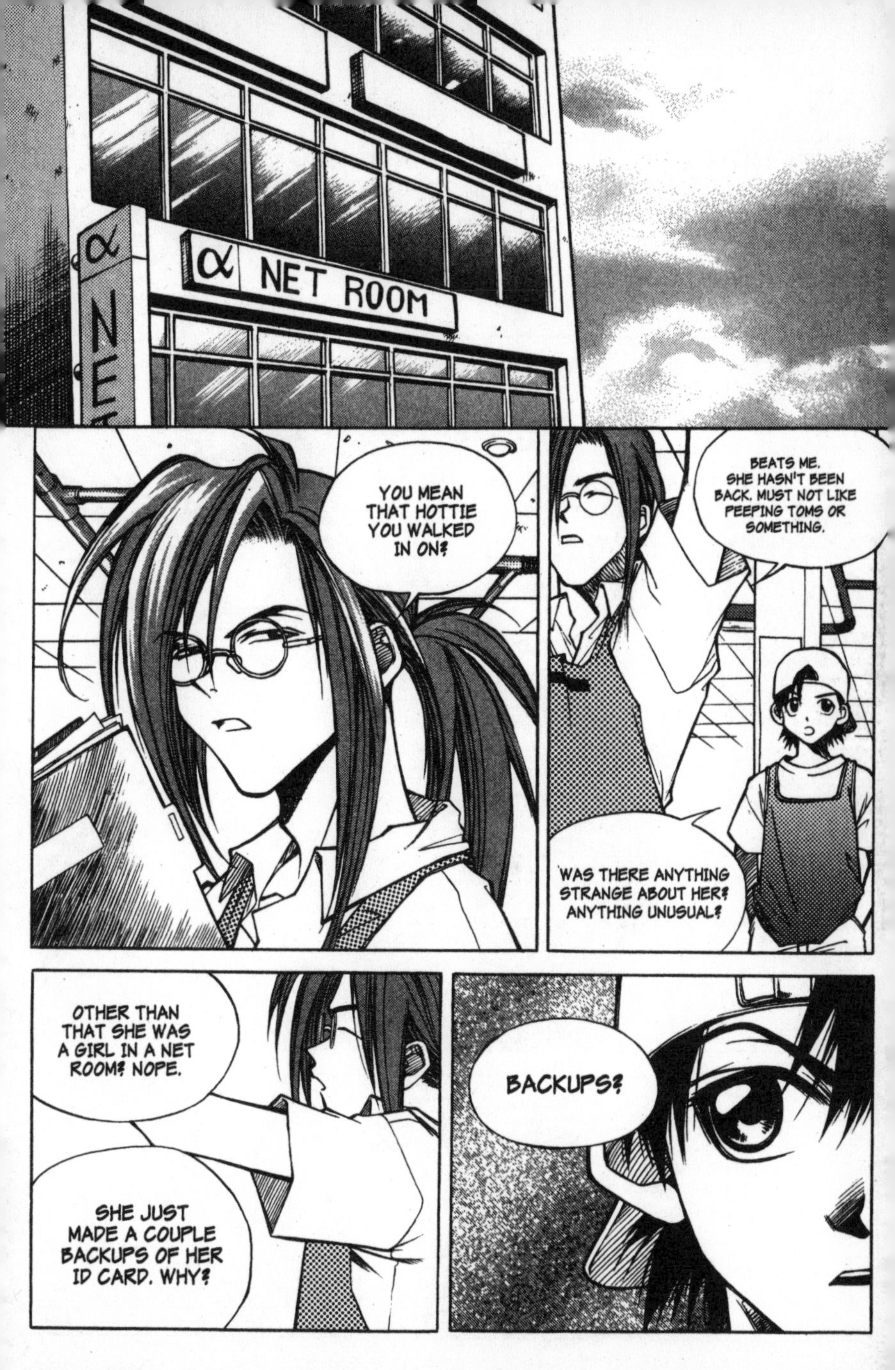
α
NE
α NET ROOM
YOU MEAN THAT HOTTIE YOU WALKED IN ON?
BEATS ME. SHE HASN'T BEEN BACK. MUST NOT LIKE PEEPING TOMS OR SOMETHING.
WAS THERE ANYTHING STRANGE ABOUT HER? ANYTHING UNUSUAL?
OTHER THAN THAT SHE WAS A GIRL IN A NET ROOM? NOPE.
SHE JUST MADE A COUPLE BACKUPS OF HER ID CARD. WHY?
BACKUPS?

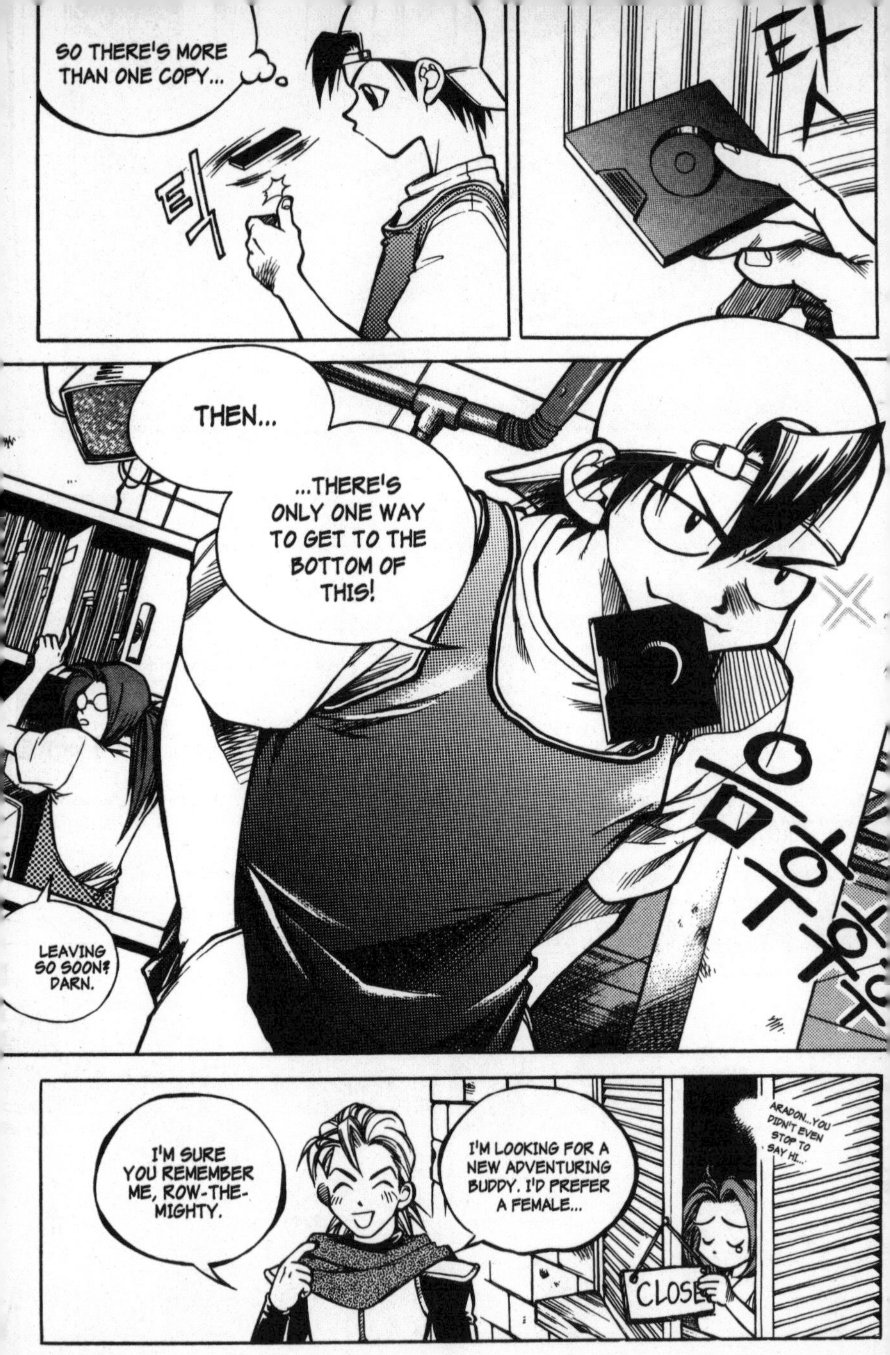
SO THERE'S MORE THAN ONE COPY...
THEN...
...THERE'S ONLY ONE WAY TO GET TO THE BOTTOM OF THIS!
LEAVING SO SOON? DARN.
I'M SURE YOU REMEMBER ME, ROW-THE-MIGHTY.
I'M LOOKING FOR A NEW ADVENTURING BUDDY. I'D PREFER A FEMALE...
ARADON...YOU DIDN'T EVEN STOP TO SAY HI...
CLOSE

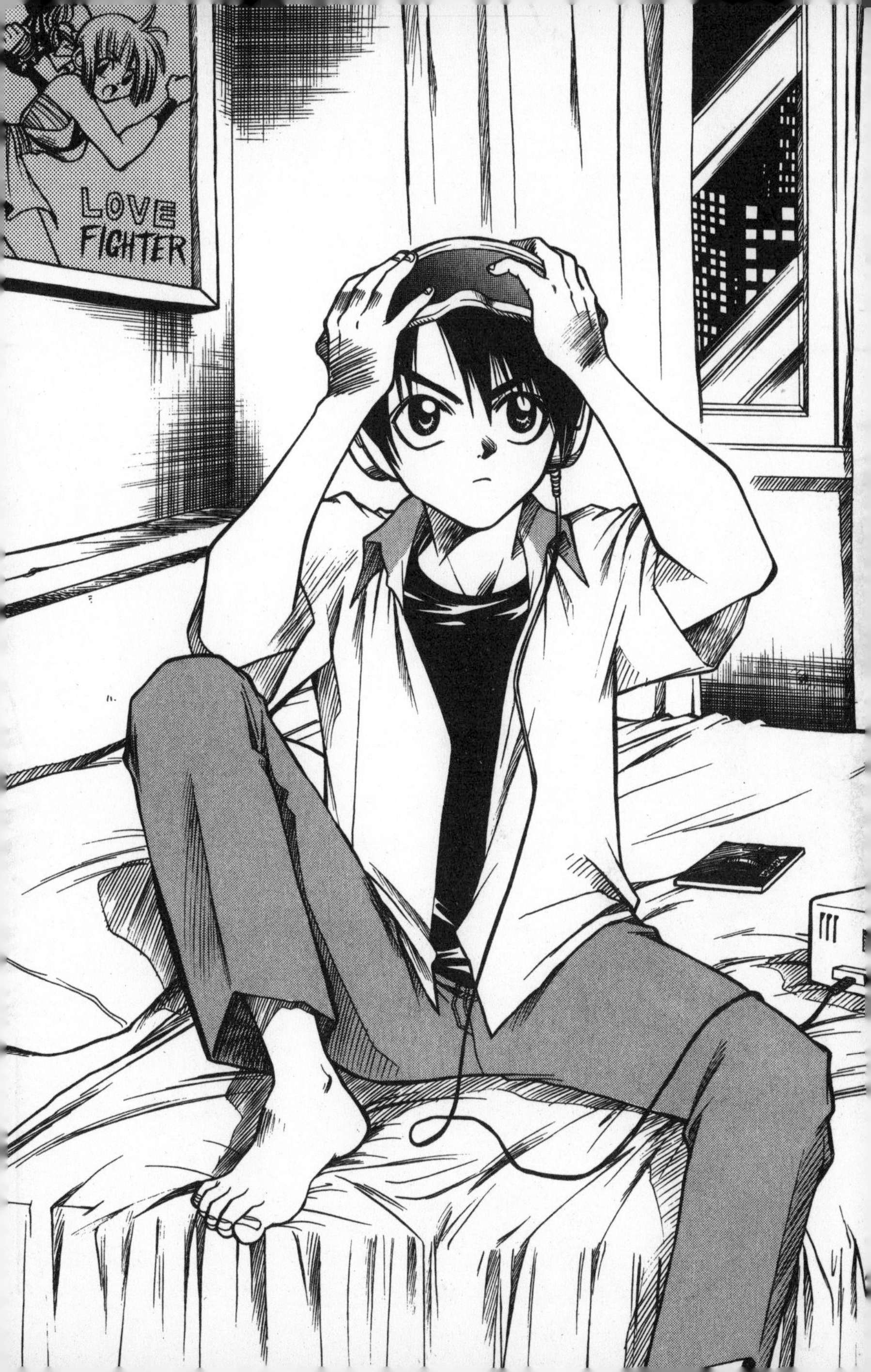
LOVE
FIGHTER

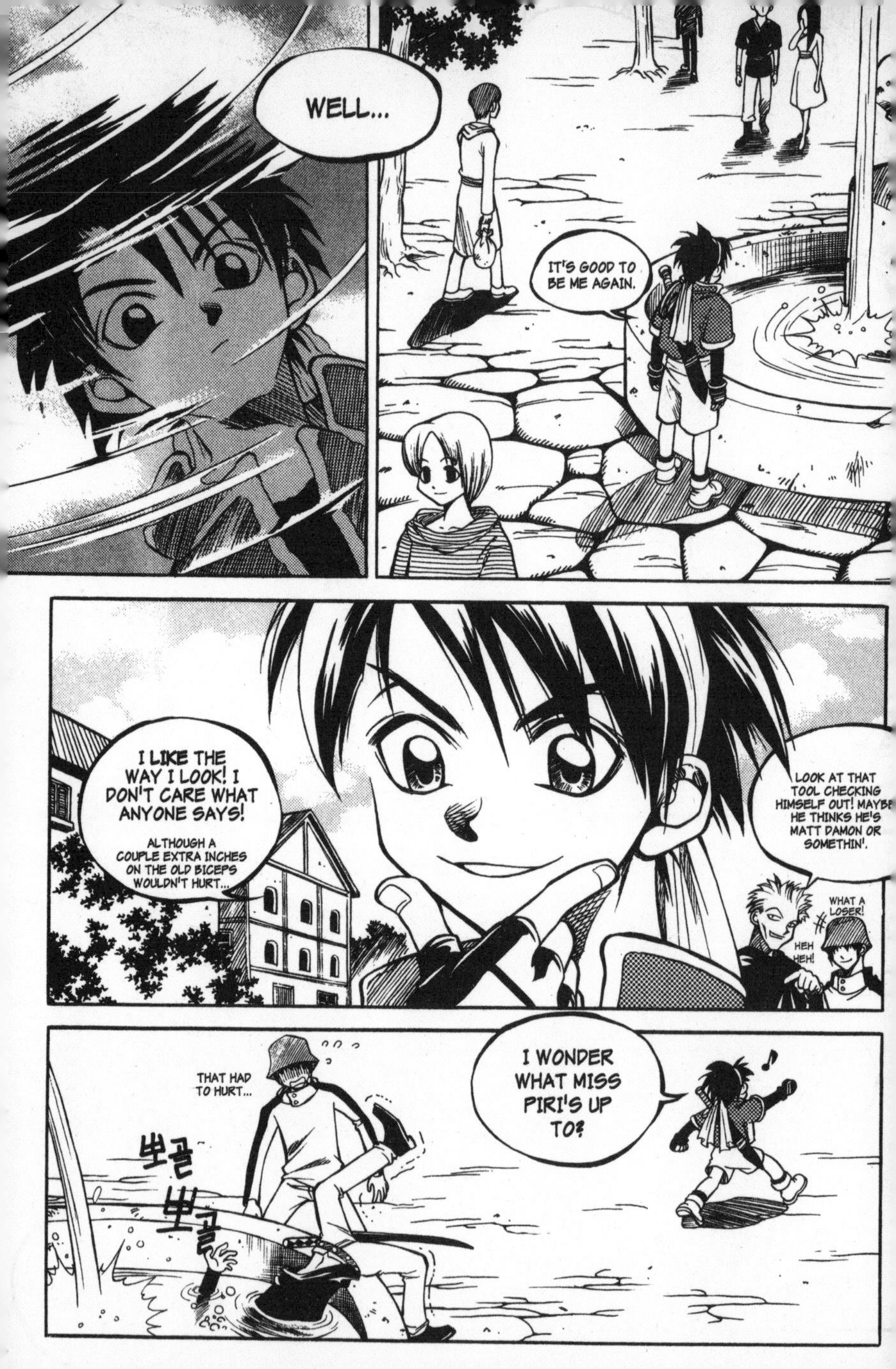
WELL...
IT'S GOOD TO BE ME AGAIN.
I LIKE THE WAY I LOOK! I DON'T CARE WHAT ANYONE SAYS!
ALTHOUGH A COUPLE EXTRA INCHES ON THE OLD BICEPS WOULDN'T HURT...
LOOK AT THAT TOOL CHECKING HIMSELF OUT! MAYBE HE THINKS HE'S MATT DAMON OR SOMETHIN'.
WHAT A LOSER!
HEH HEH!
THAT HAD TO HURT...
뽀골 뽀골
I WONDER WHAT MISS PIRI'S UP TO?

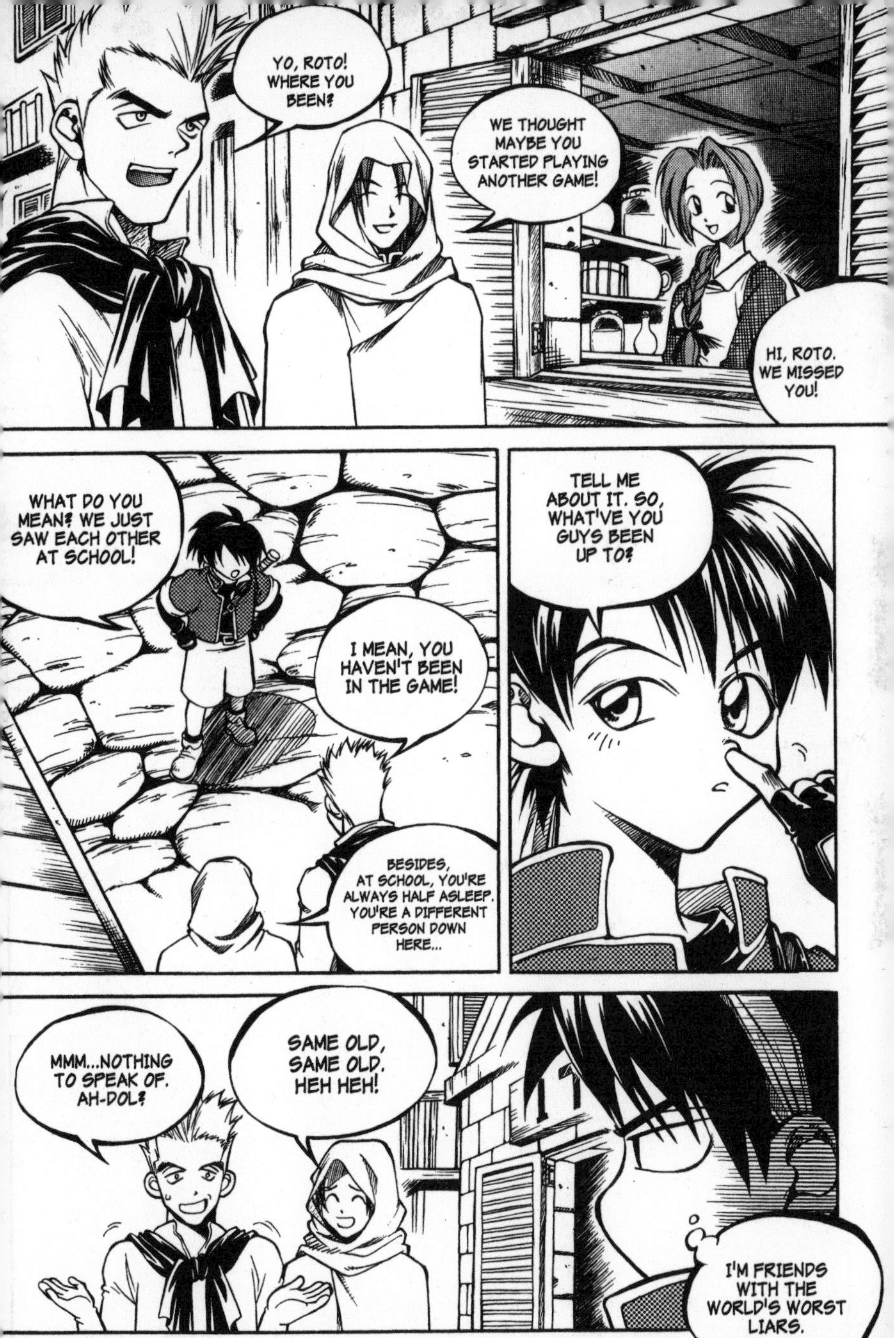
YO, ROTO! WHERE YOU BEEN?
WE THOUGHT MAYBE YOU STARTED PLAYING ANOTHER GAME!
HI, ROTO. WE MISSED YOU!
WHAT DO YOU MEAN? WE JUST SAW EACH OTHER AT SCHOOL!
I MEAN, YOU HAVEN'T BEEN IN THE GAME!
BESIDES, AT SCHOOL, YOU'RE ALWAYS HALF ASLEEP. YOU'RE A DIFFERENT PERSON DOWN HERE...
TELL ME ABOUT IT. SO, WHAT'VE YOU GUYS BEEN UP TO?
MMM...NOTHING TO SPEAK OF. AH-DOL?
SAME OLD, SAME OLD. HEH HEH!
I'M FRIENDS WITH THE WORLD'S WORST LIARS.

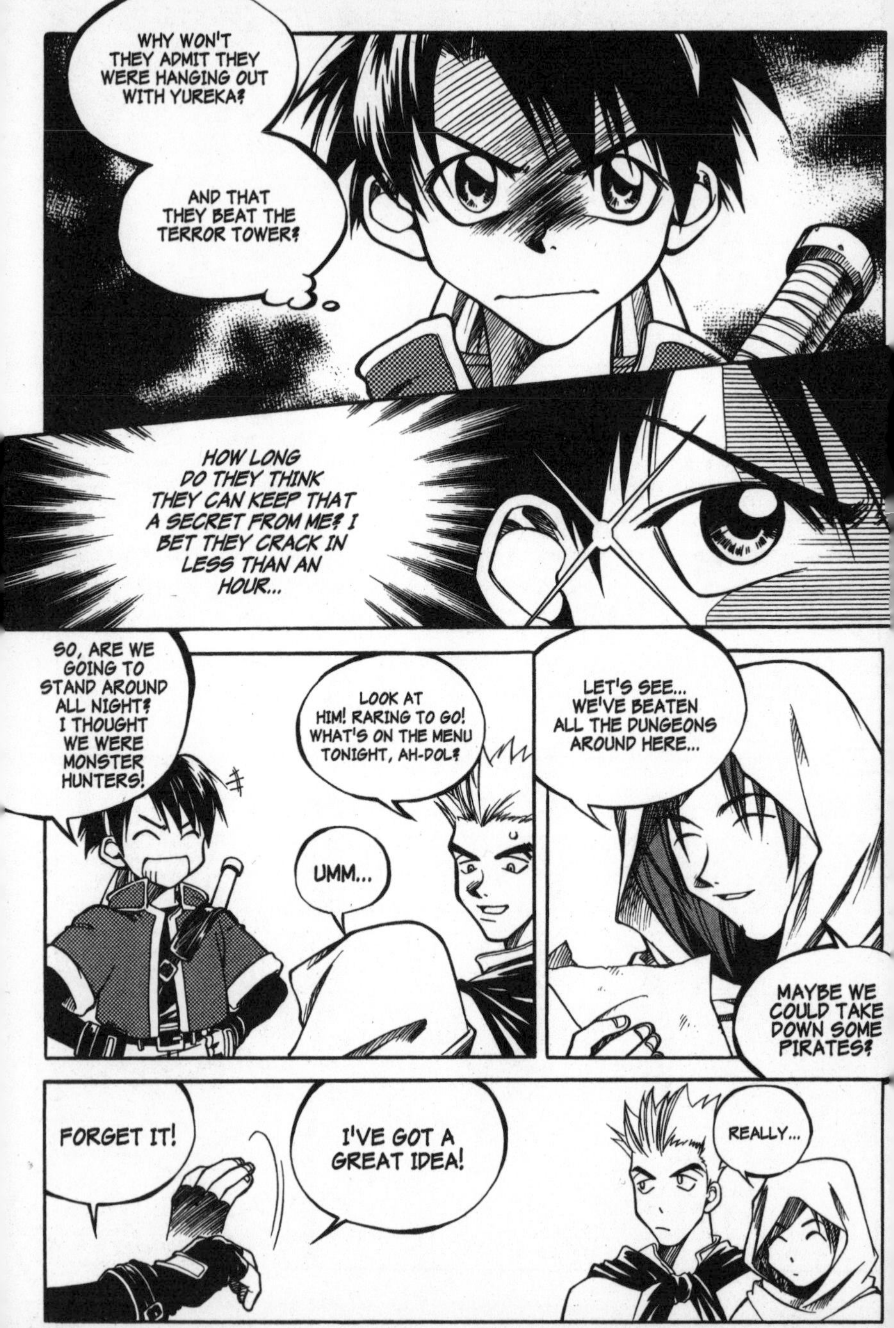
WHY WON'T THEY ADMIT THEY WERE HANGING OUT WITH YUREKA?
AND THAT THEY BEAT THE TERROR TOWER?
HOW LONG DO THEY THINK THEY CAN KEEP THAT A SECRET FROM ME? I BET THEY CRACK IN LESS THAN AN HOUR...
SO, ARE WE GOING TO STAND AROUND ALL NIGHT? I THOUGHT WE WERE MONSTER HUNTERS!
LOOK AT HIM! RARING TO GO! WHAT'S ON THE MENU TONIGHT, AH-DOL?
UMM...
LET'S SEE... WE'VE BEATEN ALL THE DUNGEONS AROUND HERE...
MAYBE WE COULD TAKE DOWN SOME PIRATES?
FORGET IT!
I'VE GOT A GREAT IDEA!
REALLY...

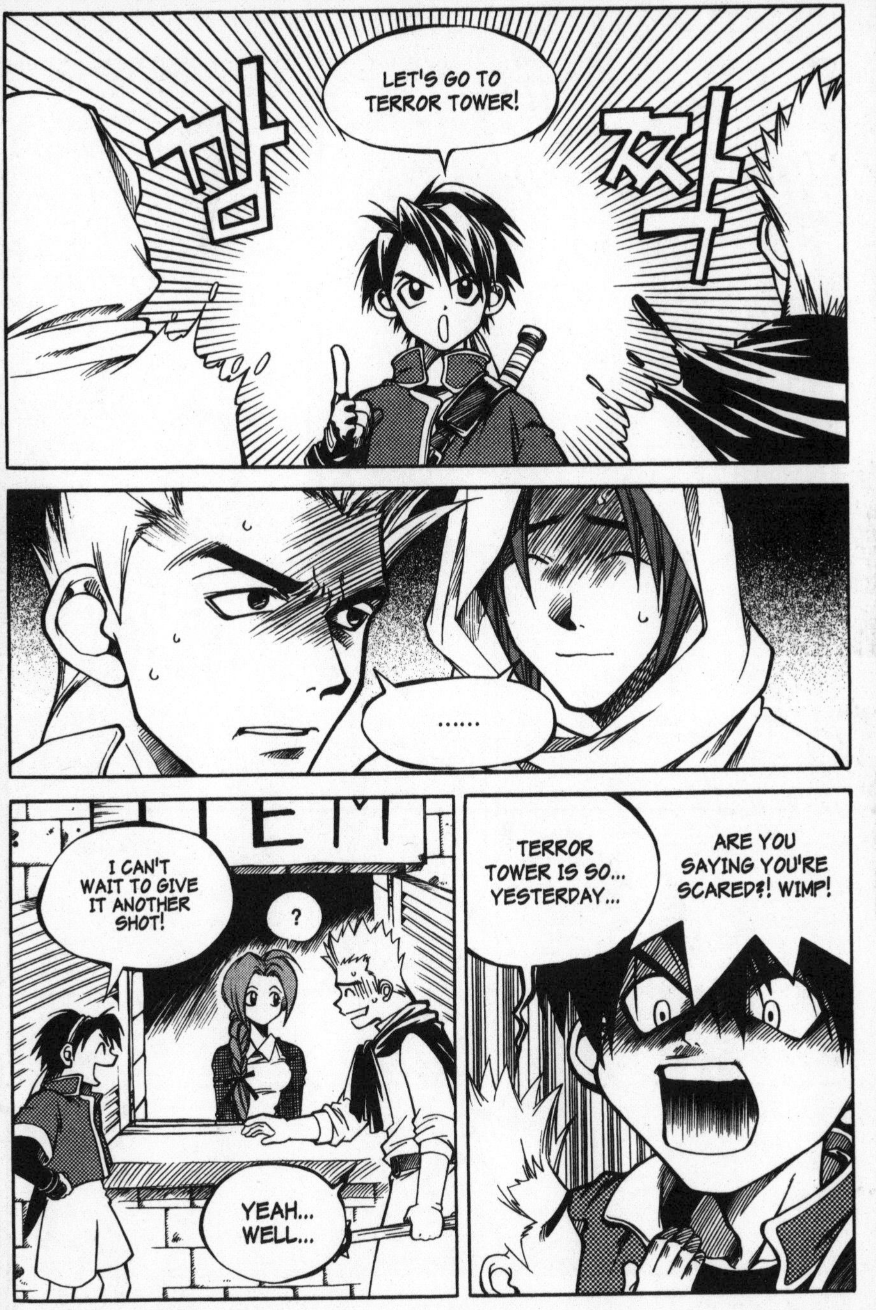
LET'S GO TO TERROR TOWER!
......
I CAN'T WAIT TO GIVE IT ANOTHER SHOT!
?
YEAH... WELL...
TERROR TOWER IS SO... YESTERDAY...
ARE YOU SAYING YOU'RE SCARED?! WIMP!

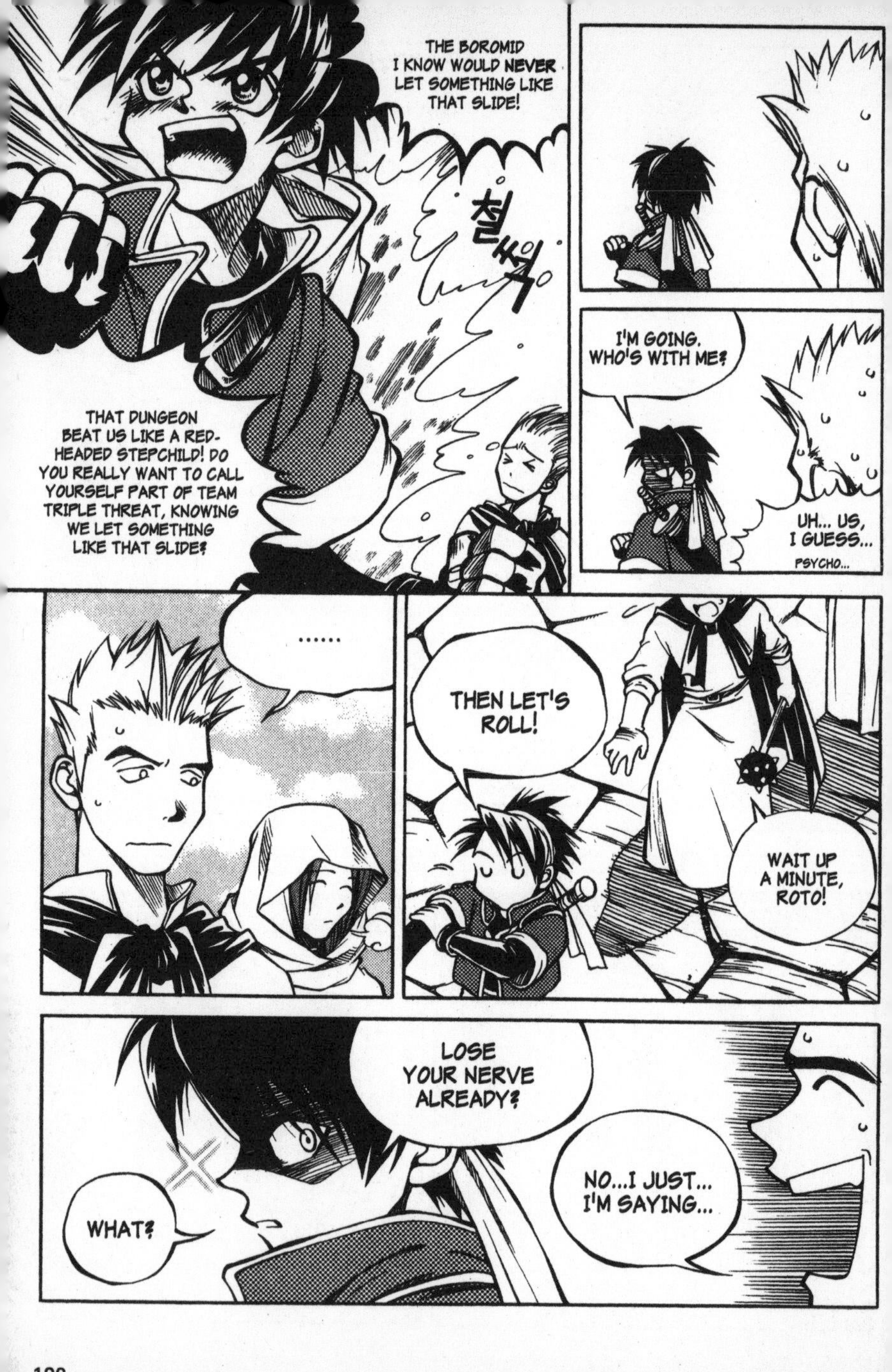
THE BOROMID I KNOW WOULD NEVER LET SOMETHING LIKE THAT SLIDE!
철썩
THAT DUNGEON BEAT US LIKE A RED-HEADED STEPCHILD! DO YOU REALLY WANT TO CALL YOURSELF PART OF TEAM TRIPLE THREAT, KNOWING WE LET SOMETHING LIKE THAT SLIDE?
I'M GOING. WHO'S WITH ME?
UH... US, I GUESS...
PSYCHO...
......
THEN LET'S ROLL!
WAIT UP A MINUTE, ROTO!
LOSE YOUR NERVE ALREADY?
WHAT?
NO...I JUST... I'M SAYING...

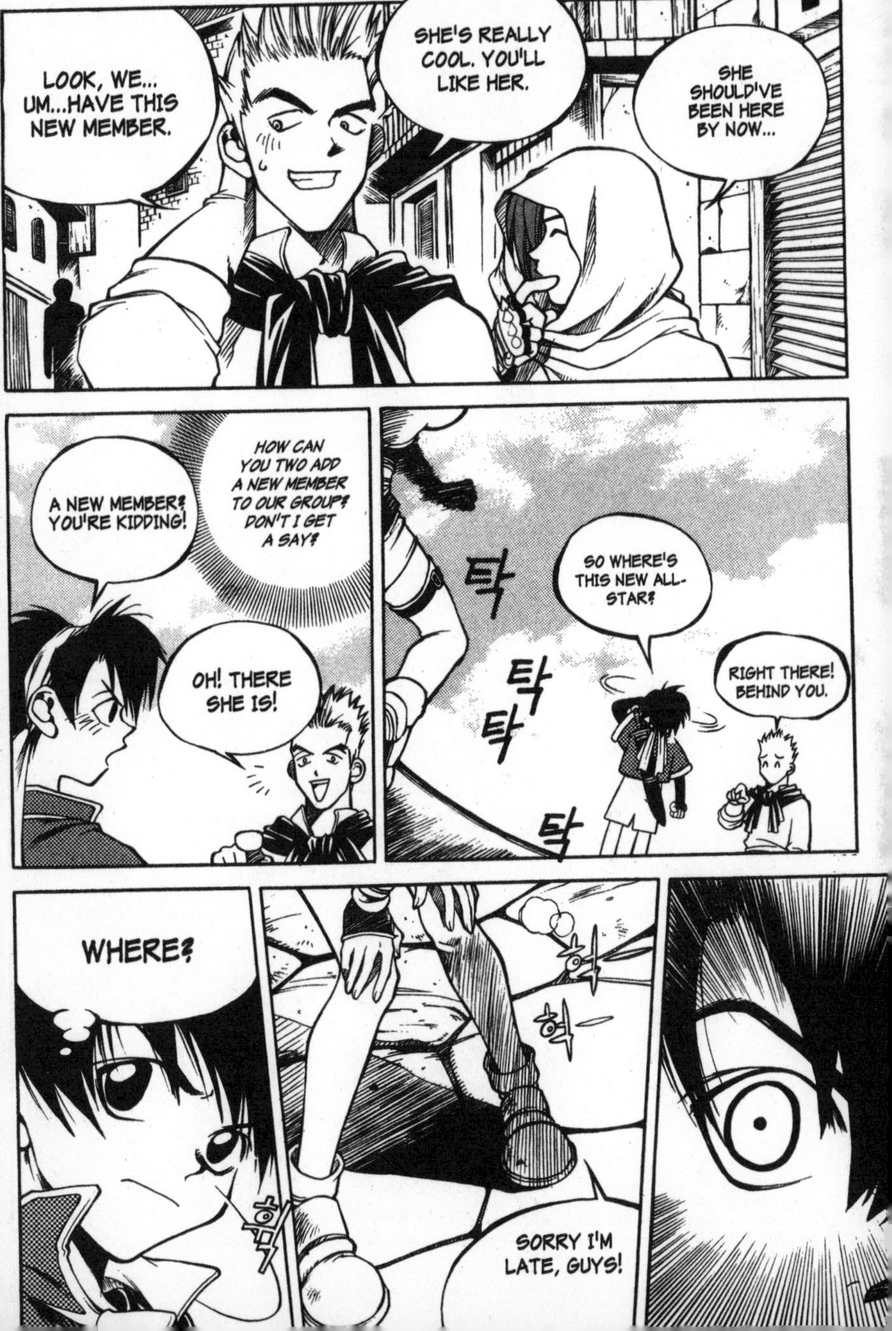
LOOK, WE... UM...HAVE THIS NEW MEMBER.
SHE'S REALLY COOL. YOU'LL LIKE HER.
SHE SHOULD'VE BEEN HERE BY NOW...
A NEW MEMBER? YOU'RE KIDDING!
HOW CAN YOU TWO ADD A NEW MEMBER TO OUR GROUP? DON'T I GET A SAY?
OH! THERE SHE IS!
탁
탁
탁
탁
SO WHERE'S THIS NEW ALL-STAR?
RIGHT THERE! BEHIND YOU.
WHERE?
SORRY I'M LATE, GUYS!

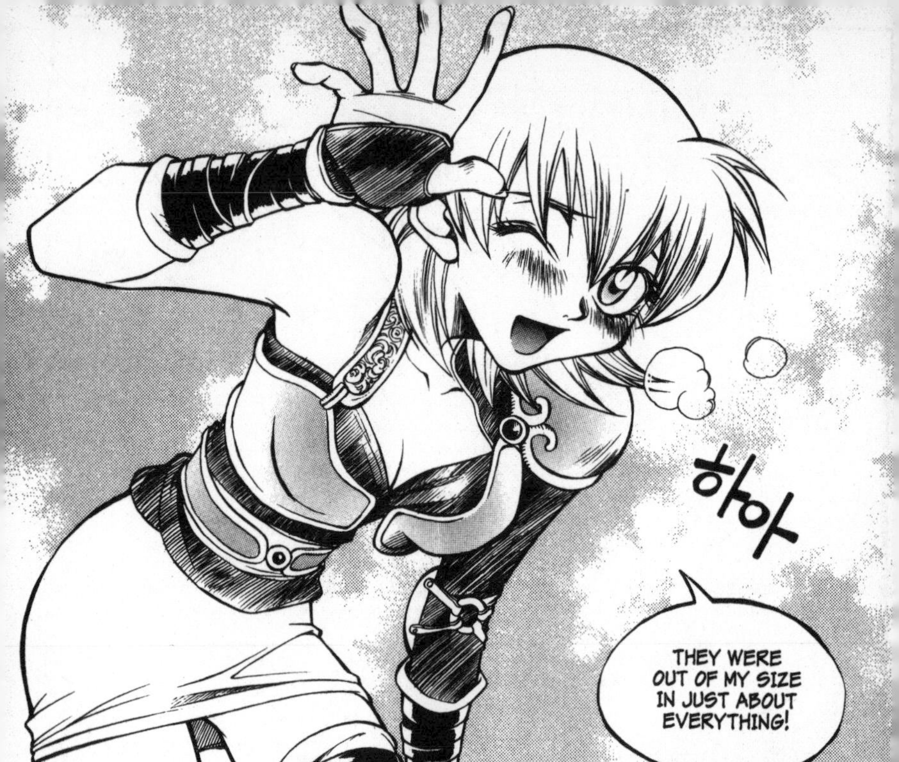
하아
THEY WERE OUT OF MY SIZE IN JUST ABOUT EVERYTHING!

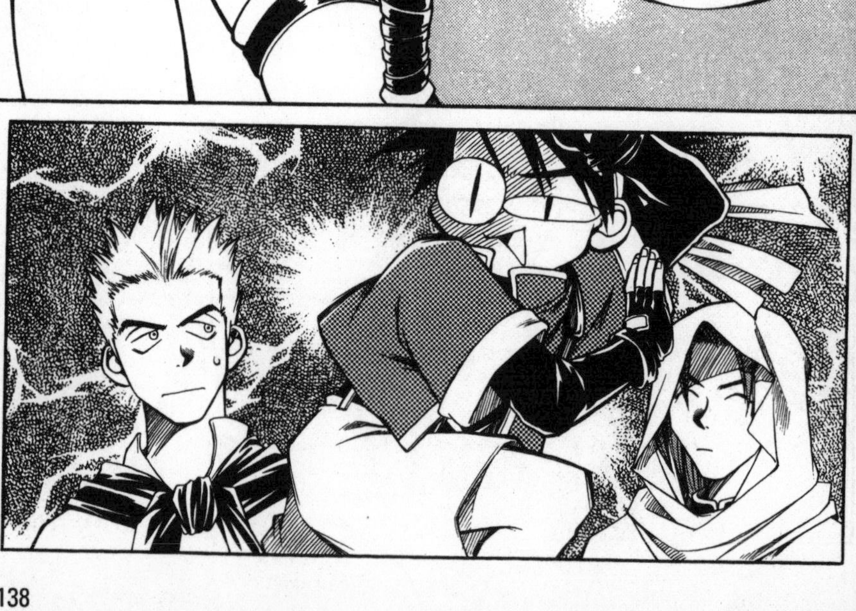

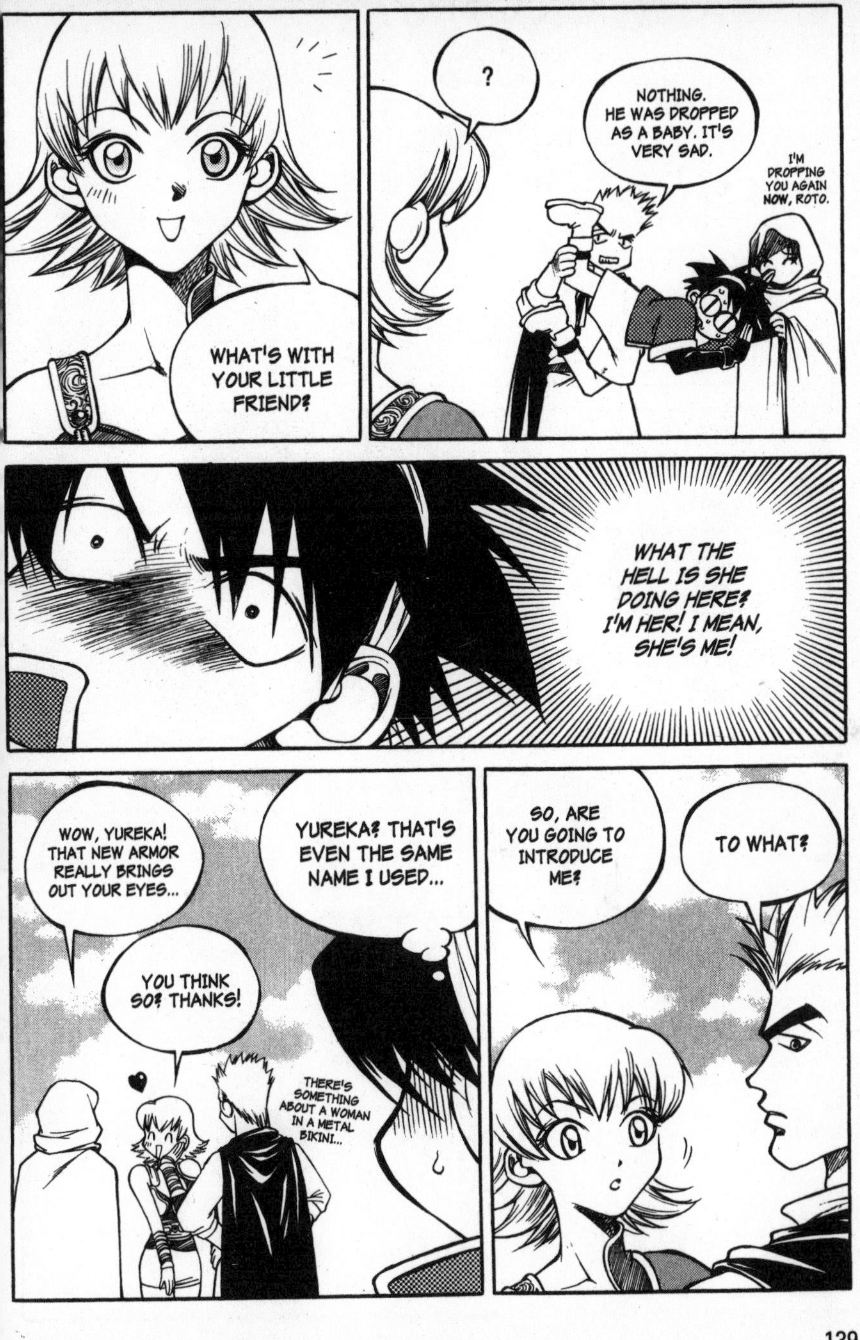
WHAT'S WITH YOUR LITTLE FRIEND?
?
NOTHING. HE WAS DROPPED AS A BABY. IT'S VERY SAD.
I'M DROPPING YOU AGAIN NOW, ROTO.
WHAT THE HELL IS SHE DOING HERE? I'M HER! I MEAN, SHE'S ME!
WOW, YUREKA! THAT NEW ARMOR REALLY BRINGS OUT YOUR EYES...
YUREKA? THAT'S EVEN THE SAME NAME I USED...
YOU THINK SO? THANKS!
THERE'S SOMETHING ABOUT A WOMAN IN A METAL BIKINI...
SO, ARE YOU GOING TO INTRODUCE ME?
TO WHAT?

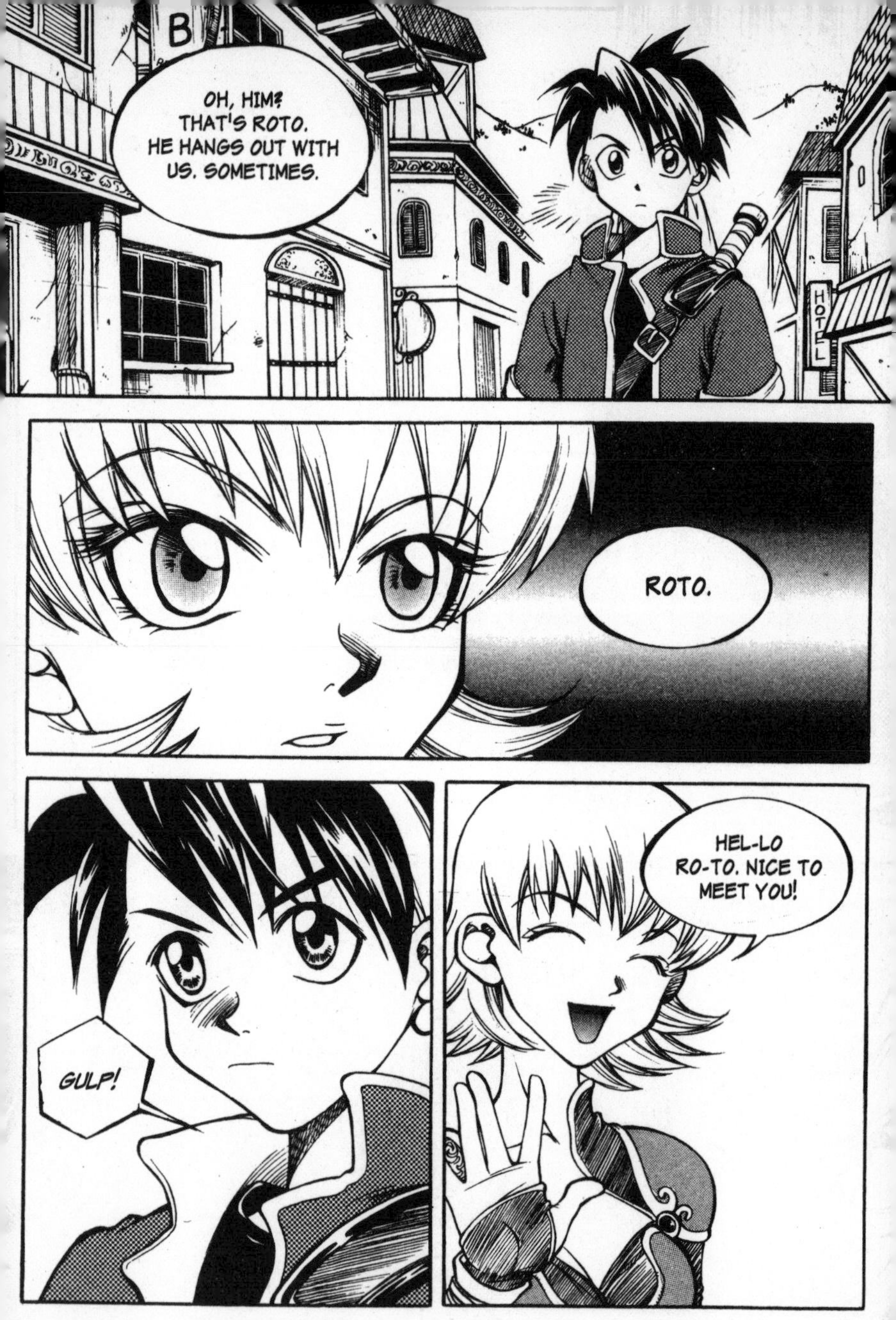
OH, HIM? THAT'S ROTO. HE HANGS OUT WITH US. SOMETIMES.
B
HOTEL
ROTO.
GULP!
HEL-LO RO-TO. NICE TO MEET YOU!

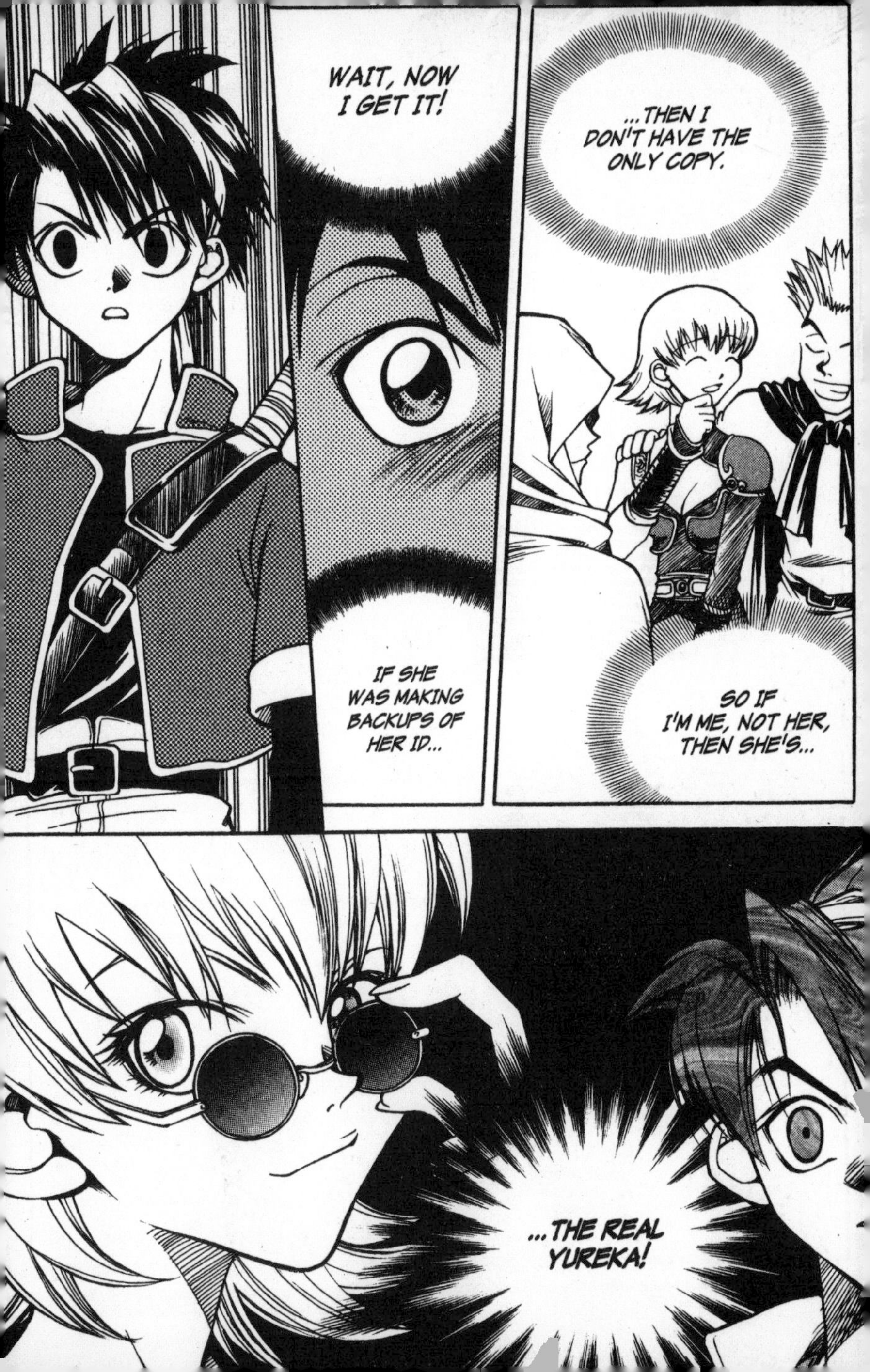
WAIT, NOW I GET IT!
IF SHE WAS MAKING BACKUPS OF HER ID...
...THEN I DON'T HAVE THE ONLY COPY.
SO IF I'M ME, NOT HER, THEN SHE'S...
...THE REAL YUREKA!

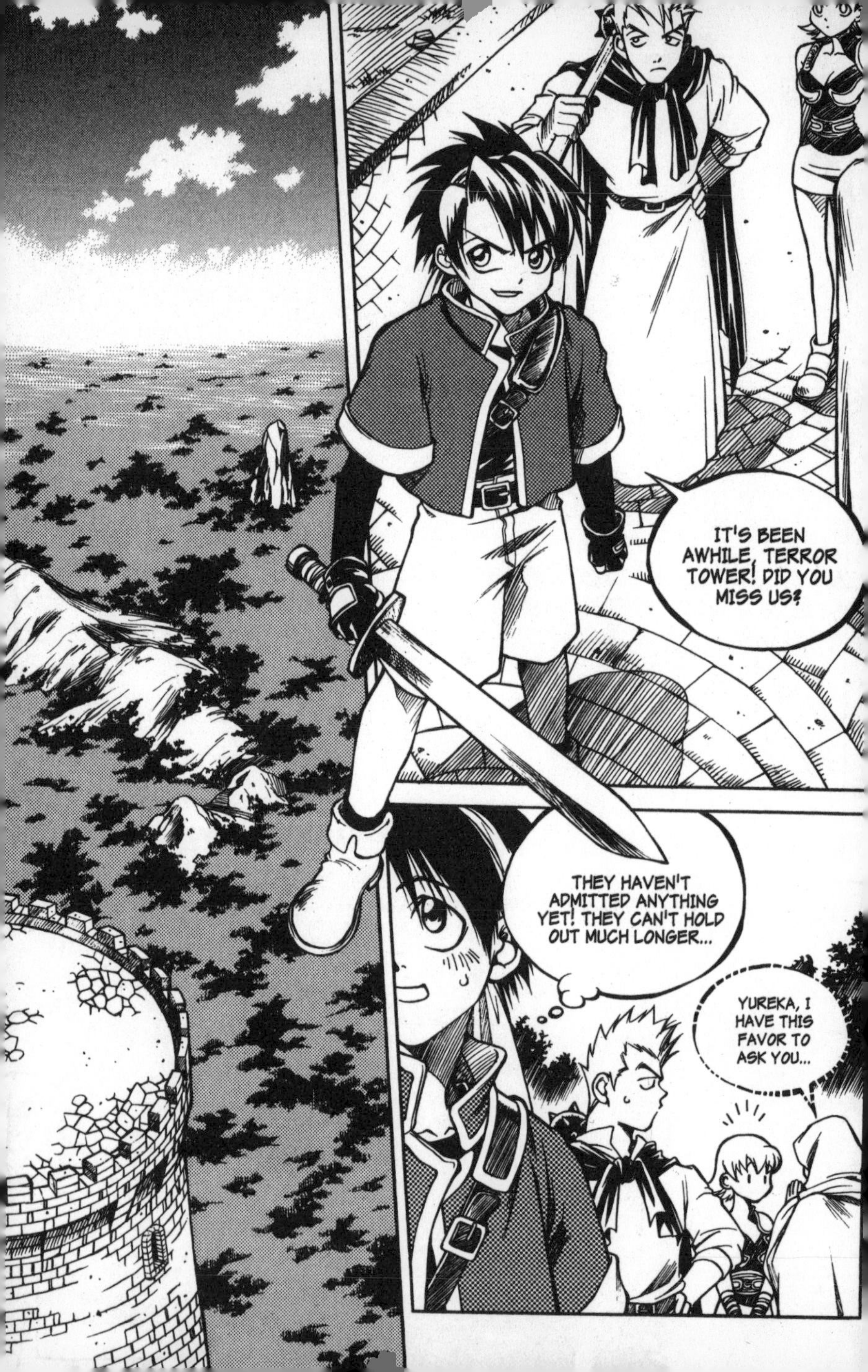
IT'S BEEN AWHILE, TERROR TOWER! DID YOU MISS US?
THEY HAVEN'T ADMITTED ANYTHING YET! THEY CAN'T HOLD OUT MUCH LONGER...
YUREKA, I HAVE THIS FAVOR TO ASK YOU...

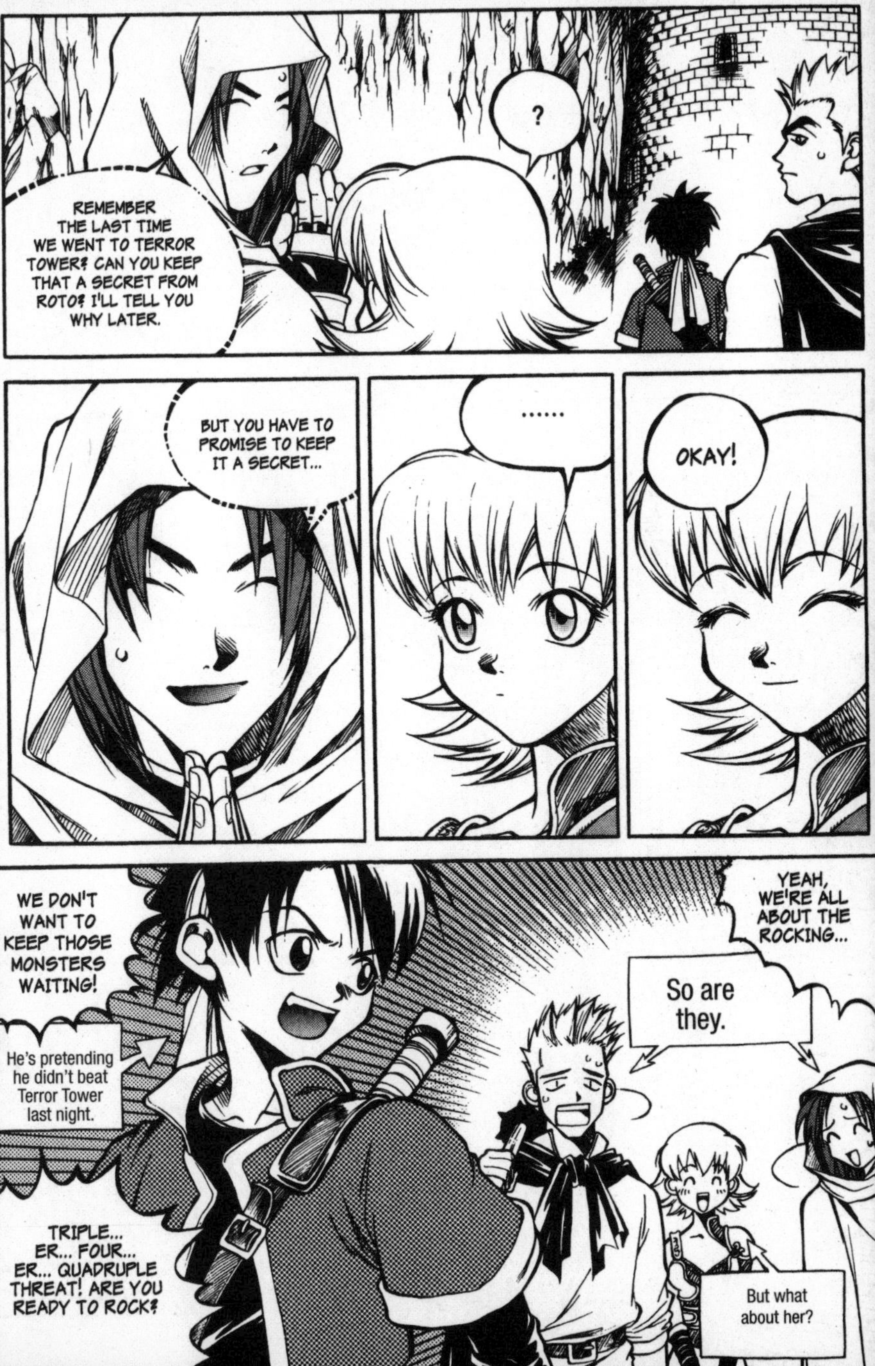

REMEMBER THE LAST TIME WE WENT TO TERROR TOWER? CAN YOU KEEP THAT A SECRET FROM ROTO? I'LL TELL YOU WHY LATER.
?
BUT YOU HAVE TO PROMISE TO KEEP IT A SECRET...
......
OKAY!
WE DON'T WANT TO KEEP THOSE MONSTERS WAITING!
He's pretending he didn't beat Terror Tower last night.
TRIPLE... ER... FOUR... ER... QUADRUPLE THREAT! ARE YOU READY TO ROCK?
YEAH, WE'RE ALL ABOUT THE ROCKING...
So are they.
But what about her?

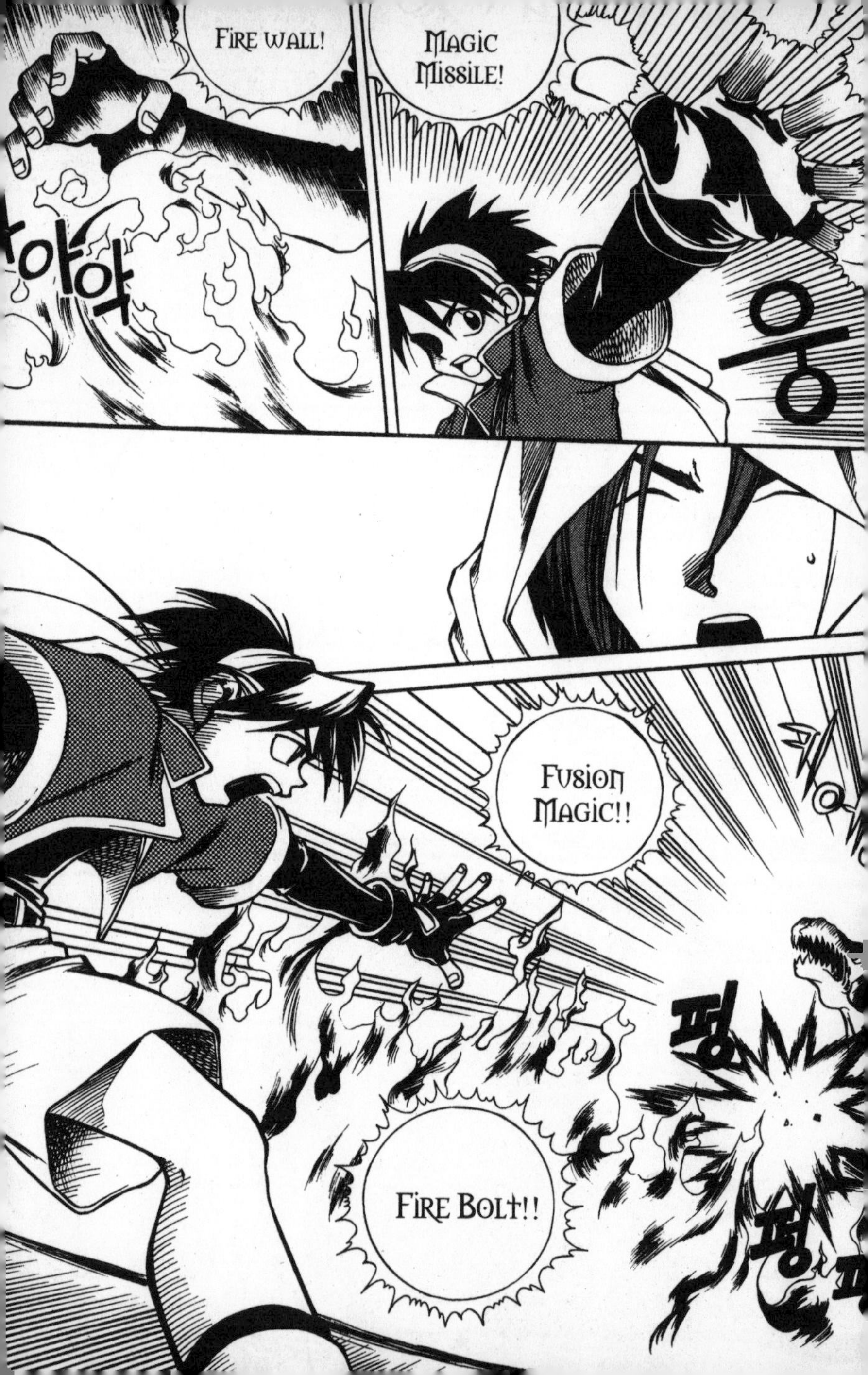

Fire wall!
아악
Magic Missile!
우웅
Fusion Magic!!
Fire Bolt!!
펑
펑

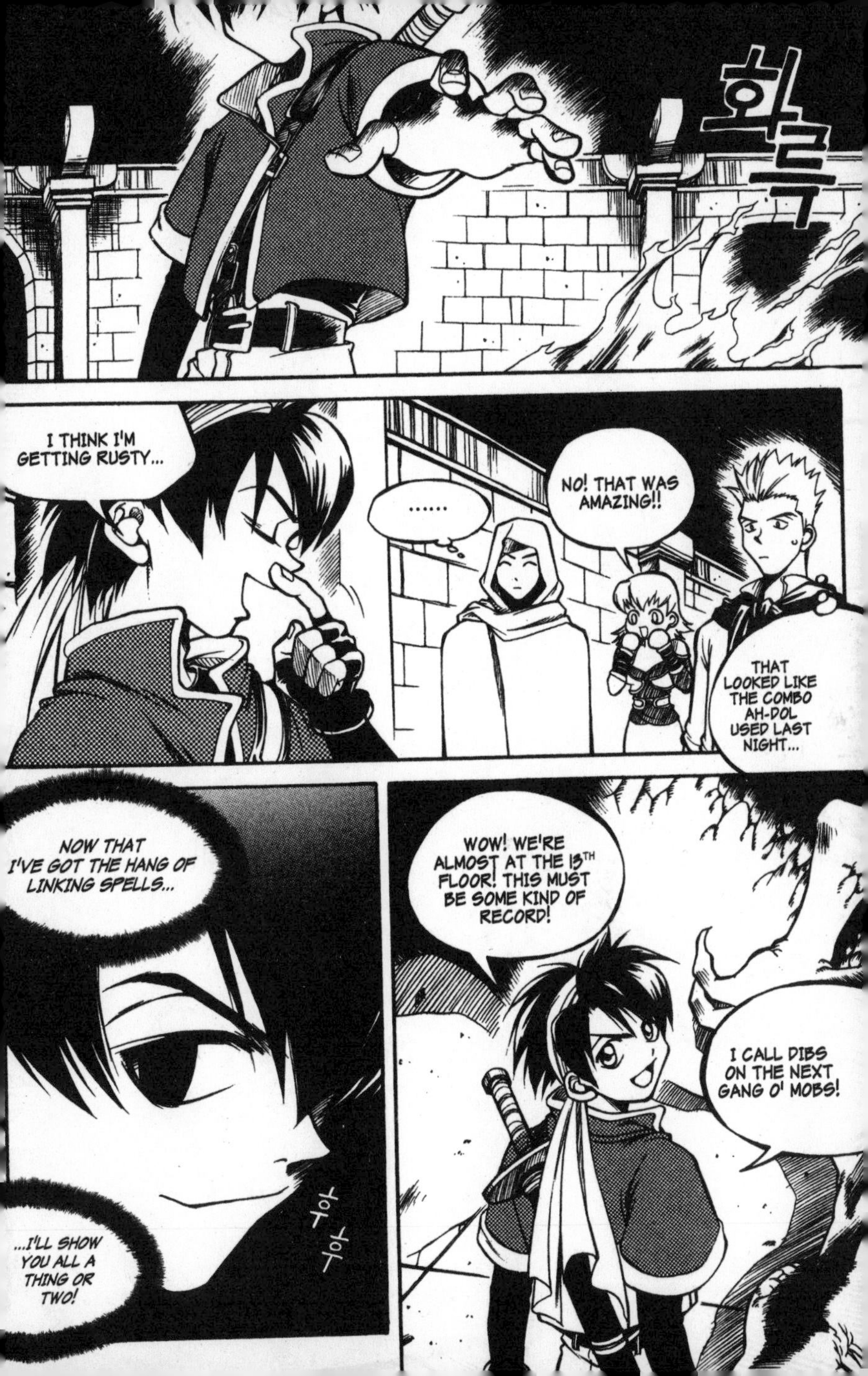
I THINK I'M GETTING RUSTY...
......
NO! THAT WAS AMAZING!!
THAT LOOKED LIKE THE COMBO AH-DOL USED LAST NIGHT...
NOW THAT I'VE GOT THE HANG OF LINKING SPELLS...
...I'LL SHOW YOU ALL A THING OR TWO!
WOW! WE'RE ALMOST AT THE 13TH FLOOR! THIS MUST BE SOME KIND OF RECORD!
I CALL DIBS ON THE NEXT GANG O' MOBS!

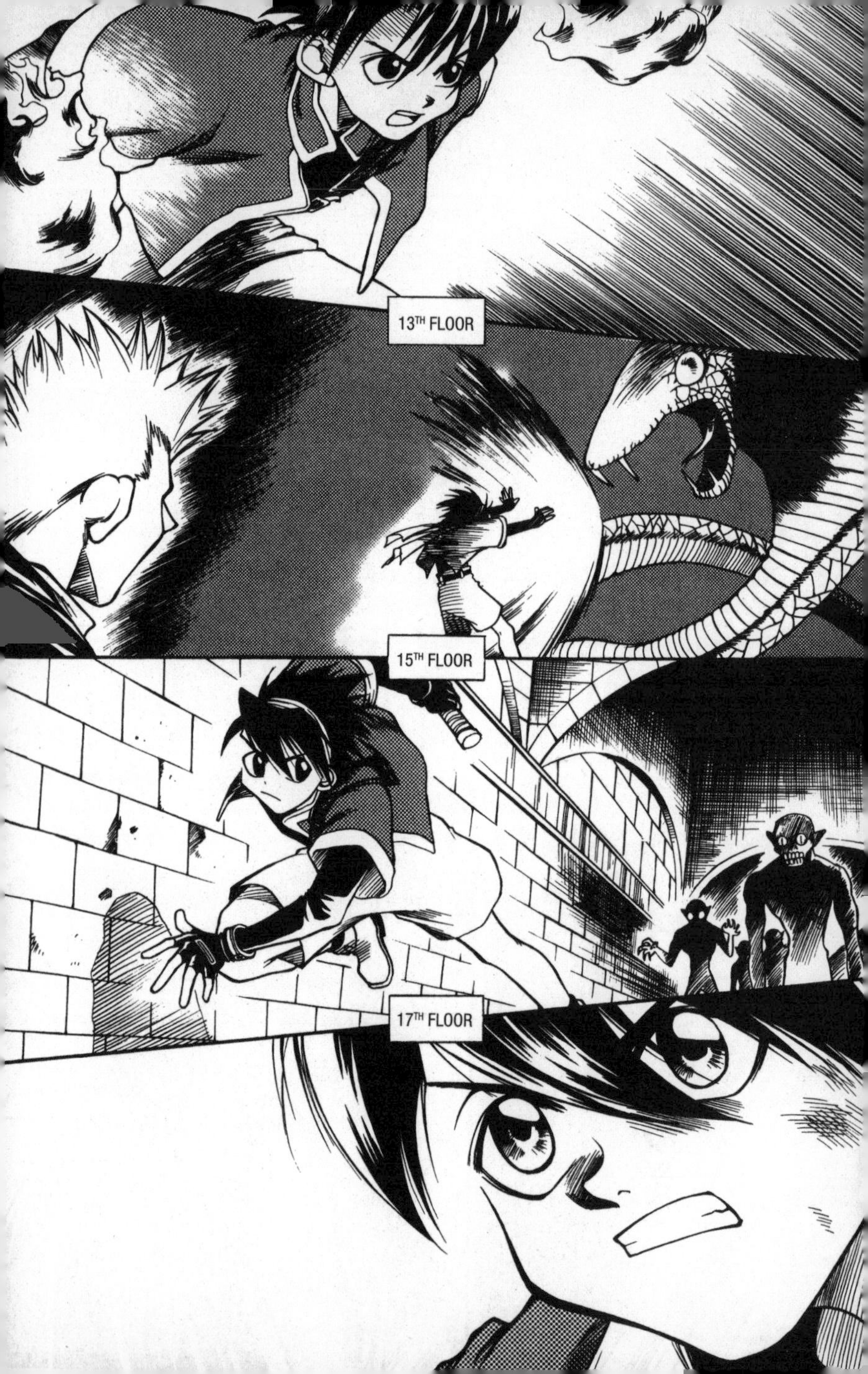
13TH FLOOR
15TH FLOOR
17TH FLOOR

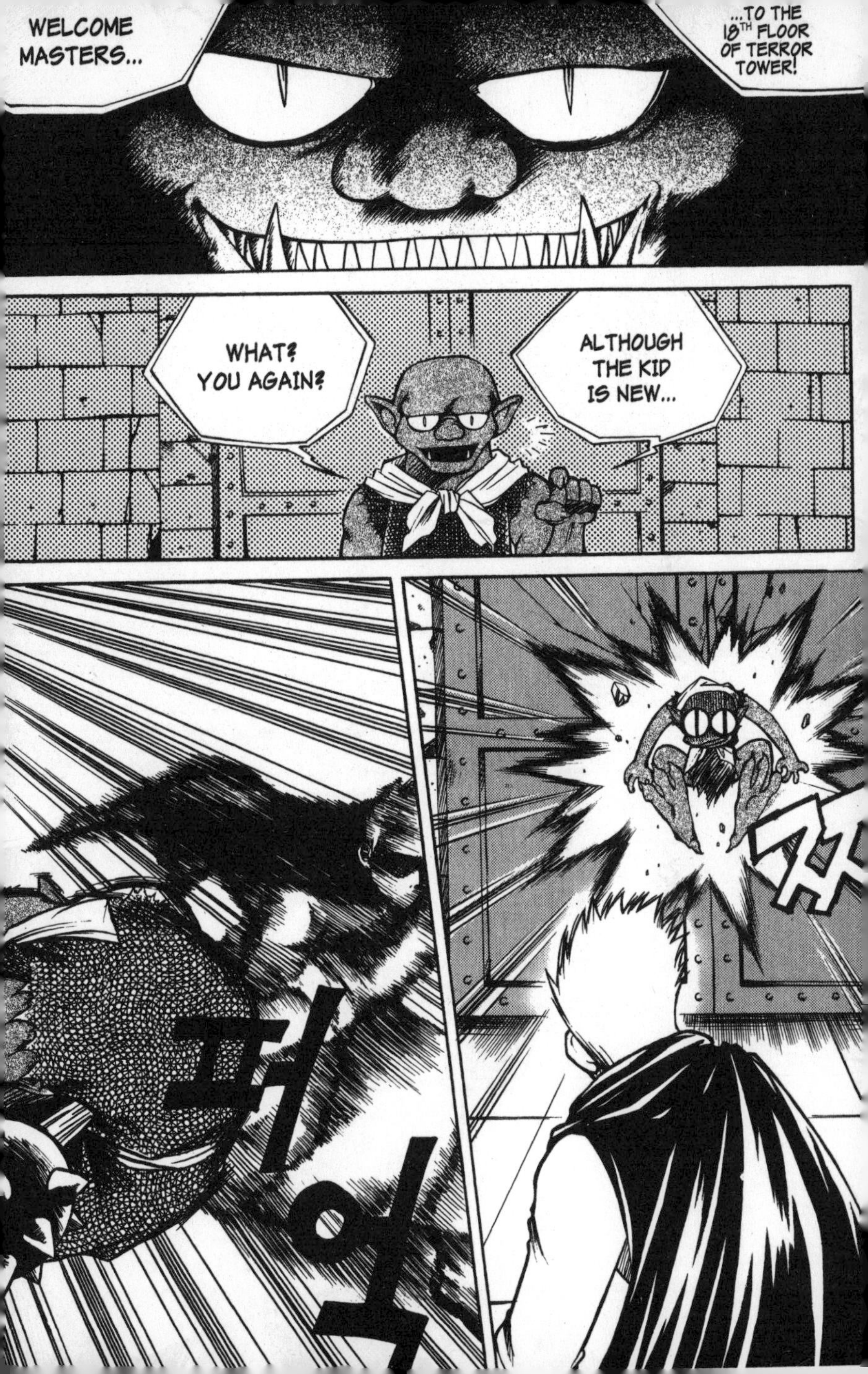
WELCOME MASTERS...
...TO THE 18TH FLOOR OF TERROR TOWER!
WHAT? YOU AGAIN?
ALTHOUGH THE KID IS NEW...

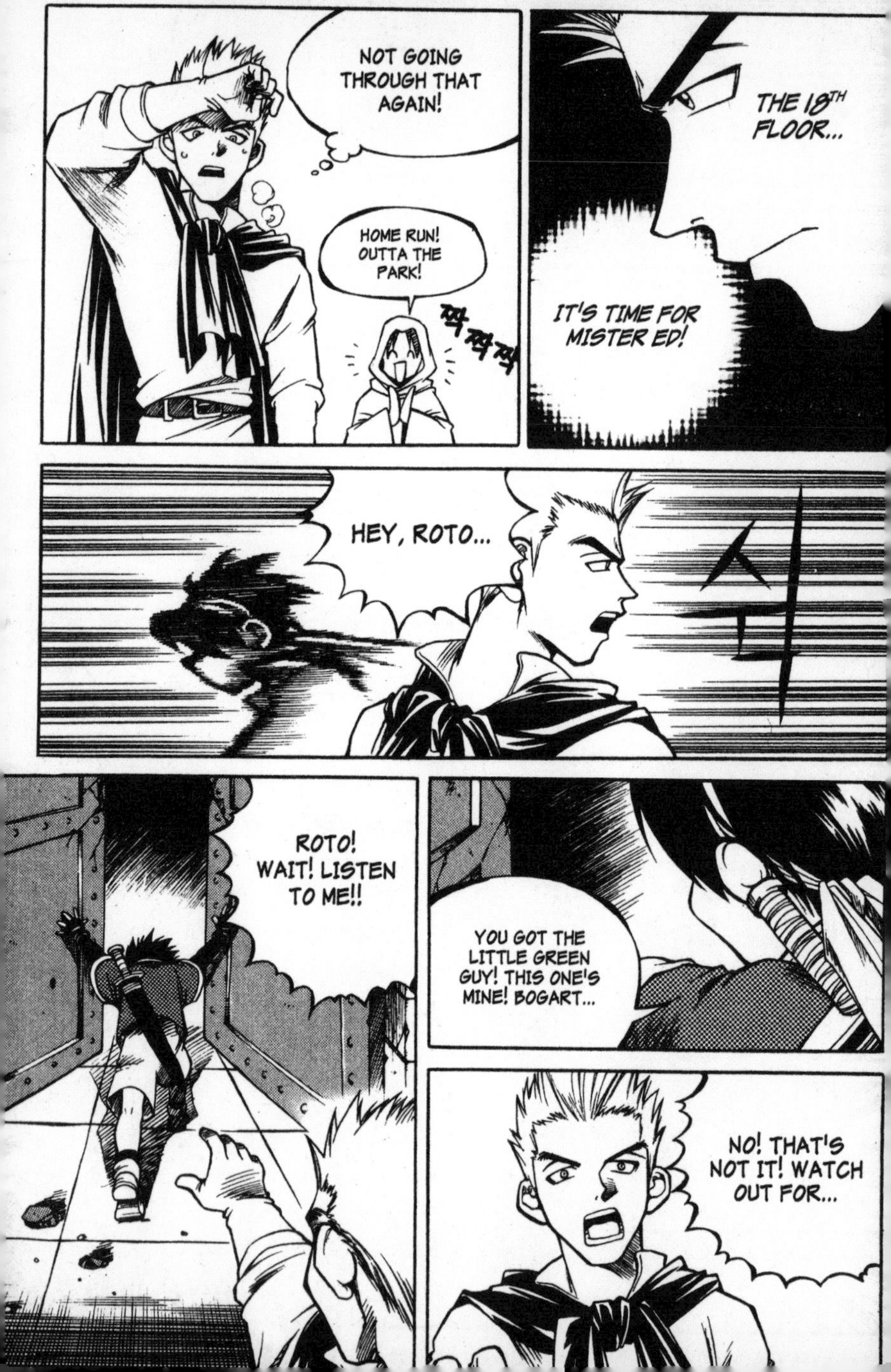

NOT GOING THROUGH THAT AGAIN!
HOME RUN! OUTTA THE PARK!
짝짝짝
THE 18TH FLOOR...
IT'S TIME FOR MISTER ED!
HEY, ROTO...
ROTO! WAIT! LISTEN TO ME!!
YOU GOT THE LITTLE GREEN GUY! THIS ONE'S MINE! BOGART...
NO! THAT'S NOT IT! WATCH OUT FOR...

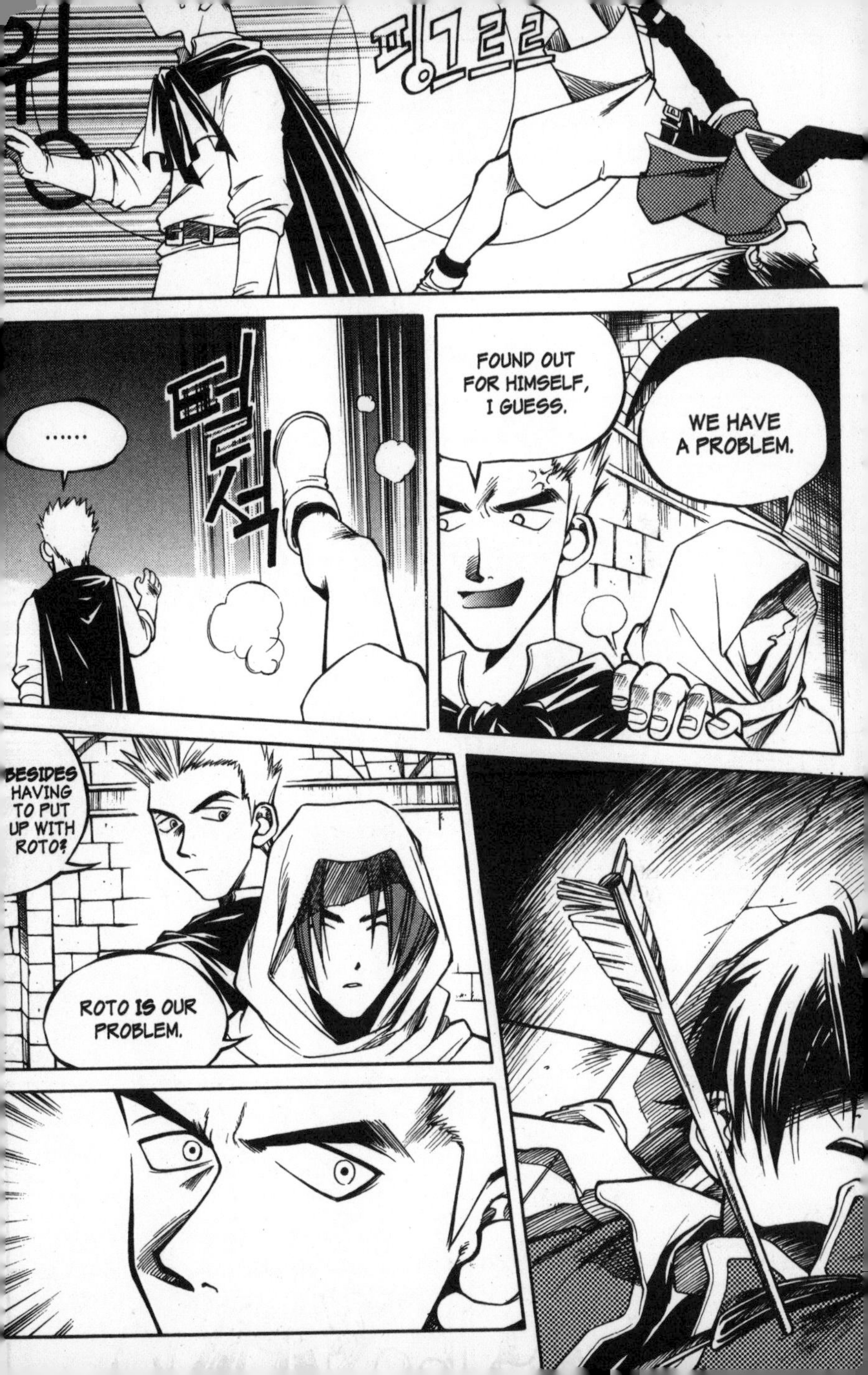
......
FOUND OUT FOR HIMSELF, I GUESS.
WE HAVE A PROBLEM.
BESIDES HAVING TO PUT UP WITH ROTO?
ROTO IS OUR PROBLEM.

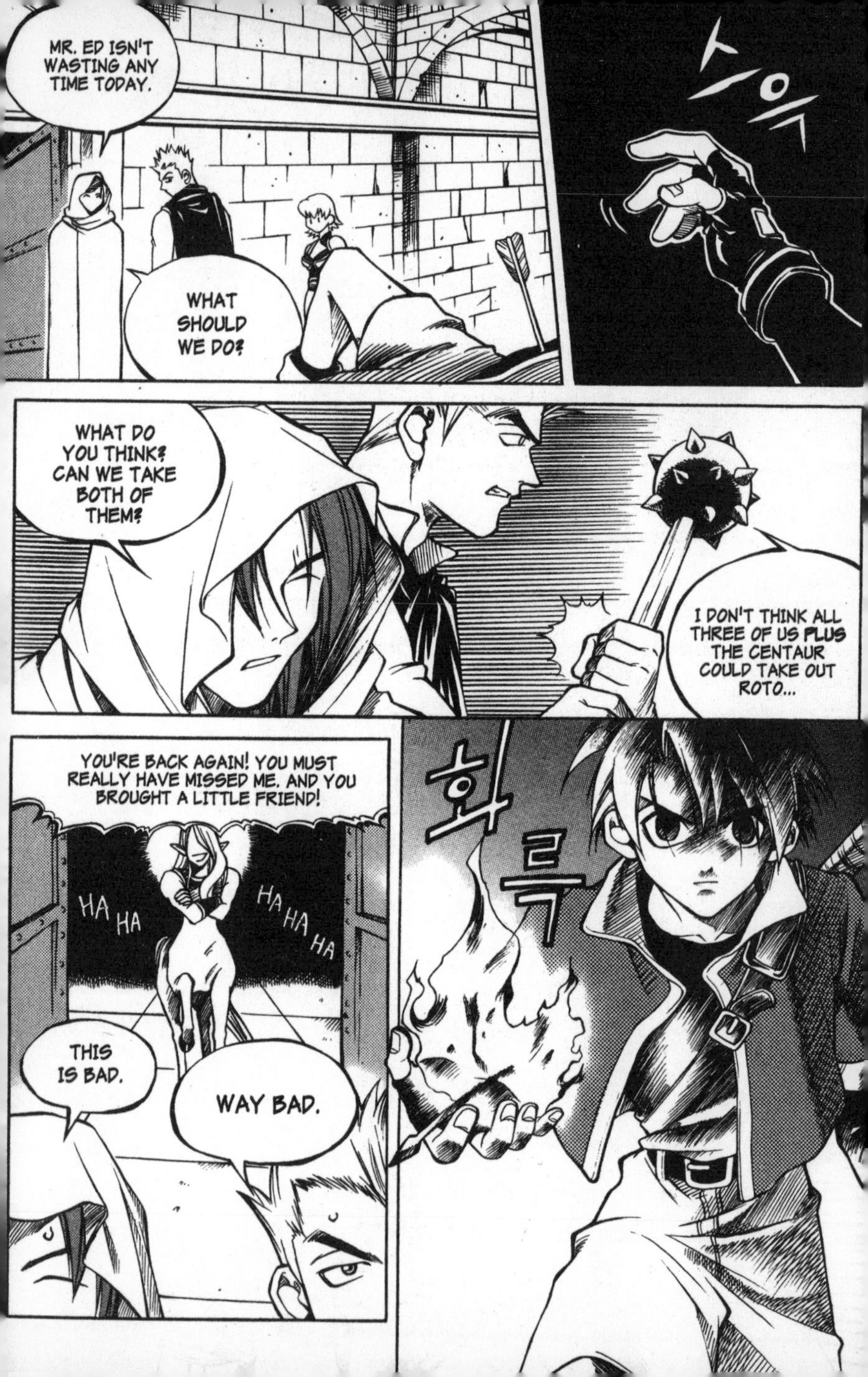
MR. ED ISN'T WASTING ANY TIME TODAY.
WHAT SHOULD WE DO?
WHAT DO YOU THINK? CAN WE TAKE BOTH OF THEM?
I DON'T THINK ALL THREE OF US PLUS THE CENTAUR COULD TAKE OUT ROTO...
YOU'RE BACK AGAIN! YOU MUST REALLY HAVE MISSED ME. AND YOU BROUGHT A LITTLE FRIEND!
HA HA
HA HA HA HA
THIS IS BAD.
WAY BAD.

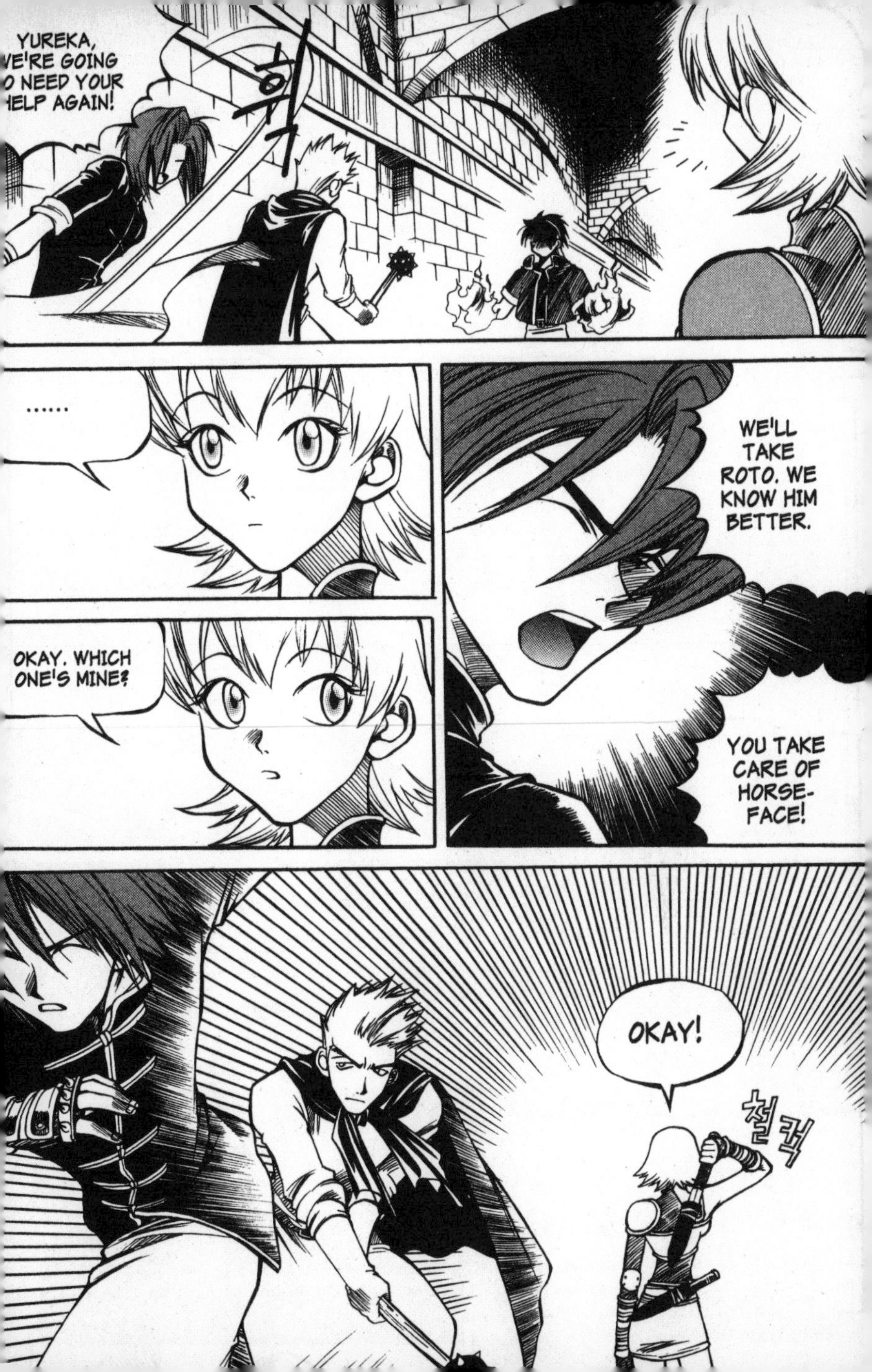
YUREKA, WE'RE GOING O NEED YOUR HELP AGAIN!
......
OKAY. WHICH ONE'S MINE?
WE'LL TAKE ROTO. WE KNOW HIM BETTER.
YOU TAKE CARE OF HORSE-FACE!
OKAY!
철컥

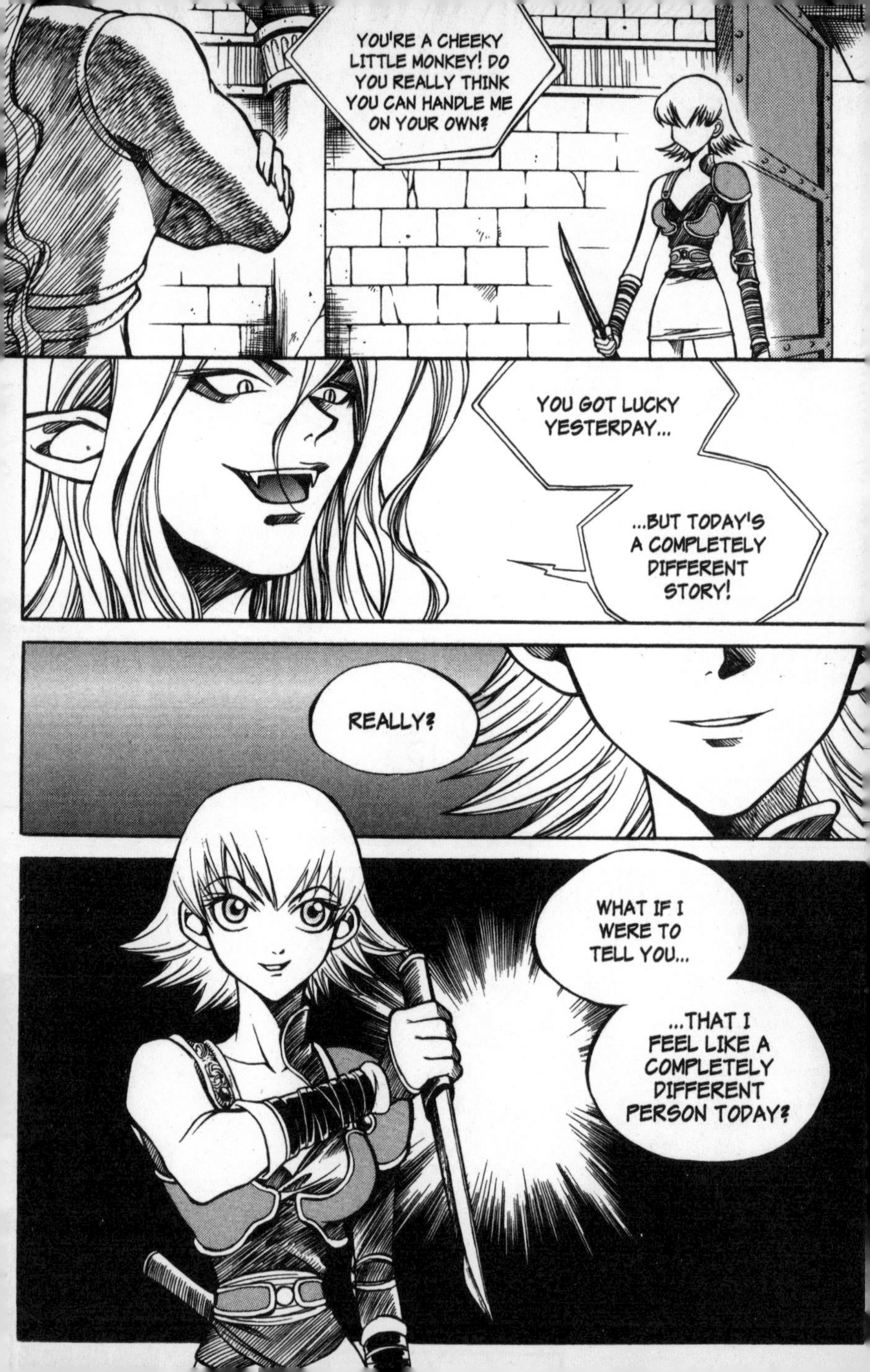
YOU'RE A CHEEKY LITTLE MONKEY! DO YOU REALLY THINK YOU CAN HANDLE ME ON YOUR OWN?
YOU GOT LUCKY YESTERDAY...
...BUT TODAY'S A COMPLETELY DIFFERENT STORY!
REALLY?
WHAT IF I WERE TO TELL YOU...
...THAT I FEEL LIKE A COMPLETELY DIFFERENT PERSON TODAY?

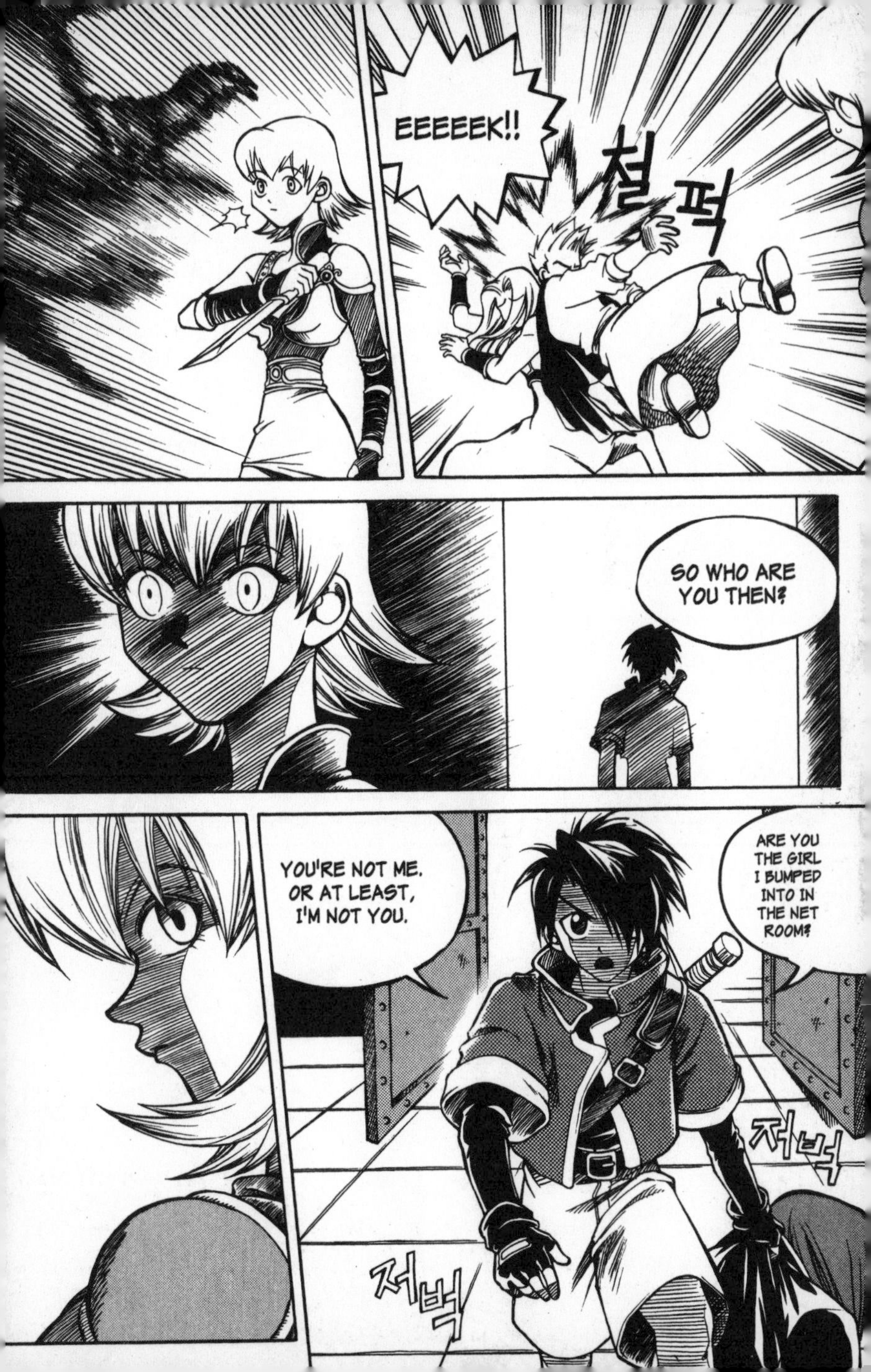
EEEEEK!!
철퍽
SO WHO ARE YOU THEN?
YOU'RE NOT ME. OR AT LEAST, I'M NOT YOU.
ARE YOU THE GIRL I BUMPED INTO IN THE NET ROOM?
저벅
저벅

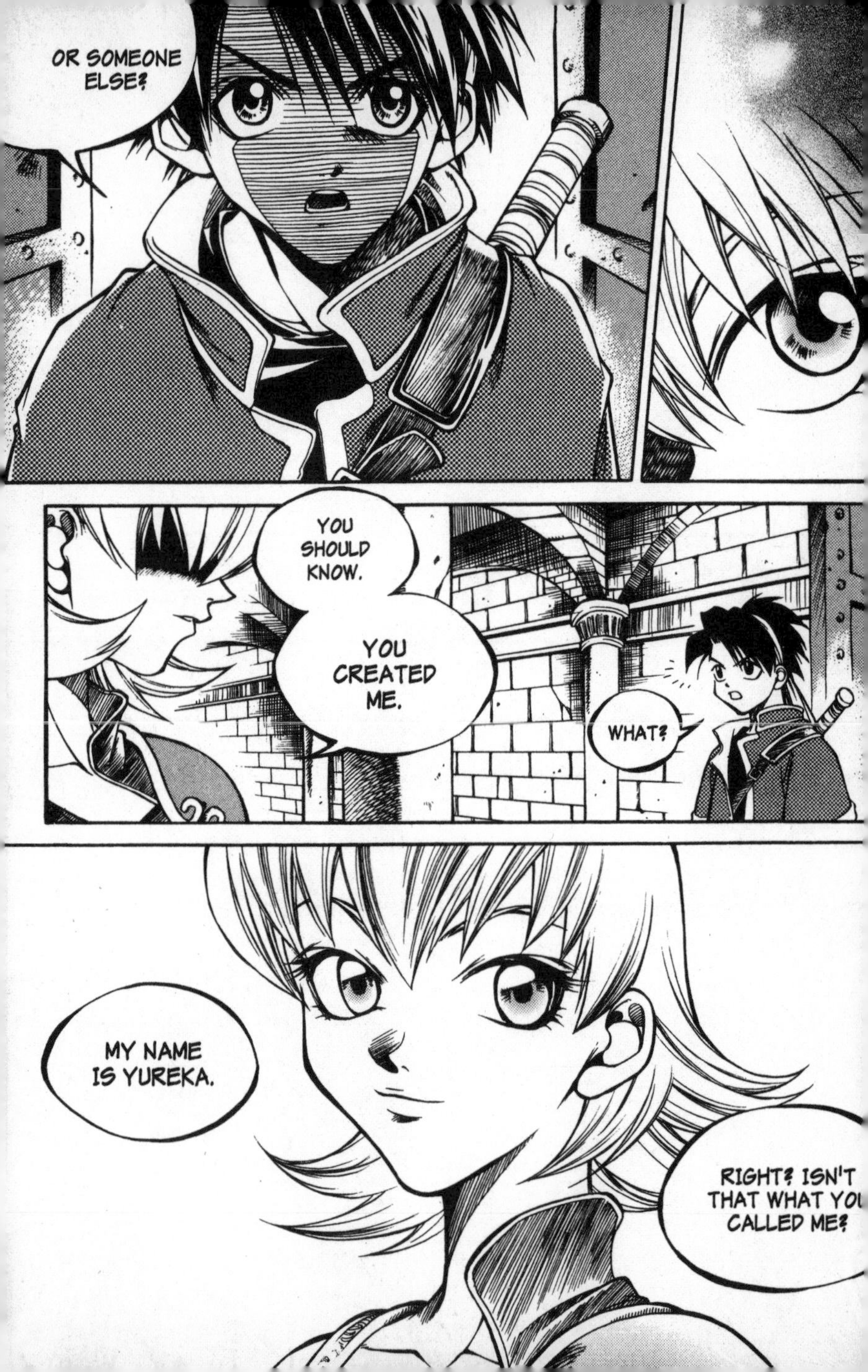
OR SOMEONE ELSE?
YOU SHOULD KNOW.
YOU CREATED ME.
WHAT?
MY NAME IS YUREKA.
RIGHT? ISN'T THAT WHAT YOU CALLED ME?

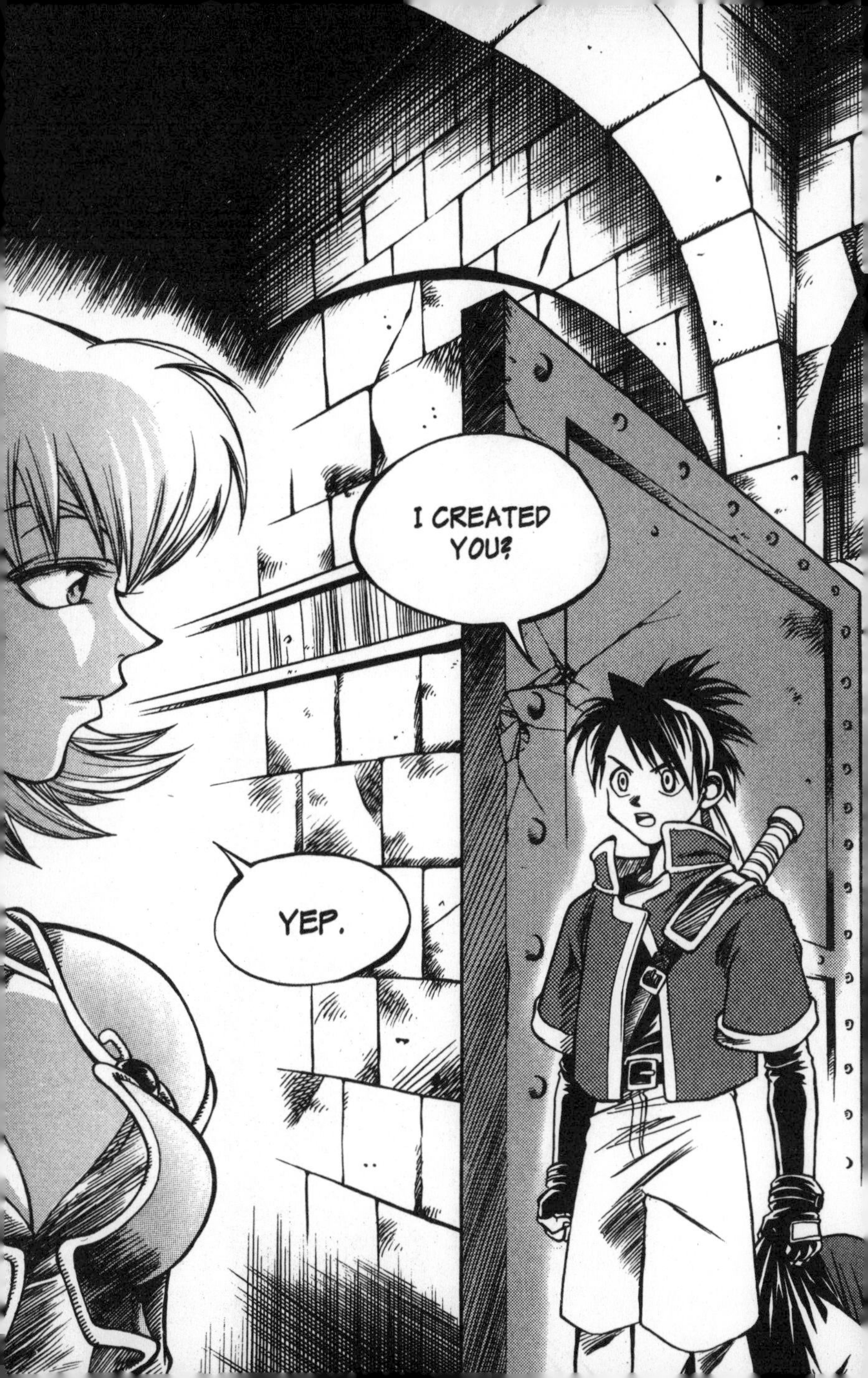
I CREATED YOU?
YEP.

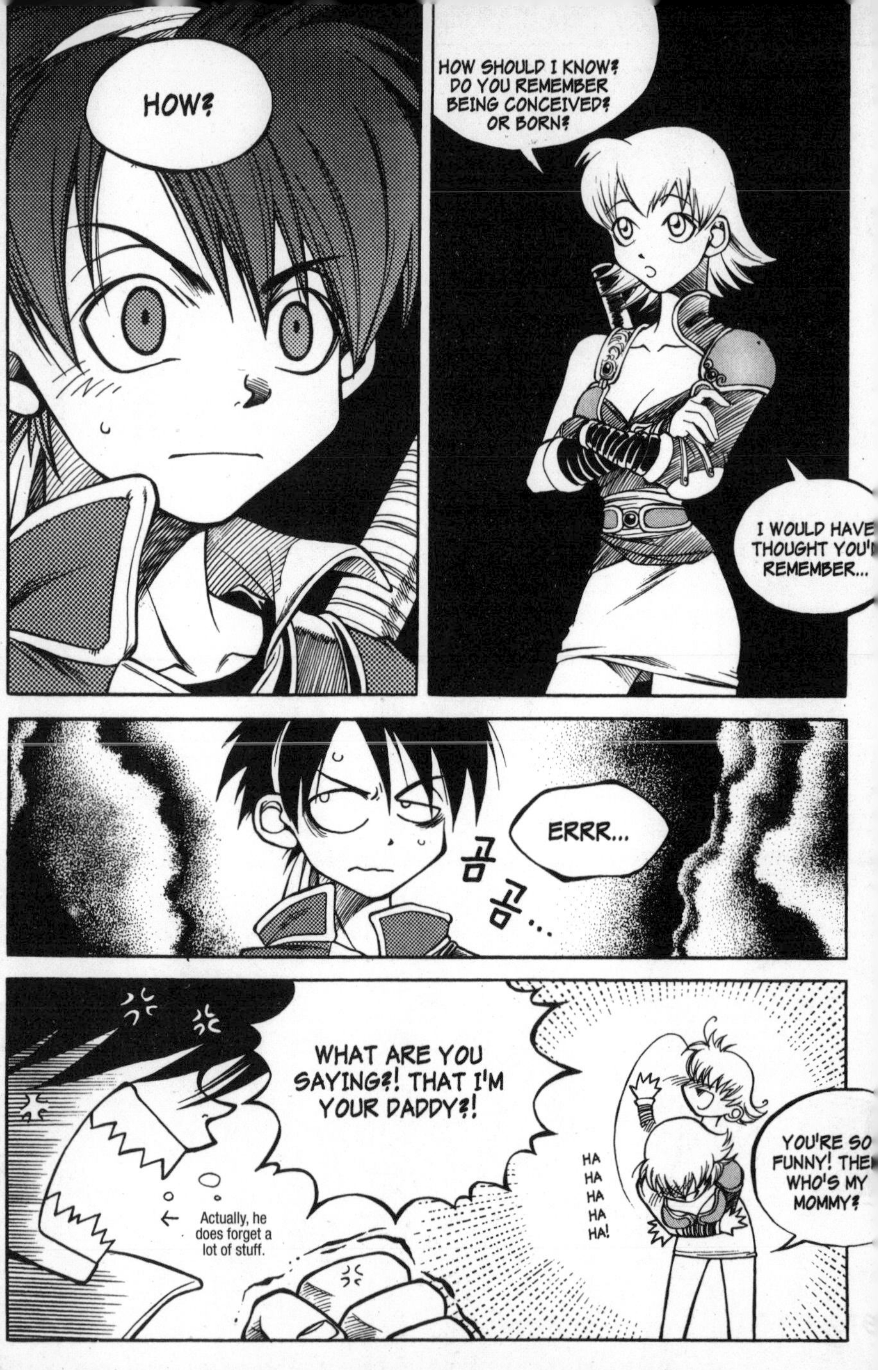
HOW?
HOW SHOULD I KNOW? DO YOU REMEMBER BEING CONCEIVED? OR BORN?
I WOULD HAVE THOUGHT YOU' REMEMBER...
ERRR...
곰 곰...
WHAT ARE YOU SAYING?! THAT I'M YOUR DADDY?!
Actually, he does forget a lot of stuff.
HA HA HA HA HA!
YOU'RE SO FUNNY! THE WHO'S MY MOMMY?

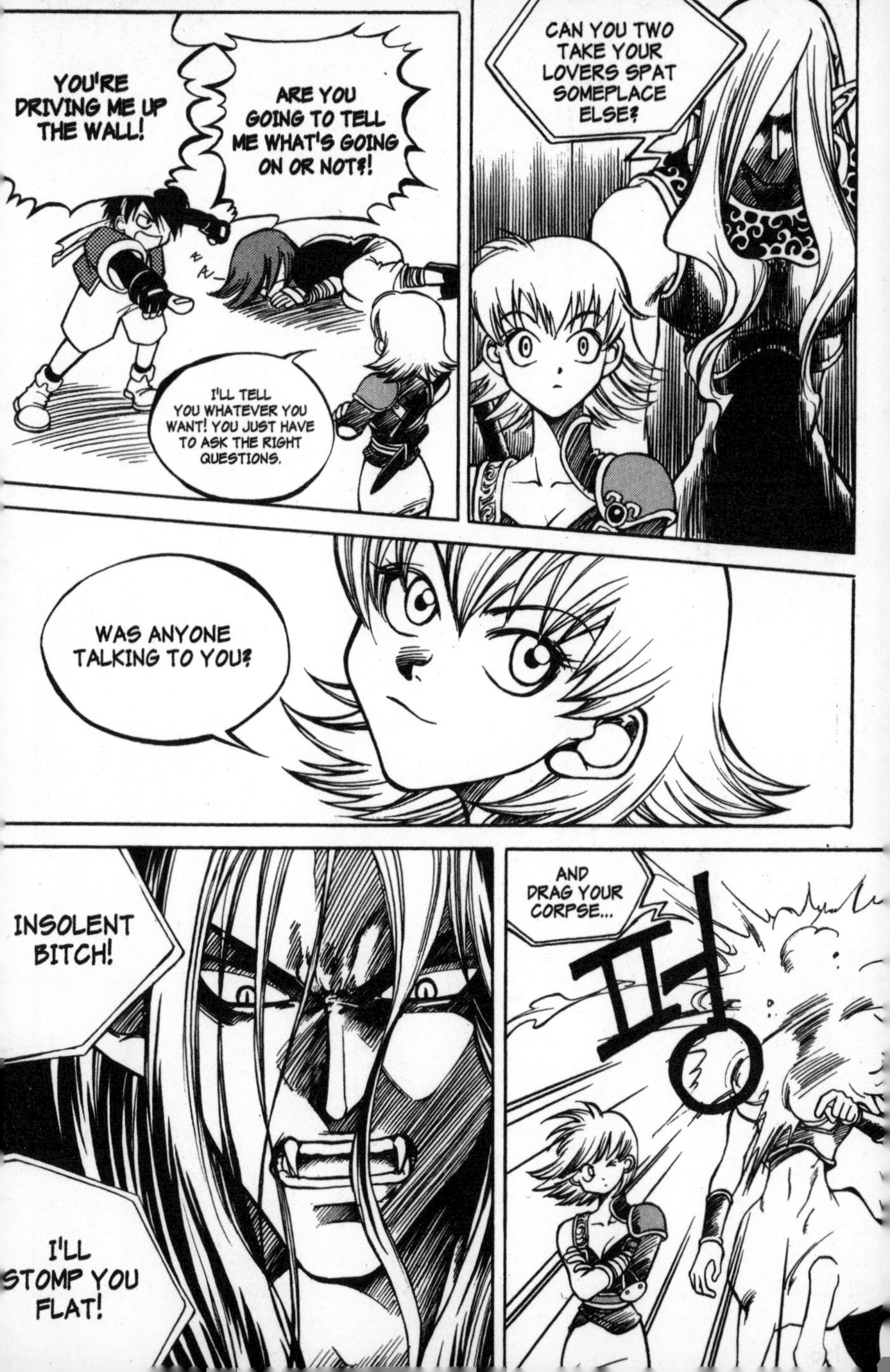
YOU'RE DRIVING ME UP THE WALL!
ARE YOU GOING TO TELL ME WHAT'S GOING ON OR NOT?!
I'LL TELL YOU WHATEVER YOU WANT! YOU JUST HAVE TO ASK THE RIGHT QUESTIONS.
CAN YOU TWO TAKE YOUR LOVERS SPAT SOMEPLACE ELSE?
WAS ANYONE TALKING TO YOU?
INSOLENT BITCH!
I'LL STOMP YOU FLAT!
AND DRAG YOUR CORPSE...

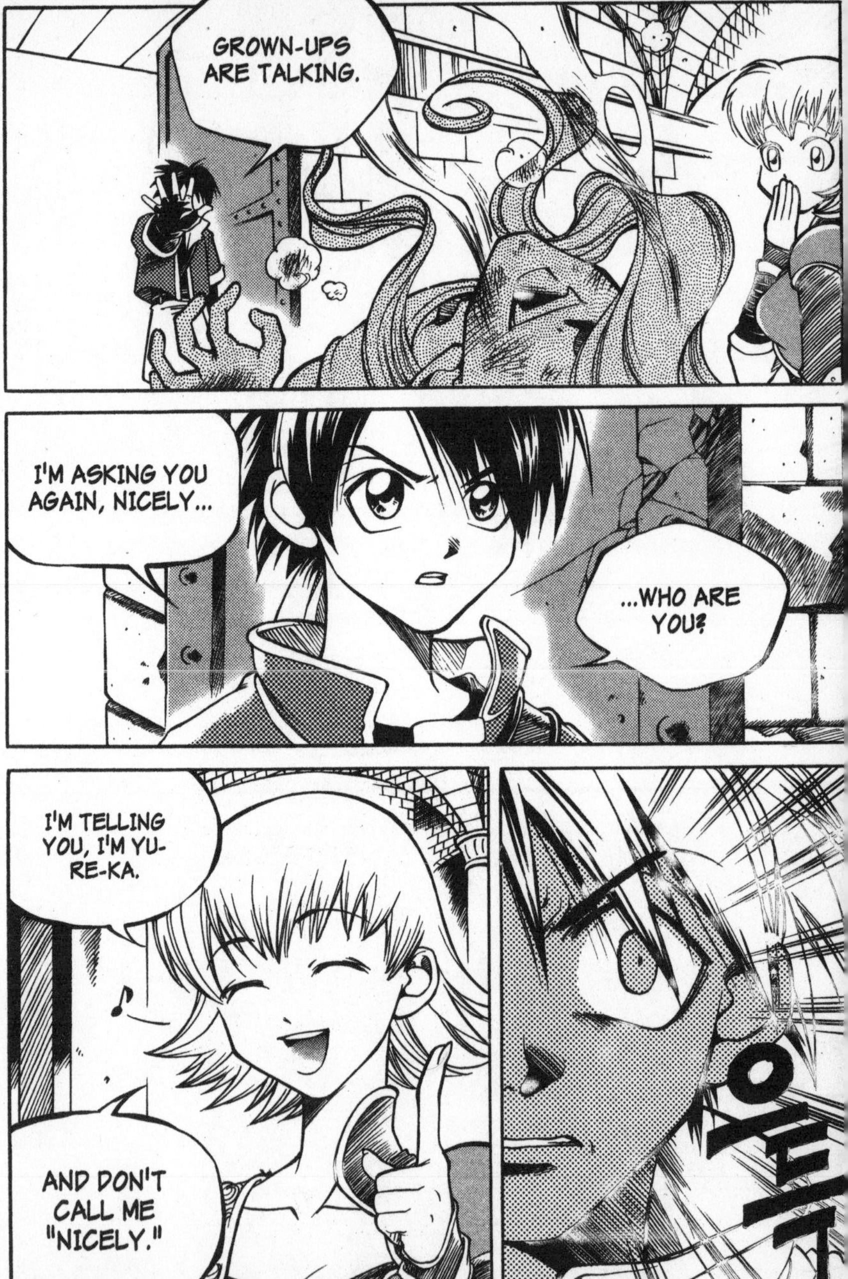
GROWN-UPS ARE TALKING.
I'M ASKING YOU AGAIN, NICELY...
...WHO ARE YOU?
I'M TELLING YOU, I'M YU-RE-KA.
AND DON'T CALL ME "NICELY."

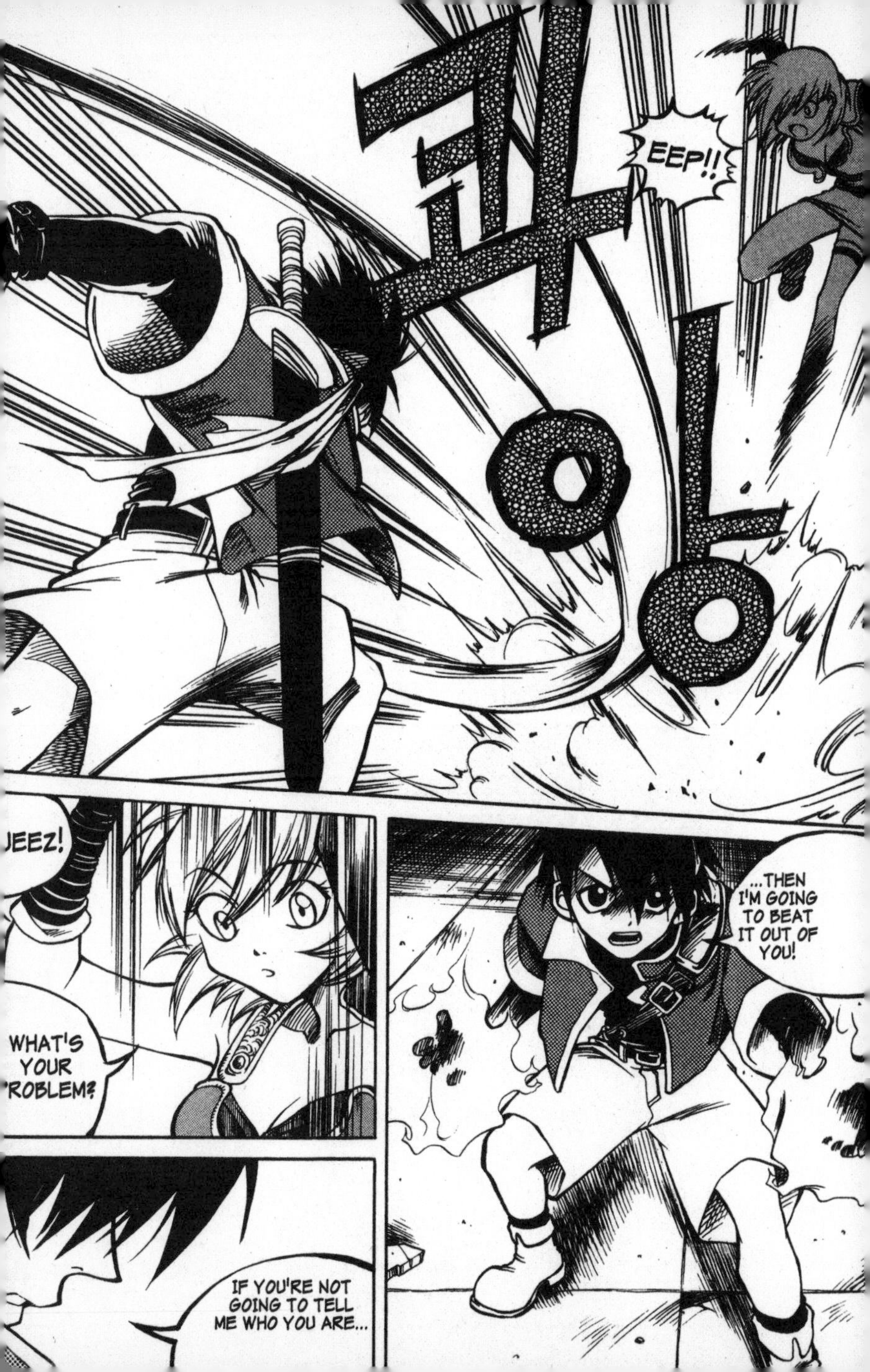
EEP!!
JEEZ!
WHAT'S YOUR PROBLEM?
IF YOU'RE NOT GOING TO TELL ME WHO YOU ARE...
...THEN I'M GOING TO BEAT IT OUT OF YOU!

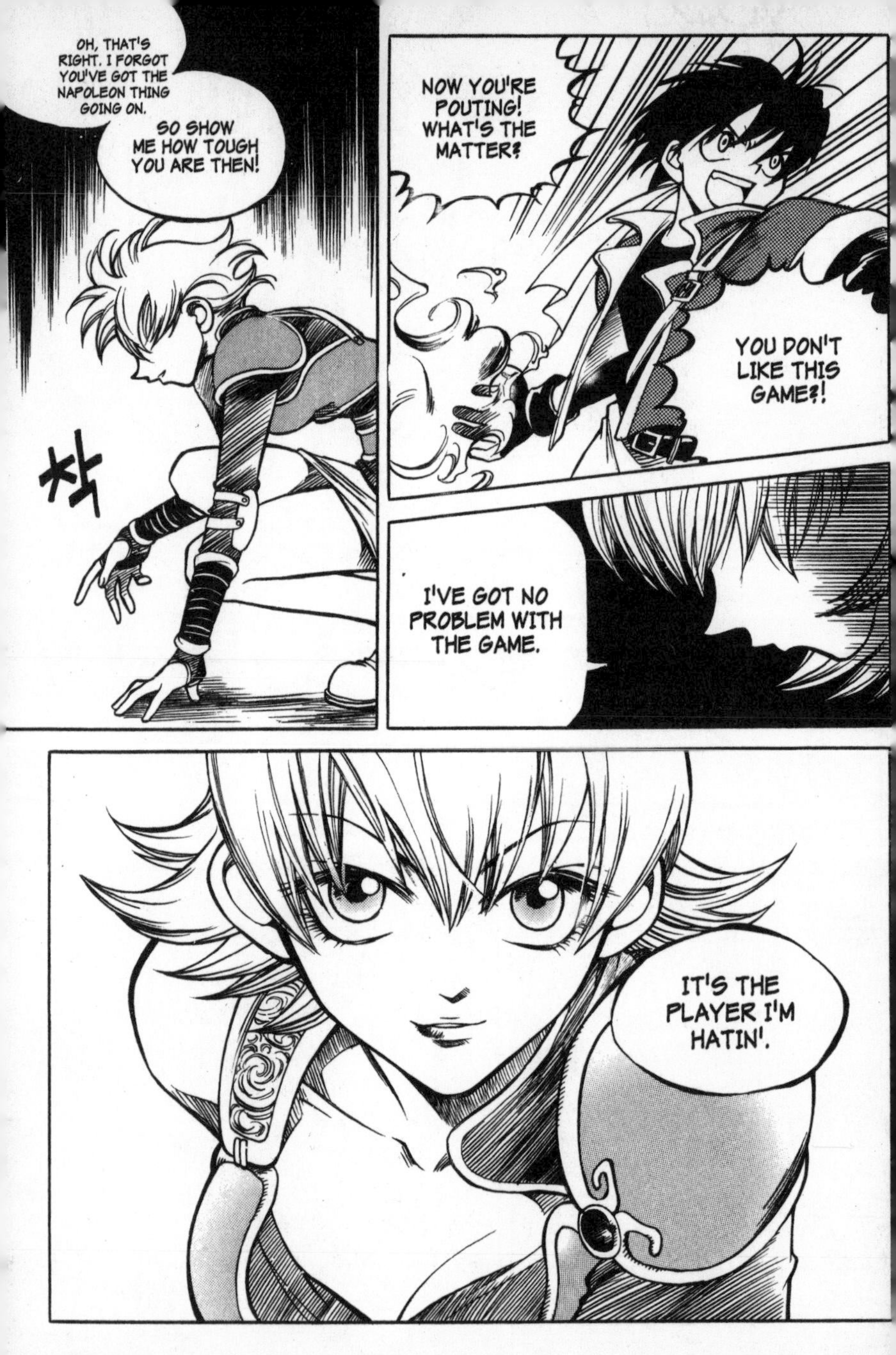
OH, THAT'S RIGHT. I FORGOT YOU'VE GOT THE NAPOLEON THING GOING ON.
SO SHOW ME HOW TOUGH YOU ARE THEN!
NOW YOU'RE POUTING! WHAT'S THE MATTER?
YOU DON'T LIKE THIS GAME?!
I'VE GOT NO PROBLEM WITH THE GAME.
IT'S THE PLAYER I'M HATIN'.

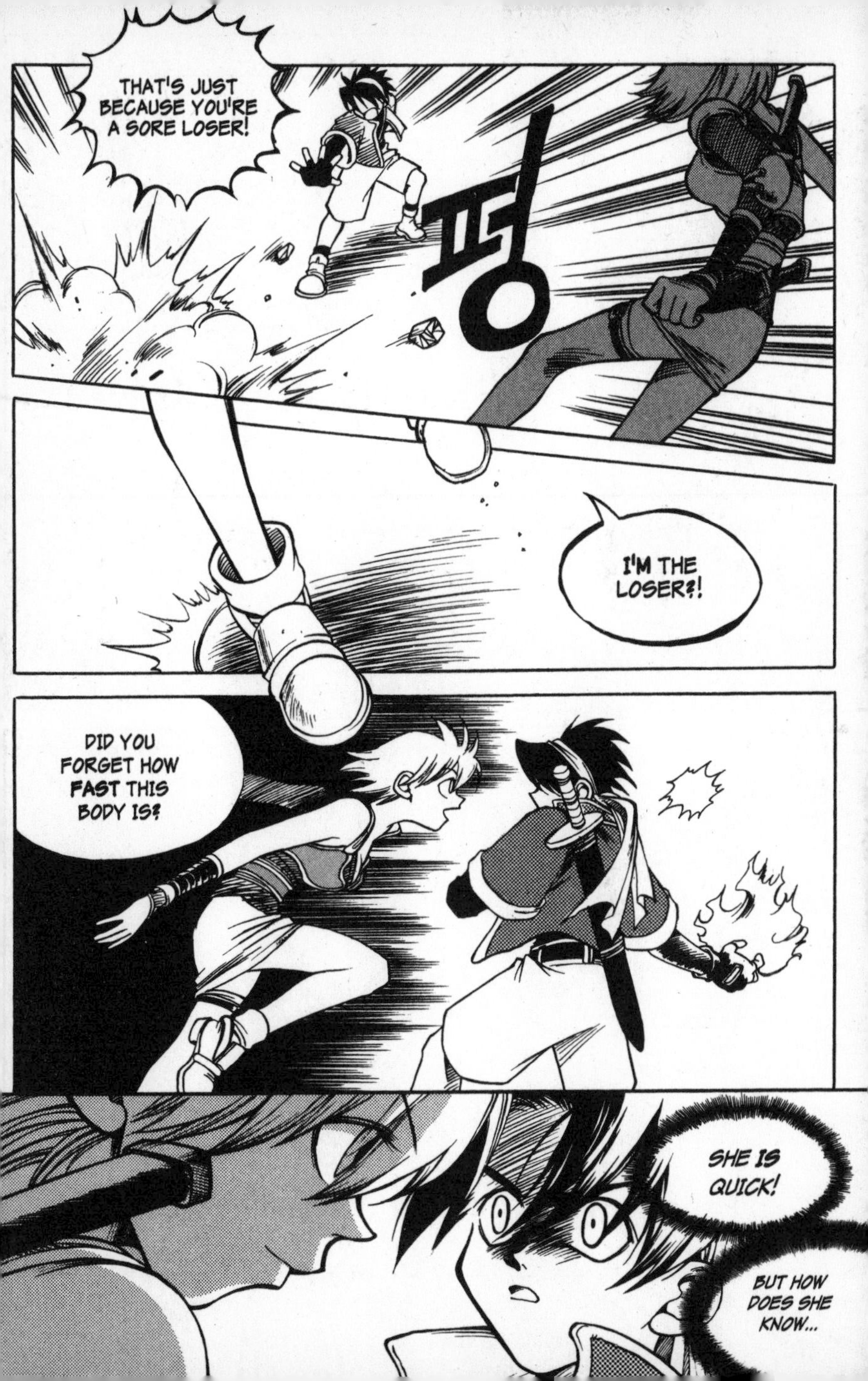
THAT'S JUST BECAUSE YOU'RE A SORE LOSER!
I'M THE LOSER?!
DID YOU FORGET HOW FAST THIS BODY IS?
SHE IS QUICK!
BUT HOW DOES SHE KNOW...

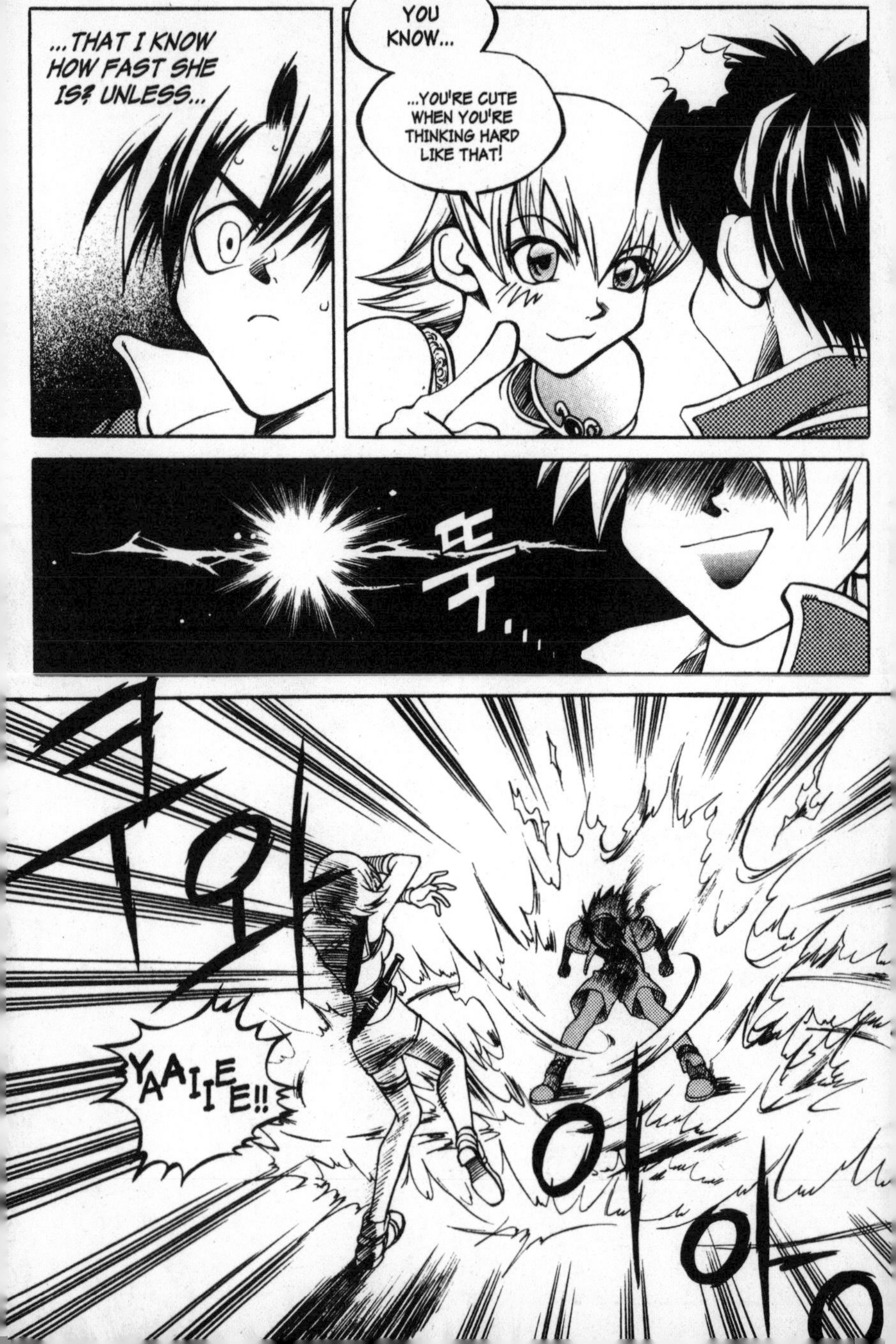
...THAT I KNOW HOW FAST SHE IS? UNLESS...
YOU KNOW...
...YOU'RE CUTE WHEN YOU'RE THINKING HARD LIKE THAT!
뚝...
YAAIIEE!!

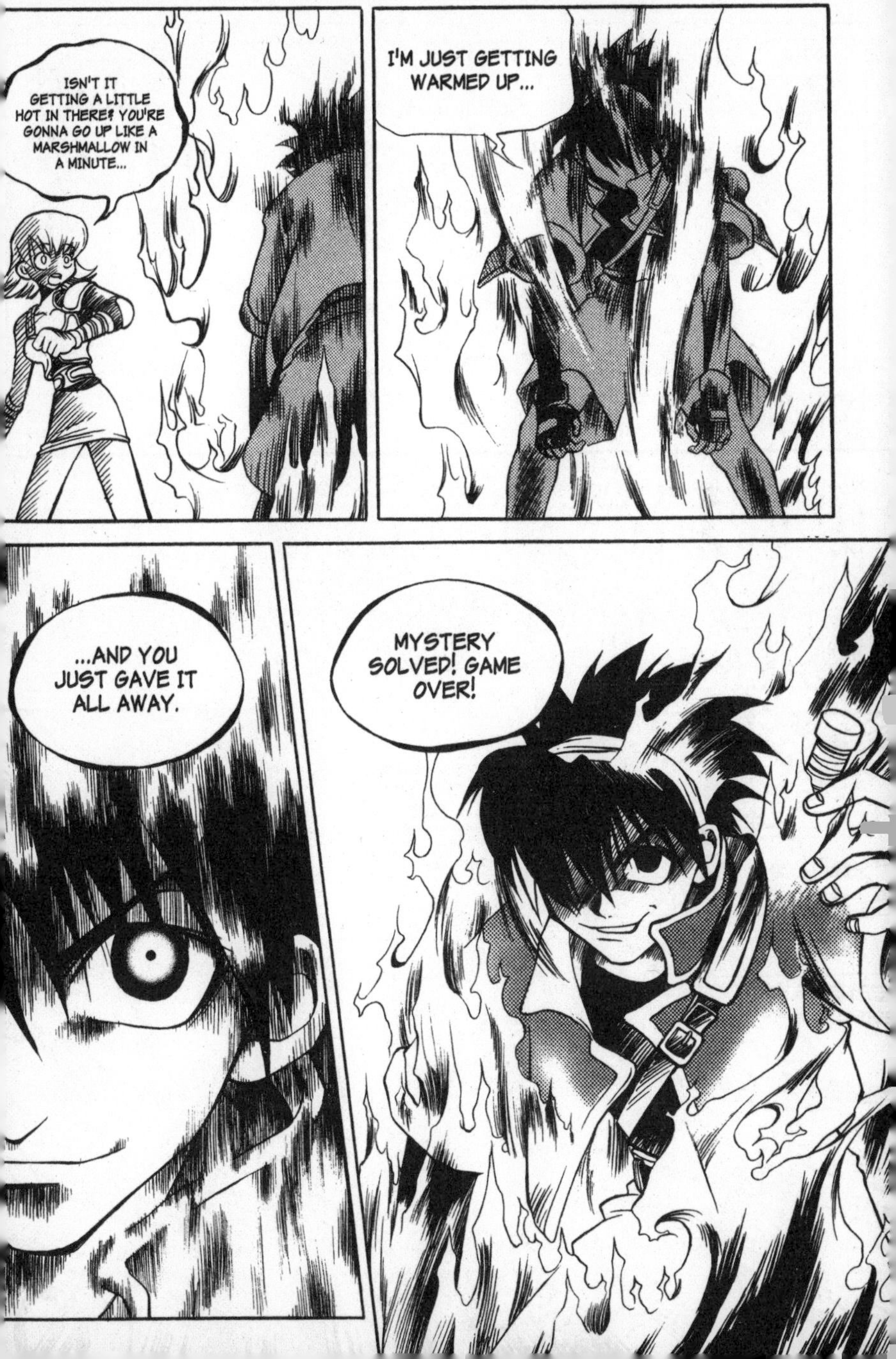
ISN'T IT GETTING A LITTLE HOT IN THERE? YOU'RE GONNA GO UP LIKE A MARSHMALLOW IN A MINUTE...
I'M JUST GETTING WARMED UP...
...AND YOU JUST GAVE IT ALL AWAY.
MYSTERY SOLVED! GAME OVER!

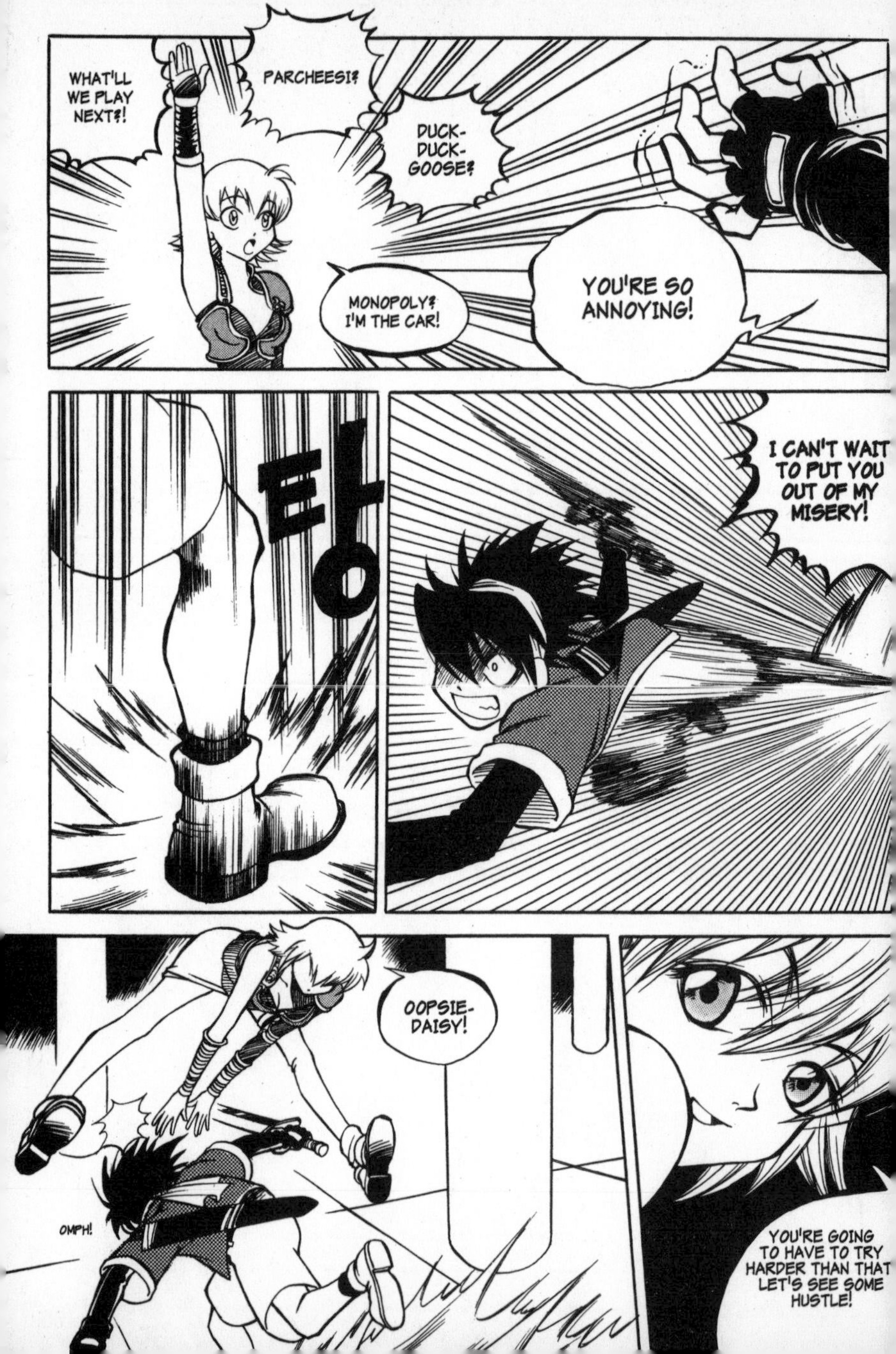
WHAT'LL WE PLAY NEXT?!
PARCHEESI?
DUCK-DUCK-GOOSE?
MONOPOLY? I'M THE CAR!
YOU'RE SO ANNOYING!
I CAN'T WAIT TO PUT YOU OUT OF MY MISERY!
OOPSIE-DAISY!
OMPH!
YOU'RE GOING TO HAVE TO TRY HARDER THAN THAT LET'S SEE SOME HUSTLE!

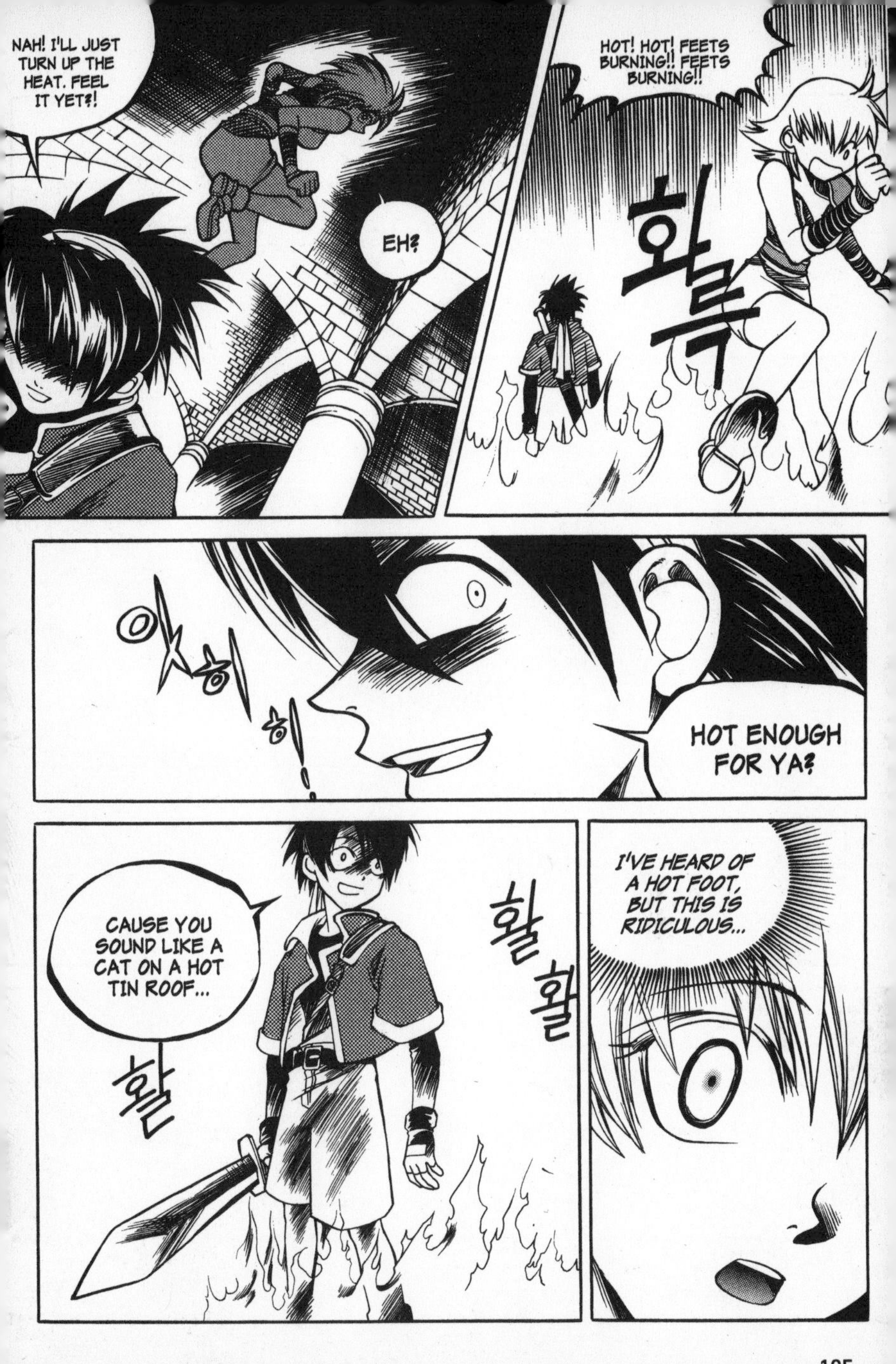
NAH! I'LL JUST TURN UP THE HEAT. FEEL IT YET?!
EH?
HOT! HOT! FEETS BURNING!! FEETS BURNING!!
화륵
HOT ENOUGH FOR YA?
CAUSE YOU SOUND LIKE A CAT ON A HOT TIN ROOF...
활
활 활
I'VE HEARD OF A HOT FOOT, BUT THIS IS RIDICULOUS...

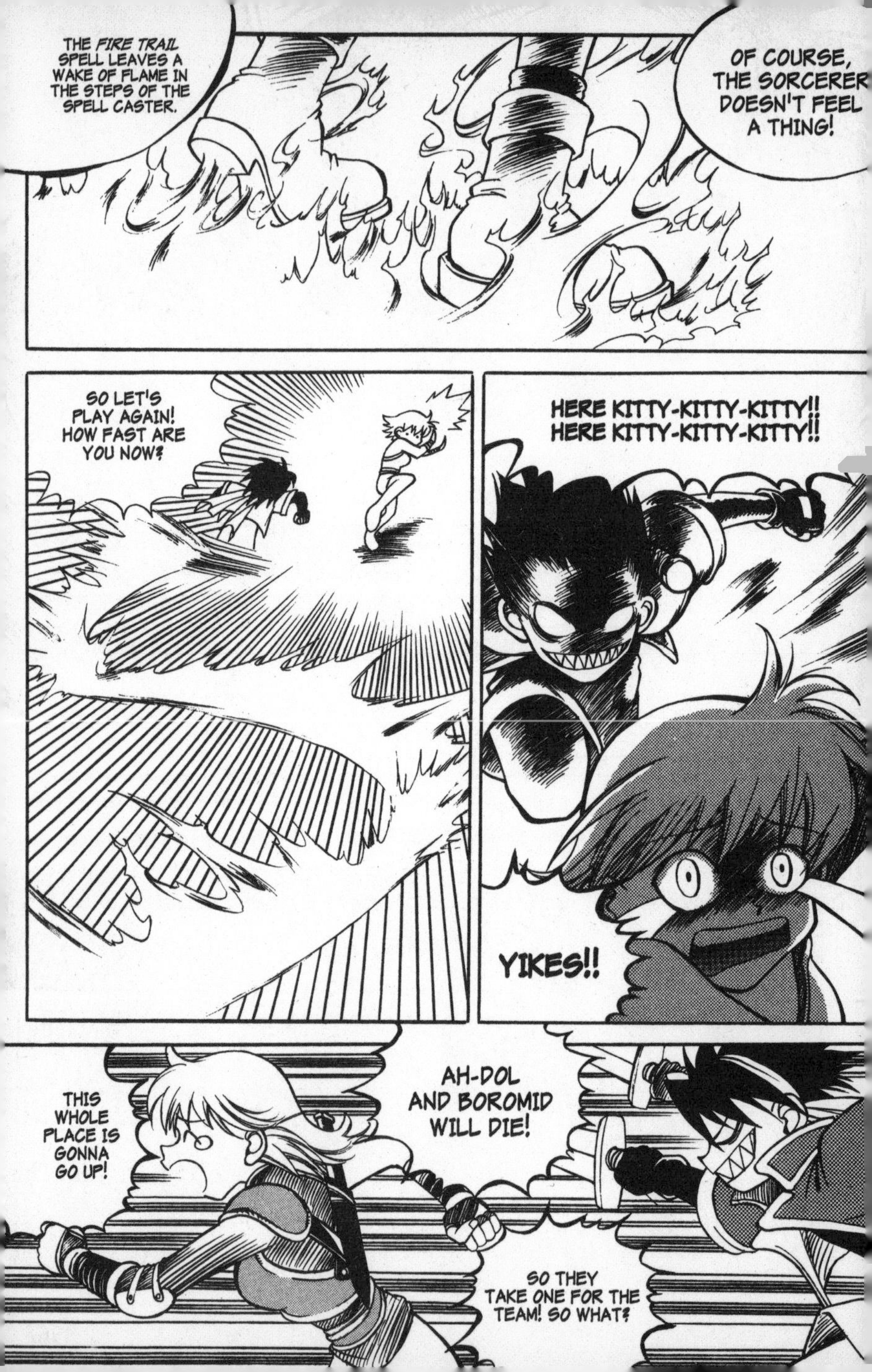

THE *FIRE TRAIL* SPELL LEAVES A WAKE OF FLAME IN THE STEPS OF THE SPELL CASTER.
OF COURSE, THE SORCERER DOESN'T FEEL A THING!
SO LET'S PLAY AGAIN! HOW FAST ARE YOU NOW?
HERE KITTY-KITTY-KITTY!! HERE KITTY-KITTY-KITTY!!
YIKES!!
THIS WHOLE PLACE IS GONNA GO UP!
AH-DOL AND BOROMID WILL DIE!
SO THEY TAKE ONE FOR THE TEAM! SO WHAT?

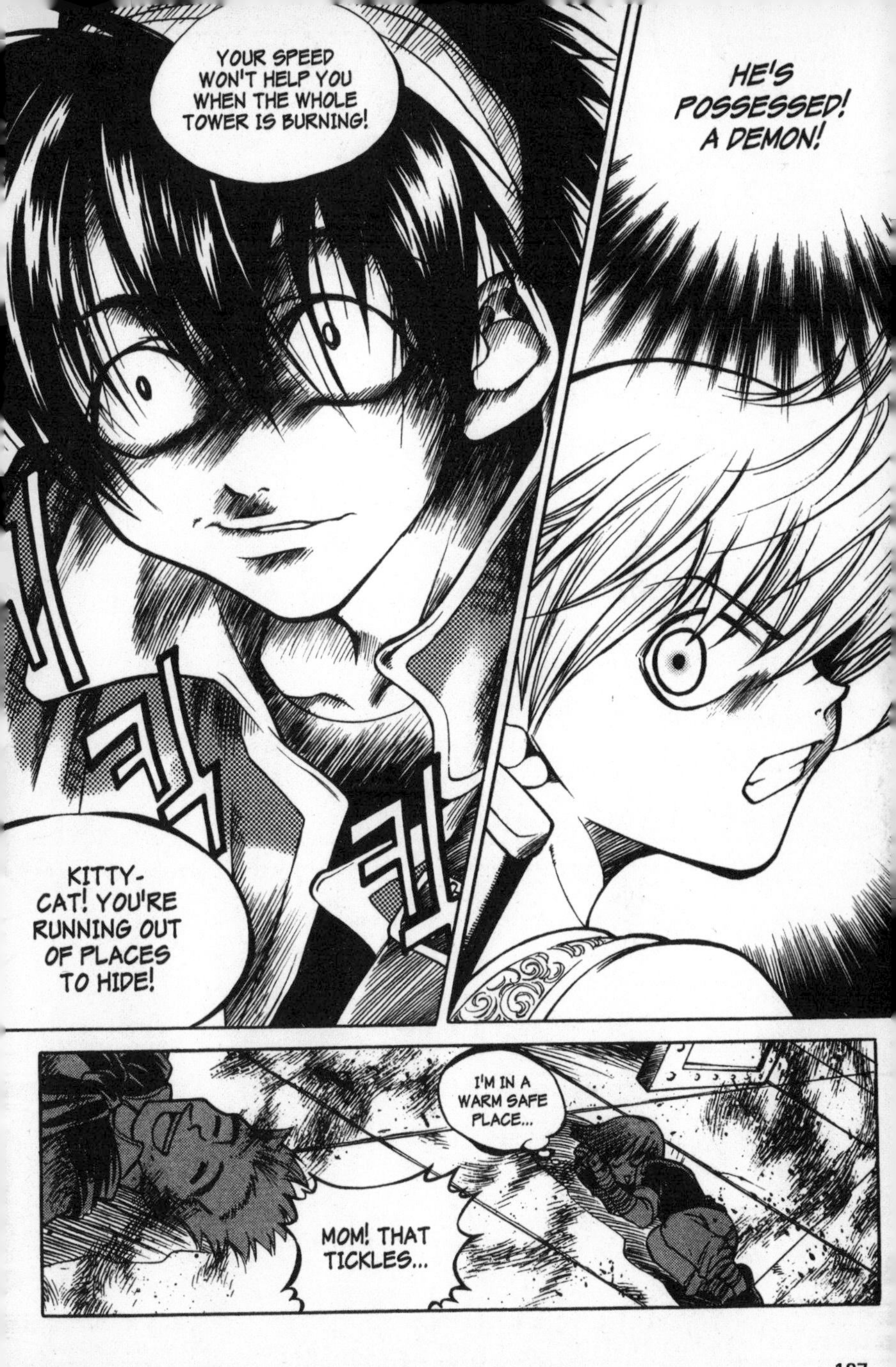
YOUR SPEED WON'T HELP YOU WHEN THE WHOLE TOWER IS BURNING!
HE'S POSSESSED! A DEMON!
KITTY-CAT! YOU'RE RUNNING OUT OF PLACES TO HIDE!
I'M IN A WARM SAFE PLACE...
MOM! THAT TICKLES...

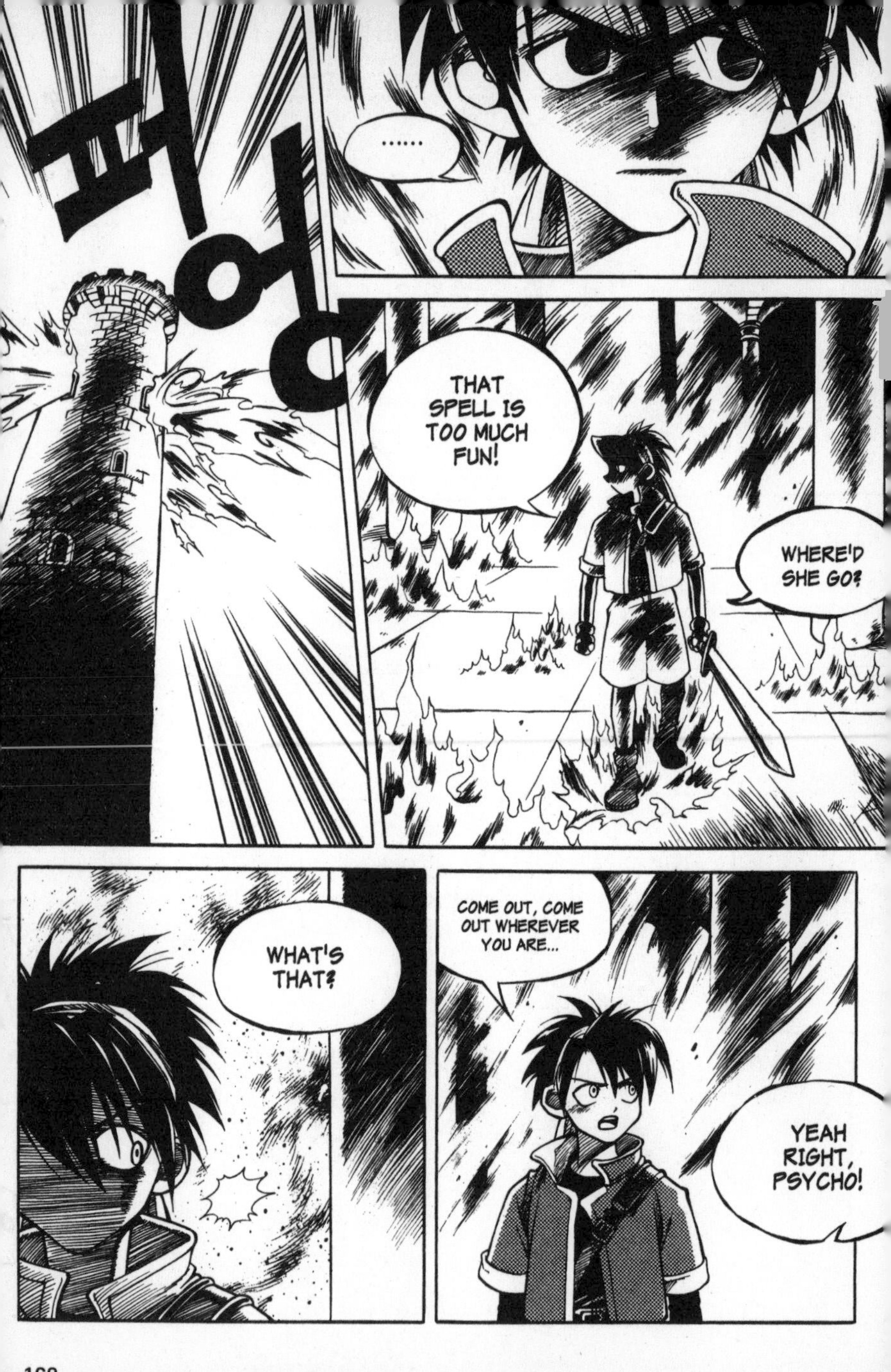
......
THAT SPELL IS TOO MUCH FUN!
WHERE'D SHE GO?
WHAT'S THAT?
COME OUT, COME OUT WHEREVER YOU ARE...
YEAH RIGHT, PSYCHO!

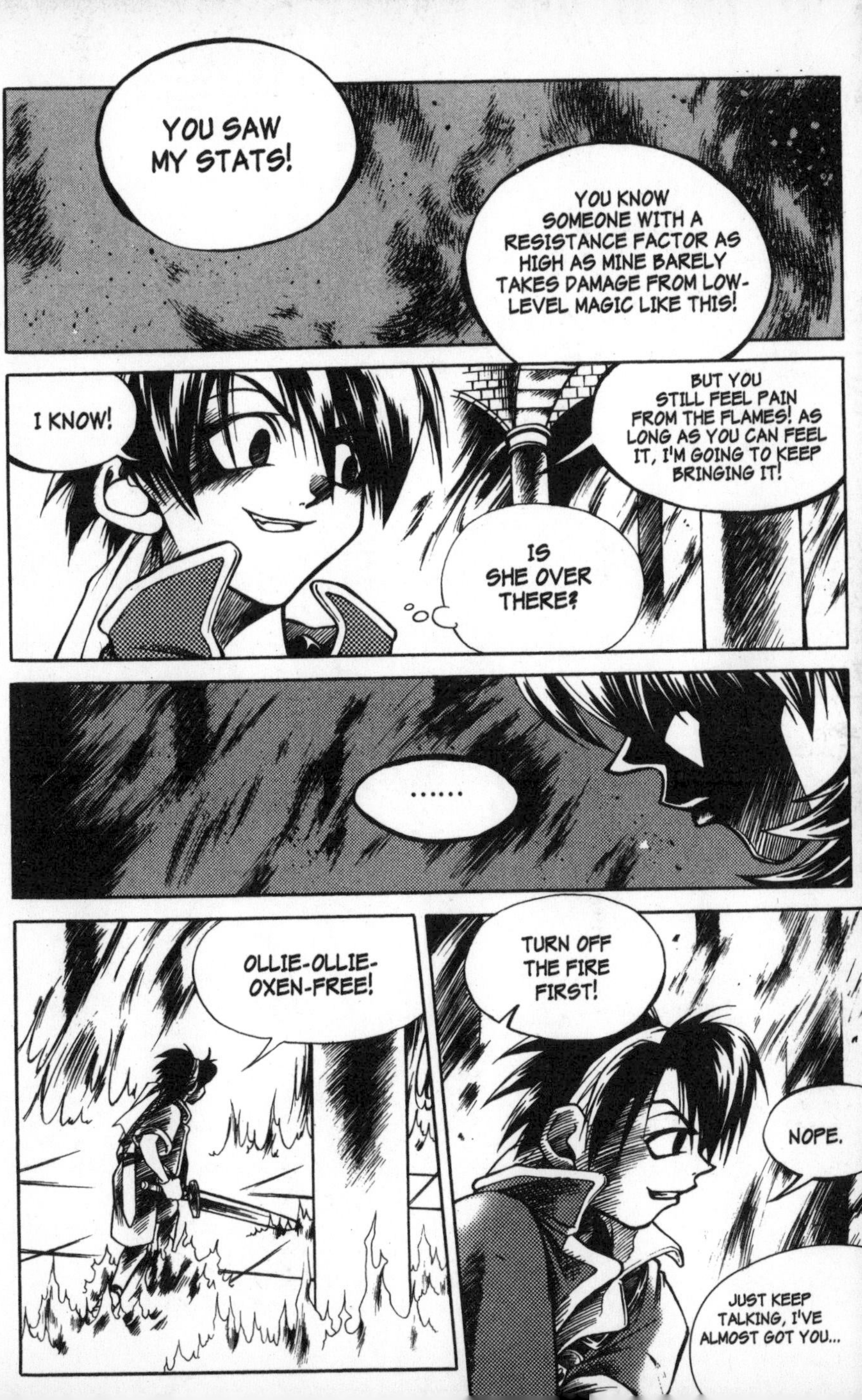
YOU SAW MY STATS!
YOU KNOW SOMEONE WITH A RESISTANCE FACTOR AS HIGH AS MINE BARELY TAKES DAMAGE FROM LOW-LEVEL MAGIC LIKE THIS!
I KNOW!
BUT YOU STILL FEEL PAIN FROM THE FLAMES! AS LONG AS YOU CAN FEEL IT, I'M GOING TO KEEP BRINGING IT!
IS SHE OVER THERE?
......
OLLIE-OLLIE-OXEN-FREE!
TURN OFF THE FIRE FIRST!
NOPE.
JUST KEEP TALKING, I'VE ALMOST GOT YOU...

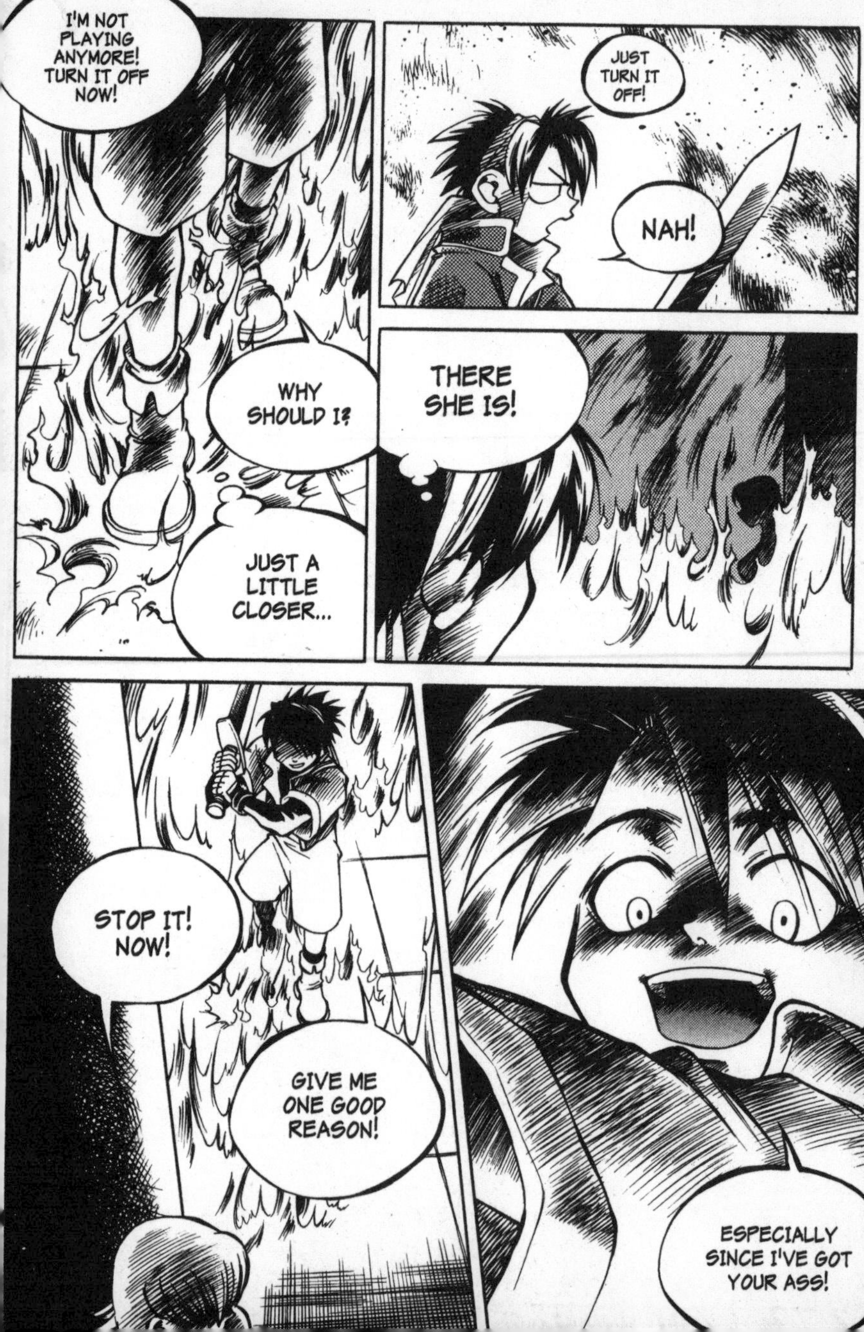
I'M NOT PLAYING ANYMORE! TURN IT OFF NOW!
WHY SHOULD I?
JUST A LITTLE CLOSER...
JUST TURN IT OFF!
NAH!
THERE SHE IS!
STOP IT! NOW!
GIVE ME ONE GOOD REASON!
ESPECIALLY SINCE I'VE GOT YOUR ASS!

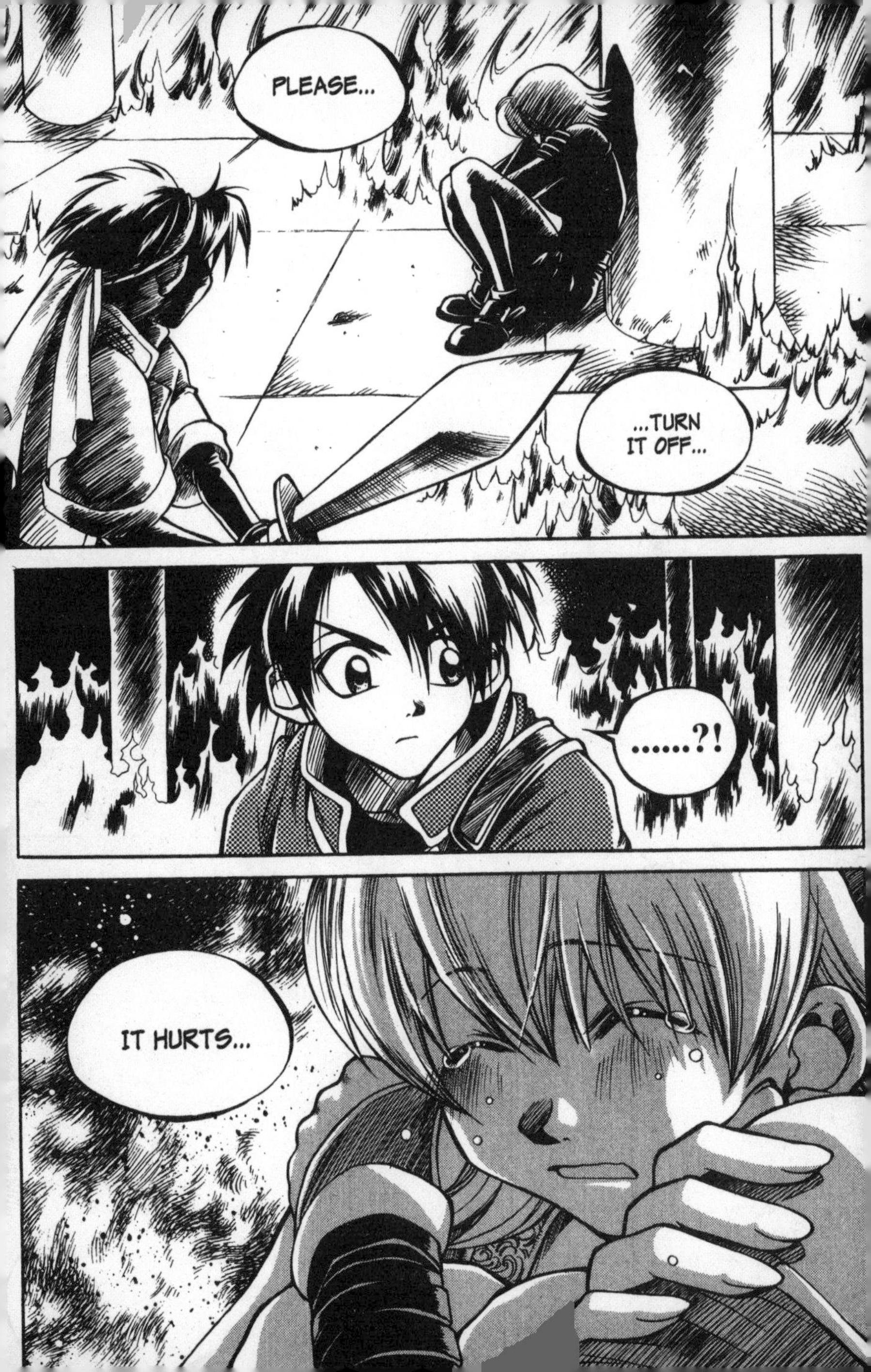
PLEASE...
...TURN IT OFF...
.......?!
IT HURTS...

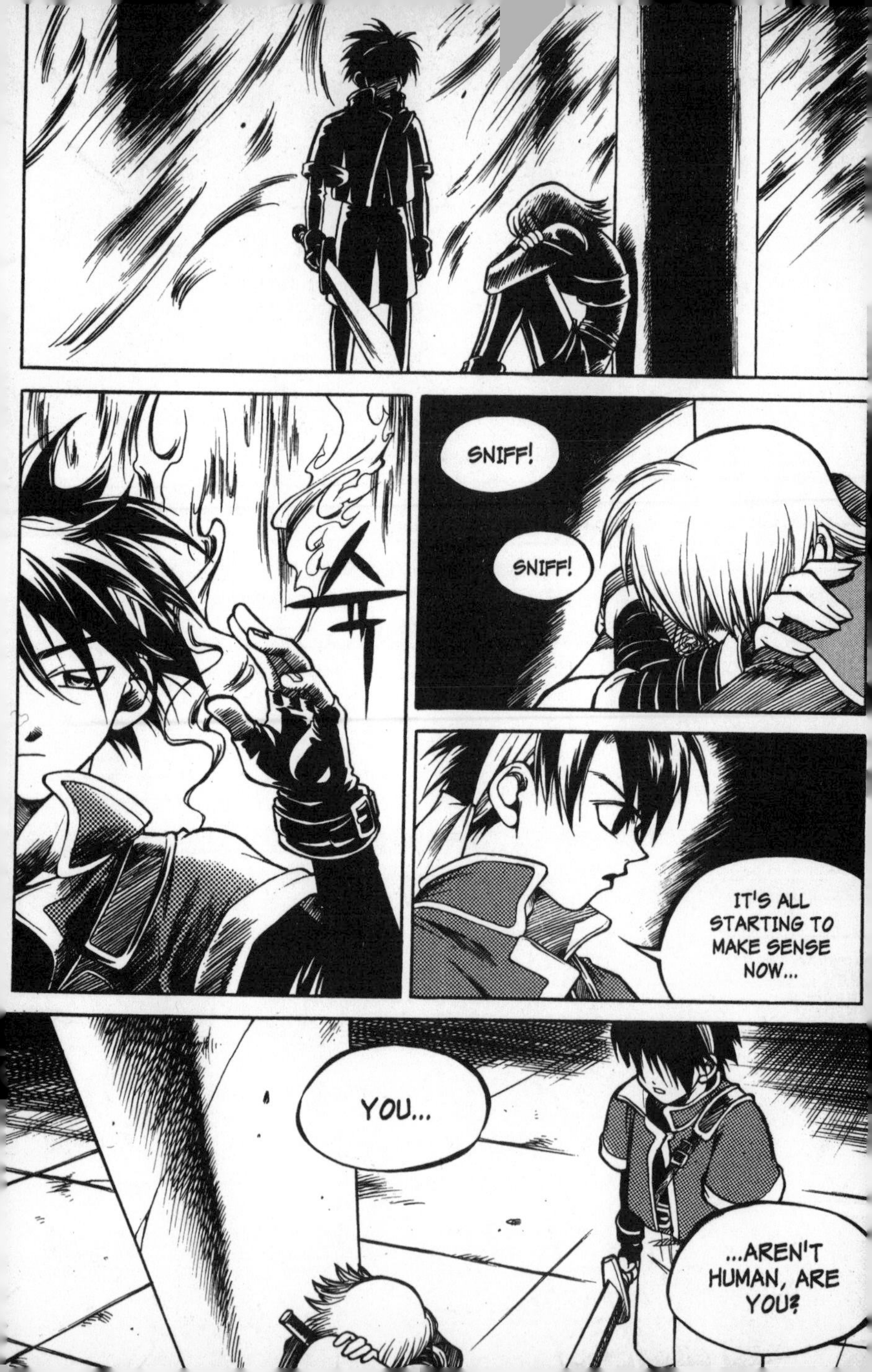
SNIFF!
SNIFF!
IT'S ALL STARTING TO MAKE SENSE NOW...
YOU...
...AREN'T HUMAN, ARE YOU?

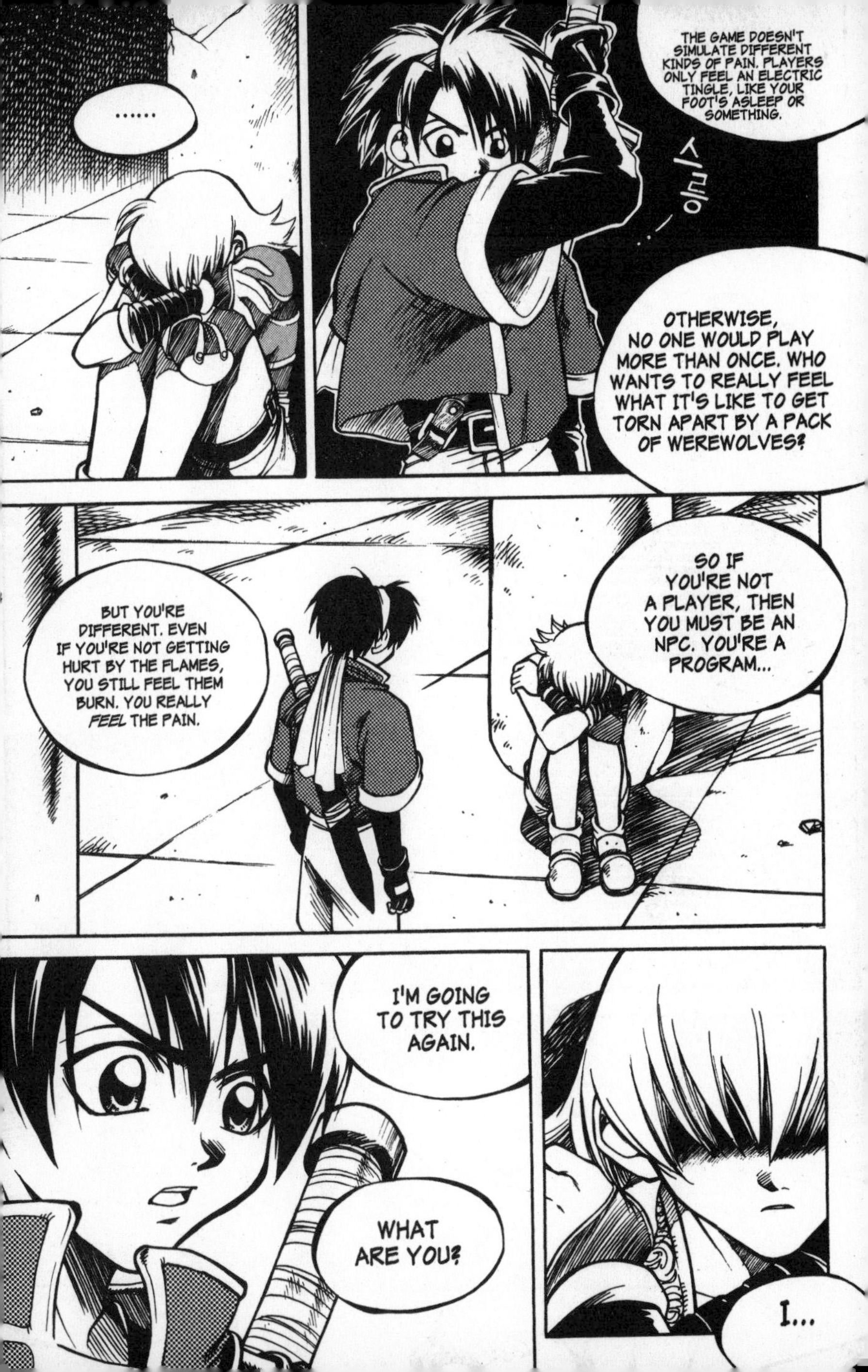
......
THE GAME DOESN'T SIMULATE DIFFERENT KINDS OF PAIN. PLAYERS ONLY FEEL AN ELECTRIC TINGLE, LIKE YOUR FOOT'S ASLEEP OR SOMETHING.
스릉
OTHERWISE, NO ONE WOULD PLAY MORE THAN ONCE. WHO WANTS TO REALLY FEEL WHAT IT'S LIKE TO GET TORN APART BY A PACK OF WEREWOLVES?
BUT YOU'RE DIFFERENT. EVEN IF YOU'RE NOT GETTING HURT BY THE FLAMES, YOU STILL FEEL THEM BURN. YOU REALLY *FEEL* THE PAIN.
SO IF YOU'RE NOT A PLAYER, THEN YOU MUST BE AN NPC. YOU'RE A PROGRAM...
I'M GOING TO TRY THIS AGAIN.
WHAT ARE YOU?
I...

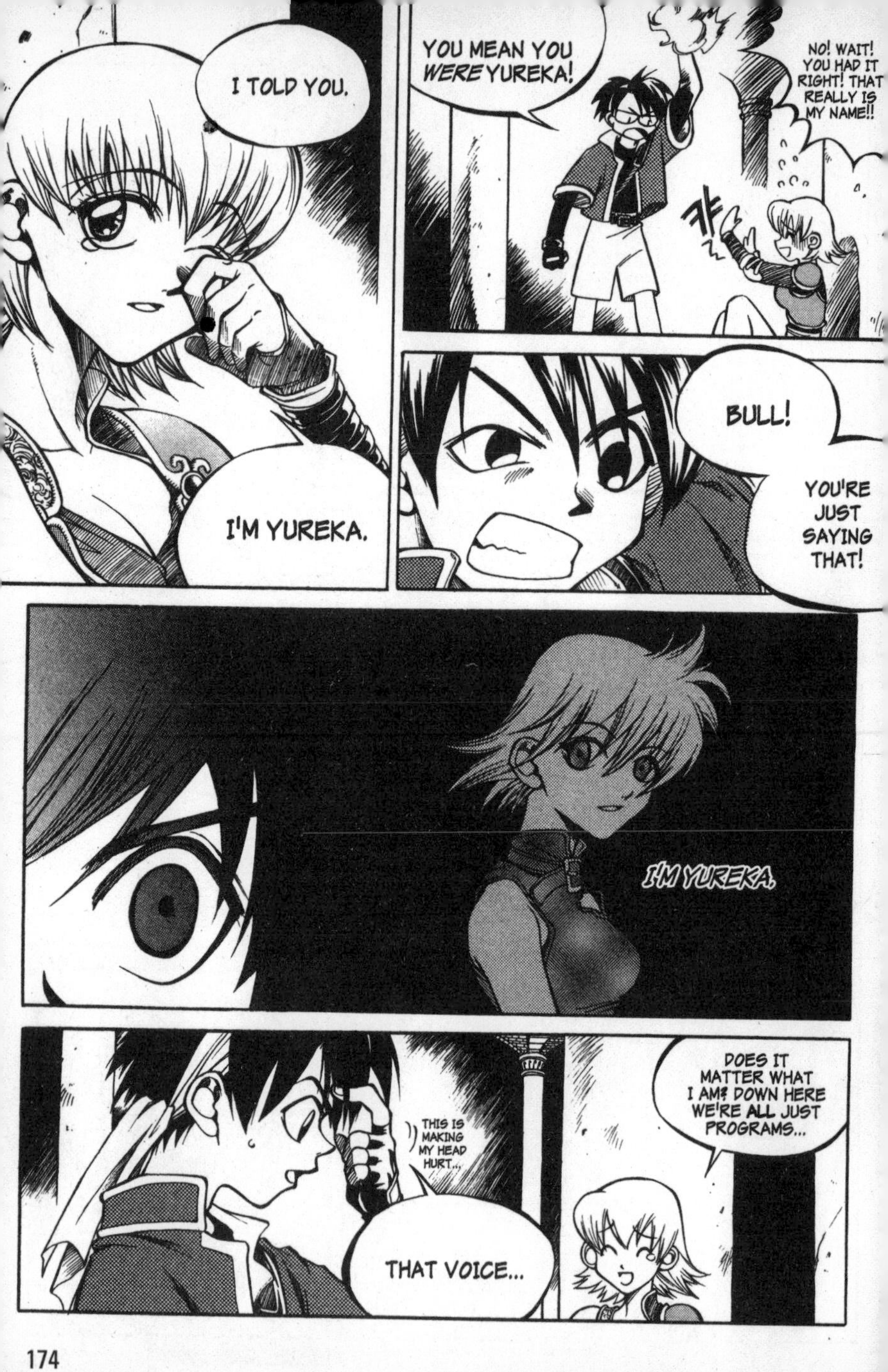
I TOLD YOU.
I'M YUREKA.
YOU MEAN YOU WERE YUREKA!
NO! WAIT! YOU HAD IT RIGHT! THAT REALLY IS MY NAME!!
BULL!
YOU'RE JUST SAYING THAT!
I'M YUREKA.
THIS IS MAKING MY HEAD HURT...
THAT VOICE...
DOES IT MATTER WHAT I AM? DOWN HERE WE'RE ALL JUST PROGRAMS...

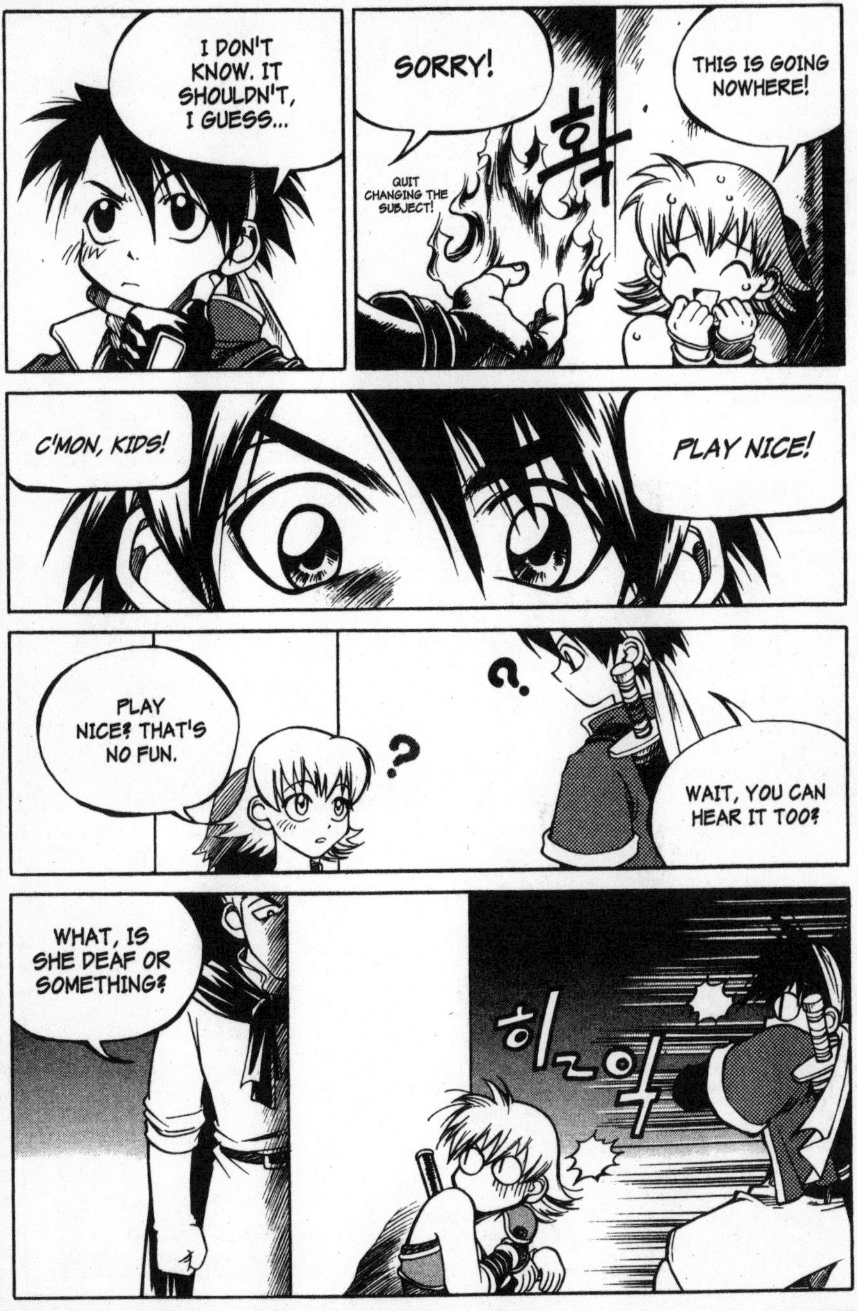
I DON'T KNOW. IT SHOULDN'T, I GUESS...
SORRY!
QUIT CHANGING THE SUBJECT!
확
THIS IS GOING NOWHERE!
C'MON, KIDS!
PLAY NICE!
PLAY NICE? THAT'S NO FUN.
?
?
WAIT, YOU CAN HEAR IT TOO?
WHAT, IS SHE DEAF OR SOMETHING?
히끄억

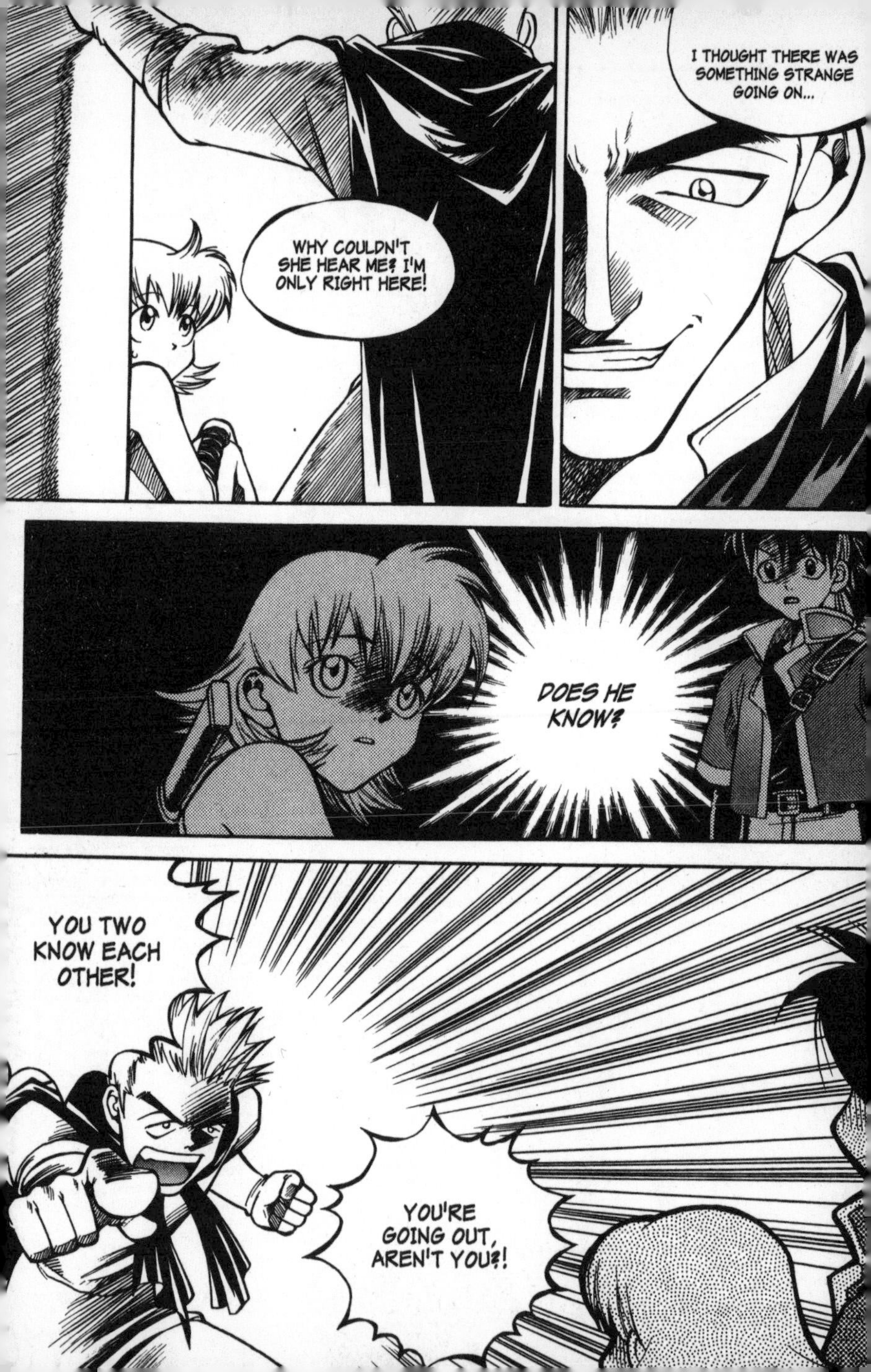
WHY COULDN'T SHE HEAR ME? I'M ONLY RIGHT HERE!
I THOUGHT THERE WAS SOMETHING STRANGE GOING ON...
DOES HE KNOW?
YOU TWO KNOW EACH OTHER!
YOU'RE GOING OUT, AREN'T YOU?!

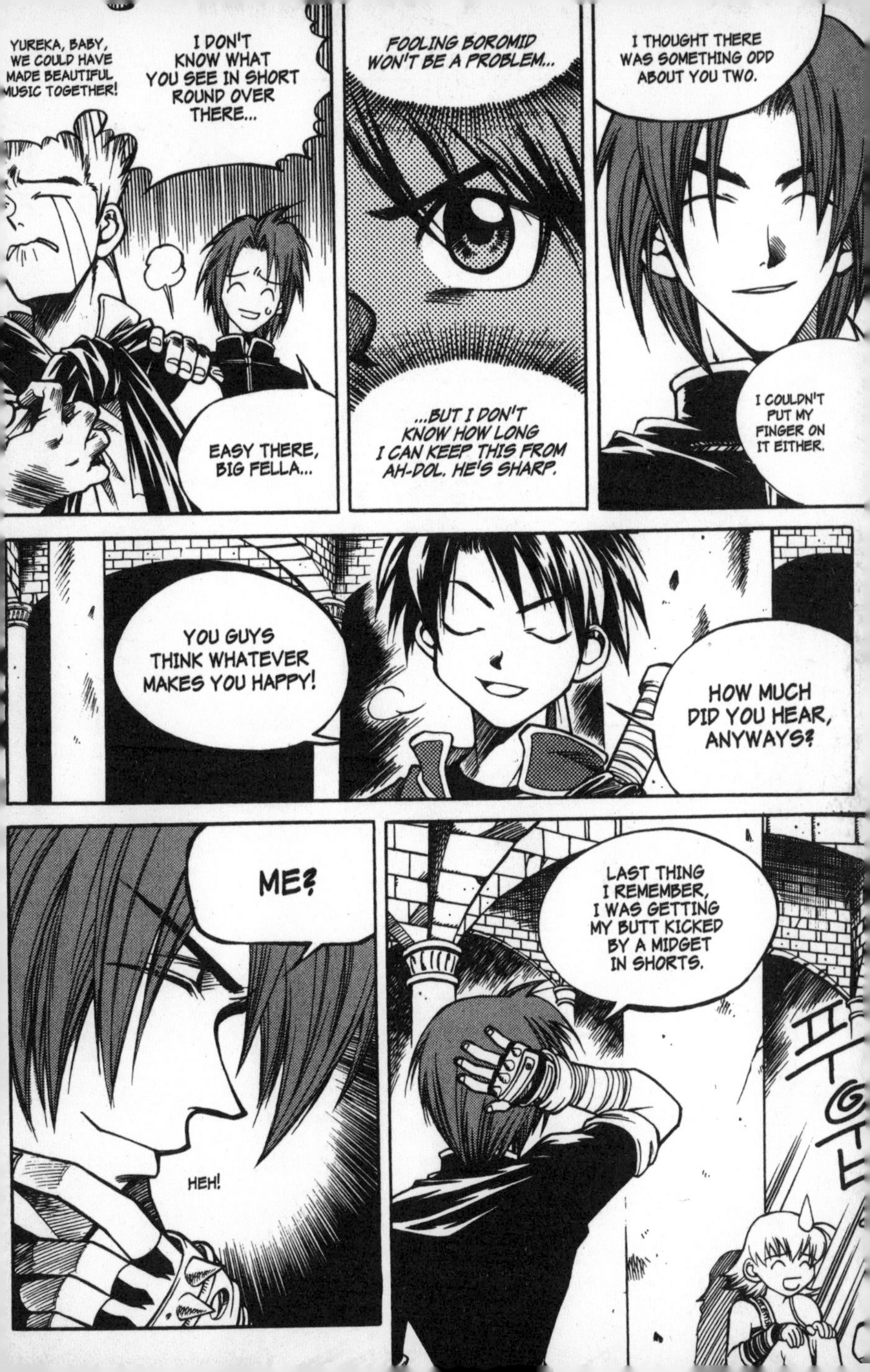
YUREKA, BABY, WE COULD HAVE MADE BEAUTIFUL MUSIC TOGETHER!
I DON'T KNOW WHAT YOU SEE IN SHORT ROUND OVER THERE...
EASY THERE, BIG FELLA...
FOOLING BOROMID WON'T BE A PROBLEM...
...BUT I DON'T KNOW HOW LONG I CAN KEEP THIS FROM AH-DOL. HE'S SHARP.
I THOUGHT THERE WAS SOMETHING ODD ABOUT YOU TWO.
I COULDN'T PUT MY FINGER ON IT EITHER.
YOU GUYS THINK WHATEVER MAKES YOU HAPPY!
HOW MUCH DID YOU HEAR, ANYWAYS?
ME?
HEH!
LAST THING I REMEMBER, I WAS GETTING MY BUTT KICKED BY A MIDGET IN SHORTS.

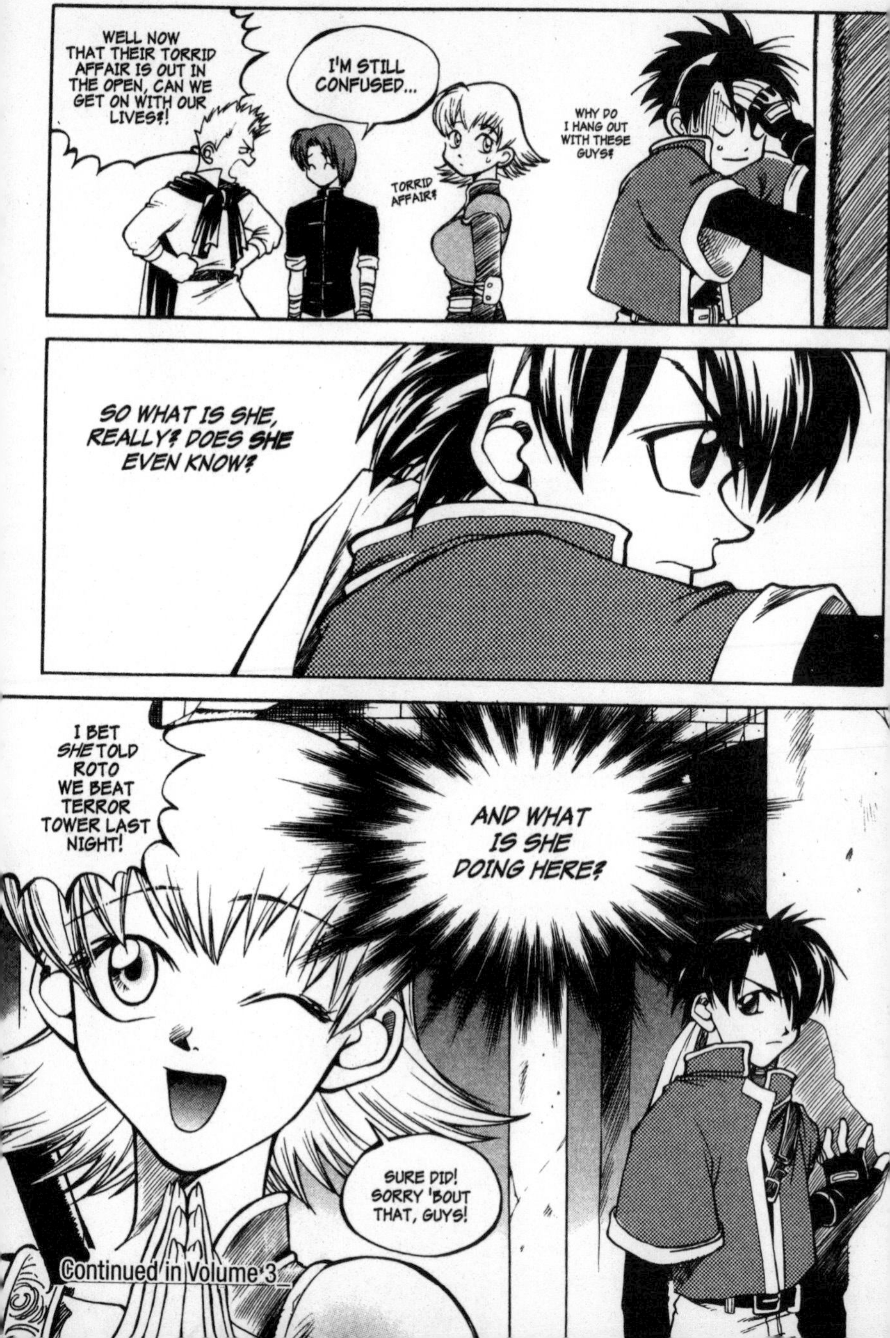
WELL NOW THAT THEIR TORRID AFFAIR IS OUT IN THE OPEN, CAN WE GET ON WITH OUR LIVES?!
I'M STILL CONFUSED...
TORRID AFFAIR?
WHY DO I HANG OUT WITH THESE GUYS?
SO WHAT IS SHE, REALLY? DOES SHE EVEN KNOW?
I BET SHE TOLD ROTO WE BEAT TERROR TOWER LAST NIGHT!
AND WHAT IS SHE DOING HERE?
SURE DID! SORRY 'BOUT THAT, GUYS!
Continued in Volume 3

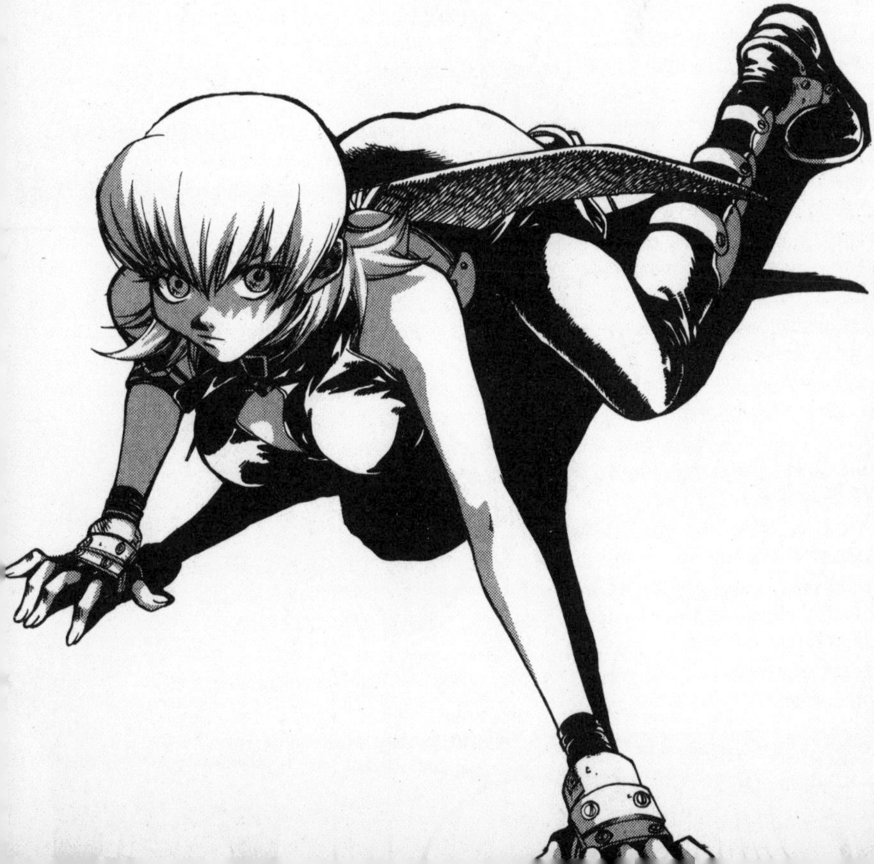

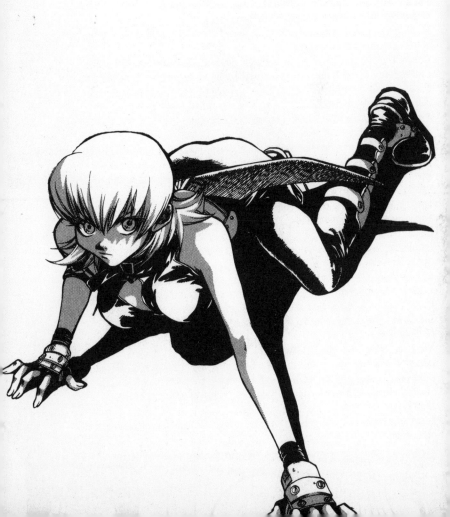

>>LEXICON

Band-aids: Healing prayers that renew a player's health. The ability to use band-aids makes a healer a vital member of a character party.

Bandwidth: The capacity of an Internet connection.

Brick: The kind of warrior a less-powerful character would prefer to be behind when faced with a particularly nasty group of monsters.

Bounty: A reward for completion of a specific deed. In *Lost Saga*, usually the apprehension or killing of a rule-breaking character.

Boss: A high-level monster at the end of a quest or campaign.

Character, ID: A player's identity in the Game.

Debugger: A Dexon employee who assumes an online identity to resolve errors or "bugs" in the *Lost Saga* environment.

Dexon: The software company that created and maintains the *Lost Saga* game.

Dial-up: A slow, old-fashioned internet connection relying on telephone technology.

Dream-mode: A method of playing *Lost Saga* that allows players to control their characters while asleep.

Dungeon chickens: Generic term for relatively harmless monsters that offer little challenge to higher-level players.

Experience: Rewards for success in combat, the accumulation of which allows characters to advance in level, which in turn rewards the character with greater abilities.

Freeze, Frozen: When a player character stops moving, because of a connection error or having been forcibly logged out.

Frag: To kill, especially another player character.

Force quit: To be logged out of the Game by external forces.

Game, the Game: *Lost Saga*, a virtual-reality environment, developed by the Dexon corporation, where players can battle monsters, search for treasure and role-play fantasy-genre characters.

Gamer: Someone for whom playing computer games is a primary leisure-time activity.

Gauntlet: A quarter-crunching mid-'80s arcade game based around seemingly endless mazes populated by teeming masses of easily-killed monsters.

Gib: To kill with gusto, reducing one's opponent to giblet-sized pieces.

Gold: Generic name for Game currency.

Hack: An illegal Game modification.

Healer: A priest-character able to heal other characters by using spell-like prayers.

High-ping bastard (HPB): A player with such a bad connection that he's often frozen, offering no help as a teammate and not much challenge as an opponent.

High priest: A high-level priest character.

Level, level-up: For a character to increase in level through the accumulation of experience.

Live-mode: Playing *Lost Saga* while fully conscious.

Log on, Log in, Drop in: To enter the Game.

Log off, Log out, Quit: To leave the Game.

Lost Saga: The fantasy-genre virtual-reality online game favored by Team Triple Threat.

Low-ping bastard (or LPB): A player who has a really fast Internet connection and low "ping" times to the game server, giving him an advantage over (better) players with slower connections.

Items: Weapons or tools that enhance a character's abilities or otherwise help them to succeed in the Game.

Kicked: To be banned from the Game.

Kill: A defeated enemy.

Medicine: A healing substance allowing characters to instantly recover from damage.

Master-level players: An elite group of players who've logged a minimum of 6,000 hours in the Game and reached a pre-determined level.

Mobs, Monsters: Computer-controlled "mobile objects" that exist solely to be killed by player characters.

Multi-channel: Using a single connection Internet connection for more than one user.

Newbie, Noob: A novice gamer.

Non-player character (NPC): A computer-controlled character.

Offline: The world outside of *Lost Saga*. For players, the "real" world, where things like school, homework and parents get in the way of Game time.

Party: A group of characters who join together to accomplish a common goal.

Patch: A legal modification of the Game.

Player characters: A character controlled by a living, breathing player, as distinguished from a computer-controlled character.

Player killer: A player character who makes a habit of killing other players to steal their items. In *Lost Saga*, this is illegal, and can result in a bounty being placed on the character.

Prayer: An invitation for divine intervention made by a priest-character with results approximating those of a magical spell.

Priest: A character with the ability to use spell-like prayers.

Power player: A player whose only goal is to advance in level as quickly as possible.

Silent step: A stealth-movement technique practiced by thief characters.

Sorcerer: A character with the ability to cast spells.

Spawn: The act of a character or monster entering the Game environment.

Spawn point: The point where a character or monster enters the Game.

Spirit master: A sorcerer adept at calling forth magical beings to do their bidding.

Sun-Bae: A Korean term used by a younger person to indicate an older colleague.

Sword master: A character with extremely high-level swordsmanship skills.

Thief: A character emphasizing dexterity, stealth and guile to succeed in the Game.

Warrior: A character relying on physical skills for success in combat.

PASSWORD RECOGNIZED...

IDENTITY CONFIRMED...

ACCESSING VOLUME 3 FILE...

Suspicious of Yureka from the start, Roto comes to believe that she's a dummy character meant to serve as a distraction while the real character hacks into the server. However, the draw Yureka has to him is undeniable. Otherwise, why would he feel confident enough to team up with her for the big *Lost Saga* tournament? With a powerful sword at stake--the Excalibur--as well as 10 million pieces of gold, the competition is sure to be fierce. Making things worse, Boromid and Ah-Dol have entered the tournament as well. With only the top team taking the prize, the boys' friendship will be sorely tested. Will this tournament spell the end for Team Triple Threat?

TRANSMISSION COMPLETE...

LOGGING OFF...

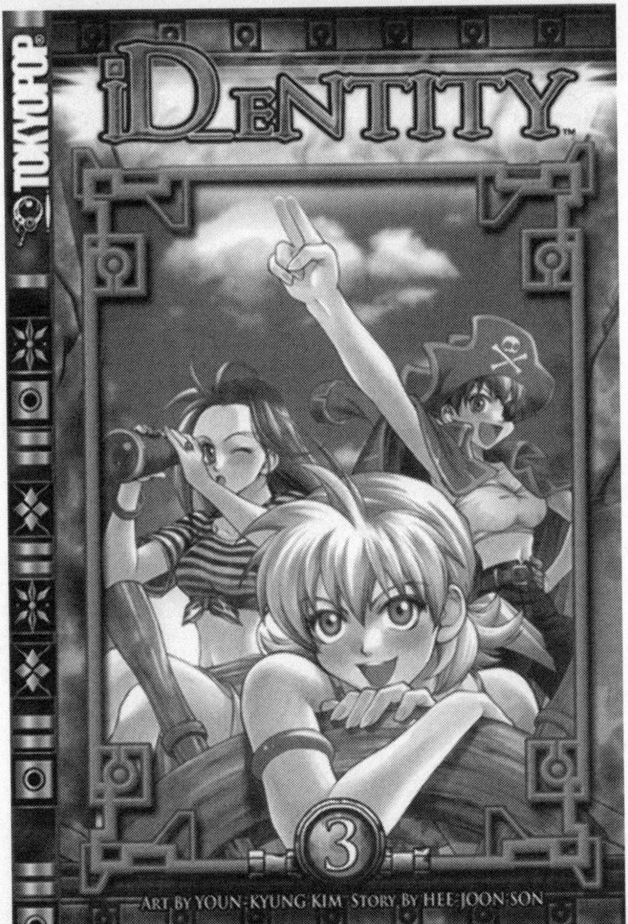
TOKYOPOP
iDENTITY
3
ART BY YOUN-KYUNG KIM STORY BY HEE-JOON SON

TOKYOPOP SHOP

SPOTLIGHT

TOKYOPOP MANGA SUPPLEMENT

SAKURA TAISEN

BY OHJI HIROI & IKKU MASA

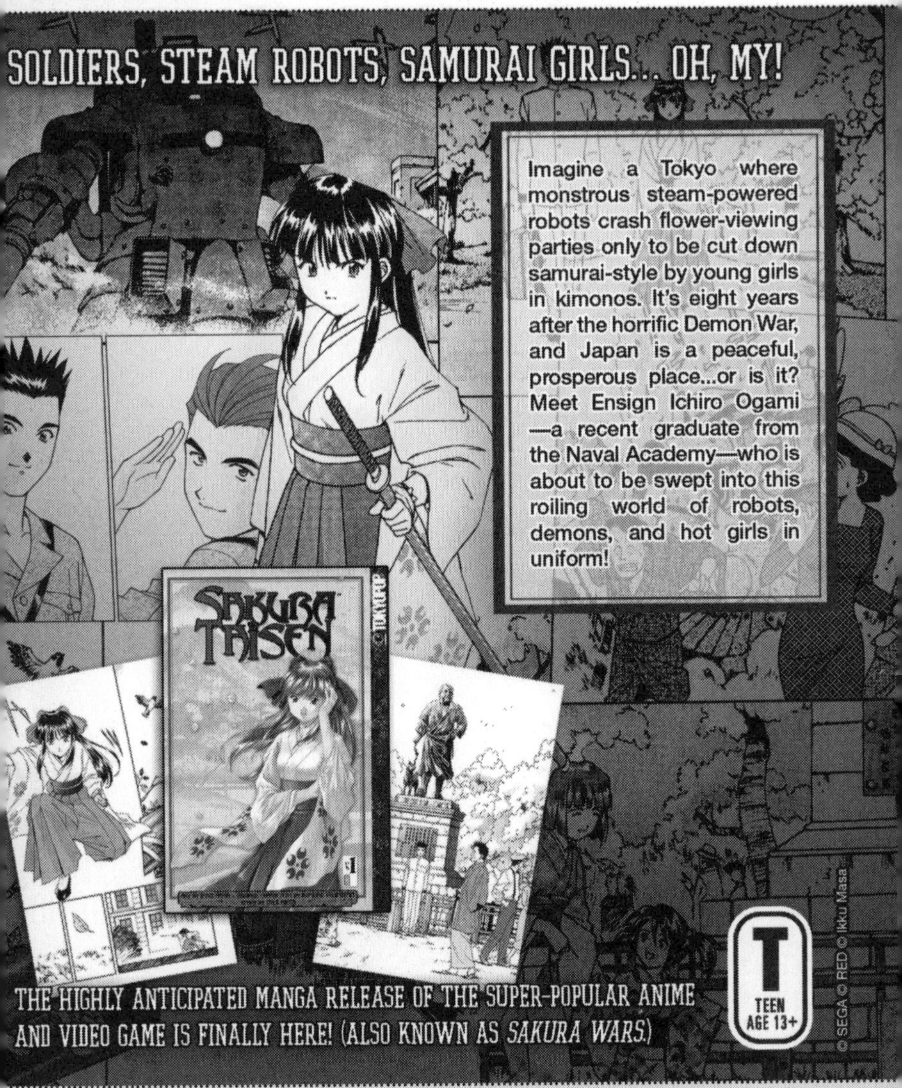
SAKURA TAISEN
TOKYOPOP

SOLDIERS, STEAM ROBOTS, SAMURAI GIRLS... OH, MY!

Imagine a Tokyo where monstrous steam-powered robots crash flower-viewing parties only to be cut down samurai-style by young girls in kimonos. It's eight years after the horrific Demon War, and Japan is a peaceful, prosperous place...or is it? Meet Ensign Ichiro Ogami—a recent graduate from the Naval Academy—who is about to be swept into this roiling world of robots, demons, and hot girls in uniform!

THE HIGHLY ANTICIPATED MANGA RELEASE OF THE SUPER-POPULAR ANIME AND VIDEO GAME IS FINALLY HERE! (ALSO KNOWN AS *SAKURA WARS*.)

T TEEN AGE 13+

FOR MORE INFORMATION VISIT: WWW.TOKYOPOP.COM

BIZENGHAST

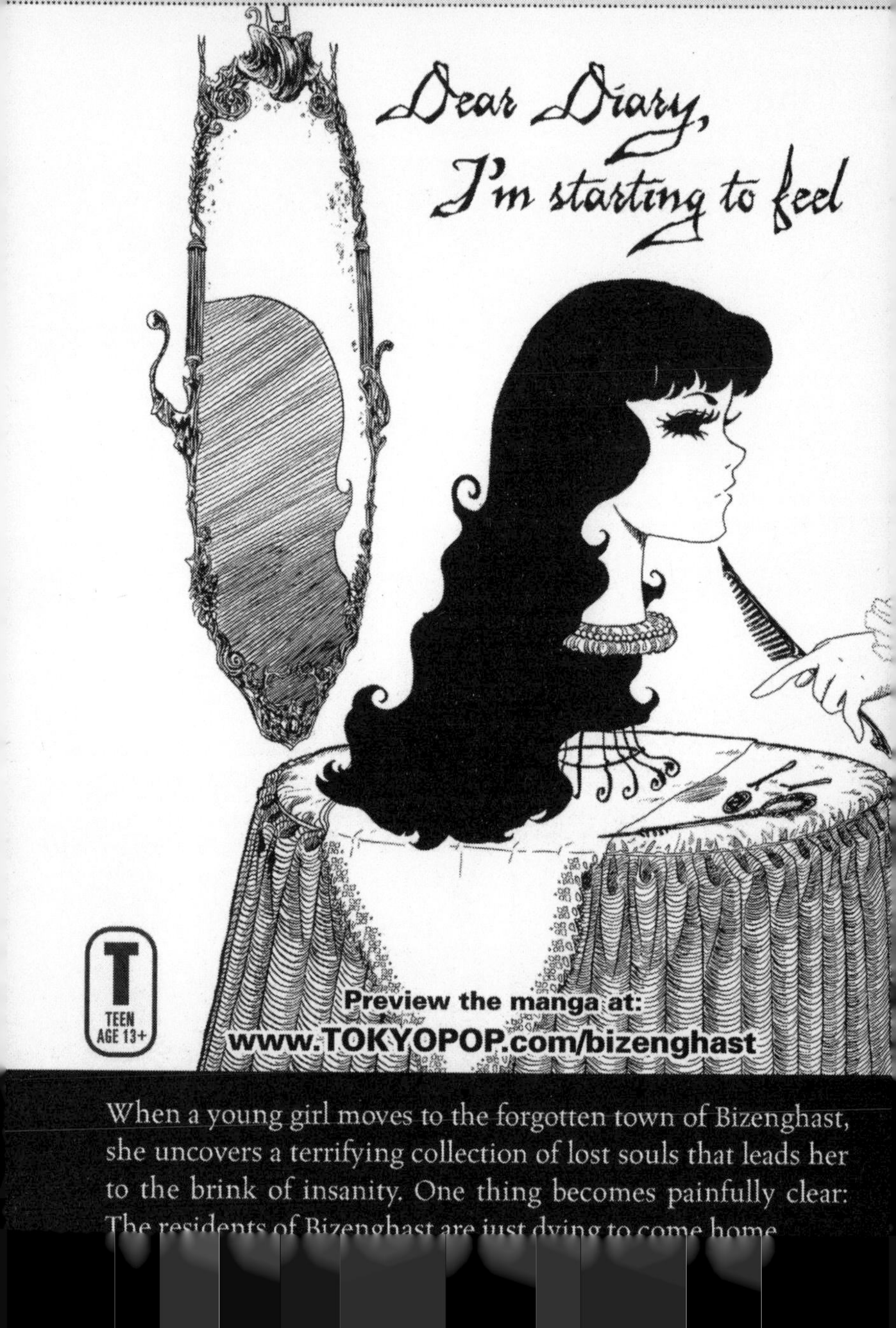
Dear Diary,
I'm starting to feel
T
TEEN AGE 13+
Preview the manga at:
www.TOKYOPOP.com/bizenghast

When a young girl moves to the forgotten town of Bizenghast, she uncovers a terrifying collection of lost souls that leads her to the brink of insanity. One thing becomes painfully clear: The residents of Bizenghast are just dying to come home.

that I'm not like other people...

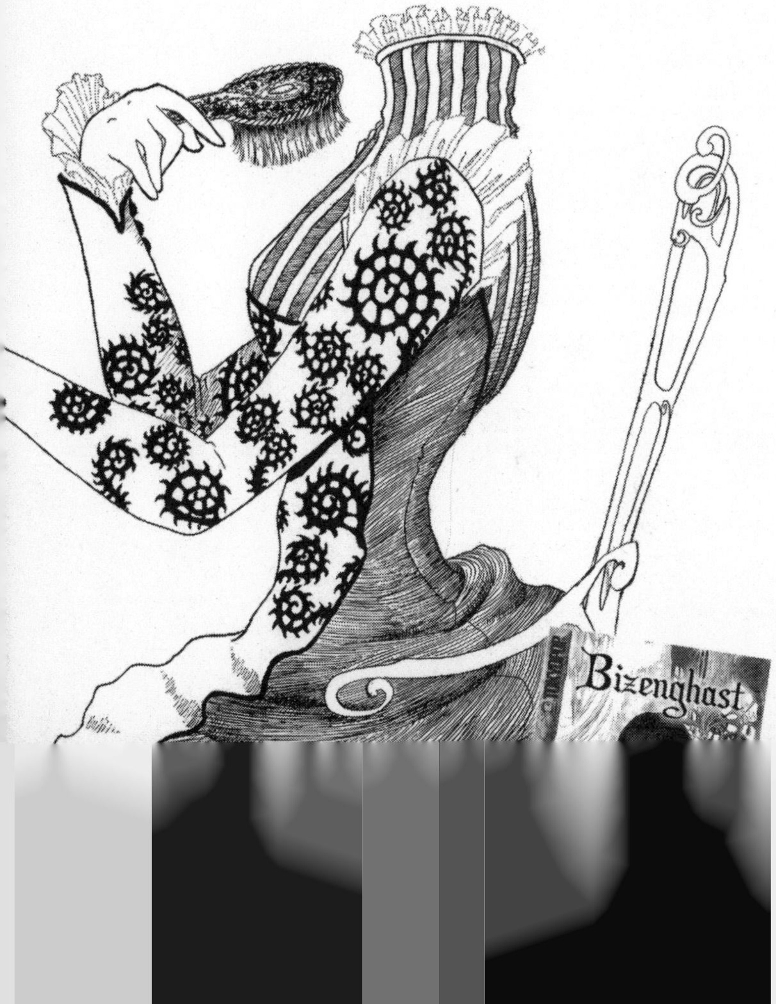
Bizenghast

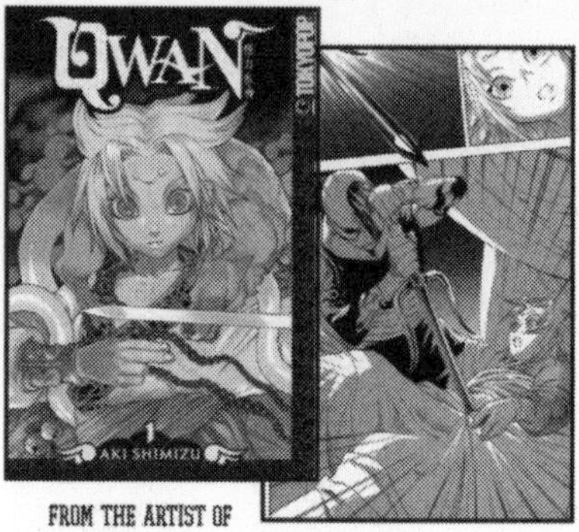
QWAN
1
AKI SHIMIZU

FROM THE ARTIST OF SUIKODEN III

BY AKI SHIMIZU

QWAN

Qwan is a series that refuses to be pigeonholed. Aki Shimizu combines Chinese history, mythology, fantasy and humor to create a world that is familiar yet truly unique. Her creature designs are particularly brilliant—from mascots to monsters. And Qwan himself is great—fallen to Earth, he's like a little kid, complete with the loud questions, yet he eats demons for breakfast. In short, *Qwan* is a solid story with great character dynamics, amazing art and some kick-ass battle scenes. What's not to like?

~Carol Fox, Editor

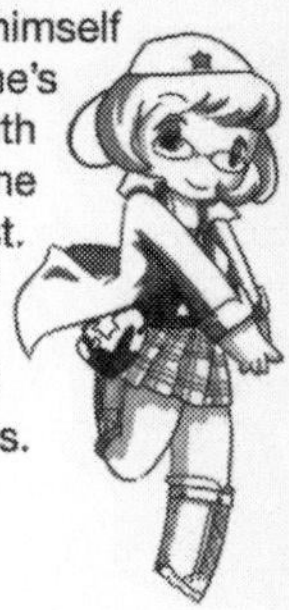

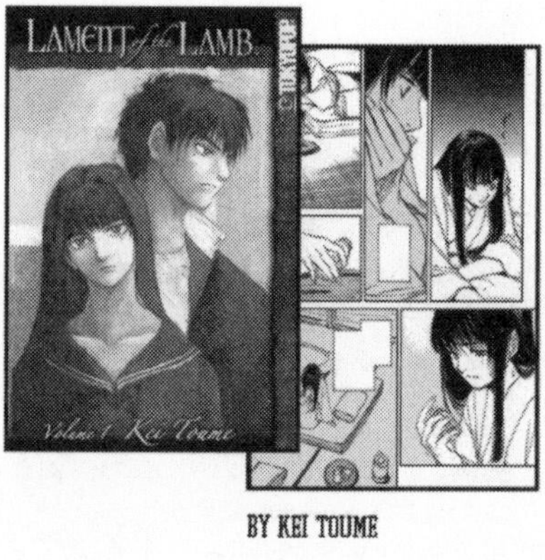
LAMENT of the LAMB
Volume 1 Kei Toume

BY KEI TOUME

LAMENT OF THE LAMB

Kei Toume's *Lament of the Lamb* follows the physical and mental torment of Kazuna Takashiro, who discovers that he's cursed with a hereditary disease that makes him crave blood. *Lament* is psychological horror at its best—it's gloomy, foreboding and emotionally wrenching. Toume brilliantly treats the story's vampirism in a realistic, subdued way, and it becomes a metaphor for teenage alienation, twisted sexual desire and insanity. While reading each volume, I get goose bumps, I feel uneasy, and I become increasingly depressed. Quite a compliment for a horror series!

~Paul Morrissey, Editor

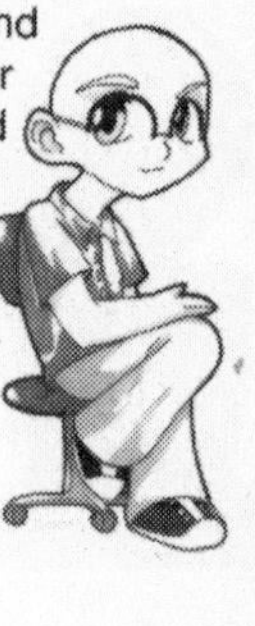

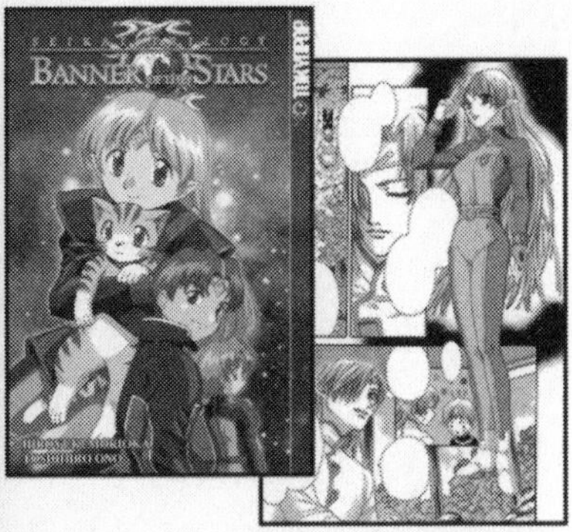

BY AYA YOSHINAGA, HIROYUKI MORIOKA, TOSHIHIRO ONO, AND WASOH MIYAKOSHI

THE SEIKAI TRILOGY

The Seikai Trilogy is one of TOKYOPOP's most underrated series. Although the trilogy gained popularity through the release of the anime, the manga brings a vitality to the characters that I feel the anime never did. The story is a heart-warming, exciting sci-fi adventure epic, the likes of which we haven't seen since *Star Wars. Banner of the Stars II*, the series' finale, is a real page-turner—a prison colony's security is compromised due to violent intergalactic politics. Each manga corresponds to the story from the novel...however, unless you read Japanese, the only way to enjoy the story thus far is through these faithful comic adaptations.

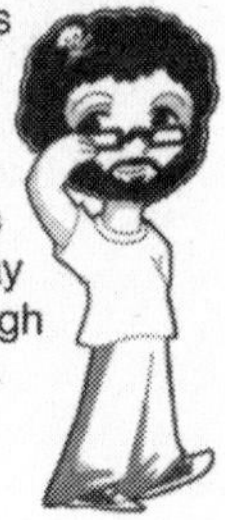

~Luis Reyes, Editor

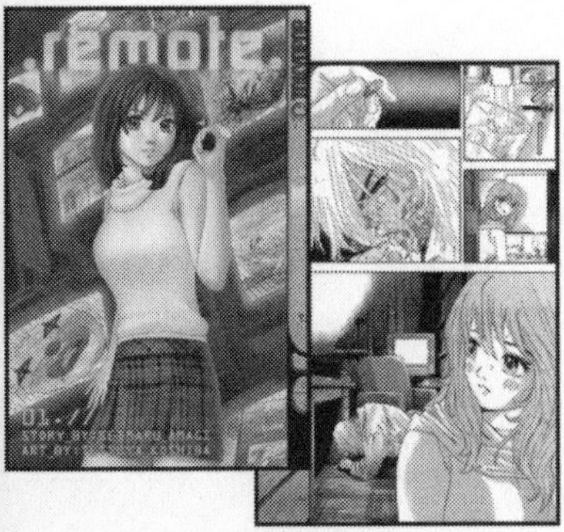
remote

BY SEIMARU AMAGI AND TETSUYA KOSHIBA

REMOTE

Imagine Pam Anderson starring in *The Silence of the Lambs* and you've got a hint of what to expect from Seimaru Amagi and Tetsuya Koshiba's *Remote*. Completely out of her element, Officer Kurumi Ayaki brings down murderers, mad bombers and would-be assassins, all under the guidance of the reclusive Inspector Himuro. There's no shortage of fan-service and ultraviolence as Kurumi stumbles through her cases, but it's nicely balanced by the forensic police work of the brilliant Himuro, a man haunted by his past and struggling with suppressed emotions awakened by the adorable Kurumi.

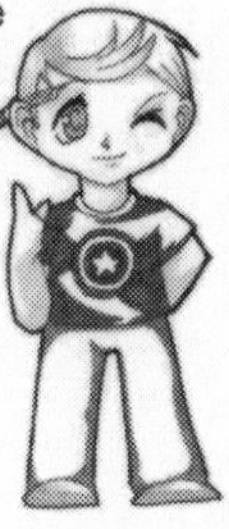

~Bryce P. Coleman, Editor

.HACK//AI BUSTER - NOVEL
BY TATSUYA HAMAZAKI

In the epic prequel to .hack, the avatar Albireo is a solo adventurer in The World, the most advanced online fantasy game ever created. When he comes across Lycoris, a strange little girl in a dungeon, he soon comes to realize that she may hold a very deadly secret—a secret that could unhinge everything in cyberspace... and beyond!

Discover the untold origins of the phenomenon known as .hack!

© Tatsuya Hamazaki © Rei Izumi

CHRONO CODE
BY EUI-CHEOL SHIN & IL-HO CHOI

Time flows like a river, without changing its course. This is an escape from the river's flow...

Three people must cross time and space to find each other and change their destinies. However, a powerful satellite, a secret code and the future police impede their progress, and their success hinges on an amnesiac who must first uncover the true nature of her past in order to discover who her friends are in the future.

T TEEN AGE 13+

© IL-HO CHOI & EUI-CHEOL SHIN, DAIWON C.I. Inc.

SAIYUKI RELOAD
BY KAZUYA MINEKURA

Join Sanzo, Gojyo, Hakkai, Goku and their updated wardrobe as they continue their journey west toward Shangri-La, encountering new challenges and new adventures along the way. But don't be fooled by their change in costume: The fearsome foursome is just as ferocious and focused as before...if not more so.

The hit manga that inspired the anime, and the sequel to TOKYOPOP's hugely popular Saiyuki!

OT OLDER TEEN AGE 16+

© Kazuya Minekura

BLADE of HEAVEN ™

THE ULTIMATE CLASH IS ABOUT TO BEGIN.

When Soma, a human, is accused of stealing the Heaven King's Sword, the otherwordly order is knocked out of balance. Heavenly beings and demons clash for ultimate supremacy. The hope for salvation rests with Soma, the heavenly princess, and the Blade of Heaven—each holds the key to preventing all Hell from breaking loose!

T TEEN AGE 13+

© 2002 YONG-SU HWANG & KYUNG-IL YANG, DAIWON C.I. Inc.